MANAGEMENT LAUREATES:

A Collection of Autobiographical Essays

VOLUME 1

Editor: ARTHUR G. BEDEIAN
Ralph and Kacoo Olinde Distinguished Professor,
College of Business Administration, Louisiana State University

MANAGEMENT LAUREATES:

A Collection of Autobiographical Essays

by

H. IGOR ANSOFF	ALFRED D. CHANDLER, JR.
CHRIS ARGYRIS	LARRY L. CUMMINGS
BERNARD M. BASS	KEITH DAVIS
ROBERT R. BLAKE	FRED E. FIEDLER
ELWOOD S. BUFFA	JAY W. FORRESTER

ROBERT T. GOLEMBIEWSKI

 **JAI PRESS INC.**

Greenwich, Connecticut   *London, England*

Library of Congress Cataloging-in-Publication Data

Management laureates : a collection of autobiographical essays / by
   Igor Ansoff ... [et al. ; editor, Arthur G. Bedeian].
      p.   cm.
   Includes bibliographical references.
   ISBN 1-55938-469-7 (v. 1)
      1. Executives--United States--Biography. 2.   Executives--Canada-
   -Biography. 3. Industrial management--United States.   4. Industrial
   management--Canada. 5. Master of business administration degree-
   -Canada. I. Ansoff, H. Igor. II. Bedian, Arthur G.
   HC102.5.A2M32   1992
658.4'092'273--dc20
[B]

CONTENTS

v

PREFACE

For many years, I have contemplated compiling a volume such as this, containing the autobiographies of the management discipline's most distinguished laureates. The impetus to do so was reinforced when, in preparing my Academy of Management presidential address, I re-read Theophile S. Krawiec's *The Psychologists* (1972-1978). Phil argues, and I agree, that "one way to learn about and understand psychology is to study psychologists as they reveal themselves in writing about their lives" (1972, p. vi). Moreover, I would make the same argument for management and its leading thinkers, since I share the belief that you cannot fully understand an individual's work without knowing a great deal about the person behind that work.

Unfortunately, the available management literature provides little insight into the personal and intellectual lives—the frustrations as well as the triumphs—of the individuals in the management discipline. Although such understanding could be conveyed in many forms, perhaps the most intimate and fascinating of these for gaining behind-the-scenes insights is the autobiography. Thus, as self-exemplifying exercises, the autobiographies in this volume, as in the two companion volumes, offer the reader not only a glimpse of the subjective determinants and personal experiences of the management discipline's most distinguished laureates, but also a deeper understanding of what management is and what it is becoming. Those who have contributed to this undertaking are all distinguished by their successes, comprising a sample of the highest achievers in the management discipline. They are widely diversified in background and involvement in various areas of management, and their experiences are indelibly marked by societal and intellectual trends that span the entire twentieth century. To borrow a term from Robert K. Merton (cited in Riley, 1988, p. 25), the management laureates included in this undertaking are "influentials." Their lives have had and continue to have significant consequences for both management and society.

The difficulty and trepidations of preparing a verbal portrait of one's life should not be underestimated. Any sincere attempt to portray an unencapsulated personal and intellectual history is risky. It requires that one stand naked in front of oneself in a state of self-communion. Such immersion in the self, with its inevitable introspection, retrospection, and interpretation, may well lead to conflict with others, as well as result in internal dissensions. Moreover, the honest reconsideration of one's own motivations and thoughts may not only influence the rest of one's career, but also impart a sense of premature semi-closure. In this sense, preparing an autobiography is an adventure.

Editorial intervention has been purposefully kept at a minimum. Although all contributions open with a photograph and conclude with a complete bibliography of the author's published works, no rigid model was specified. Thus, the various accounts reflect a diversity of approaches, interests, and experiences. Contributors were free to choose not only their manner of presentation, but also the aspects of their lives they wished to emphasize. Some have offered rounded autobiographies, while other have emphasized intellectual and scholarly achievements. Many are laced with "confessions" of one sort or another, and virtually all reflect on the many people who have influenced their lives and their work.

It is an accepted psychological fact that such personalized accounts do not proceed as mechanical reproduction, but tend toward creation (Misch, 1951, p. 11), suffering from what Lindzey (1974) has labeled an "astigmatism imposed by personal needs and too little perspective" (p. ix). For this reason, autobiographies should not be regarded as objective narratives. The lack of objectivity is offset, however, by certain advantages. In methodological terms, autobiographers are the "ultimate participants in a dual participant-observer role," having privileged (if not monopolistic) access to their own inner thoughts (Merton, 1988, p. 18). By providing insights that are direct and not secondhand, the autobiographer is better qualified than anyone else to describe his or her private feelings. Autobiographies, therefore, should be regarded not as objective narratives, but as a means for evaluating an individual's self-definition (Sjoberg & Kuhn, 1989, p. 312), documenting inner thoughts that are unobtainable from other sources.

Autobiographers, however, are not without some measure of control over errors in recollection and observation. By using historical documents and other external facts, one can transform the remebered past into what Merton (1988) has termed a "series of hypotheses to be checked" (pp. 18-19). Empirical contemplation of reality, therefore, can afford at least some protection from excessive tendentiousness. The incentive to minimize such bias is high, of course, since narrators who exaggerate their positions or engage in shallow attempts at self-justification risk damaging their professional credibility.

It is an historical truism that the past is invariably interpreted in terms of the present (Sjoberg & Kuhn, 1989). A review of the narratives in this volume, supplemented by correspondence and conversations with the authors, indicates that the narrators are no exception to this historical axiom. Each invariably interprets his reminiscences in light of what has occurred since. For virtually all, writing an autobiography has been an emotionally moving experience, leading to self-revelation as each author recalled facts and feelings, actions and reactions, the incidents that prompted him, the persons he met, and the transactions in which he was involved. Several contributors have divulged that this self-revelation has enabled, if not forced, them to perceived their lives as a single whole. As a consequence, each of this latter group has benefitted by growing in ways that others could not do for them (Misch, 1951).

Further review of the following narratives highlights a second historical truism (Riley, 1988). Though the management laureates included in these volumes are indeed "influentials," they were likewise *influenced by* the social, cultural, and environmental changes to which they were exposed. Collectively, the narratives clearly show how management thinkers living at a particular point in history have been influenced by existing social policies, practices, and structures; and how these influences have, in turn, affected their thinking. The narratives, as a group, also show that the experiences, interests, accomplishments, and failures of the various contributors were in no small way a function of the historical moment at which they entered the management discipline (Merton, 1988). For instance, those entering the discipline shortly after World War II were in an appreciably different historical context than their predecessors. As several of the contributors suggest, their common wartime experiences greatly influenced the intellectual evolution of management thinking by introducing new theoretical concepts and redirecting scientific attention to new research domains.

The relevance of historical context underscores a final point. As Phil Krawiec, for one, is found of observing, "autobiographies are an introduction to the past of our discipline" (personal interview, January 28, 1990). Contemporary as they now seem, the autobiographies in this volume are also a contribution to the history of management. Even today, readers can sense in these accounts the attitudes of earlier generations and their interpretations of changing social policies, practices, and structures. Tacitly and explicitly, the narratives also tell of dominant research philosophies and the importance of reference groups and reference individuals, the significant others who helped shape the character of contemporary management thought and inquiry.

In perusing these narratives, one might ask why only North Americans, and exclusively males at that, are included as contributors to the present volumes? Historically, the professional study of management has been predominantly American. With the spread of management training on six continents, this condition is quickly changing. Likewise, the entry over the last two decades of numerous female scholars who are now notably influencing management thought is a welcomed phenomenon. Consequently, it is hoped that any future volumes will not only be truly international, but also include distinguished female contributors. Thus, the absence of international and female contributors should not be interpreted to suggest that the editor is xenophobic or sexist, but rather to reflect an absence of appropriate candidates either belonging to the cohorts from which autobiographers were selected or who had not already prepared autobiographical memoirs.

Special thanks goes to the contributors. It is hoped that each will find some satisfaction in the immortality that the present undertaking provides. All have hereby gained a medium of access that will allow them, decades after they are gone, to speak to those management scholars who will be heirs to their intellectual legacy.

Arthur G. Bedeian
July 1991

REFERENCES

Krawiec, T.S. (1972-1978). *The psychologists* (Vols. 1-2). New York: Oxford University Press. (Vol. 2): Brandon, VT: Clinical Psychology Press.

Lindzey, G. (Ed.). (1974). *A history of psychology in autobiography* (Vol. 6). Englewood Cliffs, NJ: Prentice-Hall.

Merton, R.K. (1988). Some thoughts on the concept of sociological autobiography. In M.W. Riley (Ed.), *Sociological lives* (pp. 17-21). Newbury Park, CA: Sage.

Misch, G. (1951). *A history of autobiography in antiquity* (Vol. 1). Cambridge, MA: Harvard University Press.

Riley, M.W. (Ed.). (1988). Notes on the influence of sociological lives. *Sociological lives* (pp. 23-40). Newbury Park, CA: Sage.

Sjoberg, G., & Kuhn, K. (1989). Autobiography and organizations: Theoretical and methodological issues. *Journal of Applied Behavioral Science, 24*, 309-326.

*If I have seen farther, it is by
standing on the shoulders of giants.*

—Sir Issac Newton

A Profile of Intellectual Growth

H. IGOR ANSOFF

GROWING UP IN THE USSR

When I was eight years old, I developed a strong interest in my national origin. My mother who, like many Russians, had a lively and romantic imagination, claimed that I was born a subject of the Japanese Emperor. She based this claim on the fact that I was conceived in Tokyo, while she and my father were visiting Japan in 1918. My father, with more substance to his assertion, claimed that, according to an American law which was in force at the time, all children of American citizens, wherever born, automatically became American citizens. Thus, since he was born in Evansville, Indiana, I was an American citizen at birth.

But, at the time I was inquiring about my citizenship, both answers were academic. In reality we were living as Soviet citizens in Moscow, a short walk from the Bolshoi Theatre. I was enrolled in a primary school; wore a red kerchief around my neck which identified me as a member of the Soviet "Pioneers;" and spent a great deal of my time together with my comrades seeking profound insights in long, convoluted, and typically impenetrable speeches of our great leader Comrade Stalin.

There was no way by which I or my parents could claim right to other than Soviet citizenship, since the Soviet Union was diplomatically isolated from the "capitalist" world.

Our presence in Moscow was the result of a decision which was to have a major influence on my emotional and intellectual development during my childhood and youth. This was the decision made by my parents in 1924 to return to Moscow from Vladivostok, a city on the extreme eastern edge of Russia where I was born in 1918 after my parents' return from Japan.

At the time my father was secretary to the American Counsul General in Moscow and he had just completed a cross-Siberian trip on behalf of the American Red Cross, examining living conditions in prisoner of war camps. His assignment became meaningless because, a month before my birth, the October revolution broke out in Moscow and St. Petersburg and diplomatic relations between the Allies and the new Soviet government were broken.

Within months a civil war between the "Reds" and "Whites" was in full swing and it was only a matter of time before the Red wave was to roll across Siberia and reach Vladivostok. Thus my parents were faced with a choice to board a ship and return to the country of my father's birth, or to remain in Vladivostok and eventually become citizens of the Union of Soviet Socialist Republics.

My father wanted to go back to his American origins, and my mother, who was 600 percent Russian, wanted to return to her family in Moscow. In the end my mother prevailed. We remained in Vladivostok until it became a part of the Soviet Union and shortly thereafter travelled to Moscow traversing Siberia much under very similar conditions to those depicted in the unforgettable film *Dr. Zhivago*.

When I was four years old we arrived in Moscow in the middle of a bitter cold winter of 1924, shortly after Lenin's death, while the city was still in deep mourning. And for the next sixteen years we lived in Moscow. Legally we were Soviet citizens. But my father's American origin, and my mother's "capitalist" background (her father had owned a small samovar factory in the town of Tula some hundred miles west of Moscow) made us suspect as members of the "bourgeoisie" who were assumed to harbor their "counterrevolutionary" hopes and tendencies.

This suspicion followed me (as well as other students of similar origin) through my life in school. I was suspect because I lacked a genuine "proletarian" origin which was required for full acceptance into the "Socialist System." But I was tolerated because members of the bourgeoisie tended to be more literate, better academic performers, and able to contribute badly needed professional skills and knowledge to the task of building the Socialist Society.

As I grew and began to understand the precarious position in which students like myself found themselves, I strove to compensate for my bourgeois origins and to earn my place within the "system" in two ways: first by excelling in academic performance and, second, by becoming an activist in the Pioneers (a rough equivalent to American Boy Scouts) which were a breeding ground for the Comsomol (The Young Communist League) and eventually for The Party.

I excelled academically, but I soon found out that, for people like me, promotion within the System depended on being able to contribute a professional competence to the task of building socialism. As a result, although I excelled in all fields I studied, my parents and I decided early in my education that I should become an engineer, a goal which I later achieved and eventually abandoned in the United States.

As I now look back on the twelve years of my life spent in Moscow, I realize that the experience of never quite belonging to the Socialist System conditioned my social behavior throughout the rest of my life. This behavior expressed itself though my inability to join other "systems" in which I lived, studied and worked. It reinforced my drive to excel in order to force the systems to recognize and reward me. And, perversely, it also drove me to excel through making innovative contributions which challenged the systems' cultures.

The second major event which shaped the course of my life was the decision made by my family in 1932 to leave the USSR and return to the United States, the country of my father's birth. The decision was made possible by the resumption of diplomatic relations between the United States and the USSR in 1933. The recognition created a temporary lifting of the "Iron Curtain" and we managed to slip under the curtain just before it came down again in 1933.

With the reestablishment of the American Embassy in Moscow, my father was able to get a clerical job in the Embassy and at the same time apply for restoration of his American citizenship. The decision to use this citizenship to leave the USSR took longer. As before, my father wanted to leave the USSR as quickly as possible. My mother who, with the exception of a brief trip to Japan, had never left Russia and spoke no foreign languages, was afraid to start a new life at the age of forty and wanted to stay.

At age eighteen I became the deciding vote and sided with my father. Looking back I realize that the decision was made on very shaky grounds. After repeated exposures to news films of soup kitchens on the streets of Washington, daily newspaper stories about oppression of working people in capitalist countries, and a flood of upbeat (almost hysterical in tone) radio news broadcasts of great successes of the Soviet Society, I was firmly convinced of the evils of capitalism and had no desire to live in the United States.

However, I was a voracious reader of Western literature and in the course of my reading, I was excited and charmed by books by James Fenimore Cooper which painted a romantic picture of the heroic American Indians. This "Call of the West," combined with a natural yearning for adventure of a typical 18-year-old, led me to the following scenario: I would go to America to confirm at firsthand the evils of capitalism and to become acquainted with the American Indians and Indian culture. While in the United States, I would serve as a "foreign correspondent" to my friends and fellow students by documenting for them the evils of the capital system. And when the two tasks were completed, I would return to Moscow and resume my progress in school. I did not communicate this scenario to my parents, neither at the time the decision was made nor during the rest of their lives. But I sided with my father and together we prevailed on my mother to leave for America.

We left through Leningrad in September 1936 on a small freighter, which accommodated a dozen passengers. The ship took two weeks to cross the seasonally turbulent Atlantic and finally docked in New York.

MATURING IN THE UNITED STATES

We arrived in America, which was still recovering from the Great Depression, with very little money, no family relations, virtually no contacts, and no prospects for my father's employment. Since my father's occupation in the Soviet Union had consisted of work as an accountant (under the Soviet accounting system), and a stint as a interpreter at the American Embassy, he had no visible professional qualifications for a job in the United States.

Five years after we landed in New York, I graduated at the top of my class from Stevens Institute of Technology in Hoboken, New Jersey which, at the time, was one of three or four top engineering schools in the United States.

As I started writing about this period I was surprised that it spanned only five years. The many events and changes that shaped me and my future life during this period seemed to be sufficient to have filled a period twice as long.

Our first home in New York was two rented rooms with a gas range on 129th street which was one of the few remaining streets in Harlem occupied by white landlords and their white tenants. In those days Harlem was the poorest borough of New York but it dealt a rude shock to the expectations I brought with me about life under capitalism.

We arrived at our lodgings late in the evening and were greeted by a charming Finnish landlady who belonged to one of a few remaining enclaves of whites in a predominantly black Harlem. We had no idea that this was the case since the lodgings were arranged by one of the few American contacts of my father, whose primary concern was to find for us the cheapest possible place to stay.

We woke very early the next morning and walked down to 125th Street located in the center of black Harlem, which we found to be clean and prosperous looking compared to the streets we left behind in Moscow. We ate breakfast of coffee and rolls in a small immaculate coffee shop owned by a black proprietor, and the incredibly delicious taste of the rolls, when compared to the bread we ate in Russia, has remained one of the most vivid memories until today.

Another vivid memory is our first visit to Woolworth's Five and Ten Cent Store on 125th Street. The assortment of goods offered was a shock to my mother who used to spend hours in Moscow going from one store to another in the hope of "finding" something which would satisfy one of our urgent needs for personal goods. My strongest impression was of the large open display of goods, superficially supervised by a small number of clerks, and sparsely populated with customers. A store like this on a street in Moscow would have been mobbed and pilfered in a matter of a couple hours.

As days passed, my prior model of life under capitalism was continually bombarded with such contradictions. During the first two years in New York, my father had great difficulty in finding a steady job and part of the time we were on public relief. And yet we found that our personal comfort and standard of living exceeded those which we had experienced in our life in Moscow.

At first exposure to all these contradictions, I persisted in believing the model of American life I brought with me. Faithful to the promise to comrades in Moscow, I wrote and sent to them "news dispatches" about the shortcomings of life in America. But within a year our correspondence was cut off by the lowering of the "Iron Curtain" by Stalin. My friends in Moscow begged me to stop writing to them in order to save them from a suspicion of communicating with "the enemy." After two years my original model of capitalist exploitation lay in tatters, and I abandoned the first part of my original plan which was to return to the Soviet Union.

It should be recorded here that the second part of the plan to visit Indian territory and become acquainted with heroic Indians was also abandoned, because more immediate needs and challenges filled my life. And it wasn't until I was over seventy years old that I encountered delightful books about Indian culture by Tony Hillerman and wished again that I had stuck to the second part of my plan.

Shortly after we arrived, the problem of my education demanded attention. A Russian Orthodox priest, who helped us in many ways, took me to the Stuyvesant High School on lower Manhattan which, at the time, was one of two premier high schools in New York City.

I had completed all but one year of secondary education in Moscow with outstanding grades. With the aid of the priest, the kindly Assistant Principal at Stuyvesant translated my grades into American equivalents which made it possible for me to graduate in one year. I was given a schedule of courses and their room numbers. The priest departed, and I was left to confront one of the most traumatic experiences in my life. This trauma was my confrontation with the American language.

Prior to 1933, when our plans to go to America began to shape up, I had learned fluent German but had no knowledge of English. During the two years prior to our departure, my parents arranged for English lessons with a teacher who was educated in England. I attacked the lessons with great enthusiasm. By the time we left the USSR, I felt that I could understand English and speak it tolerably well. But I had little chance to test this opinion until, my academic schedule in hand, I showed up for my first class at Stuyvesant High. My English failed totally. I could not understand a single word spoken by my classmates and teachers.

This condition lasted for about a month. I went from class to class understanding nothing and unable to communicate to others. I discovered that my English was incomprehensible to others because of my wretched combination of Russian and English (not American) pronunciation. And the others were no more comprehensible to me because Stuyvesant was populated by students drawn from all of the boroughs of New York and New Jersey, each bringing his highly distinctive accent, none of which I had heard in the past.

Fortunately for me, the pace of Russian education was ahead of American by at least a year. Therefore, I knew most of the subjects I was required to study and could therefore devote all my energies to learning to understand, pronounce, and communicate in English.

I made the grade and graduated with the highest honors at the end of the year, which guaranteed me a four-year scholarship with all expenses paid in the New York State University system. But, as I interviewed for college, I was offered a scholarship at The Stevens Institute of Technology which was one of the most expensive and best engineering schools in the country. The scholarship was for one year and its continuation was contingent on my performing in the upper 10% of my class. Contrary to my parents' advice, who were still struggling to make ends meet, I went to Stevens. In retrospect this was one of the best decisions I made in my life.

An early experience during my four years at Stevens stands out as a major influence on my later professional development. This was a dramatic exposure to the phenomenon of complexity synthesis which was to become my major preoccupation twenty years later.

At the beginning of the freshman year, the incoming students were given an opportunity to enroll as "guinea pigs" in a basic physics course to be taught by Dr. Alan Hazeltine, one of the inventors of the modern FM radio. Dr. Hazeltine had just retired from the Hazeltine Corporation, of which he was the original founder, and decided to return to his alma mater and teach physics.

His aim was to make the subject of basic physics simple and transparent to the students. The physics department at Stevens was teaching basic physics in the traditional historical perspective, which took students through an elaborate convoluted historical evolution of the various branches of basic physics: mechanics, elasticity, electromagnetism, and electrostatics treating each of the branches as unique and different from the others. Hazeltine's proposal was to abandon the historical perspective and start with a set of simple generic parametric equations which, through simple renaming of the parameters, enabled the student to move from one branch of basic physics to another.

Understandably, the physics department was suspicious and threatened by Hazeltine's approach which it viewed as an oversimplification of an inherently complex subject. But Hazeltine was a world-renowned inventor and a major financial contributor to Stevens. Therefore, it was not possible to deny him admission to the Physics Department. The solution was to offer his course as optional to students who were prepared to retake the traditional course should Hazeltine's version fail.

The course was a smashing success. Hazeltine gave us a simple but profound "bird's eye" view of a subject which was traditionally seen by students as disjointed and convoluted. For me, the course represented a first and enormously exciting experience in complexity synthesis which identifies "the shape of a wood instead of counting its individual trees." There is a direct connection between this experience and my later 20-year-long persistence in constructing a meta model of strategic management.

By the time I received my engineering degree at Stevens, I had reached the conclusion that I did not want to practice engineering. At the time I would have been hard pressed to explain this decision. But, with the benefit of hindsight, I see that the reason was the lack of homomorphism between the natural science perspective within which engineering solves it problems and the multidisciplinary perspective which is essential if engineering solutions are to be responsive to the needs of society. Put in simpler terms, I was turned-off by the lack of "user friendliness" in engineering solutions.

Seeking a broader perspective, I took a master's degree in Modern Physics. World War II intervened, and in 1946 I went to Brown University to take a doctoral degree in Applied Mathematics. The analytic tools I learned at Brown remained unused during most of my future life. But the epistemological perspective of mathematics which taught me the meaning of scientific rigor became enormously valuable in later years in my work on complexity synthesis of multidisciplinary systems.

WORKING FOR A LIVING

My formal education was completed in 1948 when I was 30-years-old. I was married the day after defending my dissertation, and my bride and I travelled to Santa Monica, California where I was offered a job in the Mathematics Department of the Rand Corporation. It took me about four years to conclude that, while I could remain a competent mathematician, I could never become an outstanding one. And, given my drive to excel, I changed my career orientation.

I moved, laterally within Rand, to become a project manager in the large-scale project activity focused on making recommendations to the U.S. Air Force on technology and weapon systems acquisition. My first major project was a major departure from the historical emphasis on systems acquisition. Instead it was focused on vulnerability of the U.S. Strategic Air Force Command (SAC) to a Soviet attack. The two-year-long study found that SAC's defense strategy was predicated on a Soviet attack on SAC coming across the North Pole which left the southwestern approach to SAC vulnerable to a devastating attack by the Soviet bomber fleet, which had the range to deliver it. The study recommended that the early warning radar network which protected SAC be extended to cover the southwestern approach.

We took the study to SAC Headquarters in Omaha, Nebraska and presented it to the top-level commanders. At the end of the briefing, we were told by the assembled group of senior generals that, since we performed our analysis without consulting SAC, we were unqualified to analyze its problems and were escorted off the base and told not to come back. The southwestern gap in radar coverage remained open and some thirty years later I was bemused by a newspaper article reporting a new study of SAC vulnerability which arrived at exactly the same results which we obtained in the 1950s.

My second major study at Rand addressed the vulnerability of NATO Air Forces. Using lessons learned in the first study, which was done within the confines of the Rand Corporation, my team and I crisscrossed Europe interviewing senior officers and gathering information which would permit us to construct a model which included most of the important factors that determined the vulnerability of NATO Air Forces.

The model turned out to be complex and included nontechnical factors which had never been considered in prior Rand weapons selection. Among factors which we added to the technological variables were educational, cultural and political differences among the NATO nations; differences among levels of training and equipment; compatibility of the national command, control and communications systems; preparedness to deal with surprises; survivability of an airfield after an attack, and so forth.

It was the custom at the Rand Corporation to expose all major systems studies to the entire technical staff before presenting them to clients. As mentioned before, the preceding systems studies at Rand were confined to the engineering and advanced technology variables. By contrast our presentation contained no references to technologically-advanced systems such as vertical takeoff (VTOL) and short landing and takeoff (STOL) defense fighters. We excluded them because our field research had shown that within the study's ten-year time horizon such systems would remain beyond the technological state of the art; beyond NATO's means to develop them; and beyond the capability of NATO Air Force to deploy them.

Thus the Rand audience was treated to defense plans based on "soft" organizational variables. To my astonishment I found that the addition of the new variables, which made our study realistic and relevant to the needs of Nato, was treated as a deficiency and not an improvement over previous studies. Thus I learned my first lesson on organizational myopia which was to become one of my primary concerns some 20 years later.

There was a strong feeling in the audience that the study was "unrealistic" and "pedestrian" and that it should not be presented to the clients in Europe. It took much effort on the part of the team to effect a compromise under which we were permitted to present the study in Washington to a group of senior American Air Force officers. The officers' response was favorable and we were directed to take the study to Europe. European response was positive and we spent two months briefing Supreme Headquarters Allied Powers, Europe (SHAPE) and all of the regional commands. Some of our recommendations were eventually incorporated in NATO War Plans.

Although I did not realize it at the time, the rejection by SAC and near rejection by the Rand staff contained valuable insights into the manner in which organizations react to studies which contradict their historical behavior and experience. These insights surfaced from my subconscious some 20 years later and helped me understand and deal with the problem of managing resistance to discontinuous strategic changes.

At the time I felt increasingly frustrated by the difficulty I encountered as an external consultant in trying to persuade my clients and colleagues to accept recommendations whenever they were in conflict with their historical reality. As a result, I decided to join an organization in which I would be an internal actor, rather than advice-giving outsider.

In 1957 I left Rand to join the Corporate Planning Department of the Lockheed Aircraft Corporation. The timing of my move to industry was fortuitous, because it influenced my ultimate career path. It occurred at a time when American industry was increasingly confronting environmental discontinuities and turbulence. As a result, my experience at Lockheed focused my attention and trained me to deal with the problem of managing organizations in the face of environmental discontinuities which became the central focus of my attention during the following 30 years.

I entered Lockheed as a planner in its newly constituted Corporate Planning Department. At the time of my entry, corporate management of Lockheed was becoming concerned (as were a great many other corporate managements in the United States) with growth and profitability problems which stubbornly resisted treatment by management techniques which, during the preceding 80 years, made the United States the undisputed industrial leader of the world.

Lockheed's response to the problem was two-fold: (1) to start a long-range planning process for its historical business, and to (2) diversify into new businesses which offered attractive future growth and profitability. At the moment of my entry into the Planning Department, all of my fellow planners were involved in the launching of the long-range planning process and work on diversification had not yet started. Since I was the only body available, my first assignment was to develop a plan for Lockheed's diversification. Thus an almost random event determined the course of the rest of my professional and scientific life.

During my first interview with Mr. Gross, CEO of Lockheed, I asked him what was meant by diversification. His frank response was that neither he nor his colleagues had any idea of what diversification meant. Looking outside Lockheed, I found diversification activity to be widespread, but most of it consisted of opportunistic acquisitions. Very little was known about the nature of acquisition activity, its advantages and disadvantages; and few concepts and analytic tools were available for assuring success. Since Mr. Gross insisted that our diversification be planned, I spent the next year borrowing the few concepts that were available, inventing others, and building a conceptual/analytic model of diversification with assistance from two outside consultants. Next, I used the framework to analyze the entire range of manufacturing industries in the United States in order to formulate a diversification strategy for Lockheed.

The Lockheed Policy Committee accepted my recommendations and appointed me head of a Diversification Task Force charged with identifying opportunities, evaluating them, and presenting recommendations back to the Policy Committee. I spent the next two years "playing chess with companies" trying to convert our diversification strategy into concrete reality. I crisscrossed the United States visiting potential candidates, ascertaining their potential interests and terms, and evaluating them in the light of Lockheed's strategy, and presenting recommendations to the Policy Committee.

Several acquisitions were made but nowhere on a scale originally visualized by Mr. Cross. My job as Director of the Diversification Task Force ended when I was promoted to Vice President of one of the acquisitions with an assignment to turn around one of its troubled divisions.

My first impression was that the Division was going in all directions at the same time with no visible sense of purpose or strategy. A two-week strategic diagnosis exercise showed that I was presiding over a group of 100 engineers who were attempting to take the Division into seventeen different business areas. And some of these business areas were huge, such as mainframe computers, in which we were fielding 10 young and ambitious engineers against the entire IBM Company.

By the end of three years as Division Manager, I reduced the business scope of the Division from seventeen to three business areas, developed strategic plans for each, reduced the engineering staff, added marketing and production capabilities. Of the three business areas, one was abandoned and the other two began to grown and come close to the break-even point.

As I reflect on what I learned from my business experience, two important lessons come to mind. The first are the differences in the way in which staff and general managers approach problems.

In my staff role I perceived problems through the optic of the scientific disciplines in which I was trained. Thus I viewed Lockheed's diversification as a problem in cognitive logical analysis. In retrospect, I see that this narrow problem focus on analysis was responsible for the limited success of Lockheed's diversification program.

In my role as a general manager, I learned that successful solution of important management problems requires simultaneous consideration of all variables which influence a solution: cognitive, logical, psychological, sociological and political. In general management jargon, solutions of problems which have failed to include all of the relevant variables are charitably called "incomplete staff work" and, brutally, "solutions in search of a problem."

I am now convinced (and I have 30 years of experience to support this conviction) that Lockheed's diversification program would have been much more successful if I had behaved as a change agent, who takes all of the relevant disciplinary optics into account and not as a single scientific optic in which I was educated and trained.

ENTRY INTO ACADEMIA

One morning, while shaving in front of the proverbial shaving mirror, I realized that while I managed my division strategically, I had no idea of what I wanted to do with the rest of my life. My family and I were preparing for a two weeks' vacation on Cape Cod and I decided to use the time at the Cape to prepare a strategic plan for myself. As planning tools I took a half case of Scotch, grew a beard, and spent the better part of the vacation walking on the beach.

The process of strategic self-introspection turned out to be surprisingly difficult and the conclusion surprising. The resulting strategy called for a change of my career path from business to academia. The near-term action plan was to build academic visibility through publications. The long-term plan was to take early retirement from Lockheed in ten years' time and find a job in a school of management.

At the end of the vacation I went back to work. With the help and encouragement from an extraordinary secretary, Nancy Johnson, who budgeted and jealously protected my writing time, I started writing a book which would codify and generalize my experience in strategic planning of diversification and would begin to build my visibility. Within a year of my strategic decision, I was approached by The Graduate School of Industrial Administration at the Carnegie-Mellon University about my interest in joining the GSIA faculty.

I discuss this event with my students to illustrate a key purpose of an articulated strategy which is to sensitize the strategist to discontinuous and surpriseful threats and opportunities which may come his way. I am sure that, if I had not gone through the Cape Cod exercise, I would not have been interested in GSIA, because my division was beginning to make money, many exciting strategic challenges remained, and my book was making progress.

But the strategy alerted me to the fact that I was being offered a unique opportunity to join one of the three best management schools in the world. I joined the GSIA faculty in 1963. Thus, at age 45, I entered the third and final stage of my intellectual and professional development, which put me on the threshold of making contributions which eventually merited inclusion of my autobiography in this book.

When I entered GSIA, my new Dean, Richard M. Cyert, generously gave me a year free from teaching to enable me to finish the book started while

I was at Lockheed. The book, *Corporate Strategy*, appeared in 1965 and was an immediate success. Within a few years it was translated into something like fourteen different languages. It continued to sell well throughout the world, and in 1988 the Penguin Book Ltd. approached me with a suggestion that I bring the book up-to-date. A revised edition of *Corporate Strategy* was published in Britain in 1988; and in 1989 in the United States under the title *The New Corporate Strategy*.

Corporate Strategy integrated strategic planning concepts which were invented independently in a number of leading American firms, including Lockheed. It also presented several new theoretical concepts such as *partial ignorance, business strategy, capability and competence profiles*, and *synergy*. One particular concept, the *product-mission matrix*, became very popular, because it was simple and codified for the first time the differences between strategic expansion and diversification. Until today I receive requests for permission to reprint the matrix on the average of every three to four months. Although it received much less attention, the concept of partial ignorance eventually proved to be of much more fundamental, particularly in strategic planning for turbulent environments.

I remained at GSIA for the next six years. The early years were exciting— I was teaching outstanding groups of students and the stellar faculty included Herb Simon, Bill Cooper, Hal Leavitt, Vic Vroom, and a number of others.

But, as my research interest progressively developed toward a multidisciplinary perspective, I found it difficult to develop collaborative projects with most of my fellow faculty members, whose interests were confined to their own disciplines. I also began to miss the world of management.

As a result, in 1969 I accepted a position as Founding Dean of the new Graduate School of Management at Vanderbilt University in Nashville, Tennessee. I accepted the position under the condition that the school would specialize on educating change agents, a type of manager which, in my view, was badly needed in industry and not produced by any U.S. school of business.

I recruited a pilot group of faculty and together we designed an educational environment in which the word "learning" replaced "teaching," and the curriculum specialized on developing knowledge and skills needed by a change agent. Our first students graduated in 1971.

EMERGENCE OF THE CONCEPT OF STRATEGIC MANAGEMENT

One of the reasons for success of *Corporate Strategy* was that it was published at a time of widespread enthusiasm for strategic planning and an increasing number of firms were joining the ranks of its users. Thanks to the success of the book and the personal visibility it brought to me, I became known as an expert in strategic planning and planned to devote my life-long research to developing the theory and technology of strategic planning.

But, as experience accumulated, many firms found that strategic planning was not producing the hoped for improvements in their growth and profitability. One of the difficulties encountered in strategic planning was named "paralysis by analysis": Many firms found that successive annual strategic plans produced no visible impact on the firm's strategic behavior in the marketplace. In many cases the paralysis by analysis eventually led to what a colleague of mine, Hans ten Dam, called "death in the drawer": After several years of unsatisfactory experience with strategic planning, firms abandoned it and reverted, either to budgeting or to long-range planning, which they used before attempting strategic planning.

In retrospect, the incidence of strategic planning failure should not have been surprising. After all, it was a practical invention designed by staffs in business firms as a solution to a problem which was poorly understood, and in the absence of a theory which could have guided the design.

But the failures of strategic planning raised questions about their causes. One explanation, which received considerable currency, was that strategic planning was inherently a bad and unworkable invention and that it could not produce improvements in a firm's performance. Another possible explanation was that strategy was an incomplete invention, that, while it was helpful in making strategic decisions, it did not assure that decisions would be implemented. An analogy was proposed which described strategic planning as a car with an engine that generated power but without wheels to convert the power into locomotion.

I was strongly inclined to accept the second explanation. On a personal level, acceptance of the first explanation would have quickly terminated my professional aspiration to become an expert in strategic planning. On an intuitive level, I was convinced that strategic planning was an inherently useful management tool. And on a factual level, my experience in Rand and Lockheed showed me that strategic planning did not encompass all of the variables which must be managed to assure that plans will become organizational reality.

There was a way to test my conviction. This was to conduct empirical research designed to show that when, for whatever reasons, strategic planning became firmly implanted in a firm, its performance would be superior to that of other firms which did not use strategic planning.

Together with several of my colleagues at Vanderbilt, I decided to test my conviction by performing an extensive empirical study of acquisition behavior by U.S. firms between 1948 and 1968. The results gave strong support to the hypothesis that diversifying firms, which plan and act strategically, performed better than firms which used an unplanned opportunistic approach to their diversification activity. These research results, first published in 1970,[1] confirmed my opinion that an explicit strategy is a necessary but not the only factor in assuring a firm's success, and encouraged me to start a search for the other factors.

CONCEPT OF STRATEGIC MANAGEMENT

Before starting the search, I felt the need to identify a theoretical umbrella concept which would embrace all of the factors necessary for strategic success. By 1973 the Management School at Vanderbilt was launched and was producing impressive students. And I felt that pursuit of theory would have a better chance of success in Western Europe. As a result, I took my family to the European Institute for Advanced Studies in Management in Brussels, Belgium, where with a brief return to the United States, I remained for the next ten years.

In identifying the umbrella concept I was helped by an incisive phrase in one of Peter Drucker's books. According to Drucker, the ultimate concern of management is in two parts: The first is making sure that a firm is doing "the right thing," and the second that it is doing "the right thing right."

Using Drucker's dichotomy, I named the first part *strategic management.* This is the part of management which develops a firm's *future profit potential* by assuring that it does business in markets which have the potential of satisfying its objectives; that it offers products/services which these markets want; and that it offers them in a way which assures it a competitive advantage.

I named the companion "doing the right thing right" part of Drucker's dichotomy *operating management.* This is the part of management which, using the profit potential, *optimizes a firm's profitability* through efficient production, distribution and marketing its products/services generated by strategic management.

When viewed from the holistic umbrella perspective of strategic management, it becomes clear that strategic planning is a component of the overall process which develops a firm's profit potential. Its function is to choose the "right thing" through an analytic process. But, as experience has shown, choosing the "right thing" does not assure that it will be done. Therefore, my task was clear: To identify the other strategic activities which need to occur to make sure that strategy is implemented.

One such activity became evident when I used my managerial experience to construct management profiles necessary for success of a firm's strategic and operating activities. When I compared the two profiles, one fact jumped to the eye: The two organizational profiles turned out to be drastically different. Which meant that *a firm that in the past had been successful in its operating behavior, develops an management profile incapable of supporting a newly introduced strategic activity.* Thus, identification of strategic and operating managements as umbrella concepts was useful in identifying *management capability* as a second key factor necessary for success.

Before exploring the concept of management capability it is worth noting that, like many umbrella concepts, the original concept of strategic management described above was vague, "seen through the glass darkly," and that it took another 12 years to give it substance and meaning. As a result the original seven-page paper published in 1972 grew to 250 pages in 1976 and to 500 pages in 1984.[2]

CONCEPT OF MANAGEMENT CAPABILITY

I found ample confirmation of the importance of management capability in a book titled *Strategy and Structure* by Alfred D. Chandler, Jr. (MIT Press, 1972), which presents results of extensive historical research on adaptation by American firms to major discontinuities in their environments during the first half of the twentieth century. In all the firms studied, the research identified a common pattern of strategic adaptation. Typically, firms did not anticipate environmental discontinuities and responded to them after the fact.

The first phase of the response was devoted to search for a new strategy. A new strategy emerged after several years through a trial and error process. But it failed to produce satisfactory profitability. After a period of unsuccessful efforts to make the new strategy work, firms discovered that the problem no longer lay in the quality of the strategy, but in the inability of the firm's management to support it.

Once this deficiency was identified, firms in Chandler's study moved to the second phase of their response to discontinuity by changing, again through trial and error, the configuration and dynamics of their management. The most significant finding of Chandler's research was that, once both strategy and management were aligned with the new environment, all firms in his study became leading competitors in their respective industries.

Thus, I concluded that management capability was a factor which was missing from strategic planning. To operationalize the concept of capability, I constructed a profile of attributes which describe capability. It is shown in Figure 1. As the figure shows, I broke with the sociological tradition of describing a firm as a community of undifferentiated actors and separated its capability profile into characteristics of *key strategic managers*, who affect a firm as powerful individuals, and the rest of the *organization*, which exerts its influence through group action.

Furthermore, to the administrative components identified by Chandler I added *behavioral components* such as key managers' mentality, organizational culture, and the organizational power structure. Thus, the resulting profile of management capability emerges as a *multidisciplinary concept* which includes both cognitive and behavioral characteristics of management.

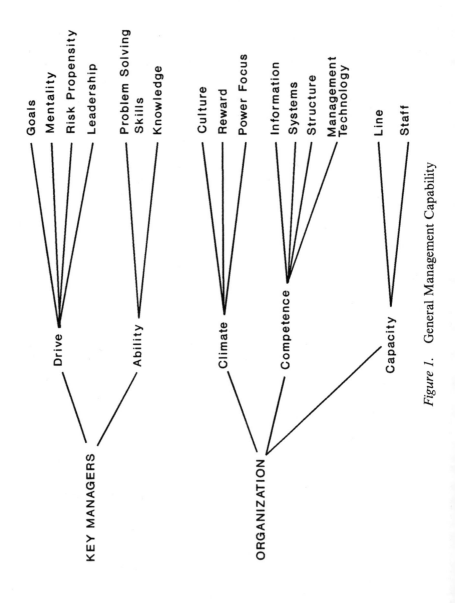

Figure 1. General Management Capability

18

CONCEPT OF ENVIRONMENTAL TURBULENCE

My next ambition was to construct a *strategic success model* which would relate strategy and capability to a firm's financial success. This ambition was an outgrowth of three factors. One was the dominant interest in success and failure of strategic behaviors developed during my experience as a general manager. The second factor was the almost total lack of interest in conditions which lead to success/failure found in both business and academic literature. The academic literature was dominated by models of organizational behavior with little concern for the consequences of this behavior. The business literature did offer prescriptions for success behaviors, but without any proof that these behaviors will, in fact, lead to success. The third factor was the early experiences with strategic planning described above which showed how organizationally disruptive unproven prescriptions can be.

As I began to work on the strategic success model, I became aware of a third factor which determines success of a firm. This factor was a firm's *environment*. This awareness was, in party, triggered by Chandler's findings that strategy/capability transformation process was triggered by an environmental discontinuity and that firms regained their profitability only when their strategy and capability were realigned with the new state of their environment. This evidence and my own experience led me to choose the concept of *environmental turbulence* as the third key factor in the strategic success model.

In addition to Chandler's influence, my choice of the concept of turbulence was influenced by two other sources. One was a seminal paper titled "The Causal Texture of Organizational Environment" by F.E. Emery and E.L. Trist, published in 1965 (*Human Relations*, Vol. 18), which proposed a taxonomy of observable environments, which are discrete and different from one another.

Emery and Trist's concept led me to what I consider to be one of my most significant contributions to the theory and practice of strategic management. This contribution was the hypothesis which states that there is no single general formula for success behavior by organizations, that there is a variety of strategic success behaviors, and that these respective behaviors are determined by the level of turbulence in a firm's environment.

In operationalizing this contingent success hypothesis I was influenced by Niels Bohr's model of the atom, which I studied in my courses in physics, in which electrons rotate around an atom in discrete orbits and jump from one orbit to another when injected with discrete amounts of energy necessary to effect the transition.

I decided to describe turbulence as a five-point scale of discrete orbits which I named *turbulence levels*. I constructed such a scale and began to test its validity by fitting real world firms on the scale. This scale is illustrated in Figure 2. As the figure shows, the respective levels of turbulence are described by a combination of *changeability* of events in the environment and by their *predictability*.

		1	2	3	4	5
DISCONTINUITY	COMPLEXITY	Economic	Business • Technology • Socio Politics			
	NOVELTY	None	Incremental Slow	Incremental Fast	Discont Familiar	Discont Novel
PREDICTABILITY	RAPIDITY	Zero	Slower Than Response	Comparable To Response	Faster Than Response	Surpriseful
	VISIBILITY	Total	Extrapolable	Predictable	Partially Unpredictable	Unpredictable
	TURB. SCALE	1	2	3	4	5

Figure 2. Scale of Environmental Turbulence

Over the past 15 years I have used Figure 2 with over a thousand senior managers around the world to help them make a quick diagnosis of the future turbulence of their firm's environments. Thus, the concept of turbulence described above can be said to have passed the test of *prima facie* acceptability by managers.

STRATEGIC SUCCESS HYPOTHESIS

Identification of turbulence completed my search for variables which determine success. The next task was to construct a *Strategic Success Hypothesis* which would identify conditions under which a firm's financial performance is optimized.

The three variables in this hypothesis are environmental turbulence, strategy, and capability. In operationalizing the hypothesis I had to define strategy and capability in terms which are on the same level of aggregation as the chosen measure of environmental turbulence.

For measuring strategy I chose the concept of a firm's *strategic aggressiveness* measured by two characteristics: *discontinuity* of a firm's consecutive strategic moves in its environment, and *timing* of the firm's strategic moves relative to the moves of other competitors in its environment. For measuring capability I used *organizational responsiveness* measured by the *openness* of an organization to its environment, and *the way the organization handles change*. Next, for each level of turbulence I drew on my management experience to construct matching descriptions of strategic aggressiveness and of organizational responsiveness which I hypothesized to optimize a firm's financial performance at the respective levels. The result was five matching "success triplets" shown in Figure 3.

The *Strategic Success Hypothesis* is implied by the table and can be expressed as follows:

Financial performance of a firm is optimized whenever the levels of its strategic aggressiveness and organizational responsiveness both match the firm's environmental turbulence level.

I need to mention that I borrowed the organization-environment matching concept from the *requisite variety theorem* by W. R. Ashby[3] which I had encountered during my studies of Applied Mathematics at Brown University.

Liberally translated, the requisite variety theorem states that, in order to succeed in its environment, an organization must match the complexity of its response to the complexity of the environment. As the reader will note, in translating Ashby's theorem into strategic management terminology, I equated Ashby's concept of environmental complexity with the concept of

ENVIRONMENTAL TURBULENCE	REPETITIVE Repetitive	EXPANDING Slow Incremental	CHANGING Fast Incremental	DISCONTINUOUS Discontinuous Predictable	SURPRISEFUL Discontinuous Partially Predictable
STRATEGIC AGGRESSIVENESS	STABLE Stable Based on Precedents	REACTIVE Incremental Based on Experience	ANTICIPATORY Incremental Based on Extrapolation	ENTREPRENEURIAL Discontinuous New Based on Observable Opportunities	CREATIVE Discontinuous Novel Based on Creativity
ORGANIZATIONAL RESPONSIVENESS	STABILITY SEEKING Rejects Change	EFFICIENCY DRIVEN Adapts to Change	MARKET DRIVEN Seeks Familiar Change	ENVIRONMENT DRIVEN Seeks Related Change	ENVIRONMENT CREATING Seeks Novel Change
LEVEL	1	2	3	4	5

Figure 3. Matching Environment—Aggressiveness Responses Triplets

environmental turbulence, and the concept of organizational complexity with the combination of strategic aggressiveness and organizational responsiveness.

PREDICTIVE AND EXPLANATORY POWERS OF THE STRATEGIC SUCCESS HYPOTHESIS

Construction of the Strategic Success Model and the Strategic Success Hypothesis was a major theoretical milestone in my progress toward understanding strategic behavior of organizations. In the language of mathematics, the Success Model would be called a *meta model* because it offers a concise high-level description of a very complex phenomenon such as strategic success. To use an apt simile, a meta model provides a "helicopter view" of the shape of a forest which cannot be perceived by remaining on the ground.

As testified by the time and effort to construct the success model, meta models are very difficult to construct. In my case, it took me 20 years of continual effort to construct the strategic success model and another 10 years to establish its validity.

Meta models are characteristically simple, but they have great predictive power. Thus, in the case of the Strategic Success Model, it takes only three variables to predict the success of a firm's strategic behavior.

Beyond prediction, a meta model usually presents a novel view of reality. Thus, the strategic success model opened my eyes to the fact that there is no single valid prescription for strategic success and that a prescription's success varies with the turbulence level of a firm's environment.

Typically a meta model does not deny validity of most prescriptions for success which had been advanced and proved by prior research. Instead it places them in a context in which each is valid and thus provides grounds for reconciling them to one another. For example, while the Strategic Success Hypothesis challenges the universal validity of prescriptions for success which have been advanced in business literature, it identifies conditions under which most of them remain valid. Thus, the popular prescription "If it ain't broke don't fix it" will bring success to organizations on Turbulence Level One; "Go back to basics" will work on Level Two; "Stick to your strategic knitting," which has been observed to bring success to many firms, works on Level Three, but becomes dangerous at Levels Four and Five.

Similarly, the multi-turbulence level concept puts strategic planning in its appropriate context. For reasons which are explored in detail elsewhere,[4] strategic planning is not useful, and can be harmful, on Levels One, Two, and Five; but it is useful on Level Three and becomes vital on Level Four.

Finally, a meta model is usually robust in the sense that it identifies new directions for exploration and research. Thus, the Strategic Success Model helped me to develop a substantial body of theory and of theory-based practical technology. I will briefly discuss the theory and technology later on. In the meanwhile we turn attention to the validity of the Strategic Success Hypothesis.

As the reader has seen, the hypothesis was suggested to me by a number of prior research efforts. But my final synthesis of these suggestions is the result of creative effort and remains speculative until shown to be valid.

A hypothesis can be validated in several ways. One way is to put the hypothesis to the test of practice. As was found in the case of strategic planning, this is a costly and organization-disturbing alternative.

Another way is to submit the hypothesis to the *test of credibility* by exposing its consequences to the judgment of experienced managers before injecting it into organizational practice.

I took the latter course as the first step toward validation of the Strategic Success Hypothesis by constructing a practical procedure called *Strategic Diagnosis* and testing it in practice. The procedure was constructed by translating the "success triplets" in Figure 3 into managerial language which permits practicing managers to assess the turbulence of their firm's environment, and diagnose the present state of its strategic aggressiveness and openness. Over some 20 years I tested the procedure with numerous managers and students who found the Strategic Diagnosis a useful management instrument. Thus the Diagnosis passed the credibility test.

EMPIRICAL TEST OF THE HYPOTHESIS

A much more conclusive test of a hypothesis is to submit it to an empirical test. An opportunity to do so presented itself to me when I returned from Europe to join the faculty of the United States International University in San Diego in 1982.

Since then nine rigorous empirical tests of the Strategic Success Hypothesis have been completed by doctoral students in the Strategic Management program at the United States International University. The tests were conducted in several countries: the United States, The United Arab Emirates, Algeria and Indonesia. The types of organizations studied were manufacturing and service firms, small and large banks, parastiatal firms, and not-for-profit organizations.

All of the tests showed that the financial success of an organization is directly and strongly related to the degree of alignment between the strategic aggressiveness/organizational responsiveness specified as optimal under the Strategic Success Hypothesis and the actual aggressiveness/responsiveness of the firm. All of the results were statistically significant at the 0.05 Level or better.[5]

CONTRIBUTIONS TO MANAGEMENT TECHNOLOGY

Both the credibility test and the empirical proof of the Strategic Success Hypothesis provided a scientific foundation for development of practical management technologies which have a much higher probability of being successful than technologies based on intuitive insights.

Over a period of some 20 years I have constructed a number of such techniques. These techniques are summarized on the left hand side of Figure 4.

The structure of Figure 4 should not deceive the reader into thinking that my intellectual development followed a linear path. On the contrary, the path was a typically convoluted one on which the respective technologies were developed in response to my current interests and demands of my teaching and consulting work. It is only in retrospect and by dint of hard work that the final logic evolved. Ironically, the empirical proof of the Strategic Success Hypothesis came last to provide a unifying and validating umbrella for the respective technologies.

A detailed exposition of the technologies can be found in my book *Implanting Strategic Management* (1990). The following briefly describes the purpose and the product of each technology.

1. *Strategic Diagnosis* is designed to be used in environments in which there is a likelihood of future shifts in the turbulence levels. The diagnosis identifies whether a shift is likely to occur, the profile of the management capability the firm will have to develop and the type of strategic planning system the firm will have to use in order to succeed on the new level of turbulence.

2. *Strategic Posture Planning* is a technology which should be used if the Diagnosis predicts Level 4 or 5. Figure 5 compares the environmental characteristics and the type of planning process appropriate to each type of environment. Strategic Posture Planning enables managers to visualize the firm's future probable environment, to create future probable success strategies and to select the strategy the firm will pursue, taxing explicit account of the entrepreneurial risk involved in making such choices. The output of strategic planning is the strategy the firm will pursue in its respective business areas, the capabilities it will develop to support the respective strategies, and the strategic investment the firm will commit to each business area.

3. *Real Time Response Technology* is in two parts. The first enables the firm to make a timely response to surprising threats and opportunities which are not captured by strategic posture planning. This technology is in two parts. The first part is called *Issue Management*. The complementary second part is *Surprise Management* which prepares a firm to deal with surpriseful threats and opportunities which escape detection by The Issue Management System.

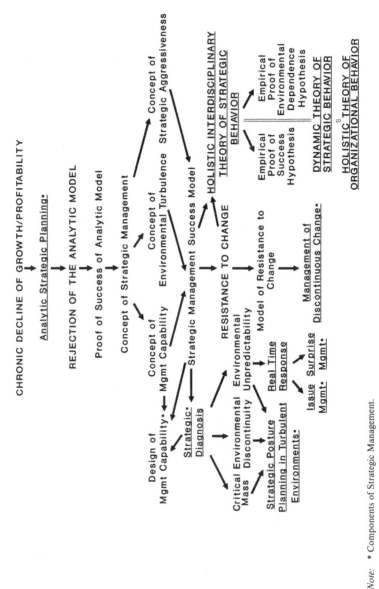

Figure 4. A Road Map of Ansoff's Contributions to Strategic Management

Note: * Components of Strategic Management.

Legend: Capital Letters = Triggering Events; Lower Case = Concepts/Models; Lower Case Underlined = Management Technologies; Double Underlining = Theories.

TURBULENCE LEVEL 1-3

- Future Demand Extrapolable
- Profits Follow Growth
- Firm's Growth Follows Market
- Historically Successful Strategies Will Remain Successful
- Historical Strengths Will Remain Strengths
- Surprises Are Few

→

STRATEGY PLANNING BY ANALYTIC EXTRAPOLATION OF FAMILIAR RISK TAKING

TURBULENCE LEVEL 4-5

- Extrapolation of Demand Is Dangerous
- Profits Do Not Follow Growth
- Firm's Demand Does Not Follow Market
- Historical Success Strategies Are Suspect
- Historical Strengths Become Weaknesses
- Surpriseful Events Are Frequent

→

STRATEGIC POSTURE PLANNING THROUGH CREATIVE VISUALIZATION OF FUTURE SUCCESS STRATEGIES AND ENTREPRENEURIAL RISK TAKING

Figure 5. Comparison of Strategic Planning at Different Turbulence Levels

4. *Management of Discontinuous Change* is a technology for anticipating, managing, and minimizing organizational resistance which inevitably arises when a firm is forced to transform its strategic behavior from one level of turbulence to another.

The Strategic Diagnosis, Strategic Posture Planning, Real Time Response and Management of Discontinuous Change are complementary component technologies of *Systematic Strategic Management* on turbulence levels 4 and 5.

STRATEGIC MANAGEMENT AS A HOLISTIC/CONTINGENT AND MULTIDISCIPLINARY CONCEPT

American management literature has a long history of putting old wine into new bottles. When a particular management technique has been around for a while and lost the blush of novelty, the frequent solution is to rename and advertise it as a new development.

This certainly is the case with the concept of strategic management. Since the concept was first proposed in 1972, there has been a proliferation of books and articles on "strategic management" which, in fact, continue to deal with analytic strategic planning. Even the annual congresses of the Strategic Management Society continue to focus on very worthwhile research on strategy formulation, strategic planning, organizational design, and cultural change. But there are very few papers on the holistic interdisciplinary process of strategic management, in the spirit of the definition I originally proposed in 1972.

Therefore, I feel that it is necessary to review the distinctive concepts of strategic management which integrate the component technologies into a coherent whole.

1. The strategic management concept is *holistic* in the sense that it concerned with strategic behavior of a firm as a whole, starting with sensing the environment and ending with launching/divesting products/ services or entering/exiting markets, acquiring/divesting technologies, creating the new relationship with sociopolitical environment. Thus, strategic management is a systems concept and its success or failure is measured at the "bottom line" by the firm's profit potential.

2. Strategic management is also a *contingent* concept in the sense that it recognizes that there is a variety of strategic behaviors which can be successful, and that the driving contingent variable is the environmental turbulence.

3. Finally strategic management is *multidisciplinary* in the sense that it recognizes and integrates that cognitive-logical, psychological, sociological and political variables affect every phase of strategic activity,

starting with problem/opportunity sensing and ending with launching
the results of strategic activity on the market.

MANAGERIAL THEORY OF STRATEGIC BEHAVIOR

When I entered academia in 1973, I brought with me a thorough grounding
in the theoretical approach to reality, as well as first-hand experience in how
strategic behavior occurs in practice. My dominant interest was, and remained,
in improving the quality of strategic behavior through development and
application of practical technology for strategic management. At the same time,
I felt that a theory of strategic behavior would provide an important stimulus
for the development of technology. In particular, I was convinced that
technology derived from an empirically-validated theory inherits this validity
and, therefore, makes theory-based technological inventions more likely to
succeed than observation-derived inventions.

As a result, I pursued technology and development theory building in
parallel. Over the years this turned out be a fruitful path on which the two
streams of development stimulated and reinforced each other. For example,
the struggle to understand the reasons for the failure of analytic strategic
planning technology led me to the discovery of the theoretical strategic success
hypothesis. And in turn, the hypothesis led to a substantial body of technology
for management in turbulent environments which was described on the
preceding pages.

My first effort to make a coherent theoretical statement was an article titled
"Toward a Strategic Theory of the Firm" (1969).

Rereading the paper, I find it to be a "through the glass darkly" first effort
to come to grips with a very difficult problem. The "theory" presented in the
paper lacked the breadth promised in the title in the fact that it did not deal
with strategic behavior as a whole. But it did provide a pioneering description
of the innovation process which is a component of this behavior. Interestingly
enough, a close reading shows an early anticipation of the contextual
perspective, and of importance of the environment as the key contextual
variable. A self critique at the end of the paper called for further
operationalization of the hypothesis and for "modeling the relation between
external and internal stimuli to the firm and the resulting strategic action, and
modeling the relation between a given strategic action and consequent
performance as the firm" (p. 39).

As the reader already knows, I followed this advice to myself in creating
and operationalizing and testing the Strategic Success Hypothesis, which did
establish the relation between a strategic action and success. The Hypothesis
became one of the cornerstones of a book I originally titled *Applied,
Managerial, Contextual, Multidisciplinary Theory of Strategic Behavior*. For

unfortunate but understandable reasons, the publisher insisted on converting this descriptive title to the misleading *Strategic Management* (1979).

The theory treats behavior of Environment Serving Organizations (ESO) which exist for the purpose of providing goods and services to their environments. Thus, by using the ESO concept, I abandoned the historical dichotomy between (for profit) business firms and not-for-profit organizations.

This turned out to be a happy choice, because it illuminated the similarities and the differences between firms and not-for-profits, and provided a basis for a practical design technology of not-for-profit ESOs which increases their responsiveness to the needs of their client environments.

Strategic Management was written as an applied theory, an approach widely in natural sciences and largely missing from the social sciences. This is unfortunate because, if this approach had been used more widely used, social sciences would have been more responsive to concerns of practical managers, and thus would have enhanced acceptance of theory by managers as being relevant to practice.

The theory is made applicable by focussing it on strategic behaviors which lead to success or failure, and by using language and relationships which facilitate translation of theoretical hypotheses into practical technology. (For example, translation of the Strategic Success Hypothesis into Strategic Diagnosis.)

Strategic Management is "managerial" in the sense that it departs from the tradition of treating organizations as undifferentiated collections of individuals by singling out general managers as a distinctive and influential group of actors.

The word "contextual" in my preferred title describes another break with sociological tradition of assuming that an observed pattern of behavior is applicable to all organizations (for example, the revealing title of the classic *The Behavioral Theory of the Firm*, by Cyert and March). The first contextual aspect of my theory is that it identifies different behaviors by different ESO's. And the second is that it makes success/failure of these behaviors contingent on the characteristics of the environment of an ESO.

The final "Multidisciplinary" descriptor in my preferred title calls attention to the range of types of variables which are used to describe ESO's and their behavior. This range consists of cognitive-rational, psychological, sociological and political variables.

Within the above framework the theory answers the following questions:

1. What is the range of observable strategic behaviors among ESOs?
2. What determines the behavior of an ESO?
3. What behaviors result in success/failure?
4. Why do many observable behaviors differ from success behavior?

The answers to these questions are in the form of hypotheses, and the processes by which ESOs choose their behavior is described by flow charts and simple parametric equations.

The logic of the book is built on six Axioms which give rise to the hypotheses. I named after distinguished scientists whose writings helped me give the book a multidisciplinary perspective. These Axioms are:

- *Whitehead's Axiom* about influence of individuals on ESOs
- *Machiavelli's Axiom* about the workings of power in ESOs
- *J. V. Thompson's Axiom* about determinants of ESO behaviors
- *Emery-Trist's Axiom* about influence of environment in ESOs
- *Chandler's Axiom* about ESOs adaptation to the environment
- *Ashby's Axiom* about success behaviors

The Hypotheses scattered throughout the book trace their origins to one or more Axioms.

A BROADER PERSPECTIVE

The privilege of writing this autobiography gave me an opportunity to relive my past and to identify the pattern and trend of my intellectual and professional life. Of necessity, such focus made this paper personal and egocentric. Before signing off, I want to take a broader look at the state of the academic study of management in its relation to the future challenges which confront the practice of management.

As discussed in detail in this paper, at the level of decision making, future environment of most organizations will, at best, be partially predictable and will require creative vision and bold entrepreneurial risk taking by mangers. But at the meta level the characteristics of the foreseeable future are clear: The environment will be turbulent, discontinuous, surpriseful, and complex. Thus, in addition to creativity and entrepreneurship, management will need skills in management of complexity. Furthermore, complexity of environments of most organizations will change with time, and managers will need skills for frequent adaptation of their organizations to the new complexity levels. Thus, management will require a combination of holistic skills in managing organizational complexity and in transforming complexity from one level to another.

As I survey the present state of knowledge and research trends, I am reluctantly forced to a conclusion that management academia in the United States is in danger of failing to meet the challenges described above. The first requirement in management of complexity is inclusion in decision making of all the important variables which make up the complexity. But a majority of academic research pays little attention to this requirement. Rather than let reality determine the scope of their research, a majority of researches let the scope be determined by the limits of the discipline or function in which they specialize.

To do this is to emasculate reality and to produce results which may be of interest to other members of one's discipline, but will have little interest and utility to managers who have to cope with the complete range of complexity. As mentioned before, in management practice such results are called "solutions in search of a problem."

A similar state of affairs is found in management training and education. Students are taught by specialists who illuminate parts of the total complexity through the optic of their respective disciplines. And the integration of the parts is left either to the existential case method, or to a computer simulation, and, therefore, in all cases to the students' subconscious.

In fairness to the field of management, this state of affairs pervades much of the scientific community which prefers in-depth research on partitioned complexity to holistic research at the requisite level of complexity. All of this is done on the implicit assumption that if enough different scientific bricks are made, the architecture of the house of science will reveal itself. But the urban blight of contractor-designed and built houses illustrates the fact that absence of an architect makes for ugly homes.

Unfortunately, in the field of management the problem of managing complexity becomes even more difficult. Management is both a cognitive and a social process. As a result most complex problems require a multi-disciplinary integration of the scientific branches which contribute to it: cognitive-administrative, psychological, sociological, political, and anthropological. Thus complexity management is also multidisciplinary management.

I am not advocating an abandonment of the current preoccupation with deep insights in partitioned pockets of complexity. But I am concerned that if management academia fails to develop a breed of multidisciplinary complexity synthesizers, and fails to legitimize and encourage research on holistic theory building, the bulk of academic contributions will become increasingly peripheral to the key problems which confront general managers during the 1990s.

PUBLICATIONS

1948

Stability of linear oscillating systems with constant time lag (Paper No. 48-A-22). *Journal of Applied Mechanics.*

A general stability criterion for linear oscillating systems with constant time lag. *Quarterly of Applied Mathematics* (October).

1957

Strategies for diversification. *Harvard Business Review* (September-October).

1958

A model for diversification. *Management Science, 4*(July).

1959

With T. Andersen, F. Norton, & J.F. Weston. Planning for diversification through merger. *California Management Review, 1*(4).

1962

A quasi-analytic method for long range planning. In M. Alexis & C. Wilson (Eds.), *Organizational decision-making.* Englewood Cliffs, NJ: Prentice-Hall.
With F. Weston. Merger objectives and organization structure. *Review of Economics and Business* (August).
Company objectives: Blueprint-or-blue sky? *Management Review* (September).

1963

Management participation in diversification. In *Proceedings of Client Conference.* Menlo Park, CA: Long Range Planning Service, Stanford Research Institute, 1963.

1964

Planning as a practical management tool. *Financial Executive* (June).
Evaluation of applied research in business rirms. In J.R. Bright (Ed.), *Proceedings of the Conference on Technological Planning on the Corporate Level.* Homewood, IL: Richard D. Irwin.
A quasi-analytic Approach to the Business Policy Problem. *Management Technology, IV* (June).

1965

Corporate Strategy. New York: McGraw-Hill.
The firm of the future. *Harvard Business Review* (September-October).

1966

Planning at the level of and enterprise in the USA. In *Proceedings of the Conference.*

1967

With R.G. Brandenburg. Research and development, planning. In *Handbook of Business Administration.* New York: McGraw-Hill.

With R.G. Brandenburg. Design of optimal business planning system: A study proposal. *Journal for Cybernetics of Planning and Organization* (March).

The expanding role of the computer in managerial decision-making. *Informatic.*

With R. G. Brandenburg. The general manager of the future. *California Management Review, 11*(3).

With R. G. Brandenburg. A program of research in business planning. *Management Science, 13*(February).

With D. Slevin. An appreciation of industrial dynamics. *Management Science, 14*(March).

The evolution of corporate planning. In *Report of the SRI long range planning service.* Palo Alto, CA.

With J.M. Stewart. Strategies for a technology-based business. *Harvard Business Review* (November-December).

1968

Vers une theorie strategique des enterprises [Toward a strategic theory of the firm]. *Economics et Societes, II*(3).

With R. G. Brandenburg. A language for organizational design. *Perspective of planning* (pp. 349-398). Proceedings of OECD Working Symposium on Long Range Forecasting and Planning, Bellagio, Italy. [Reprinted in *Management Science, 17*(12)].

[Review of the *Study of Policy Formation*]. *Journal of Business, 43*(4).

1969

Managerial problem-solving. In J. Blood, Jr. (Ed.), *Management science in planning and control* (The Technical Association of the Pulp and Paper Industry, Special Technical Association Publication No. 5). New York. [Reprinted in *Journal of Business Policy, 2*, (1, Autumn 1971)].

Issues in national policy on growth of firms. In J.F. Weston & S. Peltzman (Eds.), *Public policy toward mergers* Pacific Palisades, CA: Goodyear Publishing Co.

The innovative firm. *Journal of the PE Consulting Group.* (Reprinted in *Long Range Journal, 1*, [2]).
Business strategy. Middlesex, England: Penguin Books.
Long range planning in perspective. In *Proceedings of the 15th CIOS International Management Congress.* Tokyo: Kogakusha C. Limited.

1970

With J. Anver, R. Brandenburg, F. Portner, and R. Radosevich. Does planning pay? The effect of planning on success of acquisitions in American firms. *Long Range Planning Journal, 3*(2).

1971

Corporate strategy. Paper presented at the First European Management Symposium, Dayos, Switzerland.
With D. Lebell. Institutional factors in strategic decision-making. *Journal of Business Policy, 1*, (3).
Strategy as a tool for coping with change. *Journal of Business Policy, 1*, (4).
Acquisition behavior of U.S. manufacturing firms, 1946-65. Vanderbilt University Press.

1972

Dolgosrochnoe planirovanie v perspective. In G.K. Popov (Ed.), *Sovremennye Tendenzyi v Upravlenie v Capitalisticheskikh Stranakh* (pp. 51-72G). Moscow: Izdatelstvo Progress.
With R. J. Brandenburg, F. E. Portner, & H. R. Radosevich. The concept of strategic management. *The Journal of Business Policy, 2*(4).
From strategic planning to strategic management. *Proceedings of the International Conference on Strategic Management*, Unternenhmungs-planung, Hahn/Taylor, Physica-Verlag, Wursburg, Wien.
The next twenty years in management education. *The Library Quarterly, 43*(4).
Corporate structure, present, and future. In *Proceedings of the Third International Conference on Corporate Planning.* Brussels.

1974

Management en advieswerk: de derde generatie. *Overdruk uit TED.*

1975

La structure de l'enterprise aujourd'hui et demain. *Cahier de Fondation National pour l'Enseignement de la Gestion.*

La structure de l'entreprise, aujourd'hui et demain (premiere partie). *Cheft, Revue Suisse du Management* (February).
The knowledge professional in the post-industrial era. *Bedrijfskunde, 47,* 88.
The state of practice in management systems. Paper presented at the Second US-USSR Conference on Planning, New York.
An applied managerial theory of strategic behavior. EIASM Working Paper No. 75-12.
Management Under Discontinuity. In H.I. Ansoff (Ed.), *Proceedings from a Conference at INSEAD.*
The concept of strategic management. Managerial problem solving. Le concept de gestion strategique. La resolution des problemes de management. *African Administrative Studies.*

1976

With Declerck and Hayes (Eds.). *From strategic planning to strategic management.* New York: John Wiley.
Managing strategic surprise by response to weak signals. *California Management Review, XVIII*(2), 21-33.

1977

The state of practice in planning system. *Sloan Management Review* (Winter).

1978

With J. Eppink & H. Gomer. Management of strategic surprise and discontinuity: Improving managerial decisiveness. *Marknads Vetande, Utgiven av Sveriges Marknadsforbund,* 4/78 argang 9.
Corporate capability for managing change. *SRI, Business Intelligence Program, Research Report No. 610.*
The future of corporate structure. *Journal of General Management* (Autumn).
Functions of the executive office in a large conglomerate. *EIASM Working Paper, No. 75-42.*
With H. T. Thanheiser. *Corporate planning: A comparative view of the evolution and current practice in the United States and Western Europe.* EIASM, Working Paper No. 78-10.
Management in unpredictable environments. *The Intercontinental Advanced Management Report, 1*(7).
With J. C. Leontiades. Strategic portfolio management. *Journal of General Management, 4*(1).

1979

Strategic management. New York: John Wiley.
Societal strategy for the business firm. EIASM Working Paper No. 79-24.
Planning management of turbulent change. *Encyclopedia of Professional Management.* New York: McGraw-Hill.
Changing shape of the strategic problem. *Journal of General Management,* *4* (4).
Proposal for Research on Future Legitimacy (Role) of the Business Firm in Europe. EIASM Working Paper.
Strategic Business Areas. *Tehokas Yritys,* Johtamistoimen Ammattilehiti.
Aspirations and culture in strategic behavior. EIASM Working Paper No. 79-12.
Strategic issue management. *Strategic Management Journal, 1,* (2).
ABC of strategic management. EIASM Working Paper No. 79-25.

1980

With W. Kirsch & P. Roventa. *Dispersed positioning in strategic portfolio analysis.* EIASM Working Paper No. 80-12.
Managing the process of discontinuous change–Part 1–Behavioral resistance. EIASM Working Paper No. 80-26.
Managing the process of discontinuous change–Part 2–Systematic resistance. EIASM Working Paper No. 80-36.
Managing the process of discontinuous change–Part 3–Alternative approaches. EIASM Working Paper No. 80-37.
Managing the process of discontinuous change–Part 4–The Learning-action approach. EIASM Working Paper No. 80-38.

1983

With P. Achleitner & G. Haskins. The firm: Meeting the legitimacy challenge. *European Management Journal, 2*(1).
With P. Achleitner. Die bedeutung soziopolitischer strategien. *Harvard Manager Magazine,* 4 IV. Quartal.
With R.P. Declerck & R. L. Hayes. *El planteamiento estrategico.* Primera edicion.
Administracao estrategica, Sao Paulo, Brazil: Editora Atlas.
With W. Kirsch & P. Roventa. *Bausteine eines strategischen managements.* Unscharfenpositionierung in der Strategischen Portfolio-Analyze. New York: Walter de Gruyter.
Societal strategy for the business firm. In R. Lamb (Ed.), *Advances in strategic management* (Vol. 1). Greenwich, CT: JAI Press.

1984

Implanting strategic management in the firm. Englewood Cliffs, NJ: Prentice-Hall.

Methoden zur Verwirklichung Strategischer Anderungen in der Unter Nehmung. *Schriften zur Unternelmens Fuhrung.* Strategisches Management 1, 29, Gabler.

Implanting strategic management. Englewood Cliffs, NJ: Prentice-Hall.

1985

Conceptual underpinnings of systematic strategic management. *European Journal of Operational Research, 19.*

Laestrategia de la empresa. New York: McGraw-Hill.

La perspectiva cambiante del problema estrategico. *Sinergia, 3.*

1986

Competitive strategy analysis on the personal computer. *Journal of Business Strategy, 6* (Winter).

The firm: Meeting the legitimacy challenge. The European Institute for Advanced Studies in Management and the European Foundation for Management Development.

With T.E. Baker. Is corporate culture the ultimate answer? In R. Lamb & P. Shrivastava (Eds.), *Advances in strategic management* (Vol. 4). Greenwich, CT: JAI Press.

With J.M. Stewart. Strategies for a technology-based business. *Harvard Business Review, The Management of Technological Innovation.*

Competitive strategy analysis on the personal computer. In *The international management development review* (Vol. 2).

Bases conceptuales de la administracion estrategica sistematica. *Sinergia (Estudios En Administracion, Economia Y Ciencias Del Comport Amiento Humano).*

1987

The emerging paradigm of strategic behavior. *The Strategic Management Journal, 8.*

Strategic management of technology. *The Journal of Business Strategy* (Winter).

Que es la estrategia de la empresa? *Enciclopedia De Direccion Y Administracion De La Empresa.*

The pathology of applied research in social science. In *The use and abuse of social science.* Beverly Hills, CA: Sage.

1989

Strategicheskoe Upravalenie Moscow.
The new corporate strategy. New York: John Wiley.

1990

Implanting strategic management (2nd ed.). Englewood, Cliffs, NJ: Prentice-Hall.
Implanting strategic management. (Japanese Edition).
A nova estratejic emprescrial. Sao Paulo, Brazil: Editora Atlas A.S..
With P.A. Sullivan. Competitiveness through strategic response. In R. Gillman (Ed.), *Making organizations more competitive.* San Francisco, CA: Jossey-Bass.
[Rejonder to "The design school: Reconsidering the basic principles of strategic management," by Henry Mintzberg]. *Strategic Management Journal.*
Strategic management in a historical perspective. In D. Hussey (Ed.), *International review of strategic management.*

1992

With P.A. Sullivan et al. Empirical Proof of Paradigmic Theory of Strategic Success Behaviors if Environment Serving Organizations.

NOTES

1. "Does Planning Pay? The Effect of Planning on Success of Acquisitions in American Firms" (1970); "Corporate Strategy" (1971).
2. "The Concept of Strategic Management" (1972); *From Strategic Plannning to Strategic Management* (1976); *Implanting Strategic Management in the Firm* (1984).
3. *Introduction to Cybernetics* (Wiley, 1956).
4. *Implanting Strategic Management* (Japanese Edition, 1990).
5. "Strategic Management in a Historical Perspective" (1990); "Empirical Research on Strategic Success Hypothesis" (1991); The following unpublished doctoral dissertations at the School of Business and Management, United States International University: P. Hatziantoniou, *The Relationship of Environmental Turbulence, Corporate Strategic Profile and Company Performance* (1986); H. Chabane, *Restructuring and Performance in Algerian State-Owned Enterprises: A Strategic Management Study* (1987); T.T. Salameh, *Analysis and Financial Performance of the Banking Industry in United Arab Emirates: A Strategic Management Study* (1987); P.A. Sullivan, *The Relationship Between Proportion of Income Derived From Subsidy and Strategic Performance of a Federal Agency Under the Commercial Activities Program* (1987); R. Jaja, *Technology and Banking: The Implications of Technological Change to Financial Performance of Commercial Banks* (1989); A. Lewis, *Strategic Posture and Financial Performance of the Banking Industry in California: A Strategic Management Study* (1989); S. Djohar, *The Relationship Between General Management Capability and Performance of Indonesian Firms* (1991).

Chris Argyris

Looking Backward and Inward in Order to Contribute to the Future

CHRIS ARGYRIS

The organization of this paper begins with a description of the factors that sustained my scholarly inquiry. Then, I look inward to examine some early-life personal factors that may have influenced my scholarly concerns. The former provides a map of the ideas that challenge me. The latter provides insight into some of the sources of energy for the ideas that go beyond intellectual curiosity. Finally, I will try to make the connections between these two features more explicit.

THE FACTORS THAT SUSTAINED MY SCHOLARLY INQUIRY

Problem Oriented: Especially Puzzles, Dilemmas, and Paradoxes

I have always thought of our problems, challenges, and dilemmas that human beings express as being important in living and managing their lives. I have especially been concerned about individuals and organizations. Both seem to me to have a "right" to health, each to be managed in ways that actualize their potential and fulfill their stewardship. Effectively performing individuals and organizations are required for a sane society; without both we could go out of control.

Problems that persist and plague human beings are of special interest to me. My attention is especially caught by a problem that is described as having existed for years and unlikely ever to be solved. The idea of tackling a problem that is compulsively repetitive and protected by status quo norms is exhilarating. It is as if, were I to help solve the problem, I might help reduce the societal shackles restraining human beings. These problems come "in pairs." One is the problem itself; the other is that the problem *persists* with support from the status quo.

Looking backward, I think one of the fascinating features about problems that are compulsively repetitive and protected by the status quo is how they are often related to designed disempowerment. More fascinating is that the disempowerment is taken for granted. And even more fascinating is that designed disempowerment is often a societal mechanism to maintain order that contains its own seeds for slow but sure disorder.

Finding and doing something about inner contradictions is especially appealing. This is why, I have always been more interested in double-loop rather than single-loop learning. The latter leads to changes in action; the former requires changes in the underlying human and societal programs that guide the actions in the first place.

Theory-oriented

I have always been interested in theory. Theory provides an orderly explanation for potential and actual processes that are counterproductive. It is psychologically safer to examine disorder when I can see the orderliness of disorder and when I can help to create a new order. Both of these conditions require theory.

Theory also helps to keep me intellectually honest. In building theory, I have to make my premises and inferences explicit. I have to make public the reasoning that leads to whatever argument I am making. I also have to find ways to publicly test my conclusions.

Theory is a public way to continually reflect and monitor my thinking. This publicness helps to assure me that others would also help me to see gaps, inconsistencies, and errors.

Looking backward, this is especially important to a person such as me who feels strongly about the problems he studies. At times my emotional commitment outdistances my reasoning and data. If there is risk from my emotional commitment to problem solving, there is safety in a theory that can help make explicit and manage my unintended distortions.

For theory to act as a safety control to my personal blindness and to the unrecognized gaps in my ideas, it is important to conduct research in the everyday world. To make it more likely that the users of my theory will not be shortchanged, I feel compelled to design theory that the users can test while they are using it. I want to provide the users with as many ways that I can think of to help them be in control of their own destiny.

From the outset of my career, my research has always been guided by concern for internal and external validity. External validity meant that the research had to be relevant to the everyday world; there had to be a fit between the results and practice. As my inquiries progressed, I became increasingly fascinated with what people took for granted and how unaware they seemed to be when they were acting upon what they took for granted. This led to a line of research that suggested that behind what is taken for granted is highly skillful behavior, and behind this skillful behavior is acculturation of social virtues (for example, honesty, caring, and integrity). The internalization of the social virtues and the becoming skillful at using them leads to unawareness. The unawareness is not caused by ignorance; it is not due to a hole in people's heads. Unawareness is the price of acting skillfully and the result of internalizing the social values in which we develop and live.

If this is true, then testing these ideas in the everyday world would likely require new skills, such as how to become aware of that which you are unaware when this unawareness is due to skill. This means that "relevance" and "fit" are necessary but insufficient. Therefore, I have recently made the distinction between applicability and useability. Applicability is related to external validity; useability is to implement what is relevant and fits. For example, I believe most scholars would attribute high external validity to empirical research methods. Yet, we all know that there is a gap between these ideas and how empirical research is conducted. Filling that gap is related to useability.

The gap varies depending upon the concepts being used. For example, producing a regression analysis can be spelled out in detail. If we follow the directions correctly, we will always come out with a similar answer. If two people produce different answers, they can trace back to see where the "errors" were committed. This is an example of knowledge that is applicable and useable. It is useable because there are rules that specify how to produce it.

On the other hand, the gap between applicability and useability, let us say, on how to produce commitment so that those we study will be motivated to cooperate and give us as much valid knowledge as they can, is much larger. The more I study how to close that gap, the more I realize that researchers try to close it in all sorts of informal ways that are rarely included in the articles that are published. This knowledge is part of useability but, to my knowledge, is rarely contained in the books on research methods. As a result of my inquiries, I now also believe that a nontrivial amount of the gap between applicability and useability is produced by following the formal rules of conducting empirical research correctly.

Theory and Research: Methods that Enhance Validity and Generalizability as well as Useability

Rigorous research methods, for example, place subjects in a top-down situation that is consistent with the psychosocial structures of pyramidal organizations and, what I came to realize later, the unilaterally controlling defensiveness producing theories-in-use that most of us hold. How can scholars interested in discovering truth design research methods create conditions for limited learning, especially about how to change the nature of the universe? How can scholars who espouse objectivity and description use methods that would likely lead to describing the world as it is, that would unrealizingly lead to colluding with what the subjects take for granted, and that would help the researchers to be unaware of the collusion?

This points to what I feel is a root cause of some of the features that limits social science research in discovering knowledge that is valid and useable. The features above are normative in that they take a position about the proper condition for placing people and positioning researchers, vis-à-vis subjects, in order to get at truth. Their features are consistent with the theories-in-use (individual through organizational) that dominate human activity. If true, then the admonition to be descriptive could lead researchers to design research that unrealizingly colludes with the status quo. The collusion occurs because the research methods we use are consistent with features of the status quo that permits subjects and researchers to take the collusion for granted.

A second problem that I study is what are the features of useful conceptualizing of the knowledge that we produce. If human beings are to use knowledge produced by scholars, then the knowledge that is produced should be understandable, storable, and retrievable by the human mind under conditions of everyday life. I have always been bewildered how this "obvious" requirement is often downplayed if not ignored. For example, I recall a complex model of organizational behavior that the authors admitted (at the end of their book) was unlikely to be used in its full-blown capacity. The practitioners, they said, would have to simplify and thereby, "degrade" (their words) the model. It never occurred to these scholars that the degraded model may be closer approximation to the truth than their own. In this connection, I am impressed with Kurt Lewin's ethnographic descriptive approach and his use of topological diagrams to capture the essence of the generalizable. His topological maps are, the forerunners of the many different "action maps" that are central to my work and to the work of others.

A third problem is the degree to which knowledge produced by researchers, when used correctly, can create conditions that are questionable, if not unethical. For example, I reviewed how some of the best known literature in social psychology and sociology, if used as the authors recommend, will likely lead to cover-up and cover-up of cover-ups. Indeed, in many cases the researchers advised social lying in order to achieve objectives of getting people to do what they want them to do.

Intervention

These kinds of concerns have led to my focus on intervention in the field as a mode of inquiry. The purpose is to create rare events which (1) inform us descriptively about how the status quo reacts when it is being threatened, (2) thereby testing hitherto untested features of the status quo, and (3) at the same time produce knowledge about alternatives that can liberate human beings from features of the status quo.

Donald Campbell once told me during a debate at Northwestern that my argument was not so much against experimentation as it was an argument for how to enhance learning, especially of the double-loop variety. He pointed out that my interventions are field experiments where I try to design them to minimize some of the unintended consequences of the rules to produce rigorous research.

I found his point helpful. It freed me to focus on the features of field experiment that could begin to minimize some of the dysfunctional features that I had described. For example, (1) identifying problems that could not be solved without colluding with the status quo; (2) involving subjects as clients where there is a commitment to be of help (3) which, in turn, requires developing of rigorous theories about the way the world as is, the way it should be, and how to get from here to there; (4) which, in turn, means that researchers have to develop skills to translate practical problems into opportunities for rigorous tests of social science theories without losing the theories' connectedness to the problems; (5) researchers who have the interpersonal skill to deal with organizational, inter-group, group, and individual defenses as well as (6) the courage to hang in there even when they feel threatened, which is likely because in order to study the undiscussables, they will have to surface the culturally sanctioned by-pass and cover-up activities, which is a violation of the by-pass and cover-up activities.

Early in my career, the National Institute of Mental Health (NIMH) sponsored a small and private conference on my work. It invited scholars and a few senior executives. The lessons I remember from that conference were that even though both groups evaluated my work positively, when it came time to recommend action they recommended different strategies, both of which were self-limiting. The scholars recommended more descriptive research before my work was used in the real world. Lewin's admonition that we can learn by changing something did not seem applicable to them. Ironically, the conference was held at the Institute of Social Research at Michigan.

The executives recommended immediate field testing but not in their organizations. Their problem was not the ideas but their organizations' capacity to internalize the ideas for use in everyday life. They, and their fellow executives at the top, did not have the learning capabilities that would be required to experiment with the ideas. The biggest gap in capability was not the difficulty or the primitiveness of the ideas, but were the defensive routines within their organizations, groups, and (less so) individuals.

During this time, I was exposed to T-groups. It seemed that they represented a social science technology that could be used with organic groups at the highest levels of organization. The intervention strategy would be to begin at the top and expand downward as the values and actions of those at the top supported a new type of learning.

I soon became frustrated with the experiential movement because too many of its senior practitioners seemed not to be interested in subjecting their ideas to empirical test. An increasing number operated on tacit theories; indeed, some believed that they should not have theories or, if they did, they should remain tacit. I remember one senior professional who said that he did not think about what he was doing because he might lose his creativity! Here were scholars acting as if emotions could be distinguished from thinking; feelings could be studied separately from thinking and by a mode that somehow did not include thinking. These scholars took us from the excesses of rationality to the excesses of emotionality.

There were many idiosyncratic reasons for this trend but there were two that were systematic. I believe the lack to theory was less of an anti-thinking mentality and more that there was no theory available on how to combine the cognitive and emotional. I also believe that many of those practitioners would have found it threatening if ideas and feelings could be genuinely integrated because their coping mechanisms required the maintenance of the split. This is one reason that many of the original participants in experiential learning left the field and why the field became largely and ideology not seeking to be tested.

About this time, Donald Schön and I began to collaborate. Both of us were interested in theory, practice, and the defenses (our own and others) that may impinge on research, and both of us trusted data that were relatively directly observable. I believe that our line of inquiry points to a way that thinking and feeling can be integrated by studying them as they exist in action.

RECOLLECTIONS FROM MY PERSONAL LIFE

I was one of three boys who were born in the United States, moved to Greece for several years, and returned in time to begin their schooling in the United States. I grew up in Irvington, New Jersey. After being discharged as an officer in the Signal Corps, I attended Clark University where I received a B.A. in psychology and business (1947). I then went to the University of Pennsylvania for six months. Next, I obtained a Masters degree from Kansas University in psychology and economics (1949). I completed my formal education by obtaining a Ph.D. at Cornell University (1951).

There are two recollections that I have of these early years of my life that are relevant to this story. First, I could not speak English very well. I recollect even more vividly how unconflicted my teachers were in confirming my fears that I was, indeed in trouble. Their advice was simple: Learn English and learn it fast.

Second, I remember prejudice against our family. Comments were made to me about the fact that the neighborhood did not desire "greasy Greeks." The prejudice continued for years, although at a decreasing rate. For example, I remember wanting to buy some land at Lake Mohawk, New Jersey after World War II. I was turned down because, my sponsor told me, I was a minority.

During all those episodes, the reaction of my parents was that I should act in ways that proved the majority to be wrong. It was not so much that prejudice was wrong (they had their own prejudices), but that I was expected to show the majority members that I could meet and surpass their standards. In effect, their theory was that in the United States—the land of freedom—prejudice is lessened when the recipients of the prejudice prove that the stereotype is incorrect and therefore wrong. The impact on me was to be less angry at prejudice per se and more committed to showing it up. I think that this was a source of courage and commitment that eventually helped me out in the field, especially when powerful people rejected the use of social scientists in their organizations. I did not like the rejection: my reaction was to act in ways that proved their prejudice about social science to be mistaken.

But in order for this strategy to work, I had to perform. And because I had more than my share of warts, I had to look inward and work hard to reduce them. This is a source of my continual interest in self-inquiry and my taking it for granted that others should have the same interest, especially if they have power over others.

I became interested in an academic career in organizational studies largely by an unforgettable event. Toward the end of World War II, I was the officer in charge of several large Signal Corps depots in Chicago. I had formal awards to show that I was a very effective leader in terms of technical performance and efficiency. After I was discharged I visited the depots as a civilian. I then found out that the employees had serious doubts about my human skills. Consistent with my early upbringing, my reaction was that I had better learn more about myself. Hence, when I returned to continue my university education, I studied psychology and business administration.

During this time I interacted with Roger Barker, Fritz Heider (who was at Smith), and had a few contracts with Kurt Lewin at MIT. Although each was a very different person, they all saw the world of everyday life as the place in which to discover problems and from which to infer theory. Each, in his own way, was mounting a revolution in the discipline of psychology. Each, in his own way, gave me friendly advice to question the status quo, to make problem solving the test of the discipline, and to feel free to question theorems of the scholarly community. These values agreed with mine and I prospered. Not surprisingly, I chose the School of Industrial and Labor Relations at Cornell to do my Ph.D. It was a new school that was problem-centered and which encouraged questioning the traditional discipline boundaries. William F. Whyte was a true embodiment of those values.

My first academic appointment was at the Labor and Management Center at Yale University. Wight Bakke, its director, also encouraged a problem focus: the questioning of disciplinary boundaries. He also placed great importance on theory building. During my first year, I was given the opportunity to assess the status of research on organization in the United States. It was an excellent opportunity to interview the "big names" in the field. I learned a lot from that research. The most important personal learning was related to the internal dynamics (politics) of the field. I learned that the big names were very bright, committed to their research and, for the most part, to teaching.

I also learned that they privately criticized each other's work, yet they were poorly informed about it. This stunned me. The academic community was supposed to be an unfettered activity of inquiry for truth.

I presented my substantive findings in a conference chaired by Douglas McGregor. He began by asking me to say one or two things that I wanted to highlight. Without hesitating, I told the group that my biggest learning was how little they knew about each other's work, how insulated they were, and how their behavior did not match their espoused theories about integration and progress. I asked them how progress was to be made if they did not take the lead in modelling how criticism can feed progress.

There was a deafening silence when I finished. Doug made some important comment to the effect that this young scholar was being impertinent (said in a supportive manner) but probably was saying something that we should take seriously. A few comments followed. Soon the attention was focused on the substantive findings.

Later, several big names advised me that what I observed was probably correct. They also added that it may have been a poor career strategy to discuss those ideas publicly. Such discussions, they advised, were best done discreetly. Those who know my work, know that I have not followed that advice.

As I write this, I am scheduled to attend a conference of ten big names in our field. Now I am one of them. Each of the participants wrote a short paper. Five of these papers complained about the norms of scholarly community against confronting each other's work. They suggested that our field was dominated largely by scholars following their personal ideas and not showing much concern about monitoring the progress in the field. The other five contributors turned in papers that illuminated this concern! When it came my turn to speak about why I accepted the invitation to attend, I told the story that is written above. I then put in a plea for this group, taking the lead to provide a model of how the big names could help reduce the norms of scholarly community that produced the very concerns that many of us wrote about in our papers. There was no loud, deafening silence this time. The next scholar immediately began to talk. He described his reasons for coming. I wondered if that would end the idea of questioning our norms and practices. I am pleased to say it did not. Several of the subgroups have been given tasks which would require examining these issues.

CONNECTION

Problem-Centered

I seek to study problems in everyday life that contain puzzles, dilemmas, paradoxes, and all that challenges the status quo. I enjoy working toward producing valid knowledge, enhancing human beings' competence, and strengthening justice.

These scholarly activities produce conditions where I am seen as helpful and caring. Helpfulness and caring should be in the service of human growth and autonomy. At the early stages there is dependency but in the service of growth. When individuals ask how they can repay me, I ask that they help someone else.

I also value research that questions the status quo, especially how it disempowers human beings, and how, in turn, human beings disempower organizations. The personal dimension of this is related to my early experience of feeling disempowered by ethnic prejudice. I also felt disempowered at home because I was one, among three brothers, to confront injustice on our family. Both combined to create conditions where I felt rejected and alone; but, I reacted by "hanging-in." Looking backward, the persistence was probably due to struggling not to be permanently cut off and, at the same time, to plead my case. As best as I can remember, I acted in ways that often made the situation worse which, in turn, increased the likelihood of cut-off. Maybe the emphasis on being helpful was another way to reduce the likelihood that I would be in episodes where injustice was occurring.

The Importance of Theory

Theories organize knowledge so that it is publicly testable, thereby reducing the likelihood of unrecognized gaps, holes, and inconsistencies. Empirical research then can test to access possible unrecognized distortions as well as to provide evidence of the difficulty to falsify them.

Early in my career, I became aware that the research methods I was taught to maximize internal validity created a world where researchers were unilaterally controlling, designedly distancing from their subjects, and made both undiscussable until the end of research.

My dilemma was that I valued internal validity and equally abhorred those conditions. The abhorrence was at two levels. First, those conditions could actually be counterproductive to the objective of producing valid information. Second, I did not like being in a top-down situation. It produced the dependence that I disliked. I was in a double bind. If I followed the accepted rules, I would feel unauthentic. If I embraced the ideas of those who were against positivism, I found myself in a humanistic world that seemed not to care very much for tough public tests of their ideas. This is what has led me to attempt to create research methods that maintain the importance of internal and external validity while, at the same time, require less top-down and distancing relationships.

Unintended Consequences

Trying to redesign research methods and social virtues (such as help, respect, concern, honesty, and courage) placed me in the situation of being a deviant. I was in a minority position. Such a situation was reminiscent of my early life. It activated my sense of courage to confront resistance to change through the use of evidence. But it probably also activated the sense of frustration, loneliness, and self-depreciation that often goes along with being a minority. This, in turn, could lead to feelings of people being unappreciative, if not against me. These feelings had a social basis in the intergroup rivalries I described at the outset. This connects back to my bewilderment about scholars discriminating against each other's work. I recall that one reviewer of my article on the unintended consequences of rigorous research methods had to plead with several other reviewers that raising such questions was not an act of disloyalty. Again, to illustrate my defenses, I was surprised that even such a plea had to be made.

Finally, a word about the role of feelings in my work. Feelings are central to all my models. Equally central is the assumption that there are reasons behind all feelings. People should be encouraged to express their feelings and to take responsibility for them. The way to take responsibility is to make explicit the reasons behind them and then test publicly the validity of the reasoning.

I combine, therefore, a strong emphasis on expressing feelings with an equally strong emphasis on understanding them and testing the validity of the understanding. The later has a cognitive focus, the former an emotional one. The scholarly reasons for the cognitive focus are related to internal validity and disconfirmability. The personal reasons are related to dislike of feeling out of control. If I have the freedom to express my feelings, then I have the equivalent obligation to put the reasons for them to a test that is public and tough.

I value highly acts of being helpful and caring. Indeed, acts of helpfulness and caring by other can bring tears; in my own acts of the same behavior the tears are usually hidden (except in my family). I believe that the greatest likelihood of being powerfully helpful and caring is to focus on a difficult problem that human beings face; hence, my emphasis on studying puzzles, dilemmas, and paradoxes. Even a more likely connection to feelings of being helpful and caring is to study how the status quo can disempower, and how humans collude (often unrealizingly) to maintain their own disempowerment, and how the taken-for-granted need no longer be taken for granted.

Studying my own capacity to be designedly unaware, to distort, and to created gaps and inconsistencies without knowing I was doing so was, as I noted above, partially motivated by learning how to perform more effectively. Hence, my scholarly interests in competence and justice have as their base reducing the injustices that I created and enhancing my competencies required to reduce those injustices in the future.

If one examines the differences between the presently accepted content of such virtues as caring, support, honesty, integrity, and strength with those that Schön and I recommend, the latter can be characterized as more in the "tough love" domain than are the former. The latter encourage courage and assume that others have it or can develop it. Thus, the coping mechanisms I used early in life to deal with prejudice and other such experiences find their way in my normative view of a better world.

But the stance of "tough love" also recreates the tension for potential rejection. For example, students often attack Model II social virtues as being too tough. Or, they interpret the emphasis on disconfirmability as being too rational, especially when it is applied to feelings. I believe that collaboration between some of my colleagues never materialized because they found my confrontational stance uncomfortable. Some found it inept and incompetent. I know this is true in some cases. I also believe it is not in other cases.

The point is that in taking these stances I have recreated some of my early-life tensions. But, as long as I choose to learn from them, I could use that learning to build a normative theory about a world that values valid information, informed choice, personal responsibility, and double-loop learning.

There is another way that I recreated early-life tensions. By choosing to be problem-centered and not discipline-centered, I believe that I became a deviant to those of my colleagues those identity was connected with psychology, sociology, anthropology, or any other discipline. For example, two students, who are now big names, told me years ago that they could not include my ideas in their doctoral research in sociology because they were not seen as sociological. I do know that a president of the American Sociological Association was saddened when he realized (during an interview) that I did not consider myself to be *first* a sociologist. I also recall my first encounter with one of Harvard's most eminent social psychologists. He said, "It's so good to meet you. I have enjoyed your work. I must say I have always wondered, what do you consider yourself to be: a philosopher?"

I do believe that whatever the degree of commitment that exists to remain within discipline boundaries, it is decreasing. The graduate students and young scholars who are among the best and the brightest are increasingly concerned with understanding and solving real problems. What is especially comforting is that many of them are bright enough to pull off a genuine breaking down of the disciplinary walls. The problem will be if they can combine their brightness with the courage required to make the changes persist.

It is here where I believe that professional schools provide a more user-friendly environment. As I look at professional schools, they are developing their own identity. They are increasingly unconflicted about the importance of scholarship that is problem-centered. They are increasingly proud of teaching about a world of practice. They are increasingly providing the conditions where the best and the brightest who seek to be problem-centered can flourish.

PUBLICATIONS

1951

A note on a research technique: The flow chart. *Human Organization, 10*(4), 37-38.
With G. Taylor. A report of the member-centered conferences. In *Frontiers of personnel administration*. New York: Columbia University Press.
With G. Taylor. The member-centered conference as a research method: II. *Human Organization, 9*(4), 5-14.
With G. Taylor. The member-centered conference as a research method: II. *Human Organization, 10*(1), 22-27.
Member-centered training. *Personnel*(November), 236-246.

1952

The impact of budgets on people. New York: Controllership Foundation, Controllers Institute.
Member-centered training. In M.J. Doohrer & V. Marquis (Eds.), *Development of executive talent* (pp. 147-159). Washington, DC: American Management Association.
Diagosing defenses against the outsider. *Journal of Social Issues, 8*(3), 1-10.
Understanding personality and personnel administration. In W. Waite & D.N. Edwards (Eds.), *Personnel practices.* New York: Columbia University Press.

1953

Executive leadership. New York: Harper.
An introduction to field theory and interaction theory (rev. ed.). New Haven,
    CT: Labor and Management Center, Yale Univeristy.
Characteristics of successful executives. *Personnel*(June).
Human problems with budgets. *Harvard Business Review, 31*(1), 97-110.

1954

With E.W. Bakke. *Organizational structure and dynamics.* New Haven, CT:
    Labor and Management Center, Yale University.
The present state of research in human relations in industry. New Haven, CT:
    Labor and Management Center, Yale University.
*Organization of a bank: A study of the nature of organization and the fusion
    process.* New Haven, CT: Labor and Management Center, Yale
    University.
Human problems in bookkeeping. *Banking*(January).
Human relations in a bank. *Harvard Business Review, 32*(5), 63-72.
The fusion of an individual with the organization. *American Sociological
    Review, 19*(3).

1955

Organizational leadership and participative management. *Journal of Business,
    28*(1), 1-7.
Problems in human relations research. *Journal of the School of Higher
    Administrative Studies, 12*, 85-88.
Top management dilemma: Industrial development vs. company needs.
    Personnel(September).

1956

Diagosing human relations in organizations: A case study of a hospital. New
    Haven, CT: Labor and Management Center, Yale University.
Research trends in executive behavior. *Advances Management*(March), pp.
    6-9.
Some unsolved problems of executive development programs. *Journal of
    Educational Sociology*(September).
Some unsolved problems of executive development programs.
    Persoonnel(September).
The individual and organizational structure: Recent research findings. Personnel
    Series No. 168. Washington, DC: American Management Association.

Latest findings in human relations research. Paper presented at the 38th Silver Bay Conference.

Educating the whole man. *Vantage Points.*

Leadership pattern in a plant. In E.C. Bursk (Ed.), *Human relations for management.* New York: Harper.

1957

Personality and organization. New York: Harper.

The individual and organization: Some problems of mutual adjustment. *Administrative Science Quarterly, 2*(1), 1-24.

How human can a supervisor be? *Journal of National Society of Industrial Management Clubs*(January).

Organization and the human being. *Product Engineering*(December 30), pp. 26-29.

New approach to employee relations. *Nations Business*(January).

1958

Creating effective research relationships in an organization. *Human Organization, 17,* 34-40.

Some problems in conceptualizing organizational climate: A case study of a bank. *Administrative Science Quarterly, 2*(4), 1-16.

The organization: What makes it healthy? *Harvard Business Review, 36*(6), 107-116.

Management implications of recent social science research. *Personnel Administration, 21*(3), 5-10.

1959

Individual-organizational actualization. *Administrative Science Quarterly* (September).

The individual and organization: An empirical test. *Administrative Science Quarterly, 4*(2), 146-167.

Understanding organizational change. *General Systems Yearbook.*

Executive development and organizational effectiveness. *Advanced Management, 24*(12).

1960

Organizatinal development: An inquiry in the Esso approach. City/State: Esso Research Division, Emplyee Relations.

Understanding organizational behavior. Homewood, IL: Dorsey Press.

Understanding human behavior in organizations: One viewpoint. In M. Haire (Ed.), *Modern organization theory.* New York: Wiley.
Individual actualization in complex organization. *Mental Hygiene, 44*(2), 226-237.
Do-it-yourself executive development. *Think, 26*(5).
Organizational effectiveness under stress. *Harvard Business Review, 38,* 137-145.
Self-development in organizations. *Think.*
Human behavior in organizations. *Yale Sceintific Magazine, 34*(5), 40-51.

1961

Explorations in client-consultant relationships. *Human Organization, 20*(3), 121-133.
Organizational leadership. In L. Petrullo & B. Bass (Ed.), *Leadership and interpersonal behavior.* New York: Holt, Reinhart, & Winston.
Interpersonal relationships in organizations. In D.H. Fenn, Jr. & L. Fernberger (Eds.), *Management of materials research* (Vol. 14). New York: Intersceince.
A Model for relating interpersonal competence to organizational effectiveness. In *Mental health in industry.* Ann Arbor, MI: Foundation for Research in Human Behavior.
Employee apathy and non-involvement: The house that management built? *Personnel, 38*(4), 8-14.
Puzzle and perlexity in executive development. *Personnel, 39*(11).

1962

Interpersonal competence and organizational effectiveness. Homewood, IL: Irwin-Dorsey.
The integration of the individual and the organization. In *Social science approaches to business behavior.* Homewood, IL: Irwin-Dorsey.
Beehavior of executives within the organization. In *Behavioral science research in industrial relations.* Industrial Relations Monograph No. 21. New York: Industrial Relaitons Counselors, Inc.
A new era in personnel relations. *Dun's Review, 79,* 40-41.

1963

A brief description of laboratory education. *Training Directors, 17,* 31-32.
A comment on George Odiorne's paper. *Training Directors, 17,* 31-32.

1964

Integrating the individual and the organization. New York: Wiley.

The process of influence and manipulations within the organizational setting. *Industrial Medicine and Surgery, 33*(12), 899-928.

The process of influence and manipulations within the organizational setting. *Engineering of Human Behavior*(Special Supplement, December).

Being human and being organized. *Trans-Action, 1,* 3-6.

T-group for organizational effectiveness. *Harvard Business Review, 42,* 60-74.

1965

Organization and innovation. Homewood, IL: Irwin-Dorsey.

Leadership pattern in a plant. *Harvard Business Review, 32,* 63-70.

Explorations in interpersonal competence I. *Journal of Applied Behavioral Science, 1*(1), 58-83.

Explorations in interpersonal competence II. *Journal of Applied Behavioral Science, 1*(3), 255-269.

1966

Explorations in human relations training and research. *NTL, 3.*

Interpersonal barriers to decision making. *Harvard Business Review, 44*(2), 841-898.

Interpersonal competence, organiztional milieu, and innovation. *Research Management, 9*(2), 71-99.

1967

On the future of laboratory education. *Journal of Applied Behavioral Science, 3*(2), 153-210.

Today's problems with tomorrow's organizations. *Journal of Management Studies, 4*(1), 31-55.

Do you recognize yourself? *Foreign Service Journal, 44*(1), 21-26.

How tomorrow's executive will make decisions. *Think, 33*(6), 18-23.

We must make work worthwhile. *Life*(May 5), pp. 56-61.

1968

On the effectiveness of research and development organizations. *American Scientist*(December), pp. 344-355.

Issues in evaluating laboratory education. *Journal of Applied Behavioral Science, 8*(1), 28-40.

Some consequences of separating thought from action. *Ventures, 8*(1), 68-72.
Organization: Effectiveness and change. In *International Encyclopedia of Social Sciences*(pp. 311-319). New York: Macmillan/The Free Press.
Some unintended consequences of rigorous research. *Pyschological Bulletin, 70*(3), 185-197.
Interpersonal competence asquisition vs. therapy. *Journal of Applied Behavioral Science, 4*(2), 147-177.
Students and businessmen: The bristling dialogue. *Think*(July-August), pp. 26-31.

1969

Using qualitative data to test theories. *Administrative Science Quarterly*(December).
The incomleteness of social-psychological theory. *American Psychologist,24*(1), 893-908.

1970

Intervention theory and method. Reading, MA: Addison-Wesley.
Students and businessmen: The bristling dialogue. *Yale Scientific Magazine, 44*(5), 7-10.

1971

Management and organizational development. New York: McGraw-Hill.
Essay review on *Beyond freedom and dignity. Harvard Educational Review, 41*(4), 550-567.
Management information systems: The challenge to rationality and emotionality. *Management Science, 17*(6), B275-B292.

1972

The applicability of organizational sociology. London: Cambridge University Press.
The company president: Effective leadership today and tomorrow. *Enterprise*(Fall), pp. 9-20.
Do personal growth laboratories represent an alternative culture? *Journal of Applied Behavioral Science, 8*(1), 7-28.

1973

On organizations of the future. Sage Professional Paper in Administration and Policy Studies No. 03-006. Beverly Hills, CA: Sage.

Some limits on rational man organizational theory. *Public Administration Review*(June).
Personality and organization revisited *Administrative Science Quarterly, 18*(2), 141-167.
The CEO's behavior: Key to organizational development. *Harvard Business Review, 51*(2), 55-64.

1974

Behind the front page. San Francisco, CA; Jossey-Bass.
With D. Schön. *Theory in practice.* San Francisco, CA: Jossey-Bass.
Alternative schools: A behavioral analysis. *Teachers College Record, 75*(4), 429-452.
Changing communities by changing organizations. In W. Hawley(Ed.), *1974 urban annual review: Improving the quality of public services.*
Conversations with Chris Argyris. *Organizational Dynamics*(Summer), pp. 45-62.
Personality vs. organization. *Organizational Dynamics, 3*(2), 3-17.
Personality vs. organization. *Organizational Dynamics*(Fall), pp. 3-17.

1975

Learning environment for increased effectiveness. In C.L. Cooper (Ed.), *Theories of group processes.* London: Wiley.
Dangers in applying results from experimental social psychology. *American Psychologist, 30*(4), 469-485.
Problems and new directions for industrial psychology. In M. Dunnette (Ed.), *Handbook of industrial and organizational psychology.* Chicago, IL: Rand-McNally.

1976

Increasing leadership effectiveness. New York: Wiley-Interscience.
Theories of action that inhibit individual learning. *American Psychologist, 31*(9), 638-654.
Leadership, learning, and changing the status quo. *Organizational Dynamics, 4*(3), 29-43.
Single- and double-loop models in research on decision making. *Administrative Science Quarterly, 21*, 363-375.

1977

Organizational learning and management information systems. *Accounting, Organizations, and Society, 2*(2), 113-123.
Double-loop learning in organizations. *Harvard Business Review, 55*(5), 115-125.

1978

With D. Schön. *Organizational learning.* Reading, MA; Addison-Wesley.
Is capitalism the culprit? *Organizational Dynamics*(Spring), pp. 21-37.
Ineffective regulating processes: A theory of action perspective. In *Regulating business: The search for an optimum.* San Francisco, CA: Institute for Contemporary Studies.
Media's capacity for self-destruction. *Neiman Reports, 31*(4), 17-20.

1979

How nornal science methodology makes leadership research less additive and less applicable. In J.G. Hunt & L.L. Larson (Eds.), *Crosscurrents in leadership.* Carbonndale, IL: Southern Illinois University Press.
Psychological defenses, system intervention, and preventative mental health. In C. Alderfer & C.L. Cooper (Eds.), *Advances in experiential social processes*(Vol. 2). London: Wiley.
Reflecting on laboratory education from a theory of action perspective. *Journal of Applied Behavioral Science, 5*(3), 296-310.

1980

Inner contradictions of rigorous research. New York: Academic Press.
Some inner contradictions in management information systems. In H.C. Lucas (Ed.), *Proceedings of IFIP WG8.2 Bonn Working Conference on the Information Systems Environment.* Amsterdam: North-Holland.
Some limitation of the case method: Experience in a management development program. *Academy of Management Review, 5*(2).
Making the undiscussable and its undiscussability discussable. *Public Administration Review*(May).
Educating administrators and professionals. In *Leadership in the 80s: Essays on higher education.* Cambridge, MA: Harvard University Press.

1981

Teaching and learning in design settings. In W. Porter & M. Kilbridge (Eds.), *Architecture education study*(pp. 551-660). New York: Andrew W. Mellon Foundation.

1982

Reasoning, learning and action: Individual and organizational. San Francisco, CA: Jossey-Bass.

Research as action: Useable knowledge for understanding and changing the status quo. In N. Nicholson & T.D. Wall (Eds.), *The theory and practice of organizatinal psychology.* London: Academic Press Ltd.

The executive mind and double-loop learning. *Organizational Dynamics*(Autumn), pp. 5-22.

Why individuals and organizations have difficulty double-loop learningg. In P.S. Goodman (Ed.), *Change in organizations.* San Francisco, CA: Jossey-Bass.

1983

With D. Schön (Eds.). Organizational learning [Special issue]. *Journal of Management Studies, 20*(1).

Useable knowledge for double-loop problems. In R.H. Kilman, K.W. Thomas, D.P. Slevin, R. Nath, & S.L. Jerrell (Eds.), *Producing useful knowledge for organizations* (Vols. 1 & 2). New York: Praeger.

Action science and intervention. *Journal of Applied Behavioral Science, 19*(2), 115-135.

1984

How strategy professionals dealeith threat: Individual and organizational. In J.M. Pennings (Ed.), *Strategic decision making in complex organizations.* San Francisco, CA: Jossey-Bass.

1985

Strategy, change and defensive routines. Boston, MA: Ballinger.

With R. Putnam & D.M. Smith. *Action science.* San Francisco, CA: Jossey-Bass.

Organizational defensive routines. In R.W. Boss (Ed.), *Academy of Management OD Newsletter.* Boulder, CO: University of Colorado Press.

Interventions for improving leadership effectiveness. In A. Kieser, G. Reber, & W. Wunderer (Eds.), *Encyclopedia of leadership.* Stuttgart: Poeschel Verlag.

1986

Skilled incompetence: An organizational paradox. *Harvard Business Review*(September/October), pp. 74-79.

1987

First and second order errors in managing strategic change: The role of organizational defensive routines. In A. Pettigrew (Ed.), *Managing strategic change.* Oxford, England: Basil Blackwell.

Making knowledge more relevant to practice: Maps for action. In E.E. Lawler & Associates (Eds.), *Doing research that is useful for theory and practice.* San Francisco, CA: Jossey-Bass.

Bridging economics and psychology: The case of teh economic theory of the firm. *American Psychologist, 42*(5).

1988

Problems in producing usable knowledge for implementing liberating alternatives. In D.E. Bell, H. Raiffa, & A. Tversky (Eds.), *Decision making*(pp. 540-561). Cambridge, England: Cambridge Univeristy Press.

Crafting a theory of practice: The case of organizational paradoxes. In R.E. Quinn & K. Cameron (Eds.), *Paradox and transformation: Towards a theory of change in organization and management*(pp. 255-278). Boston, MA: Ballinger.

Reasoning, action strategies, and defensive routines: The case if the OD practitioners. In W. Passmore & R. Woodman (Eds.), *Research in organizational change* (Vol. 1). Greenwich, CT: JAI Press.

Reciprocal integrity: Creating conditions that encourage personal and organizational integrity. In C. Argyris, D. Schön, & S. Srivastva (Eds.), *Executive integrity.* San Francisco, CA: Jossey-Bass.

*The industrial sociologist as an academic researcher in organizations.*Professional Development Series. Washington, DC: American Sociological Association.

1989

Strategy implementation: An experience in learning. *Organizational Dynamics* (Winter), pp. 5-15.

Participatory action research and action science compared. *American Behavioral Scientist, 32*(5), 612-623.

1990

Overcoming organizational defenses. Needham, MA: Allyn & Bacon.

Managers, workers, and organizations. *Society*(September/October), pp. 45-48.

How the media continue to reduce their credibility. *Neiman Reports*(Winter).

1991

The dilemma of implementing controls: The case of managerial accounting. *Accounting, Organizations and Society.*

A Transformational Journey

BERNARD M. BASS

On a hot afternoon in Tokyo in July 1970, I was riding in a taxi with my Japanese host. He mentioned that his grandfather, Admiral Togo-Heihachiro, had led the Japanese force which destroyed the Russian fleet at the Battle of Tsushima in 1905. "Tanakasan," I said, "your grandfather's victory resulted in the pogram fomented by the Czarist government to distract the populace which forced my grandfather, Mordko Bass, to flee from Kiev." Accompanying him were his wife, Bertha, and two sons, one of whom was seven-year-old Alexander, my father-to-be.

THE MUSICAL CONNECTION

In addition to being long-lived, musicians tended to run in the Bas family. My paternal great-grandfather, Meir, played the bass violin (bas in Russian, whence came the family name; the second s was added several years before leaving Russia). My grandfather played the mandolin. My father was a professional pianist who appeared in silent films as such, played in house orchestras in the days of vaudeville, and in club dates thereafter. My uncle Abrasha studied cello at the St. Petersburg Conservatory, and completed a long career with the New York Philharmonic and the Denver Symphony. He also had a coterie of dedicated students until he died in his nineties. His son played trumpet in the Minneapolis Symphony (and married its harpist; a grandson is carrying on the tradition on the piano).

My mother, Clara Helen Abrams, was two years old when her larger family emigrated in 1902 from Bialystok Poland. My maternal grandfather was a tailor. Some of his sons became owners of women's wear manufacturing establishments and retail shops. One son had a long career as a school principal in a Harlem Junior High School. My maternal cousins included Ph.D.s, metallurgists, and other professionals; my paternal cousins included architects and musicians, so the genes were promising on both sides of my family. America, the land of opportunity, clearly provided the context to make use of the potential they represented.

THE PRECOCIOUS KID

From an early age I enjoyed playing with ideas rather than mechanical gadgetry. Playing "make-believe" was a favorite pastime. By age 6 or 7, I was doing long division, drawing fantasy maps, and making up accompanying stories. I already had a public library card and was a regular patron. I still remember the title of the first book I borrowed from the library. It was the medieval romance (in modern English), *The Song of Roland.* My recreational reading still includes a lot of biographies of historical figures.

I was proud of my first research efforts. I was about age 12 or 13 when I was hired by a neighborhood policeman to assist him by identifying sociological studies in journals and books at the New York Public Library which were relevant for the M.A. thesis on which he was working.

I was hardly ever given any toys for the Great Depression had begun when I was four years old. I just imagined or created what I needed for fun and games. Also, my friends and I designed and constructed group games. For instance there was cardboard baseball. For an entire real baseball season, we took on the roles of owner-managers. Each of us were responsible for a competing major league team. Games were played with spinners to denote strikes, balls, hits, base-on-errors, and so forth. Detailed statistics were kept on teams and players. Players were traded but we did not have free agents to contend with. (The games and exercises I developed many years later for management education may have had some of their seeds in this child play.) I also enjoyed the many traditional group games that used to be played on the streets of New York City (for example, see Peter Breughel's paintings). Team sports of adolescence were also played in the streets or gymnasiums.

Except for a few occasions, I never ventured outside the New York metropolitan area until I left for military service. Often living in tenements with windows of apartments opening on back alleys and playing on streets without trees, shrubbery, or grass, I felt somewhat deprived of the sights, smells, and sounds of Nature. I still have fond memories of a third grade teacher who took the class on a nature walk in a small park near our school one fine spring morning. No doubt, I have treasured both world travel and camping, hiking, scuba diving and skiing all the more as an adult as a consequence of the felt confinement as a youngster.

I grew up with a neighborhood circle of 10 to 15 boys who remained together as a formal club of our own, the Rangers, until World War II sent us all off in different directions. Early on, we became masters of presiding at meetings, taking minutes, scheduling games with other "sandlot" teams, and organizing money- raising raffles, all without any noticeable adult intervention.

By 1930, my father had lost permanent work with the demise of the silent film and vaudeville show in neighborhood theaters which had required live music. He was insistent that I should not become a professional musician. To earn a living, he thought it would be better if I learned a skilled trade. My older brother, in sales all of his life, was more impressed by my father's emphasis on making as much money as soon as possible being the prime goal of any career. Fortunately, my mother had a different idea. She had recognized that I enjoyed school and that I was an "A" student from the first grade on. There never was any question in her mind, nor mine, that some day I would go to college. She died, at age 42, just after I had entered college but her unquestioning love, affection, and support as I was growing up were the most important determinant in me of a sense of security and self-confidence that stood me in good stead in later life. However, neither my parents nor any other of my immediate contacts could give me much advice or advance information about college or career. How to pay for college was not given much thought. It was just assumed to be there for me when the time came to go.

LOOK TO YOUR LEFT; LOOK TO YOUR RIGHT . . .

So, I moved ahead without much guidance, and did not apply for college scholarships but just went along into the College of the City of New York which was completely free at the time, if you were in the top 10% of your class in high school grades. I graduated in 1941 (at age 16) from DeWitt Clinton High School in the top 1% in grades. CCNY was no haven for the so-so scholar. Given the high school grade requirement, CCNY had an extremely bright and highly competitive student body. It had to be. During our first weekly convocation of all the Arts and Science students in the Great Hall at CCNY, the dean declared "Look to the student on your left; look to the student on your right; only one of you will be here next year." The competition was stimulating. It also led some students to attempt (and sometimes succeed) at catching their professors in intellectual traps.

On the one hand, CCNY was supposed to be a hotbed of radicalism. On the other hand, Bertrand Russell, one of the intellectual giants of the twentieth century had been fired because he professed the value of "free love." One of my French professors was an ardent supporter of Vichy France.

A high school chemistry teacher had made chemistry most attractive, so I enrolled in CCNY's chemical engineering program in 1941. (To illustrate what times were like, CCNY had been forced in 1941 to admit its first females. The seven were admitted to the Engineering School because our free New York City sister institution for women only, Hunter College, had no engineering program.) Although my grades were good, I could not stand the frustration of the introductory chemistry lab which I could not connect systematically with the chemistry lectures. I switched to history because I found the first year of world history most exciting. (I had already read a lot of history on my own and have continued to do so ever since.) I would have continued in history except for being discouraged by a terribly boring American history teacher in a course focused on the post-Civil War period. At that point, I was given vocational counseling by a young Ph.D. student from Columbia, Robert Watson. (He subsequently became a well-known authority on the history of psychology.) He counseled me into psychology. A classmate sitting next to me in my first psychology course (which at CCNY you only were allowed to take as a sophomore), described industrial psychology to me. After that, I was hooked, although at the time (1942), I saw myself starting the preparation for a career as a professional in personnel management. The psychology faculty was excellent. Most prominent was Gardner Murphy, in personality, whom I assisted in running totally unsuccessful experiments in extrasensory perception.

INTO THE AIR, JUNIOR BIRDMAN

By 1943, all my close friends who were about two years older than me had enlisted or been drafted into the military services. I was eager to sign up and was accepted by the Army Aviation Cadet program. My two years of duty were spent in air crew training programs; I never saw overseas service for the projected losses of bombers in 1944 over Germany based on the 1943 record did not materialize as longer-range fighter-plane escorts became available to protect the bombers.

It was quite an experience for a bright but brash kid learning how to get along in the military. I had never been more than 35 miles from New York City. Military service provided the opportunity to learn what life and values were like in one of the world's greatest bureaucracies as well as in small towns from Florida to Texas. I saw Jim Crow first hand in the Deep South; how Mexican-Americans and Native Americans were treated in Texas, and got myself slugged by a South Carolinian for saying, "But we (the North) had won the Civil War." I learned from a number of such experiences the value of self-monitoring.

HELLO, COLUMBUS

After discharge in Sioux Falls, South Dakota, in November 1945, with a net worth of $50 and the G.I. Bill in the offing I hitchhiked to New York City, stopping to enroll at Ohio State University in Columbus, known to me primarily because of its football team and program in industrial psychology. I met my wife, Ruth Rothschild, at Ohio State and was introduced to a wider world of good taste, fine arts, and classical literature. She was 19, I was 21 when we married. Her father was graduate chemist who owned and managed a small cosmetics manufacturing firm; her mother was a medical technician with scholarly interests who introduced me to a broader range of literary magazines and books in philosophy and social science.

Rather than return to CCNY for my B.A., as I mentioned earlier, I began classes again in January 1946 at Ohio State to continue as an undergraduate since it was there I planned to get a Master's Degree to help me get an entry job in personnel management, but I quickly realized that I was more interested in an academic career. Thanks to Sidney Pressey who was a strong proponent of accelerated education, and full-time summer programs, I entered Ohio State in January 1946 as a junior, received the M.A. in industrial psychology in August 1947 and the Ph.D. in industrial psychology in 1949. The Ph.D. would have been earned at age 22 but I had to take two years off for service in the U.S. Army Air Force.

Ohio State, in the late 1940s was a hotbed of dustbowl empiricism and Hullian behaviorism. My one course in social psychology was with a young instructor from Berkeley, Donald T. Campbell, who had just received his Ph.D. under the direction of E.C. Tolman and Egon Brunswick. Don's mentalism (as I saw it) was heresy at OSU. Unfortunately, I lost an opportunity at that time to become open to learning about the importance of cognitive theory. I was more interested in arguing and trying to correct Don. But this was just the first of many times I missed a great learning opportunity. A second was failing to study factor analysis with Bob Wherry who came to Ohio State in 1948 just as I took off for a consulting internship at the Ohio Boxboard Company.

Most of the time as a student at Ohio State, I held down two or three jobs, starting with washing dishes at a fraternity house and keeping rat cages clean and ending with teaching 10 hours a week and consulting to design a personnel system to select apprentices. One cherished extracurricular learning experience was attending the Friday night coffee-klatches, intellectual salons of graduate students, held in Jean and Leo Chall's book-filled one room apartment just above ours. (Jean is now a distinguished Harvard professor in readability research; Leo founded *Sociological Abstracts*.) The discussions widely broadened my knowledge in the social and political sciences.

Another extracurricula developmental experience came from living in 1946 in an interracial Rochdale cooperative. We certainly were not the neighborhood's most popular student house in Columbus in 1945. I met my first Chief Executive Officer, Murray D. Lincoln of the Farm Cooperative in trying to get assistance in handling our co-op house's mortgage. He read a newspaper on his desk throughout the brief interview. Needless to say, we received no help from him.

To a considerable degree, my career has involved chance encounters and events on a larger stage along with the opportunities to work with numerous friends and associates.

Following Cal Shartle's[1] lead, we were directed toward a behavioral approach to the study of leader behavior. This set me, in 1948, looking for some behavioral elements in the leadership situation. R.S. Urbrock, the Procter & Gamble industrial psychologist, was invited by Cal to give a seminar to the Personnel Research Board. Urbrock had just returned from England where he had observed the British country house technique and the uses of the leaderless group discussion (LGD).[2] As it was used in assessment, the LGD appeared terribly subjective. As an ardent behaviorist, I wanted to look at the LGD from a "muscle twitch" point of view. Some kitchen clocks were purchased and attached to on-off switches to be activated by military-surplus throat microphones. (At first, I activated the clocks myself with a panel of on-off switches.) One clock was assigned to each participant in a group. The group was given a problem to discuss. No leader was appointed. Who did what to whom in the group setting was observed and the time each participant spent talking was measured. And, of course, what emerged was a phenomenon nobody wanted to accept. Even now, there are many who will reject the idea out of hand. Yet, as in every study of the LGD since then, when the relation is rediscovered,[3] a correlation of about .9 was found between the amount of time spent by participants talking in these initially leaderless group discussions and their influence as rated by both their peers in the session as well as by observers.[4]

My dissertation dealt with the leaderless group discussion. After five years of publication on the subject, a swan song was published in 1954 in the Psychological Bulletin in the belief that nobody was listening.[5] Two years later, however, Bray, Campbell, and Grant[6] began their assessment center program at AT&T. The leaderless group discussion was one of its features and has continued to be. One thing that puzzles me is that little attention has been paid to the correlation of .75 between performance in a one-hour leaderless group discussion and such outcomes after three days of assessment. This was demonstrated in Vernon's[7] South African assessment studies as well as in the OSS *Assessment of Men.*[8]

Like the fisherman who brags about the one that got away, I have found years later how many half-baked ideas I unsuccessfully tried to use were rudimentary forms of important innovations pursued more doggedly by other investigators with more appropriate disciplinary knowledge. Because I lacked further implementation, some of these ideas fortunately died aborning as they should have. For example, as an undergraduate in 1942, as an effort to cure the Great Depression I wrote a paper in economics proposing a plan for nationalizing all wholesale and distribution firms, but allowing manufacturing and retailing to remain free enterprises.

In graduate school, during the late 1940s, I spent many an hour on a fruitless search for a graphic solution to multiple regression. As Sidney Pressey's graduate assistant, I informed him that teaching machines were not theoretically sound and would never work well so I asked and received a transfer of assignment.

THE BAYOU CHALLENGE

The Department of Psychology at Louisiana State University in the Fall of 1949 was a great opportunity and challenge for a new assistant professor even though I taught 12 class hours regularly plus three extra hours of any subject in psychology that needed teaching including statistics, clinical psychology, educational psychology, and social psychology, not to mention tests and measurements and industrial psychology. (I also taught a seminar on the History of Ideas in the Middle Ages and Renaissance to an honors group of freshmen.) As a result, I was forced to learn a broad swath of psychology. In the preceding spring, the entire department had resigned, and Paul Young, a clinician had been asked to return as chairman. A fellow 1949 Ohio State graduate, Bill Hurder, in physiological psychology, had sent me a telegram of encouragement and along with Henry Shanklin, a new Ph.D. from Purdue and Ray Schrader, an instructor, we manned the entire program. I had four graduate assistants! The challenge was the teaching load; the opportunity was to have four assistants working on my research with me. I named my first son, Robert Cecil after two of my assistants, Robert McGehee (later to become a Vice President at Boeing) and Cecil Wurster (later to become a high-level federal government administrator).

Back to some of the fish that got away as well as some that were caught. If the probability of one event was .1 and the probability of a second event was .1, the joint probability, I believed, was the product of $.1 \times .1$ or .01. This was my form of meta-analysis that I used in the late 1950s in an unpublished book in which I replicated small group experiments four or five times, then multiplied the product of their probabilities of rejecting the null hypothesis. Too little, too early. In these same experiments, I used cross-lagged correlation of two individual members' decisions before and after discussion. I correlated the first member's first set with the second member's second set, then compared the correlation with the reverse to determine whether the first or second member had been more influential. I even corrected the difference for the changes in each member's sets. This was cross-lagged correlation vintage 1957.[9] (More about this approach later on assessing objectively who influenced whom).

As early as 1949, I moved away from raw empiricism toward conceptual analyses, then theory construction. My first attempt was a paper at the 1949

APA convention in Denver in which I conceived attitude as a type of sHr, a Hullian habit strength, in which response acts back on stimulus. The effort was totally ignored except that I got a nice long supportive letter from Clark Hull.

By 1951, I had completed half a book integrating the fields of psychology which was never published as my collaborator failed to complete his half. But it was a rewarding experience. In addition to learning a lot about fields such as the psychology of music, my writing skills improved immensely as a consequence of the careful editing of the incompleted manuscript received from the copy editor, to whom I must remain eternally grateful.

As part of a study of stress that began in 1952, we obtained films of the LSU football games and played back to designated players selected episodes asking them with a brief questionnaire how they felt emotionally as particular actions were replayed. Bill Hurder, Norman Ellis, and I were interested in the differential experiences of approach-approach conflict, approach-avoidance frustration, avoidance-avoidance fear, and generalized anxiety. The method and results were buried in a final report to the Air Force Aeromedical Laboratory which had sponsored the research. (Nowadays, films and videotapes of stressful episodes are used for selection and training.)

The overall research investigation was directed at the study of human stress under extraordinary environments. I did not fully appreciate what the Air Force meant by extraordinary environments. I thought they were talking about high-flying jets. They were really talking about space; however, space research was still science fiction for me in 1952.

My heightened sense of research ethics would prevent me from doing this research today. We used bladder stress as the stressor. We were assured by a urologist that we would not hurt our subjects. We first fed a gallon of ice water to a South African student. After drinking the gallon, he shivered somewhat, put on a stiff upper lip, and indicated it was an uncomfortable but tolerable experience. Subsequently, we found that just a quart of lukewarm water would force 10% of our freshman male students, denied a toilet during a two-hour program of testing, to urinate uncontrollably. That was our criterion for breakdown under stress.

The task for all subjects was to complete Ed Fleishman's psychomotor battery involving steadiness, tapping, eye-hand coordination, and so forth. One of the 10 "tests" was a fairly complete physiological battery. A Latin square design was employed so that all 200 subjects went through the order of nine Fleishman[10] aptitude tests and the physiological battery in a random sequence. We then could calculate how each skill or physiological response changed as the stress from the intake of water and pills, perceived to be diuretics, built up over the 10 periods.

There were five treatments. We fed 80% of the subjects pills, supposedly diuretic, but actually placebos. To generate conflict stress, pills were given for supposedly doing well to 20% of the subjects. Another 20% in a fear group, received pills for supposed failure. Anxiety was throughout to be generated in the 20% who received pills randomly. A control group of 20% did not get the pill. A final 20% got neither the pill nor the water. Most higher-order interactions were significant. This is one of the reasons this line of investigation was not continued. We got so many significant results, they were impossible to understand. In other words, to understand what urine stress under these pill conditions would do depended on whether the pill was punishing or whether it was rewarding. It depended as well as on which psychomotor test was involved. For example, steadiness improved dramatically throughout the entire two hours of testing.[11]

Although 'subordinate' satisfaction was required of Japanese feudal leaders by the twelfth century, in the West, employee satisfaction was regarded even by "human relationists" as a means to an end. Although evidence was mixed, in mid-century, it was argued that employee satisfaction generated better job performance. (Actually, the two could be independent, or the reverse might even be true.) Again, prematurely in 1952 in an article "Ultimate Criteria of Organizational Worth,"[12] I argued that the ultimate objectives of a firm should be to satisfy its various constituencies including its owners, managers, customers and employees. Better job performance was good in its own right; so was employee satisfaction. When I presented this idea to groups of U.S. managers in the 1950s to whom the bottom line was the sole criterion of organizational success, I was usually laughed at. Industrial psychologists seemed equally uninterested, although in the past ten years, every once in a while, I see a reference made to the article. With their emphasis on harmony, Japanese managers, if they had known of the article, might have subscribed to its point of view.

A particularly significant event in my career occurred in the summer of 1952 at Dartmouth. Supported by a grant from the Social Science Research Council, I was invited with five other young scholars, the sociologists, Seymour Martin Lipset and Alvin Gouldner, and the psychologists, John Hemphill, Cecil Gibb, and the late Ben Willerman to spend six weeks working on the problem of leadership. Generally, I was both frustrated and educated by the experience. Then and there I began to formulate the theory of leadership based on a behavioristic reinforcement model that took eight years to complete as a book, *Leadership, Psychology, and Organizational Behavior*.[13] That book had considerable implications for what I did subsequently in the use of organizational simulations and in current research on management styles. Some of the ideas in the book were taken up again in my revisions of *Bass & Stogdill's Handbook of Leadership*.[14] Also as a consequence, I engaged in a series of small group experiments,[15] testing aspects of the theory. We received generous financial and intellectual support from ONR's Luigi Petrullo and later on from John Nagay and Bert King for this level of work well into the 1960s.

Experimental social psychology was new and exciting in the 1950s. It rivaled physics in attracting science enthusiasts. I made various attempts to explore and verify some of the propositions derived in *Leadership, Psychology, and Organizational Behavior*. Still trying to be objective and highly measurement conscious, with the assistance of Frank Farese, we built an early transistorized analog-digital converter and computer, the "metagnosiometer." Using it, we directly measured in electric current the differences in the ranking decisions before-and-after discussion of five group members. We measured in this way how much each changed, how much they influenced each other, and how much each improved in accuracy. Also obtained was how much the group changed, coalesced in opinion, and improved as a group.[16] Thirty years later special computers are being marketed having aspects similar to those of the metagnosiometer to provide summary data to each member of a group on how the rest of the group feels about a particular matter. The Decision Room, a network of PCs, and a summary display is the latest version. We are now beginning to use one in the Center for Leadership Studies for training and research.

A CHANGE OF VENUE

My one big career shift occurred in 1962 when I moved from the Department of Psychology at Berkeley where I was visiting into the Graduate School of Management at the University of Pittsburgh. I felt I shared more interests in common with problem-oriented management faculties than with discipline-oriented psychology faculties. This was at the time that graduate business education was giving a strong boost to math, economics and psychology in its curricula.

When I moved to the University of Pittsburgh in 1962, I was faced with a hundred MBA students at a time in classroom settings. This generated my interest in business gaming for experimentation as well as education.

One experience stands out. In 1963, I developed a business game called The University of Pittsburgh Production Organization Exercise.[17] I asked Paul Lawrence and Ralph Stogdill to visit Pittsburgh to develop a "top-down" organization of the student players that would maximize their success in the exercise. In the exercise, companies actually manufactured cut, folded, and stapled items from IBM cards, then sold their production. I also asked Murray Horowitz and Hal Leavitt to do the same, but with a "bottom-up" organization. They spent an entire Friday morning instructing the teams of students who were to be responsible for the bottom-up and top-down organizations competing in a common market. Action started at 1:00 p.m. At 1:15 p.m., one of the student's radios announced that President Kennedy was assassinated.

As the news was devastating, the experiment was called off. We repeated the effort the following year, however, with a variety of interesting results.[18]

In 1962, I began writing a book to try to integrate industrial psychology. By 1965, I had already finished a book-length manuscript with only about one-third of the field covered, the organizational portion. Hal Leavitt[19] had coined the term *organizational psychology* in a speech on Walter V. Bingham Day at the then Carnegie Institute of Technology and it seemed appropriate to my manuscript. As a consequence, in 1965, I published the first hardback titled *Organizational Psychology*.[20] Ed Schein completed a paperback with that title about the same time.[21] (We have crossed paths many times in workshops and conventions since then including being inducted at the same time into the Fellows of the Academy of Management in 1989.) The industrial psychology book was finally completed with the collaboration of Jerry Barrett.[22]

I developed a small group exercise for each of the chapters in the organizational psychology book to generate phenomena dealing with the content in each chapter. For example, the first chapter dealt with objectives, so I constructed an "Exercise Objectives." It was a budgeting problem with alternative objectives requiring five individual and group decisions. It was like a leaderless group discussion except that the problem was completely structured. Revealed by the exercise were managers' goals and whether they were pragmatic or idealistic in their budgeting decisions; for example, whether their company ought to continue to pollute a stream or take a chance on being fined. (This was early in the era of ecological consciousness-raising, an activity which became more prominent in the years following.) The exercise provided for individual and team data collection. Copies of what the managers did were summarized, analyzed, and fed back to the participants along with the implications of what had been involved. The other exercises in this "Program of Exercises for Management Development" featured personal, interpersonal, and organizational problems involving attitude change, motivation to work, supervision, group processes, design of work, communications, negotiations, and evaluative problem-solving.[23] The exercises made it possible to research managerial attitudes and behavior at the same time the exercises provided a learning experience for the participants.[24]

THE SENSITIVE TRAINER

Equally important to the construction of the exercises was the fact that I was persuaded to attend (reluctantly) a sensitivity training session in 1959. As a hard empiricist and an experimenting social psychologist, I thought no good could come out of a sensitivity training effort. But, Paul Baker, working at the time for Standard Oil of New Jersey, and Frank Cassens, also of the Baton Rouge refinery, who had been at Ohio State with me, suggested "Try it, you'll like it." Well, it turned out that I liked it very much. In my first experience, I served as a junior trainer depending on my background in small group research. The senior trainer was Hal Leavitt who always was a pleasure to work with. I became a trainer without having been a participant.

We did a pretty good job. One of our participants was a young engineer named Cliff Garvin, who eventually reached the top of the EXXON hierarchy as Chairman of the Board. So the participants may have learned something. Many programs later, Bob Blake, with his innovations in instrumenting sensitivity training, who acted like a program dean for the Bayway program for Standard Oil of New Jersey, set me to structuring and instrumenting sensitivity training activities. I developed various experimental exercises with measurement and feedback to go along with sensitivity training programs, and completed a number of evaluative studies.[25] The combined interest in experimental exercises and sensitivity training led to a set of twelve integrated self-guided exercises providing a trainerless group with a T-group experience.[26] Other spinoffs were into awareness and attitude change about upgrading women[27] and blacks.[28]

Continued research with sensitivity training led me to the conviction that under certain conditions sensitivity training might be contraindicated in terms of contribution to organizational effectiveness.[29] Much more is required for it to make a positive contribution to organizational effectiveness. But it helped to loosen me up enough to look at myself and my relations with others as well as at futurism, humanism, social impacts, business policy questions, the science of social science, and a variety of other research topics.

THE INVISIBLE NETWORK

I can cite many other examples of how much I was influenced by colleagues. Sometimes the influence went unrecognized. I cannot stress how important to me has been the invisible network built up over 45 years in determining my professional agenda.

In the mid-1950s, Irv Berg, a colleague at Louisiana State University, was finding that considerable variance in personality assessment was due to response set rather than substantive factors. I became convinced that the Adorno et al. F-scale was mainly a measure of acquiescence. I was so convinced that I accepted a factor analysis of the data by Lee Cronbach, an editorial reviewer that gave me the results for which I was looking.[30] Unfortunately, Lee's analysis was in considerable error. Instead of there being 75% acquiescence on the F-scale, there was only 25%. I pushed on, however, into personality assessment and appraisal by means of response set analysis and related means.[31] I still remain interested in response bias. Recently, my colleagues and I have been trying to deal with correcting for same-source bias.[32]

Muzafer Sherif had an important impact on me as he did on so many other scholars. His Robber's Cave experiment in the early 1950s coupled with Robert Blake's applications to management training initiated my experimental studies in intergroup competition.[33] Later on, results of a simulated nuclear site negotiation.[34] were published[35] showing how polarized groups can be coalesced by selected doses of social psychological manipulation. We take two polarized groups, engage them in a set of experiences so that when they finish they are less polarized, more knowledgeable, and closer together in attitude.

In *Leadership, Psychology, and Organizational Behavior*, I had made the proposal that attempted leadership is strongly associated with whether one is self-oriented (self-concerned), interaction-oriented (relations-oriented), or task-oriented. (Self-oriented individuals climb mountains for personal recognition and fame; interaction-oriented individuals climb mountains to enjoy the companionship and task-oriented individuals climb mountains because they are challenges to be overcome.) Societies cycle from task-orientation to interaction-orientation to self-orientation, then begin a new cycle again starting with task orientation. At the time of its writing in the late 1950s, I saw the United States as having left the pre-1950s task-oriented phase, and expected it would remain for many decades to come in an interaction orientation phase. Self-orientation as a development was expected to become dominant in the distant future, not as it actually took hold in the late 1960s. I underestimated the speed of societal change again in 1968 and 1973 when forecasting what work would be like in the year 2000.[36] Much has already come to pass; for instance, supervision by means of electronic mail, the rise of a leisure class of senior citizens, yuppies with challenging jobs, and an underclass without interesting work.

With the assistance of a graduate student, Helen Wambach, I developed scales for measuring the three orientations.[37] Numerous evaluative studies were completed.[38] A summary of this work appeared in 1967 showing the contribution of these orientations to the understanding of leadership behavior. In line with theoretical expectations, task orientation was found positively associated with work performance and leadership in a variety of laboratory and field settings.[39]

Hal Leavitt was a particularly important figure in my career development. I have already mentioned how I came to work together with Hal in my first management sensitivity training program. Subsequently, Hal put me together with Marshall Robinson, then Dean at the Graduate School of Business at the University of Pittsburgh. The result was a move to that institution in 1962, shifting my career from industrial psychology to organizational behavior.

Hal completed a European tour in 1964 for the Ford Foundation to determine the state of research and education on organizational behavior in Europe. There was $8,000 left over in his budget which Vic Vroom was administering as Hal had moved on from then Carnegie Institute of Technology to Stanford. With that $8,000, Hal and Vic subsidized my launching in Europe

of the Program of Exercises for Management Development which I have
mentioned earlier. These exercises had been used first in the executive
development program at the University of Pittsburgh. About 25% of the
managers attending the program at that time came from abroad. As I
administered the exercises to them, I was amazed at the extent of variations
that emerged as a consequence of the origins of the managers. Although
American managers more or less performed in the ways that I had expected,
foreign managers did not. A group of 30 European social scientists met with
me at the Playafels Hotel near Barcelona to discuss the introduction of the
exercises into Europe. (I was teaching at the Instituto de Estudios Superiores
de la Empresa (I.E.S.E.) in Barcelona in the Spring of 1966. I had stepped
on a sea urchin in the Virgin Islands just before the three-day meeting and
was still limping. Reg Revans of the University of Manchester introduced me
to the assembly as one limping into Barcelona with a package of exercises in
the footsteps of Ignatius Loyola for Loyola had come into Barcelona 450 years
earlier, with his famous Spiritual Exercises, limping from war wounds.) We
obtained a $300,000 grant from the Ford Foundation to study managers in
countries (ultimately 20) handling the phenomena that appeared in the
exercises. At the time, such exercises and participative education, in general,
were novelties in management education, particularly outside of the United
States.

I felt that I would not be able to complete this project in less than five years.
The Foundation was only willing to provide support for three years. It took
15 years. Analysis is still incomplete. Some of the exercises are still in use in
1990 for management training in many different countries ranging from Italy
to Singapore. The book, *Assessment of Managers: An International
Comparison*,[40] reviewed the research results in 12 of the 20 countries or groups
of countries in which we were involved. The book covered the data collected
between 1968 and 1972. Analyses reported concern differences between
nationalities as well as the relation between managers' performance in
budgeting decisions, setting objectives, planning and so on, and their rate of
advancement in their own countries. Universal as well as localized effects
emerged which varied across countries. The International Institute for
Organizational Development which was created under the direction of Leopold
Vansina in Louvain, Belgium, in 1966 to handle the distribution of the exercises,
data collection, and training of trainers celebrated its twenty-fifth anniversary
in 1991 as an important European management consulting firm.

In 1977, Ralph Stogdill asked me to collaborate with him on the second
edition of the *Handbook of Leadership*, unfortunately he died before we could
begin to work together so I had to take the full responsibility for revising the
original as well as for the expansion in text and references in two subsequent
editions.[41] It took four years for me to complete the expanded second edition
which appeared in 1981 but nine more years to complete the further expanded

third edition. I was delighted to be able to hand a signed copy of this book to John W. Gardner to whom I had dedicated it when I met him in San Francisco at the 1990 Academy of Management convention.

Bert King, another professional friend of long acquaintance, asked me to prepare a state-of-the-art paper on organizational decision making. The end product was a model and the book on that subject.[42]

Bob House, Henry Tosi, and I were having dinner together in Montreal in 1987 when I dropped into the conversation the idea for *The Leadership Quarterly*. The first issue appeared in 1990.

A QUESTION OF STYLE

Since 1970, I have actively pursued a line of research and development about different aspects of management styles. In each instance, colleagues and I have begun with available empirical evidence, developed factored scales, and created feedback instruments used by three or more colleagues. The first product of this research was the *Management Styles Survey*.[43] The originating ideas came from *Leadership, Psychology, and Organizational Behavior* and a task force led by Enzo Valenzi at the Management Research Center to review leadership research with situational implications.[44] The survey focused on 22 organizational, work group, task, personal, and interpersonal factors, along with five leadership styles and four outputs of satisfaction and effectiveness. The five leadership styles were: direction, negotiation, consultation, participation, and delegation. The *Management Style Survey* was evaluated by a report from the Center for Creative Leadership as one of the best feedback instruments available. Such feedback instruments formed the basis of a considerable data bank and numerous research reports.[45] One of my many ideas which never has caught on was to pursue a new generation of feedback from discriminant functional analyses of data that compare individual managers with effective and ineffective managers in the management styles data bank. A manager can be provided with a set of prescriptions based on these analyses. If managers would like to increase their effectiveness scores to some higher point, according to normative data and according to designated manager's data, they must make appropriate changes in antecedent scores such as their leadership style, interpersonal behavior, or in various aspects of the task, group, or organization. For example, given a manager's leadership style, and his or her subordinates' commitment to the group, regression analyses may suggest that to increase effectiveness the manager should increase consultation and reduce delegation.[46]

Another seemingly still-born idea built into the survey measurements and validated with smallest space analyses by Zur Shapira[47] was that manager and subordinate each can vary in how much power they have over each other in reaching decisions as well as how much information each has relevant to the decisions. (This was an extension of systems theory that explains input, throughput, and output in terms of flows of energy [power] and information.) Manager direction is appropriate when the manager has more power and information. Manager consultation is appropriate when a manager has more power but less information. Persuasion and negotiation are appropriate when the manager has the information, but subordinate has more power. Delegation would seem most appropriate when a subordinate has both more power and more information than a manager.

Rudi Klauss was an MIS Ph.D. student who had tried to survey 400 Kodak engineers about which documents they found most important in making their decisions. Instead he found that 85% of the weight about decisions lay in interpersonal communication, not formal documents. And so efforts in 1975 were redirected toward individual managers' communication styles and their credibility, informativeness, and role clarification as well as the consequences. A summary of research with the 11-factor model was completed.[48] Path analyses showed, for example, that open two-way communication led to more credibility and trustworthiness which in turn enhanced effectiveness and satisfaction with the communicator. Strong communalities were found among the various communication and management styles. Thus directive managers used one-way communication; participative managers, two-way communication. Consultative managers were seen to have more trustworthy and credible communications than did negotiative managers.

A MOST IMPORTANT TRANSFORMATION FOR ME

The third survey feedback instrument grew out of my interest in transformational leadership starting with a chance encounter with John A. Miller, one day in 1979. A former Ph.D. student of mine, John, now the Chairman of Management at Bucknell University, asked me if I had read James McGregor Burns' new book *Leadership*[49] which at that time was the rage in Washington. I confessed that I had not, but immediately bought and read a copy. I become enamoured with the concept of transformational leadership thereafter for it offered the opportunity to bridge the gap between small group studies of leadership and the leadership of the world's movers and shakers. It linked together my continuing interests in psychology, psychodynamics, and history.

In the summer of 1980, I had the chance to ask 70 senior executives at the University of South Africa in Pretoria if during their careers, anyone had transformed them in Burns' terms (raised awareness, raised their needs on Maslow's hierarchy, and moved them to transcend their self-interests). All 70 described someone, usually their organizational superior. They also informally talked about their heightened motivation and performance. So was born the beginning of the development of the psychometrics and surveys of transformational leadership in military, industrial, and educational organizations and the model construction of models which in 1985 formed the book *Leadership and Performance Beyond Expectations*[50] and the line of investigation with my colleagues Bruce Avolio, David Waldman, Fran Yammarino, Leanne Atwater, and Don Spangler that has continued into the 1990s.[51] Some twenty doctoral dissertations have been completed at other universities so far using our models and instruments; others are in progress.

One morning in May 1989, I received a surprise telephone call from Italy. "Hello, this is Gianfranco Gambigliani. You remember me? We worked together as trainers in Rome in 1970. I am now the Chairman of the Board of Isvor-Fiat (the wholly-owned training arm of the Fiat Corporation). I came across a reference in a thesis by Steve Pile to your name and work on transformational leadership and I am convinced this is just what we need for our 20,000 Fiat executives, managers, and supervisors. Can you meet me in New York next week to get started." The result is the Italian version of the *Transformational Leadership Development Program*[52] whose American development Avolio and I had begun in 1985.

CULTURE SHOCKS

I cannot resist mentioning some of my experiences that have occurred in many of the forty-or-so countries in which I have presented papers, lectured, or conducted workshops. For example, I was thrown out of stride on my first lecture in India to an audience of 150 managers in Madras. After many of the best of my choice comments, they waggled their heads from side-to-side which I interpreted as negative feedback instead of affirmation of what I was saying. Recently in a two-hour lecture to 200 Japanese managers in Fukuoka, using the slower consecutive translation (which took up one of the hours), again I felt I had lost the audience early on because so many kept their eyes closed. My host, Jyugi Misumi, was probably being kind about it, and assured me the audience had their eyes closed to concentrate better.

I was alarmed in Utrecht, Holland, when at 7:55 a.m. there was no sign of 20 workshop participants. I looked out from the window to the street to see the 20 approaching from a variety of directions. At 8 a.m. sharp, not one minute before nor after, they all arrived, shook hands all around, and were ready to begin. Shortly after in Mexico City for the same kind of workshop, advertised to begin at 9 a.m., I could not begin until 10 a.m. because most of the participants arrived an hour late.

After I had conducted a workshop in Manila, my sponsor answered a telephone call which turned him ashen white. As the conversation was in

Tagalog, I did not know why and asked what had happened. "Oh," he said, "I was told that if I do not fork over $5,000 on Monday evening to a political faction, they'll kill me."

Earlier on that same trip, I had stopped in Tokyo for a week. I had left the United States without the cholera shots required for travel in the Phillipines. On arrival in Tokyo I asked my host to take me to get my first dose as soon as possible. He whisked me off to a department store. When we reached the men's department, he proudly pointed to the great display of colored shirts from which I could choose. I did finally make it clear that I needed a cholera shot, not a colored shirt. When I deborded in Manila and indicated I needed a second shot, I was grabbed by the arm and immediately rushed into the Public Health Service room and given it. (The Phillipine Public Health Service was reported to be the most efficient public agency in the Phillipines.)

On another note: I often completely midjudged what was really going on in a country. My ignorance was sometimes appalling as I ventured into different countries. I conducted a workshop in Teheran just a few months before the Shah was overthrown. I was in Lebanon just before the Civil War broke out where my taxi driver assured me I was being driven across the Switzerland of the Middle East. I was in Paris just before the 1968 student revolution and was completely unaware of the pent-up frustrations with academia there. I had no inkling of the feelings of the Flemish toward the Walloons in Belgium until I began working there nor did I appreciate the strength of separation among French Canadians until I was in a workshop with them. Similarly, I never realized that Chileans and Argentinians regarded themselves as Europeans (of a higher status) while they regarded Venezuelans and Peruvians as Latin Americans (lower in status). Nevertheless, I generated with some ideas for management in some of these countries. Thus I proposed in Singapore that because of its Chinese culture, personnel programs be family-oriented, for instance, organizing visits of the whole family to the workplace. Recently, I learned that in mainland China, the family is often involved by factory supervisors in dealing with problems of worker motivation.[53]

THEN AND NOW

I would like to conclude with some thoughts about how our world of research has changed since when I first began. I chuckle when I hear complaints from younger colleagues about problems in getting their research done and their lack of time and needed resources.

In the 1940s, Herbert Toops at Ohio State University kept an IBM accounting machine (as large as a modern main frame computer) in his office, using what he called Hollerith cards (the 80 column IBM cards) after Herman Hollerith who created the cards for the 1890 census. With its use, it still required six months for me to complete my first large-scale factor analysis replete with errors. We learned how to wire the machine to total up sums, sums of squares, and sums of cross-products from which we could calculate one product-moment correlation coefficient at a time between two variables. We could also use hand-cranked Monroe Calculators for the same purpose.

At Louisiana State University in 1949, we began with one telephone for the whole department. In writing Leadership, Psychology and Organizational Psychology, I searched by hand for the 400 references and made notes on 3×5 cards. I used absorbent wrist cuffs to keep the perspiration from the paper on which I was writing in a hot, humid world without air conditioning.

Duplication usually involved typing masters and hand-cranking mimeograph or ditto machines. Photocopying was expensive and rare. My wife, Ruth, typed my doctoral dissertation on multilith stencils (difficult to make corrections) so I could have more and better copies than possible with carbon paper.

Although unrecognized at the time unless you were in a major department at a major university, you were much more isolated than nowadays. Regional meetings made more sense. It might take several days to get to a national meeting by train or automobile. International meetings required even longer time in transit. The roundtrip for letters with a colleague in Europe took at least two weeks without the availability of BITNET or FAX. Difficult to handle magnetic wire was required for audiorecording, or phonograph or dictograph records had to be cut. Videotaping was in the distant future; filming, of course, was much more expensive and hard to manage. But there was much less competition for publication space in the better journals.

I never had been career-conscious, as such, in academia. That is, I assumed that promotion would come as rapidly as possible as a function of my efforts and performance. I never even had heard about or paid attention to tenure until long after I was serving without tenure as an assistant professor. I became a tenured associate professor in 1952 and a tenured full-professor in 1956 without ever having given much thought to either promotion or tenure. Shortly after, I listened to a lecture on the demotivating aspects of becoming a tenured full-professor by 33. I was only 31. My students, many of whom had been veterans, were finally beginning to become younger than me. This cavalier attitude toward tenure got me and my group into trouble later on when I joined a business school in which organizational behavior came to be treated as a heresy.

I only really woke up to the importance of tenure at the University of Rochester after I found myself in a management school in 1972 in which the dominant powers reached the judgment that organizational behavior was without validity or relevance for management. Life was a matter of trade-offs. The economic dynamics of the free market outside the firm could be used in the same way to fully explain the competitive dynamics inside the firm. However, the threat was turned into an opportunity. In a belated effort at self-defence and in reaction to what I judged to be the "scientism" of extreme monetarist economists for whom price theory seemed to be the only basis for understanding human behavior, in 1974, I published "The Substance and the Shadow" in the American Psychologist in which I argued that much of "scientific" research in social science is scientism and not scientific. An investigator can be too rigorous rather than not rigorous enough. It depends on where one is in a line of investigation. Early in a line of investigation, one should be open to reality and "hang loose." One should "wallow around in reality." Late in investigation, research should meet higher standards of rigor.

As I look back, I am reminded of the short time span in the development of industrial psychology and modern management. One of my mentors at Ohio State, Harold Burtt received his Ph.D. under Hugo Munsterberg, who at the turn of the century, introduced industrial psychology into the United States from Germany. Walter V. Bingham told me in 1952 about his attending the first meeting of the American Psychological Association in 1892. I listened in 1968 to Lillian Gilbreth, then 98 years old, commenting on presentations at an American Management Association meeting.

. . . AND TOMORROW

As I look ahead, I continue to feel that I am on a fast track, with many things to do still ahead. With the support of a large grant from the Kellogg Foundation, I am committed with Bruce Avolio and our staff at the Center for Leadership Studies to train 400 community leaders by 1993. Bruce and I have a similar commitment to Fiat. A transformational leadership training organization is being envisioned and articulated. *The Leadership Quarterly* has been launched but still depends on CLS's management. Invitations have been received to visit institutions in countries ranging from Indonesia to Finland and from Norway to New Zealand. And I have a long list of other things I feel I must do: become PC-literate, learn some more Italian and German, go through the Straits of Magellan, trek in the Himalayas, walk the Milford Track in New Zealand, visit the Galapagos, and climb the same mountain in Rocky Mountain National Park again with Ruth on our 50th wedding anniversary in 1996 as we vowed to do on our 25th in 1971.

PUBLICATIONS

1946

The Jew and higher education. *Chicago Jewish Forum, 4*, 246-250.

1948

Application of addends to sales and clerical occupational classification. *Journal of Applied Psychology, 32*, 490-502.

1949

An analysis of the leaderless group discussion. *Journal of Applied Psychology,* *33,* 527-533.

1950

Selecting personnel by observation. *Personnel, 26,* 269-272.
The leaderless group discussion technique. *Personnel Psychology, 3,* 17-31.

1951

Situational tests: I. Individual interviews compared with leaderless group discussions. *Educational and Psychological Measurement, 11,* 67-75.
Situational tests: II. Leaderless group discussion variables. *Educational and Psychological Measurement, 11,* 196-207.
Intra-university variations in grading practices. *Journal of Education Psychology, 42,* 366-368.
With F-T. M. Norton. Group size and leaderless discussions. *Journal of Applied Psychology, 35,* 397-400.
With R.E. Stucki. A note on a modification of the Purdue Pegboard. *Journal of Applied Psychology, 35,* 312-313.
With O.L. White. Situational tests: III. Observers' ratings of leaderless group discussion participants as indicators of external leadership status. *Education and Psychological Measurement, 11,* 355-361.
[Review of *The group approach to leadership-testing*]. *Personnel Psychology, 4,* 306-311.

1952

Ultimate criteria of organizational worth. *Personnel Psychology, 5,* 157-173.
With C.N. Coates. Forecasting officer potential using the leaderless group discussion. *Journal of Abnormal and Social Psychology, 47,* 321-325.
With S.H. Klubeck. Effects of seating arrangement on leaderless group discussion. *Journal of Abnormal and Social Psychology, 47,* 724-727.
With C.R. McGehee & R. B. Marston. Selecting wage-earning employees for the chemical and chemical process industries. *Chemical and Engineering News, 30,* 2980-2982.

1953

With C.R. Wurster. Effects of company rank on LGD performances of oil refinery supervisors. *Journal of Applied Psychology, 37,* 100-104.

With C.R. Wurster. Situational tests: IV. Validity of leaderless group discussions among strangers. *Educational and Psychological Measurement, 13*, 122-132.

With S. Klubeck & C.R. Wurster. Factors influencing the reliability and validity of leaderless group discussion assessment. *Journal of Applied Psychology, 37*, 26-30.

With C.R. McGehee, W.C. Hawkins, P.C. Young & A.S. Gebel. Personality variables related to leaderless group discussion behavior. *Journal of Abnormal and Social Psychology, 48*, 120-128.

With C.R. Wurster. Effects of the nature of the problem on LGD performance. *Journal of Applied Psychology, 37*, 96-99.

With C.R. Wurster, P.A. Doll, & D.J. Clair. Situational and personality factors in leadership among sorority women. *Psychological Monographs, 67*, 1-23.

1954

With S. Klubeck. Differential effect of training on persons of different leadership status. *Human Relations, 7*, 59-72.

Feelings of pleasantness and work group efficiency. *Personnel Psychology, 7*, 81-91.

Leaderless group discussion as a leadership evaluation instrument. *Personnel Psychology, 7*, 470-477.

The leaderless group discussion. *Psychological Bulletin, 51*, 465-492.

With B. Karstendick, G. McCullough, & R. C. Pruitt. Policemen and detectives, public service. Validity information exchange. *Personnel Psychology, 7*, 159-160.

With C. H. Coates. Advanced Air Force and Army ROTC cadets. Validity information exchange. *Personnel Psychology, 7*(279), 553-554.

[Review of *Group relations at the cross roads*]. *Journal of Applied Psychology, 38*, 378-379.

1955

Authoritarianism or acquiescence? *Journal of Abnormal and Social Psychology, 51*, 616-623.

1956

With E.L. Gaier. Effects of city familiarty on size estimation. *Psychological Reports, 2*, 35-38.

With D.A. Dobbins. The role of the statistician in correlational administration and guidance. *American Journal of Correction, 18*(12), 24-25.

Reducing leniency in merit ratings. *Personnel Psychology, 9*, 359-369.
Leadership opinions as forecast of supervisory success. *Journal of Applied Psychology, 40*, 345-356.
Development of a structured disguised personality test. *Journal of Applied Psychology, 40*, 393-397.
[Review of *Leadership qualities: A theoretical inquiry and an experimental study of foremen.*] *American Sociological Review, 21*, 407-408.
Development and evaluation of a scale for measuring social acquiescence. *Journal of Abnormal and Social Psychology, 53*, 296-299.
With C.R. Wurster. Using "mark sense" for ratings and personal data collection. *Journal of Applied Psychology, 40*, 269-271.
With D.A. Dobbins. IBM "mark sense" cards in prison classification and criminological research. *Journal of Criminal Law, Criminology and Police Science, 47*, 436-443.

1957

With E.E. Gaier, F.J. Farese, & A.W. Flint. An objective method for studying behavior in groups. *Psychological Reports, 3*, 265-280.
Reply to Messick's and Jackson's comments on acquiescence or authoritarianism. *Journal of Abnormal and Social Psychology, 5*, 426-427.
Iterative inverse factor analysis—a method for clustering persons. *Psychometrika, 22*, 105-107.
Undiscriminated operant acquiescence. *Educational and Psychological Measurement, 17*, 83-85.
With J. Dawson, C.R. Wurster and F.H. Hine. Measurement of symptomatic changes in hospitalized psychiatric patients. *Diseases of the Nervous System, 18*, 58-62.
With W. Flint & M. Pryer. *Esteem, status, motivation, and attraction to the group* (Tech. Rep. No. 9).
With W. Flint & M. Pryer. *Effects of status-esteem conflict on subsequent behavior in groups* (Tech. Rep. No. 10).
With W. Flint & M. Pryer. *Esteem and successful leadership* (Tech. Rep. No. 11).
With W. Flint & M. Pryer. *Group effectiveness as a function of attempted and successful leadership* (Tech. Rep. No. 11).
Validity studies of a proverbs personality test. *Journal of Applied Psychology, 41*, 158-160.
Leadership opinions and related characteristics of salesmen and sales managers. In R.M. Stogdill & A.E. Coons (Eds.), *Leader behavior: Its description and measurement* (*Personnel Board Monograph* No. 88). Columbus, OH: Ohio State University Press.

Test of a proposed theory of leadership. *Behavior in Groups* (3rd Annual Rep.).
Faking by sales applicants of a forced choice personality inventory. *Journal of Applied Psychology, 41*, 403-404.

1958

With D.A. Dobbins. Effects of unemployment on white and negro prison admissions in Louisiana. *The Journal of Criminal Law, Criminology and Police Science, 48*, 522-525.
With M. W. Pryer, E.L. Gaier, & A.W. Flint. Interacting effects of control, motivation, group practice and problem difficulty in attempted leadership. *Journal of Abnormal and Social Psychology, 56*(6), 352-356.
With D.F. Pennington & F. Haravey. Some effects of decision and discussion on coalescence, change and effectiveness. *Journal of Applied Psychology, 42*, 404-408.
Famous sayings test: General manual. *Psychological Reports, 4*, 479-497.
Leadership opinions as forecasts of supervisory success: A replication. *Personnel Psychology, 11*, 515-518.
Social and industrial psychology: 2000 B.C.-4000 B.C. *The American Psychologist, 13*, 78-79.

1959

An approach to the objective assessment of leadership. In B.M. Bass & I.A. Berg (Eds.), *Objective Approaches to Personality Assessment* (pp. 146-168). New York: Van Nostrand.
With E.L. Gaier. Regional differences in interrelations among authoritarianism, acquiescence and ethnocentrism. *Journal of Social Psychology, 49*, 47-51.
With M.K. DiStefano, Jr. Prediction of an ultimate criterion of success as a lawyer. *Journal of Applied Psychology, 42*, 404-445.
With M.W. Pryer. Some effects of feedback on behavior in groups, *Sociometry, 22*, 56-63.
Effects of motivation on consistency of performance in groups. *Educational and Psychological Measurement, 19*, 247-252.
Great men or great times? *Adult Leadership, 8*, 7-10.
The 1959 LSU Department of Psychology symposium on leadership and interpersonal behavior. *Journal of Counseling Psychology, 6*, 157-159.
Go west, *CP*, go west. *Contemporary Psychology, 4*, 92.
With I.A. Berg (Eds.). *Objective approaches to personality assessment.* New York: Van Nostrand.

1960

Leadership, psychology, and organizational behavior. New York: Harper.
[Review of *Creativity and its cultivation*]. *Personnel Psychology, 13*, 105-108.
Measures of average influence and change in agreement of rankings by a group
of judges. *Sociometry, 23*, 195-202.
The management training laboratory: A way to improve organizational
effectiveness. *Advanced Management, 25*(7), 11-15.
With R.N. Vidulich. Relation of selected personality and attitude scales to the
Famous Sayings Test. *Psychological Reports, 7*, 259-260.

1961

[Review of *An anatomy of leadership: Princes, heroes, and supermen*].
American Journal of Psychology, 74, 322-323.
[Review of *The dynamics of discussion*]. *Contemporary Psychology, 6*, 208-
209.
Conformity, deviation and a general theory of interpersonal behavior. In I.A.
Berg & B.M. Berg (Eds.), *Conformity and Deviation* (pp. 38-100). New
York: Harper and Bros.
Some aspects of attempted, successful and effective leadership. *Journal of
Applied Psychology, 45*, 120-122.
Some observations about a general theory of leadership and interpersonal
behavior. In L. Petrullo & B.M. Bass (Eds.), *Leadership and
interpersonal behavior* (pp. 3-9). New York: Holt, Rinehart & Winston.
Some observations about a general theory of leadership and interpersonal
behavior. In W.R. Lassey & R.R. Fernandez (eds.), *Leadership and
Social Change* (2nd ed., pp. 64-79). LaJolla, CA: University Associates,
1976.
With L. Petrullo (Eds.). *Leadership and interpersonal behavior.* New York:
Holt, Rinehart & Winston.
With I.A. Berg (Eds.). *Conformity and deviation.* New York: Harper & Bros.
An experimental approach to teaching personnel selection. *Personnel
Psychology, 14*, 101-104.
With E.B. Gurman. Objective compared with subjective measures of the same
behavior in groups. *Journal of Abnormal and Social Psychology, 63*, 368-
374.
With C.R. Wurster & W. Alcock. A test of the proposition: We want to be
esteemed most by those we esteem most highly. *Journal of Abnormal
and Social Psychology, 63*, 650-653.
Some recent studies in social acquiescence. *Psychological Reports, 9*, 447-448.

1962

The Orientation Inventory. Palo Alto, CA: Consulting Psychologists Press.
Further evidence on the dynamic character of criteria. *Personnel Psychology,*
    15, 93-97.
[Review of *Training in business and industry*]. *Management Science, 8,* 372-
    373.
Reactions to "Twelve Angry Men" as a measure of sensitivity training. *Journal*
    of Applied Psychology, 46, 120-124.
Mood changes in a management training laboratory. *Journal of Applied*
    Psychology, 46, 361-364.
With P. Baker. A secretary's lot is a happy one: Or is it? *The Secretary, 22*(April
    2), 4, 6, 8.
Are motor response elements additive? *Perceptual and Motor Skills, 15,* 433-
    434.
[Review of *Leadership and Organization*]. *Journal of Business, 35,* 324-325.
With M.W. Pryer & A. W. Flint. Group effectiveness and consistency of
    leadership. *Sociometry, 25,* 391-397.

1963

Some experimental approaches to the study of organizational psychology.
    Management International, 3, 90-97.
Experimenting with simulated manufactured organizations. In S.B. Seels (Ed.),
    Stimulus determinants of behavior (pp. 117-196). New York: Ronald
    Press.
With F.H. Kanfer & I. Guyett. Dyadic speech patterns, orientation and social
    reinforcement. *Journal of Consulting Psychology, 27,* 199-205.
With G.H. Dunteman. Supervisory success and engineering assignment
    associated with the Orientation Inventory. *Personnel Psychology, 16,* 13-
    22.
With G.H. Dunteman, R. Frye, R. Vidulich & Helen Wambach. Self,
    interaction, and task orientation inventory scores associated with overt
    behavior and personal factors. *Educational and Psychological*
    Measurement, 23, 101-116.
With G.H. Dunteman. Biases in the evaluation of one's own group, its allies
    and opponents. *Journal of Conflict Resolution, 7,* 16-20.
With G.H. Dunteman. Behavior in groups as a function of self, interaction
    and task-orientation. *Journal of Abnormal and Social Psychology, 66,*
    419-428.
Amount of participation, coalescence and profitability of decision-making
    discussions. *Journal of Abnormal and Social Psychology, 67,* 92-94.

With M. D. Dunnette. Behavioral scientists and personnel management. *Industrial Relations, 2*(3), 115-130.
With H.J. Leavitt. Some experiments in planning and operating. *Management Science, 9,* 574-585.
With R. Frye. Behavior in a group related to tested social acquiescence. *Journal of Social Psychology, 61,* 263-266.
With H.A. Bryant & D.A. Dobbins. Group effectiveness, coercion, change and coalescence among delinquents compared to nondelinquents. *Journal of Social Psychology, 61,* 167-177.
Simulating the micro-economy of the farmer. In *The management input in agriculture.* Agricultural Policy Institute, South. Farm. Mgmt. Res. Comm. Farm Foundation.

1964

With R.B. Morton. The organizational training laboratory. *Training Directors Journal, 18*(10), 2-18.
Industrial organization for the space age. *Pittsburgh Business Review, 34*(1), 5-13.
With D.A. Stimpson. Dyadic behavior of self, interaction and task-oriented subjects in a test situation. *Journal of Abnormal and Social Psychology, 68,* 558-562.
Business gaming for organizational psychology. *Management Science, 10,* 545-556.
With H.J. Leavitt. Organizational psychology. *Annual Review of Psychology, 15,* 371-398.
Defensiveness and susceptibility to coercion as a function of self, interaction and task orientation. *Journal of Social Psychology, 62,* 335-341.
With M.D. Dunnette. Criticism and comment. Behavioral scientists in personnel management. *Industrial Relations, 3,* 109-118.
Some current research in individual and group behavior. *Pittsburgh Business Review, 34*(3), 3-5.
Socio-psychological implications of disarmament. *Pittsburgh Business Review, 34*(8), 4-5, 11.
With J.A. Vaughan. *Psychology of Learning for Managers.* New York: American Foundation for Management Research.
Studying performance under various organizational structures. In *Management Games in Selection and Development* (pp. 31-47).
With W.W. Cooper, H.J. Leavitt, & M.W. Shelly, II (Eds.). Production organization exercise: An application of experimental techniques to business games. In *New perspectives in organization research* (pp. 97-114). New York: Wiley.

1965

A program of exercises for management and organizational psychology.
Pittsburgh, PA: Management Development Associates.
Organizational psychology. Boston, MA: Allyn & Bacon.
The psychologist and the business school. *The Industrial Psychologist, 2*(3),
14-18.
Reply to Naylor's criticism. *The Industrial Psychologist, 2*(4).

1966

Effects on the subsequent performance of negotiators of studying issues or
planning strategies alone or in groups. *Psychological Monographs, 80*(6).
A plan to use programmed group exercises to study cross-cultural differences
in management behavior. *Industrial Journal of Psychology, 1,* 319-322.
With J.A. Vaughan, *Training in Industry: The Management of Learning.*
Belmont, CA: Wadsworth.

1967

Administrative training and research using small group exercises. *Pittsburgh
Business Review, 37*(4), 1-4.
Combining management training and research. *Training and Development
Journal, 21*(4), 2-7.
The anarchist movement and the t-group: Some possible lessons for
organizational development. *Journal of Applied Behavioral Science, 3,*
211-230.
Social behavior and the orientation inventory: A review. *Psychological
Bulletin, 68,* 260-292.
With S. Deep & J.A. Vaughan. Some effects on business gaming of previous
quasi-T group affiliations. *Journal of Applied Psychology, 51,* 426-431.
With J.A. Vaughan. A comparison of bottoms-up vs. top-down management
organizations in a noncomputer business game. *Transaction, 5*(1), 50-
52.
Some effects on a group of whether and when the head reveals his opinion.
Organizational Behavior and Human Performance, 2(4), 375-382.

1968

The interface between personnel and organizational psychology. *Journal of
Applied Psychology, 52*(1), 81-88.
How to succeed in business according to business students and managers.
Journal of Applied Psychology, 52(3), 254-262.

Implications of the behavioral sciences in the year 2000. In *Management 2000* (pp. 101-107). Hamilton, NY: American Foundation for Management Research.
With G.V. Barrett. Comparisons of managerial values and behavior. *Naval Research Review, 21*, 8-13.
Ability, values and concepts of equitable salary increases in exercise compensation. *Journal of Applied Psychology, 52*, 299-303.

1969

With R.J. Lee. *Il dirigente e medio livello: Ruoli presenti e futuri.* Milan: Franco Angeli Editore.
With K. M. Thiagarajan. Differential preferences for long- vs. short-term payoffs in India and the United States. *Proceedings of the XVIth International Congress of Applied Psychology* (pp. 423-428). Amsterdam: Swets & Zeitlinger.
Planning for research. In *Proceedings of the OAR Symposium on Research Management* (pp. 65-76). Washington, D.C.

1970

When planning for others. *Journal of Applied Behavioral Science, 6*, 151-171.
With R.C. Cooper & J.A. Haas (Eds.). *Managing for accomplishment.* Lexington, MA: Heath/Lexington.
With S.D. Deep (Eds.). *Current Perspectives for Managing Organizations.* Englewood Cliffs, NJ: Prentice-Hall.
On becoming a psychologist in industry. 5. The role of the business school. *Personnel Psychology, 23*, 208-212.
The task-oriented manager. In B.M. Bass, R.C. Cooper, & J.A. Haas (Eds.), *Managing for Accomplishment* (pp. 5-12). Lexington, MA: Heath/Lexington.
With G.V. Barrett. Comparative surveys of managerial attitudes and behavior. In J. Boddewyn (Ed.), *Comparative Management Teaching, Training and Research* (pp. 179-217). New York: Graduate School of Business New York University.
Errata: How to succeed in business according to business students and managers. *Journal of Applied Psychology, 54*, 103.

1971

The American advisor abroad. *Journal of Applied Behavioral Science, 2*, 285-308.

With G.V. Barrett & J.A. Miller. Combatting obsolescence using perceived discrepancies in job expectations of research managers and scientists. In S.S. Dubin (Ed.), *Professional obsolescence* (pp. 59-71). London: English Universities Press.

With J. Krusell & R.A. Alexander. Male managers' attitudes toward working women. *American Behavioral Scientist, 15*(2), 221-236.

With R.A. Alexander, G.V. Barrett, & E.C. Ryterband. Empathy, projection and negation in seven countries. In L.E. Abt & B.F. Reiss (Eds.), *Progress in clinical psychology: Industrial applications* (pp. 29-49). New York: Grune & Stratton.

1972

Organizational life in the 70's and beyond. *Personal Psychology, 25* 19-30.

With G. V. Barrett. *Man, work and organization: An introduction to industrial and organizational psychology*. Boston, MA: Allyn & Bacon.

With S.D. Deep (Eds.). *Studies in organizational psychology*. Boston, MA: Allyn & Bacon.

With R.H. Franke. Societal influences on student perceptions on how to succeed in organizations: A cross-national analysis. *Journal of Applied Psychology, 56*, 312-318.

With R.A. Alexander. Climate, economy, and the differential migration of white and non-white workers. *Journal of Applied Psychology, 56*, 518-521.

With K.M. Thiagarajan. Preparing managers for work in other countries. *European Training, 1*(2), 117.

Greater productivity and satisfaction through self-planning. In *Proceedings of the First International Sociological Conference on Participation and Self Management*. Dubrovnik, Yugoslavia.

1973

With E.C. Ryterband. Work and non-work: Perspectives in the context of change. In M.D. Dunnette (Ed.), *Work and non-work in the year 2001*. Monterey, CA: Brooks-Cole.

With E.C. Ryterband. Work and organizational life in the year 2000. In M.D. Dunnette (Ed.), *Work and non-work in the year 2001*. Monterey, CA: Brooks-Cole.

With L.D. Eldridge. Accelerated managers' objectives in twelve countries. *Industrial Relations, 12*, 158-171.

With F.L. Vicino, J. Krusell, E.L. Deci, & D.A. Landy. The impact of PROCESS: Self-administered exercises for personal and interpersonal development. *Journal of Applied Behavioral Science, 9*, 737-756.

With G.V. Barrett. Comparative surveys of managerial attitudes and behavior. *Quarterly Journal of Management Development, 4*(1), 1-28.

With E.C. Ryterband. Management development. In J. McGuire (Eds.), *Contemporary management: Issues and viewpoints.* Englewood Cliffs, NJ: Prentice-Hall.

With W.F. Cascio & E. O'Connor. Magnitude estimations of frequency and amount. *Journal of Applied Psychology, 59*, 313-320.

With R. Klauss. Group influence on individual behavior across cultures. *Journal of Cross-Cultural Psychology, 5*, 236-246.

With D.C. King. Leadership, power and influence. In H.L. Fromkin & J.J. Sherwood (Eds.), *Integrating the organization.* New York: The Free Press.

Managerial style as a function of personal and situational factors. In K.W. Tilley (Ed.), *Leadership and management appraisal.* London: English Universities Press.

With E. Valenzi. Contingent aspects of effective management styles. In J.G. Hunt & L.L. Larson (Eds.), *Contingency Approaches to Leadership* (pp. 130-157). Carbondale, IL: Southern Illinois University Press.

Unternehmungsspiel fur die organizationsforschung. In F. Eisenfurh, D. Ordelheide, & G. Puck (Eds.), *Unternehmungsspiele in Ausbildung und Forschung.* Betriebswirtschafleicher Verlag Dr. Th.Gabler: Weisbaden.

The substance and the shadow. *American Psychologist, 29*, 870-886.

1975

With Z. Shapira. Settling strikes in real life and simulations in North America and different regions of Europe. *Journal of Applied Psychology, 60*, 466-471.

With R. Klauss. Communication styles, credibility and their consequences. *Personnel Administrator, 20*(6), 32-35.

With H.R. Valenzi, D.L. Farrow, & R.J. Solomon, Management styles associated with organizational, task, personal and interpersonal contingencies. *Journal of Applied Psychology, 60*, 720-729.

1976

With R. Bass. Concern for the environment: Implications for industrial and organizational psychology. *American Psychologist, 31*, 158-166.

With R. Bass. Concern for the environment: Implications for industrial and organizational psychology. In P.J. Woods (Ed.), *Career opportunities for psychologists* (pp. 197-210). Washington, D.C.: American Psychological Association.

With G.V. Barrett. Cross-cultural issues in industrial and organizational psychology. In M. D. Dunnette (Ed.), *Handbook of industrial and organizational psychology* (pp. 1639-1686). New York: Rand-McNally.

Self-managing systems, Z.E. G. and other unthinkables. In Meltzer & F. Wickert (Eds.), *Humanizing organizational behavior* (pp. 134-157). Springfield, IL: C.C. Thomas.

Life goals and career success of European and American managers. *Rivista Internationazionale di Scienze Economiche e Commerciali, 23*(2), 154-171.

With W.F. Cascio. The effects of role play in a program to modify attitudes toward black employees. *Journal of Psychology, 92*, 261-266.

A systems survey research feedback for management and organizational development. *Journal of Applied Behavioral Science, 12*, 215-229.

Environmental psychology. Comment. *American Psychologist, 31*, 679.

With W.F. Cascio, J.W. McPherson, & H.J. Tragash. PROSPER—Training and research for increasing management awareness about affirmative action in race relations. *Academy of Management Journal, 19*, 353-369.

With C.W. Mitchell. Influence on the felt need for collective bargaining by business and science professionals. *Journal of Applied Psychology, 61*, 770-773.

Italian managers compared with managers from elsewhere in Europe. *Rivista Internazionale di Scienze Economiche e Commerciali, 23*(9), 849-862.

1977

Group decisions. Comment. *American Psychologist, 32*, 230-231.

With R. Bass & Z. Shapira. Environmentalists' and business executives' attitudes and information about the nuclear power controversy. *International Journal of Environmental Studies, 10*, 79-83.

With E. Rosenstein. Integration of industrial democracy and participative management: U.S. and European perspectives. In B.T. King, S.S. Streufert, & F.E. Fiedler (Eds.), *Managerial control and organizational democray*. Washington, D.C.: Victor Winston & Sons.

Ori: Manual for the orientation inventory. Palo Alto, CA: Consulting Psychologists Press.

Utility of managerial self-planning on a simulated production task with replications in twelve countries. *Journal of Applied Psychology, 62*, 506-509.

Quality standards for "ready-to-use" training and development programs. *Journal of Applied Behavioral Science, 13*, 518-532.

With D.W. McGregor & J.L. Walters. Selecting foreign plant sites: Economic, social, and political considerations. *Academy of Management Journal, 20*, 535-551.

With D.L. Farrow. Quantitative analyses of biographies of political figures. *Journal of Psychology, 97*, 281-296.

1978

With F. Vicino. Lifespace variables and managerial success. *Journal of Applied Psychology, 63*, 81-88.

1979

With E.C. Ryterband. *Organizational psychology*. Boston, MA: Allyn & Bacon.

With H.T. Reis. Changing attitudes and knowledge about nuclear energy. *International Journal of Environmental Studies, 14*, 127-138.

With P. Burger et al. *Assessment of managers: An international comparison*. New York: Free Press.

With V.J. Shackleton. Industrial democracy and participative management: A case for a synthesis. *Academy of Management Review, 4*(3), 393-404.

Het Gebruik van de Ergom-Oefeninger Als Beoordelings-Instrument van Het Managersgedrag in 12 Landen. In *Sleuthels voor morgen*. Antwerp: Reclamebureau J. Verdyck.

1980

With V.J. Shackleton & E. Rosenstein. Industrial democracy and participative management: What's the difference? *International Review of Applied Psychology, 28*, 81-92.

With E. Valenzi. Organizational psychology: A professional application. *Professional Psychology, 11*, 469-476.

Augmenting observation with objective data from small group exercises. *Assessment Newsletter* (June).

Individual capability and team performance. *Small Group Behavior, 11*, 431-508.

1981

Origins of leadership research: From leaderless group discussion to cross-cultural leadership. *Journal of Management, 7*, 63-77.

Stogdill's handbook of leadership (Rev. and expanded ed.). New York: Free Press.

With G.V. Barrett. *People, work and organizations*. Boston, MA: Allyn & Bacon.

What makes people work harder? *New York Times* (April 25).

With P.C. Burger. Multinational management: Cross-national differences. *Modern Office Procedures, 25*(9), 16-22.
With P.C. Burger. Management differences and the socialization process. *Modern Office Procedures, 25*(10), 14-20.
With P.C. Burger. Six national profiles. *Modern Office Procedures, 25*(11), 16, 18, 22.
With P.C. Burger. Six more national profiles. *Modern Office Procedures, 25*(12), 14, 16, 20.

1982

Individual capability, team response and productivity. In E.A. Fleishman, & M.D. Dunnette, (Eds.), *Human performance and productivity.* Vol. I: *Human capability assessment* (pp. 179-232). New York: Lawrence Erlbaum.
Intensity of relation, dyadic-group consideration, cognitive categorization and transformational leadership. In J.G. Hunt, U. Sekaran, & C.A. Schreisheim, (Eds.), *Leadership: Beyond established views* (pp. 142-150). Carbondale, IL: Southern University Press.
With R. Klauss. *Interpersonal communications in organizations.* New York: Academic Press.
Leadership and management in the 1980's. In A. Glickman, (Ed.). *The Changing Composition of the Work Force.* New York: Lawrence Erlbaum.

1983

Organizational decision-making. Homewood, IL: Richard D. Irwin.
[Review of *Conformity, suicide and homicide*]. *Behavioral Science Research.*
Issues involved in relations between methodological rigor and reported outcomes in evaluation of organizational development. *Journal of Applied Psychology, 68,* 197-199.
Leadership, participation and non-trivial decision-making. In J.G. Hunt & C.A. Schreisheim, (Eds.). *New frontiers in leadership research.* New York: Oxford University Press.
[Review of *Participatory management in libraries*]. *Public Libraries, 22,* 122.

1984

Leadership and supervision. In R.J. Cassini (Ed.), *Encyclopedia of psychology* (Vol. 2, pp. 286-287). New York: Wiley.
Management development. In R.J. Cassini (Ed.), *Encyclopedia of psychology* (Vol. 2, pp. 331-332). New York: Wiley.

Team Performance. In R.J. Cassini (Ed.), *Encyclopedia of psychology* (Vol. 3, pp. 406-307). New York: Wiley.
Productivity and democratic leadership. In R. Franke (Ed.), *Productivity*. San Francisco: Jossey-Bass.
Leadership and organizational decision-making. In J.G. Hunt (Ed.), *Leaders and managers: International perspectives on managerial behavior and leadership*. New York: Pergamon.
Transformational leadership and performance beyond expectations. *Singapore Psychologist, 1*, 5-34.
Foreward. In Y.U. Chandar (Ed.), *The organization men: Executives and their behavior*. New Delhi: Shri Venkot.
El estilo de direccion [Management styles]. In *Enciclopedia de Direccion y Administracion de la Empresa* (pp. 21-40). Barcelona: Ediciones Orbis.
With P.M. Piaker. Time for accountants to point the way to peace. *New York Times* (April 17).

1985

Leadership: Good, better, best. *Organizational Dynamics, 13*, 26-41.
Leaderscap: Goed, beter, best. [Leadership: Good, better, best]. *Praktish Personeelsbeleid, 19*, 99-118.
Leadership and performance beyond expectations. New York: Free Press.
[Review of *Leadership and Organizational Culture*]. *Journal of Higher Education, 56*, 592-595.

1986

With D.A. Waldman. Self-administered process and task-oriented learning groups: A comparison of expectations and outcomes. *International Journal of Small Group Research, 2*, 107-112.
Viewpoint. *International Management, 41*(7), 57.

1987

With B.J. Avolio. Charisma and beyond. In J.G. Hunt (Ed.), *Emerging leadership vistas*. Lexington, MA: Lexington.
With P. Drenth & P. Weissenberg. *Advances in Organizational Psychology: An International Review*. Beverly Hills, CA: Sage.
With B.J. Avolio & L. Goodheim. Biography and the assessment of transformational leadership at the world-class level. *Journal of Management, 13*, 7-19.
With D.A. Waldman, B.J. Avolio, & M. Bebb. Transformational leadership and the falling dominoes effect. *Group and Organizational Studies, 12*, 73-87.

With D.A. Waldman & W.O. Einstein. Leadership and outcomes of performance appraisal process. *Journal of Occupational Psychology, 60,* 177-186.

1988

With J. Hater. Superiors' evaluations and subordinates' perceptions of transformational and transactional leadership. *Journal of Applied Psychology, 73,* 695-702.

Liderazgo transformacional en la empresa Americana. In *Hombre y empresa* (pp. 67-88). Bilbao: Universidad de Deusto.

El impacto de los directores transformacionales en la vida escolar. In R. Pascual (Ed.), *La gestation education ante la innovacion y el cambio.* Narcio: Bilbao.

Evolving perspectives on charismatic leadership. In J. Conger & R.N. Kanungo (Eds.), *Charisma leadership: The elusive factor in organizational effectiveness.* San Francisco, CA: Jossey-Bass.

The inspirational processes of leadership. *The Journal of Management Development, 7*(5), 21-31.

1989

Charisma: Entwickeln und zielfuhrend einsetzen. Landsberg/Lech: Verlag Moderne Industrie.

With B.J. Avolio. Potential biases in leadership measures: How prototypes, leniency, and general satisfaction relate to ratings and rankings of transformational and transactional leadership constructs. *Educational and Psychological Measurement, 49,* 509-527.

The two faces of charisma. *Leaders, 12*(4), 44-45.

With J.G. Seltzer & R.E. Numerof. Transformational leadership: Is it a source of more or less burnout and stress? *Journal of Health and Human Resources Administration, 12,* 174-185.

1990

Bass & Stogdill's handbook of leadership: Theory, research and managerial applications (3rd ed.). New York: Free Press.

From transactional to transformational leadership: Learning to share the vision. *Organizational Dynamics, 18*(3), 19-31.

With B.J. Avolio. Training and development of transformational leadership: Looking to 1992 and beyond. *European Journal of Industrial Training, 14*(5), 21-27.

With B.J. Avolio. The implications of transactional and transformational leadership for individual, team and organizational development. In R.W. Woodman & W.A. Passmore (Eds.), *Research in organizational change and development*. Greenwich, CT: JAI Press.

With J. Seltzer. Transformational leadership: Beyond initiation and consideration. *Journal of Management, 16*, 693-703.

With D. Waldman & F.J. Yammarino. Adding to leader-follower transactions: The augmentation effect of charismatic leadership. *Group & Organizational Studies, 15*, 381-394.

With F.J. Yammarino. Long-term forecasting of transformational leadership and its effects among Naval officers: Some preliminary findings. In K.E. Clark & M.B. Clark (Eds.), *Measures of leadership*. Greensboro, NC: Center for Creative Leadership.

1991

Debate. Ways men and women lead. *Harvard Business Review, 69*(1), 150-160.

Transformational leadership and stress. In F. Heller (Ed.), *Decision-making and leadership*. Cambridge, England: Cambridge University Press.

With D.A. Waldman. Transformational leadership at different phases of the innovation process. *Journal of High Technology Management*.

With B.J. Avolio & F.J. Yammarino. Identifying common methods variance with data collected from a single source: An unresolved sticky issue. *Journal of Management, 17*, 571-587.

With B.J. Avolio. *Full range of leadership development*. Binghampton, NY: Bass/Avolio and Associatiates.

With F.J. Yammarino. Person and situation views of leadership: A multiple levels of analysis approach. *Leadership Quarterly, 2*, 121-139.

With F.J. Yammarino. Self and others' transformational leadership ratings related to Naval officers' performance. *Applied Psychology: An International Review, 40*, 437-454.

With N. Yokochi. Charisma among senior executives and the special case of Japanese CEOs. *Consulting Psychology Bulletin* (Winter/Spring), pp. 31-38.

In Press

Is there universality in the full range model of leadership? *International Journal of Public Administration*.

Assessing the charismatic leader. In M. Syrett & C. Hogg (Eds.), *Leadership in business*. London: Basil Blackwell.

With B.J. Avolio. Diffusion of transformational leadership. In M.M. Chemers (Ed.), *Festschrift for Fred Fiedler*. New York: Academic Press.

With B.J. Avolio. Transformational leadership and organizational culture. *Journal of Public Administration.*

With B.J. Avolio (Eds.). *Transformational leadership and innovation in human resources management.* Turin, Italy: ISVOR-FIAT.

Submitted

Continuity and change in the history of work. (Commissioned by the Centennial Committee of the American Psychological Association.)

NOTES

1.   C.L. Shartle (1979). Early years of the Ohio State University leadership studies. *Journal of Management, 5,* 127-134.

2.   J.M. Frazer (1947). New type selection boards in industry. *Occupational Psychology, 21,* 170-178.

3.   G. Ginter & S. Lindskold (1975). Rate of participation and expertise as factors influencing leader choice. *Journal of Personality and Social Psychology, 32,* 1085-1089.

4.   "An Analysis of the Leaderless Group Discussion" (1949).

5.   "The Leaderless Group Discussion" (1954).

6.   D.W. Bray, R.J. Campbell, & D.L. Grant (1974). *Formative years in business: A long-term AT&T study of managerial lives.* New York: Wiley-Interscience.

7.   P.E. Vernon (1950). The validation of civil service selection board procedures. *Occupational Psychology, 24,* 75-95.

8.   OSS Assessement Staff (1948). *Assessment of men.* New York: Reinhart.

9.   *Leadership, Psychology, and Organizational Behavior* (1960).

10.   E.A. Fleishman (1954). Dimensional analysis of psychomotor activities. *Journal of Experimental Psychology, 48,* 437-454.

11.   *Assessing Human Performance Under Stress* (1954).

12.   "Ultimate Criteria of Organizational Worth" (1952).

13.   *Leadership, Psychology, and Organizational Behavior* (1960).

14.   *Bass & Stogdill's Handbook of Leadership* (1981, 1990).

15.   "Some Effects of Decision and Discussion on Coalescence, Change and Effectiveness" (1958); "Some Effects of Feedback on Behavior in Groups" (1959); "Interacting Effects of Control, Motivation, Group Practice, and Problem Difficulty in Attempted Leadership (1958).

16.   "An Objective Method for Studying Behavior in Groups" (1957).

17.   "Business Gaming for Organizational Psychology" (1964).

18.   "Business Gaming for Organizational Research" (1964); "Experimenting with Simulated Manufacturing Organizations" (1963).

19.   H.J. Leavitt (1961). Walter Van Dyke Bingham lecture. Pittsburgh, PA: Carnegie Institute of Technology.

20.   *Organizational Psychology* (1965).

21.   E. Schein (1965). *Organizational psychology.* Englewood Cliffs, NJ: Prentice-Hall.

22.   *People, Work and Organizations* (1972, 1981).

23.   *A Program of Exercises for Management and Organizational Psychology* (1965).

24.   "Combining Management Training and Research" (1967).

25. "Reactions to 'Twelve Angry Men' as a Measure of Sensitivity Training" (1962); "Mood Changes in a Management Training Laboratory" (1962); "The Organization Training Laboratory" (1964).

26. J. Krussell, E. Vicino, M.R. Manning et al. (1971, 1981). *PROCESS: A program of self-administering exercises in personal and interpersonal development.* Scottsville, NJ: TPC.

27. "'Male Managers' Attitudes Toward Working Women" (1971).

28. "PROSPER—Training and Research for Increasing Management Awareness About Affirmative Action in Race Relations" (1976); "PROFAIR—An Affirmative Action Program for Women Employees" (1971).

29. "The Anarchist Movement and the T-Group" (1967); "Some Effect on Business Gaming of Previous T-Group Affiliations" (1967).

30. "Authoritarianism or Acquiescence?" (1955).

31. "Reducing Leniency in Merit Ratings" (1956); "Development and Evaluation of a Scale for Measuring Social Acquiescence" (1956); "Reply to Messick's and Jackson's Comments on Acquiescence or Authoritarianism" (1957); "Undiscriminated Operant Acquiescence" (1957); "An Approach to the Objective Assessment of Leadership" (1959).

32. "Identifying Single Source Bias Using Multiple Levels of Analysis" (1991).

33. "Biases in the Evaluation of One's Own Group, Its Allies and Opponents" (1963).

34. "Environmentalists' and Business Executives' Attitudes and Information About the Nuclear Power Controversy" (1977).

35. "Changing Attitudes and Knowledge About Nuclear Power" (1979).

36. "Implications of the Behavioral Sciences in the Year 2000" (1968); "Work and Organizational Life in the Year 2000" (1973).

37. "The Orientation Inventory" (1962, 1977).

38. "Behavior in Groups as a Function of Self, Interaction and Task-orientation" (1963); "Dyadic Speech Patterns, Orientations and Social Reinforcement" (1963).

39. "Social Behavior and the Orientation Inventory" (1967).

40. *Assessment of Managers* (1979).

41. *Bass & Stogdill's Handbook of Leadership* (1981, 1990).

42. *Organization Decision-Making* (1983).

43. "A Systems Survey Research Feedback for Management and Organizational Development" (1976).

44. E.R. Valenzi, J.A. Miller, L.D. Eldridge, P.W. Irons, R.J. Solomon, & R.E. Klauss (1972). *Individual differences, structure, task and external environment and leader behavior: A summary* (Tech. Rep. No. 49). Rochester, NY: University of Rochester, Management Research Center.

45. "Management Styles Associated with Organizational, Task, Personal, and Interpersonal Contingencies" (1975).

46. "Discriminant Functions to Identify Ways to Increase Leadership Effectiveness" (1978).

47. Z. Shapiro (1976). A facet analysis of leadership styles. *Journal of Applied Psychology, 61*, 136-139.

48. *Interpersonal Communications in Organizations* (1982).

49. J.M. Burns (1978). *Leadership.* New York: Harper & Row.

50. *Leadership and Performance Beyond Expectations* (1985).

51. "From Transactional to Transformational Leadership" (1990).

52. *Full Range of Leadership Development* (1991).

53. J.A. Wall, Jr. (1990). Managers in the People's Republic of China. *Academcy of Management Executive, 4*(2), 19-32.

The Fruits of
Professional Interdependence
for Enriching a Career

ROBERT R. BLAKE

The happiest day in my professional life came in the fall of 1987. Jane Mouton and I had just learned that we were both to be inducted into the Human Resource Development Hall of Fame on December 9. The gratification was made doubly meaningful because of the simultaneous induction; in other words, a recognition that, whatever contribution had been made, it had been made as a team, not as two separate individuals. That gave validity to the operating premise of our entire joint career.

This moment of great fulfillment was all too soon followed by ultimate sorrow. The ceremony was scheduled in New York, immediately upon our return from a trip to India, where we addressed the International Congress of Training and Development, and then to Athens, where we were scheduled for client activity. The presentation in Delhi went quite well, but at this point a difficulty arose. Jane complained of abdominal pains and, as they grew worse, it was determined she should be hospitalized. She decided to cut the trip short and returned to Austin in late November. I continued to fulfill our commitments, phoning her daily in order to stay apprised of the latest events. Though she remained hospitalized, Jane claimed to be making progress and even thought she might be able to rejoin me in New York for the Hall of Fame ceremony. She died quite suddenly, two days prior to this event, on December 7, 1987.

This tragedy symbolizes the end of a significant part of my career. Jane and I were partners, working hand in hand for 36 years. Together we formulated the Managerial Grid ®, the conceptual framework of which is contained in a book that has already exceeded sales of two million copies, and is available in sixteen languages. We also published *Synergogy*, a book that outlines a radical solution to many of the chronic problems facing teachers and educators today. These were only two of a long line of other books—38 in number—all mutually co-authored by us. Our major effort, however, involved the creation and development of Scientific Methods, Inc. and the leadership we provided that has sustained it for three decades. For all of these reasons, this autobiography can only be written by weaving the centrally important fact of our joint cooperation into the story which follows.

MY FAMILY

I was born in January 1918 in Brookline, Massachusetts, and lived in Massachusetts until I was thirteen. My family consisted of four children, three boys and a girl. I was the second in line, with an older brother, followed by my sister, and finally a younger brother. We all attended college but I was the only one who maintained my academic interests and went on to complete graduate work. My two brothers were engineers, both finding careers with Du Pont. My sister became a nurse and later went into nursing administration.

My mother and father were both critical influences in shaping my future career; my mother, particularly so, as she had enduring academic ambitions. When I showed an interest in learning, she was my number one advocate and supporter. However, I trace the issue of my interest in conceptual learning primarily to my father. He was a graduate of Harvard at both the bachelor and advanced levels. Throughout his life he maintained an abiding interest in intellectual matters, particularly as they related to world developments. He and I maintained a constant dialogue throughout our lives as to the deeper meaning of political events, considered not so much from an ideological point of view as from the standpoint of conceptual assumptions underlying political and other forms of leadership. I believe it was from him that I gained my interest in the conceptual issues of leadership.

The Depression arrived with full fury, and my family moved to Tennessee. My father became responsible for one of the major forest development projects of that era. There were no schools within fifty miles, so I attended a resident high school in Crossville, a small, closely knit school, with only nine in my graduating class.

As I look back on it, my family was one of those in the last generation of tightly knit American families. In one way, the Depression illustrated this point. The Depression provided numerous illustrations of the conditions under which family cohesion permitted its members to persist and retain their integrity. It also taught me the impermanence of material wealth and the durability of conceptual commitments and academic values. The former could disappear over night; the latter endured a lifetime, to be built upon not only for personal enhancement but for social value and applied utility as well.

Those aspiring toward a college education in my area turned their focus to Black Mountain College in North Carolina, Berea College in Kentucky, or Berry Schools in Georgia. All catered in one way or another to poor students of the Appalachian region. I was accepted in 1936 at Berea, and that became my life for the next four years.

Berea was unusual in every respect, and it continues many of its traditions even today. There was no tuition; rather, everyone worked in the college labor program. Life was simple: no cars, no smoking, no furs, no extravagances. It is still the kind of college where students can invest themselves in learning as fully as desired and with minimum interruption. I chose to major in psychology and philosophy. Both disciplines seemed central for understanding life, its institutions, and how they operate—business, government, education, religion, medicine.

In anticipation of graduation in 1940, I applied for scholarships at twelve schools—six in philosophy; six in psychology. I received a Du Pont Fellowship at the University of Virginia and was able to finish a Master's Degree before World War II. I also got married. We moved to Virginia, with the clear recognition, however, that this arrangement was to be short-lived.

Several key influences upon me from my college period derive from Charles Darwin, Sigmund Freud, and Kurt Lewin. Darwin represented, for me, the perfect scholar: investigating, investigating, investigating; seeking to establish his theory of evolution in the most complete way possible before bringing it to the attention of the world for its scrutiny. He provided such a powerful model for me that his influence on my career is without question. Though I was later to learn and commit myself to "pure" laboratory research resting on preplanned experimental designs, natural or field research provided me a model of investigation that paralleled the university laboratory. "Natural" observations were to become my model in the psychoanalytic group therapy studies at Tavistock, and after my university period it became my model for our own fieldwork over the world.

Jane shared my admiration for Darwin. As opportunities presented themselves, Jane and I replicated Darwin's travels that led to his fundamental discoveries. We went to Terra Del Fuego, the turbulent waters below the tip of South America created by the joining of the Atlantic and Pacific. We sailed those waters to gauge what he must have been up against on that voyage, particularly in view of the fact that Darwin suffered from seasickness. To do his research, Darwin served on the Beagle, where its captain sailed the vessel back and forth, back and forth in pursuit of the overriding mission of accurate cartographic mapping. As we sailed these same rough waters, we empathized with Darwin's plight. We continued on to the top of the Andes, where Darwin had been so impressed by the "contradiction" of finding sea shells high in the mountains at an altitude of 15,000 feet and, of course, we went to the Galapagos Islands to see for ourselves something of Darwin's frame of reference as he formulated the theory of natural evolution. To complete our studies of Darwin, we journeyed in England to the town of Downs where he lived in his later years; his house is now a private museum.

Much the same applies to the work of Freud. While I am reluctant to embrace his theory of the unconscious, my respect for him has steadily increased through the years as I have found myself more able to appreciate the depth and hiddenness of the phenomena he sought to explain.

Several projects provided something of an opportunity to study Freud's personal life in Vienna, which I did. I located an historically accurate novel about his life, told in chronological sequence. It reveals what Freud did, where, and with whom, and I used it in its entirety as a tour guide. This allowed me to follow many of his walks, for example, to "accompany" him from his home to the hospital. It gave me a feel for the environment in which he had operated.

Kurt Lewin pioneered a new kind of social psychology research in his investigations related to leadership climates as well as being responsible for numerous other contributions. His work influenced me by demonstrating that complex interactions are as readily subject to rigorous, controlled investigation through planned designs as are more fixed and stable phenomena of the kind studied in one cause/one effect designs. This meant that many opportunities for expanding the various areas of social psychology research could now be evaluated by such means and methods.

The advent of World War II brought an end to my youth, and from 1940 forward, every life event proved to be of serious import. While recreation and social enjoyment did not recede into the background, what did expand was my sense of purpose. Service in the Air Force during World War II permitted me to continue my conceptual and academic interest in psychology, but now it concerned applied problems of crew selection for pilots, navigators, and bombardiers. It is probable that my long-term interest in group dynamics originated at this point.

My service in the Air Force was concentrated in a Psychological Research Unit. This was an important experience for me in terms of its impact on my professional career because I was thrown together with 500 or more others in the same and other related fields such as sociology and anthropology. It was a marvelously broadening experience for a person like me who had spent four years in the simple environment of Berea College just a short time before.

I was discharged in 1945 in San Antonio, Texas. Since the closest university was the University of Texas in Austin, I found my way there and began teaching as an instructor, finishing my Ph.D in 1947. I continued as an assistant professor, associate, and finally full professor before resigning to form Scientific Methods, Inc. in 1964.

Two children were born during this period: Brooks, in 1954, currently a ranch foreman on a four-thousand acre spread just outside of Austin; and my daughter, in 1957. Cary has just completed Graduate School after completing a Bachelor's Degree in psychology, but her focus is now on music, art, and media through which therapy with children may be enhanced.

MY TWO CAREERS

My professional life has extended over two quite distinct careers. One involved teaching and research at the University of Texas. The second, of almost equal length, started with the founding of our company called Scientific Methods, Inc., initially developed as a commercial venture for delivering behavioral science applications to business on a worldwide basis. We currently have offices in over forty countries, the most recent to be opened being in Thailand and the Soviet Union.

The University Years

The university years extended from 1947 to 1964. I concentrated in social psychology. It was during these years that research and applications in this area of endeavor were at their most creative and innovative stage. Much of what is taken today as the basis for good, sound practice is based on research findings and conclusions from that era.

In 1949, I received a post-doctoral Fulbright Scholarship that took me to the University of Reading and the Tavistock Clinic in London. This 18-month stint proved to be a major turning point in my life, primarily by virtue of that unique period in time and the nature of the colleagues with whom I came to work. It was during this period that the United Kingdom had enacted medical legislation that embarked the nation on an era of socialized medicine. This included the Tavistock Clinic. As a direct result of this, the staff was able to utilize a considerable portion of its work time for research purposes. Because it was rigorously psychoanalytic in its practice, my participation offered me a dramatic contrast between psychoanalytic thinking and academic psychology. It closed the artificial separation between cognitive social psychology and underlying dynamic motivation that energize behavior.

The London experience put me in contact with Wilfred Bion, author of the famous series of articles, *Working in Groups*; John Bowlby, who became this generation's world famous child psychiatrist and father of *attachment theory*; and Eric Trist, who is known for his work with sociotechnical systems analysis. Most important to me personally, however, was Henry Ezriel, the leading investigator of psychoanalytic group therapy and the person with whom I worked day-in and day-out in a co-therapist role in his groups. This was the bridge that provided the needed connection between cognitive social psychology and psychoanalytic group dynamics.

About this time there was a sharp de-evaluation of British currency. As a result I had to live on a shoestring, with enough, however, for frugal travel to Europe and an occasional weekend in Paris. I found my work and study so engaging that a 12- to 14-hour day became the rule.

My return to the States and to my university career can best be understood by following it along two tracks: the first concerned our research and development and the second our professional collaboration with colleagues and peers.

After Tavistock, rather than returning to the University of Texas, I accepted a research appointment in the Department of Social Relations at Harvard University, where I worked closely with Jerry Bruner and also spent many hours at the Psychology Clinic with Henry Murray of *Apperception Test* fame. Because my credentials had included rigorous experimental research during my graduate school days and with a continuation in the interim years and with numerous publications, I enjoyed accessibility to Memorial Hall.

Memorial Hall was the Department of Experimental Psychology at Harvard during this period of time. The split between psychology and social relations already existed but it was the creation of these two separate departments by Harvard's academia that made it official. Thereafter, it was common knowledge that the "rigorous" people resided in Memorial Hall while those who looked on psychology in a somewhat "looser" way were housed in the Department of Social Relations.

On occasion, when I visited Memorial Hall, I would run into B.F. Skinner, who seemed to find some degree of interest in my background. This formed the basis of our association and, as a result, we talked from time to time. Sometimes we would chat while he was attending his pigeons. These pigeons lived in boxes in the basement of Memorial Hall and Skinner, anxious to assertain their response, would visit the boxes to "check them out." This effort was, of course, unnecessary as a counter maintained constant surveillance over the number of "pigeon pecks" and these were mechanically recorded. Nonetheless, Skinner avidly enjoyed monitoring this process and I would often find him standing with one foot on the box, doing his own mental arithmetic as to pigeon behavior. It was during these times that we often engaged in an inoffensive but provocative banter about psychology and social relations.

One short anecdote provides the full flavor of these exchanges I shared with Skinner. He had a Ping-Pong table which had been set up and the pigeons trained to peck the Ping-Pong ball back and forth according to a prearranged schedule. That pigeons could be taught such a "social" game as Ping-Pong via an individual reinforcement schedule and then put together in such a way as to respond to each other, not in point of fact but rather according to its own schedules of reinforcement, was regarded as an outstanding contribution for demonstrating that social relations, at least in conventional terms, do not exist. The ultimate communication was of a sign posted on the Ping-Pong table titled "Social Relations 1."

There was a poignancy in all of this, as it served to demonstrate the fundamental cleavage that existed between experimental psychology and social relations at this time. Still, it was in a disguised form which, on the one hand, taught a lesson but, on the other, was sufficiently playful so that no one felt the need to lodge any serious objections.

Another significant development in my career involved the National Training Laboratories (NTL). While in London I learned that NTL was being established in Bethel, Maine for the purpose of studying group behavior. One of my first objectives upon returning to the United States was to arrange to spend a summer there to learn more about this. That became the beginning of a 10-year, every-summer session for me, which proved to be a rich and rewarding experience in the context of the academic discipline following the psychoanalytic group therapy I had experienced at Tavistock.

Lee Bradford, one of the founders of NTL, was a unique administrative leader who did much to solve the problem of how to transfer behavioral science knowledge to applied use by "normal" people. He "protected" the T-Group by keeping it at the forefront of behavioral learning and sensitivity training for the period from NTL's inception until his retirement.

I served on summer faculties at Bethel and as a member of the NTL Board of Trustees for a decade. These provided yet another collaboration from which I learned much, mostly centered on Lee's efforts to maintain an action-oriented faculty comprised of many conflicting elements. The major polarity related to the role of theory versus common sense, or even clinical insight, in seeking to learn more about social processes created in part by an individual's own conduct. Some faculty members saw theory as a comprehensive framework within which process phenomena could be identified and understood and in this way serve as the basis for generalization. Others saw theory as an effort to intellectualize, that is, a way of deviating from the learning objective of using an activity to learn more about oneself.

This cleavage was never resolved during my tenure at NTL. However, efforts in pursuit of its resolution might be regarded as the core of Jane's and my life work. And, I think satisfaction was felt that we indeed achieved this objective.

Finally I was faced with a basic decision. The University of Texas' impatience with my frequent leaves made it necessary for me to decide where I might best spend my career. My wife, a native Tennesseean, cast her vote for the South and a warmer climate. This tipped the scales in the direction of the University of Texas where I ended up concentrating the remainder of my academic work.

In 1952 I returned to Texas and it was then that I first met Jane Mouton as one of my students. She was enrolled in the Social Psychology Doctoral program, having previously finished a Master's Degree in Mathematics at Florida State University. Jane immediately became a teaching assistant and, from that point forward, we cooperated in every pursuit. Jane received her Ph.D. in 1954 and joined the University faculty as an assistant professor. She joined me in attending the Bethel summer sessions in order to experience the T-Group training methodology then in use. This turned out to be a critical turning point for her in the area of social and group dynamics.

The following year Jane and I conducted a laboratory course to introduce T-Groups to the University. This was a major decision because it made possible our engagement in research on fundamentals of change as they relate to learning social psychology theory, reinforced by a T-Group experience. Furthermore, it led to a book jointly authored by us and published in 1961 titled *Group Dynamics: Key to Decision Making*.

Another "fall out" from these early NTL years was the development of a close acquaintance with Dr. Herbert Shepard, an early Bethel staff member but simultaneously employed by Exxon. This contact led to Jane and me conducting something approximating a 10-year experiment within the Exxon Corporation. More on this is to be said later.

As noted, previously, Jane and I had been conducting experiments in our Social Psychology Laboratory. These involved organizing students into T-Groups and then, at various points in time, arranging a competition between T-Groups as the basis for measuring team effectiveness. These experiments proved provocative and resulted in numerous publications. Several of these articles came to the attention of Exxon management. It seemed to them that this research bore some significance for reviewing basic interdepartmental and union-management attitudes.

The combination of my close friendship with Herb Shepard and the interest that Exxon had in our research findings resulted in Jane and me being invited to Baton Rouge to conduct a series of two-week seminars. The Baton Rouge Refinery was thought of at that time as being the avant-garde management development center within the Exxon system. Its readiness to try new things that might have significant implications for management and institutional effectiveness was indeed striking. Several hundred managers participated in this program.

A further experiment was built into the arrangement. The mornings were devoted to a T-Group type experience. The afternoons were to be applied to management development through case study discussions led by Harvard Business School professors. The intention of this experiment was to make possible a systematic comparison of the character of learning possible from each of the methodologies as well as from both in combination.

This experiment was eventually abandoned following the fourth seminar as a result of the evaluations by Exxon personnel. They came to the conclusion that case studies were simply not absorbing enough when compared to a T-Group experience and they therefore recommended dropping them from use. The seminars that followed, therefore, concentrated on an expanded study of behavioral theories, particularly power and authority in experiential terms and reinforced by theory. This led to the formulation of the Managerial Grid and to further intergroup study of the win-lose dynamics such as those found between departments, unions, headquarters and subsidiaries, and so on. The T-Group continued to be the centerpiece of this learning.

Jane and I accumulated a wealth of data during this time, particularly on the intergroup problem, which in turn led to the publication in 1964 of *Managing Intergroup Conflict in Industry*. This introduction to group dynamics with a significant number of Exxon managers in attendance was judged to be highly successful, particularly as it brought many new and fresh perspectives to bear on how managers looked at recurrent and chronic problems as well as crisis situations and how to resolve them.

The head of the Bayway Refinery in New Jersey attended one of these sessions as a manifestation of his general interest in management development. As he and I became well acquainted, he made it known that he wanted to do something within his own refinery that might go beyond what had been attempted at Baton Rouge. As a result, I agreed to spend two years on a full-time basis at Bayway. The objective of the effort was, "to see how effective an organization might become were it to concentrate its full human resources on the objective of excellence."

The Bayway project closely followed the completion of the one at Baton Rouge. It allowed Jane and myself, and also Herb Shepard to some degree, to reexamine what had been attempted at Baton Rouge and to answer the question, "What should we now do or what would we do differently, given this opportunity of a fresh beginning?" Several aspects were included. One was to concentrate on the Managerial Grid as the centerpiece of learning about the options for exercising leadership when working with and through others. Another was that the seminars would no longer be T-Groups conducted by trainers in a hands-on way. Rather, they would be instrumented, that is, the synergogic learning theory published by Jane and myself later on as *Synergogy*. They were attended on a diagonal-slice basis, that is, with people from all levels of management participating but with no direct boss and subordinate relationship on the same team.

The entire management component of Bayway participated and this stimulated many applications consistent with the learning. While the seminars themselves were highly successful, the hoped-for applications were slow in coming and some simply did not appear. This was disturbing to us because it suggested that the limits of development had been met, and they were insufficient to justify the effort expended. However, they also permitted an alternative conclusion. We hypothesized that the culture of most work teams is so deeply embedded that individual team members in and of themselves are unable to markedly change it, even though each may recognize the obstacles to team effectiveness that prevent them from being as effective as they might be. This led to the discovery of *Team Development*, later spoken of as Team Building. As a result, the effort that followed the basic seminar became an off-site session of each actual "corporate family," starting at the top. People were now instructed to diagnose within their own work team insights and feelings based on open and candid critique. This provided a basis of shared understanding regarding what had been done in the past that should no longer be continued and what might be done and should be done in the future that had not been a part of the past. This had a highly significant impact on team, and organization, effectiveness.

Other areas of application centered on the character of intergroup problem solving, involving such issues as turf and territory conflicts (for example, those that occur between union and management), and problems of prerogative and "ownership," such as those between divisions (for example, engineering and maintenance, manufacturing and marketing, and so forth). These applications also yielded gains in productivity for the entire organization.

A particularly significant event occurred in the top-team development phase. When this group convened, it came to the conclusion that it spent entirely too much time reporting to the top man what was transpiring in each of the operating departments. Traditionally, the boss interrogated each member one after the other. The rationale for doing so was that it kept everyone on his toes. Furthermore, it was justified in the name of good mentoring. As a result of this, however, team members spent an inordinate amount of time being briefed by their own direct reports as to what was going on so that they would be in a position to accurately defend their performance within the top team. Rather than being involved with the real business of running the company and a future corporate vision, this group of top executives busied itself with keeping track of the nitpicky details of day-to-day operations.

The upshot from this activity was important to the future of OD. This top team decided it was imperative that they stop doing what they had been doing. They determined that the appropriate business of a top team did not lie in a detailed analysis of each minute activity within the departments. Rather, there were other significant matters and many currently missed opportunities in which this top group should be engaged that held far more promise for the long-term health of the organization. This meant, however, that the power/ authority dynamics must undergo a dramatic shift, with each member solving the problems of over-centralization that had been created by the need to be knowledgeable of the small details. In other words, the problem resided not only in the top team; it had cascaded down through the organization, resulting in each level being concerned with decisions that should be made at one or two levels below. Authority had been pulled up to the top with levels below unable or unwilling to exercise initiative. In some ways the organization had become paralyzed, waiting on a nod from the top man before action could be taken.

At this point the top team decided to set a date two months out at which time the problem of centralization/delegation was to be resolved, thus freeing the top for new and more important activity. Once this action had been taken, it brought into focus an entirely new aspect of organization development. With over-centralization abandoned, the top team discovered they had nothing to do. There were no projects in which to engage that held any degree of meaning. Top team members had little experience or skill in doing anything other than managing the ongoing operation, fire-fighting, and reacting to crisis. This led to the advent of Ideal Strategic Corporate Modeling, the Phase 4 activity in Grid Organization Development; an important event in integrating sound behavioral dynamics with true effectiveness on the corporate side of decision making.

As this period of time played itself out, I constantly made notes as to the dilemmas I confronted. Upon returning to my apartment in the evenings, I would dictate these daily experiences and then send them to Jane, who remained at the University of Texas. Upon my return to Texas for the occasional weekend, we would take this opportunity to discuss my notes further and to design intervention strategies for the coming week. As a result, Jane became very involved in this project and joined me at the Bayway Refinery for purposes of systematizing the Ideal Strategic Modeling phase of this OD effort. Eventually our accumulated notes told a very significant story, which truly became the advent of Organization Development as a systematic activity. This was published in *Diary of an OD Man* by Jane and myself in 1976.

The Research Phase

The vast majority of my university period was devoted to the investigation and study of social-psychological problems from an experiment-based point of view. The character of this research can be evaluated in the appended bibliography, which identifies some 150 journal articles, almost all published jointly by Jane and myself and sometimes including other parties as well. The nature of this research centered on leadership behavior on the one hand and conformity and deviation dynamics on the other.

These two topics—leadership and conformity—became the focal points of the business we embarked on for the next twenty-five years. As I now look back, I can see how fundamental it all was to what came later. Perhaps the primary reason for this is that formulating researchable hypotheses and then, through experimental designs, testing their validity proved to be a very sobering experience. We discovered that the way things work in everyday life rarely conform with initial hypotheses as formulated. To us, this was a startling revelation. We learned the importance of expanding the time to make possible more rigorous formulation rather than just accepting commonsense explanations or what appeared to be reasonable and taking that at face value. It compelled us to engage in microscopic examination of the phenomena at hand while at the same time maintaining a macroscopic perspective; that is, seeing the problem within the class of problems of which it was but one representative.

While some professors delved only in the research angle, Jane and I were members of that smaller group that also loved to write. The danger in writing, of course, is that it submits one's thinking to the evaluation and criticism of others. This is a difficult hurdle for many to cross, but Jane and I seemed never to have a difficulty with this. We valued the enlightenment provided by constructive discourse with other professionals.

The manner in which Jane and I wrote is noteworthy as it is a bit unusual. Someone recently asked me to describe our approach. Their logic-based query was: How did the two of you write? Did you do Chapters 1, 2, and 3, and then did she take Chapters 4, 5, and 6? Did you then pass them back and forth? Did you take the lead, or did she? How did you combine effort?

This question, which in fact reveals how many jointly-authored articles and books are produced, could not have been further from the mark. Rarely did either of us compose a piece of isolated writing to be handed to the other for criticism and review. Rather, we sat together at a large writing desk, long enough that both of us could sit side by side. Then we discussed, analyzed, formulated, and finally wrote, but always simultaneously and together. Sometimes, after things had been framed to a point where they seemed to provide an acceptable formulation, I would dictate to Jane. Or, vice versa. Even this description fails to capture the full character of our work; it is difficult to convey in words the spontaneity with which we interacted. We always felt free to interrupt the other midway through a sentence in order to express the thought more clearly or to reshape it and restate it in a different way. So interdependent were our thought processes that more often than not one spoke the words that resided in the other's mind. It was a total union of effort.

Working with Others

Jane and I had every desire to keep expanding the frame of reference within which we were thinking and analyzing problems. To accomplish this end, we engaged in a series of joint projects with other professors, several of whom hold particular significance.

In 1949, I conceived of a symposium to be conducted over the entire academic year at the University of Texas consisting of nine different distinguished persons, one presentation per month. Several of these in particular merit further comment as they directly or indirectly influenced our thinking and later work. Alfred Korzybski, founder of the Institute of General Semantics, was invited to conduct one of these sessions. His contribution to my career is significant because of the fundamental character of General Semantics for understanding human thought. Only now, almost sixty years after the publication of his seminal work, *Science and Sanity* (in 1933), is he being accorded the respect that his contribution deserves.

Two illustrations provide an indication of Korzybski's thinking. One is the dictum—"The map is not the territory"—indicating that human perception of a phenomenon is not equivalent with or identical to the phenomenon itself. Therefore, it becomes imperative to understand human thought processes as they reflect how human experience comes to be represented in a "map" which represents an event rather than providing a true replica of it. It is our *interpretation* of an event rather than the event itself. Furthermore, your interpretation of an event may differ vastly from my own interpretation of the very same event.

A second contribution by Korzybski is the central emphasis placed upon processes of generalization from the concrete to the abstract, showing how abstractions necessarily omit features of a phenomenon itself. And, the higher the order of this abstraction, the greater the omission of selective character of details of that phenomenon.

The legacy of Korzybski's thinking resides in a book organized by myself and Glenn Ramsey as an outgrowth of the 1949-1950 Clinical Psychology Symposium held at the University of Texas. The book is titled *Perception: An Approach to Personality*. The distinctive aspect of Korzybski's contribution lies in the fact that he had completed the writing of his particular paper but he died eight days prior to its delivery. A close associate of Korzybski, Charlotte Schuchardt, read the paper in his behalf as originally prepared. It was a memorable occasion for all who attended, hearing described posthumously the scientific conclusions that this man had reached. This particular chapter, "The Role of Languages in the Perceptual Processes," became a classic in the field of philosophy, and more specifically among General Semanticists. It continues to be published and republished in different languages; the most recent being in Spanish, which has just been released.

The other members who took part in this symposium constitute an interesting group in the light of modern history for they turn out to have become illustrious contributors in the field of psychology. Included among these were Carl Rogers, world famous for his formulation of client-centered therapy; Norman Cameron, an important contributor to clinical and psychiatric thinking; Else Frenkel-Brunswik, a key contributor to the justly famous *Authoritarian Personality*; Jerome Bruner, one of the leading spokesmen of social psychology; Frank Beach, a leading biological level investigator of psychological phenomena. Ernest Hilgard, President of the American Psychological Association and famous author of a classic elementary psychology text; and Urie Bronfenbrenner, another world renowned child psychologist.

Although Jane arrived after Korzybski's death, she later became quite involved in General Semantics and was an ardent student and brilliant interpreter of how these processes could enrich our own formulations.

Another colleague who greatly influenced our thinking was Harry Helson, a world respected psychophysicist, whose justly famous *adaptation level theory* has stood the test of time and in many respects has led to a reformulation of psycho-physical theory. For those who knew Helson, his interests knew no bounds, spreading across all fields of human endeavor. He has, however, been most noted for his contribution to psycho-physical quantification.

Helson's interest extended into social psychology and it is in this context that he, Jane, and I began our collaborative efforts. Together we published several articles demonstrating how adaptation level theory serves to unravel the influences that determine human social conduct. Stated simplistically, the theory identifies three sources of influence on any human outcome. These can be identified as stimulus, or the focal event being attended to; background, those antecedent experiences that relate to the focal event; and residual, the enduring and more or less fixed responses operable in a person and reinforced over time that relate to the phenomena being studied. Helson accorded great significance to the second of these sources of influence, background. As a result, our experiments were ones in which we kept the stimulus constant but varied the background factor. Two illustrations provide an understanding of how this was accomplished.

In the first, students were invited to participate in a number of experiments. In each case the stimulus remained constant while the background was changed in systematic terms. For example, in one condition, students learned that if they volunteered for an experiment, the obligation of one examination would be waived. In some cases students knew this in advance; in other cases not. In still other examples, volunteering brought no particular gain; and so on. In other words, by systematically varying background, we learned that the rate of volunteering could readily be shifted. In one condition, over 80% volunteered, whereas in another, less than 20% did so.

In a second experiment, concerned with donation as an act of contribution, those to whom the request was made received a standard invitation. Under one background condition, the names of donors were added to a blank list attached to a clipboard; that is, as yet no one had been credited with the act of donation. In this case, as well as others, subjects could readily observe the clipboard. Under another circumstance, subjects were able to note that ten people had already made donations. In a third, 25 could be seen as having contributed. Therefore, the background element varied in terms of whether it indicated number of donors, who those donors were, how much donors had given, and so forth. We found that the subject was greatly affected by these variations, thus demonstrating that the same stimulus can produce different behaviors as a function of the background conditions under which the stimulus is experienced.

In summary, as a result of this collaboration, Harry and I became close friends. I found him one of the most stimulating associates of my career because of the character of his thought, the range of his interests, and his dedication of effort.

A third colleague who exerted great influence on my professional development was Muzafer Sherif. I knew Sherif in a formal way from the earliest years. Therefore, in the Fifties it seemed to Jane and me that it would provide a mutually stimulating experience for the three of us to work together. I arranged for him to come to the University of Texas as a visiting professor, which he did, during 1955-1956.

Many of Sherif's influences are of memorable importance, but two stand out in particular. One of these is his work on intergroup conflict, perhaps best known in the field as the Robbers Cave study. This consisted of an investigation of how two groups of young boys behaved toward one another on first and then upon repeated contact when neither group was previously aware of the presence of the other group within their same "psychological space." The space in this study was the Robbers Cave State Park in Oklahoma where the youngsters were encamped for a two-week summer vacation.

This experiment had just been completed when Sherif arrived in Austin. As related to Jane and myself, it had the effect of stimulating our long-term interest in this field of research and endeavor. Sherif established that conflict is the "natural" reaction of the members of a group when they come in contact with the members of another group under the conditions described above. The deeper aspect of this experiment arose in the opportunities afforded for studying strategies of deescalation. Sherif found only one condition that held the promise of significantly contributing to deescalation; that is, creating conditions under which the youngsters experienced a superordinate goal. Only then were previously held competitive attitudes diminished because of the higher stakes of cooperation with each side collaborating with the other for the purpose of superordinate goal achievement. That is, the groups came off of their fixed positions when there was more to gain by virtue of letting go than by holding on to vested interests.

A significant limitation in the Sherif approach to superordinate goals lies in how these goals come into existence. In the experiment, he found it necessary to contrive conditions that made superordinate goal achievement imperative to the youngsters. While this is an acceptable basis for experimental work, in real life it is not common nor is it desirable for someone on the outside of the circumstance to mastermind conditions that make superordinate goal achievement desirable and/or inevitable. This, however, is the only limitation as we see it in an otherwise brilliant experiment.

Over time, Jane and I sought to rectify this limitation and I believe have successfully done so. This is true at least to the point where amount of cooperation needed from any two contending groups at the beginning of superordinate goal formation is only a commitment to sit down and explore such a possibility. This extension of the Sherif work has recently been published in a *Festschrift* volume honoring Sherif's many unique contributions to the field of social psychology.

It seemed to us that Sherif had come to the heart of the matter of many of the conflicts that operate within organized society: union-management conflicts; those between departments or divisions of companies; tensions between headquarters and subsidiaries; and even the cleavages that exist between nations. Because of its importance, I arranged for Muzafer Sherif to attend sessions in some of our later work in Exxon, and he was much admired by managers from that organization for his conceptual analysis, spirited thinking, and dedication to grappling constructively with problems with which they, too, found themselves entangled.

The other significant aspect of Sherif's impact on my thinking transpired during a seminar jointly conducted by him, Jane, and myself and attended by approximately 30 graduate students. This particular seminar turned out to be one of the most stimulating of graduate courses available at the University of Texas during that time. The title of the course was "Properties of Groups," and the objective was to identify the necessary and sufficient variables for providing an inclusive framework to analyze the properties of any group. We were able to identify several of these variables which lie at the very heart of organization development. One is power and authority in that no group exists without differences and variations in the strength of influence exerted by its individual members. Another is norms and standards; that is, the traditions, precedents, and past practices groups come to accept as second-nature. A third is morale and cohesion, or the extent to which people feel drawn to the group; and, finally, goals and objectives as the identified purposes for which a group exists and toward which it strives.

Since that time we have found it necessary to add only two additional variables to complete our formulation. One of these is structure and differentiation; that is, the extent to which the roles and responsibilities of individual members are made detailed and explicit. The other is feedback and critique, or the ability of a group to make use of the reactions of its members to current and past conditions in order to determine how action should be taken in the future. These six variables characterize how a group functions and lie at the center of our approach to organization development and team building.

A fourth colleague who falls in the category of those who have significantly influenced my professional career is Jacob L. Moreno. I met Moreno—founder of sociometry, psychodrama, and action-oriented psychotherapy—during my Tavistock period.

Moreno's primary stimulation came from his hands-on approach to seeking solutions to problems of life. Currently, psychodrama is probably the best-known of his contributions, but sociometry is another seminal area, more of which will be revealed through future investigation. The same is true of a number of other areas of endeavor for Moreno.

My memories of Moreno are reflected in numerous aspects but a key one of these involved his psychodramatic sessions in which problems, personally damaging to the effectiveness of people or their spirit, were subjected to in situ recharacterization. I attended many of these Friday night sessions with him in the Fifties when I found myself frequently in New York working with Exxon on the Bayway project. The actors were called upon to portray the problem they were experiencing and then, by degrees, a stage of supporting actors was set in place. The problem was reenacted. Finally, in a third part of the psychodramatic session, the issues involved could be dealt with in a more rational manner.

Moreno's insights were not only unique, they were brilliant. Many participants felt they acquired an entirely new perspective for evaluating the dilemma they confronted by virtue of participation. For others, it was only a beginning as they embarked on the process of resolving the internal emotional struggles that would need to be resolved before they could successfully grapple with a problem only recently confronted or recognized. In either case it often proved to be the return to prior effectiveness and healthy spirits.

To illustrate the spontaneity involved in this work, I can recount one session in which I was asked to participate. Two new parents were having trouble with an unruly infant and found themselves locked in conflict as to the better approach to dealing with the problem. To reenact the situation, such an infant was required to recreate the crying and wailing in order for each parent to demonstrate his or her preferred solution. A child's bed was contrived and I became the infant in question. The learning for me was dual. Not only did I gain insight into how readily one can portray such a role, but I also gained a great appreciation for the plight experienced by parents who are unable to cope with such a situation and who, by virtue of turning their frustration toward one another, find themselves engaged in battle. One or the other parent was finally able to deal with me in a way that proved satisfactory and I quickly went to sleep to the great relief of all involved.

As I analyze these several colleagues and seek to identify what they held in common that might have appealed to me, I certainly find no immediate answer in terms of the subject matter. Helson, the rigorous psychophysicist, and Moreno, the spontaneous interventionist, stand at opposite poles. What was the appeal, then, of their thinking that caught my attention? It seems that what I admired most in each of these persons is in some way related to how they went about formulating concepts rather than the specific area of application to which these concepts had relevance. Helson's background factors are very similar to Sherif's frame of reference concept developed in the early Thirties. Korzybski's "Map is not the territory" is in many ways a restatement of what these investigators set out to demonstrate.

A second aspect of these four to which I was strongly drawn was the spirit of their dedication. Each lived his professional life to the fullest and I think found fulfillment in his respective professional work.

THE BUSINESS YEARS

The business years might be dated from 1964, when Scientific Methods was registered, to the present. I served as President from that time forward until 1984, when I vacated my position, passing it to Jane. I became Chairman, an activity which I continue to this day.

The founding of Scientific Methods, Inc. as a business entity can almost be described as a casual occurrence, responding to empirical need rather than entrepreneurial initiative. What actually happened was that I needed funds (somewhere in the neighborhood of a couple of thousand dollars) to carry on the Baytown work, primarily from the standpoint of printing and employing clerical helpers to facilitate our effort. The money could not properly be accepted by the University of Texas since it was not intended for research but had a specific non-university purpose behind it. Therefore, it was necessary as well as wise to establish a corporate shell that could receive and distribute the money independently of the public university body. We did this and it proved to be an immediate solution to the problem at hand. It is interesting to note that about this same time we were conducting experiments in which the query was whether or not the ideas inherent in the Managerial Grid and our approach to team building and organization development were more or less unique to an oil company setting and therefore restricted to its use or whether these ideas could be generated across the various categories of business.

As described earlier, the Exxon experiments coincided with the University period. In the beginning, they were activities of the summer months; this created no problem in terms of my participation. Once the Bayway project got underway, however, it called for a commitment of two years, and I arranged two successive leaves of absence in order to engage in the project. However, prior to this, I had taken an almost two-year leave of absence for the Fulbright work at the Tavistock Clinic, and it seemed to me that my outside interests were far outweighing my research and teaching career.

I finally came to terms with this problem when invited to conduct the third Exxon experiment, this time at Baytown in Texas. This was to be a totally absorbing project because these three experiments in the succession of a decade had provided a basis of building one on the other and thereby coming to a point of understanding of organization dynamics that would otherwise not have been subject to achievement.

During the Baytown project I received an invitation to carry on the same kind of work within Exxon, but now in the Far East. This too was a turning point. I decided to terminate my professorship at the University of Texas and to use Scientific Methods, Inc. as the vehicle for carrying on this applied work.

We soon found ourselves being called upon by banks, pharmaceutical companies, mining companies, chemical industries, high tech companies, service companies, private as well as non-profit enterprise and public agencies, and so forth. In responding to these invitations, it was not difficult to conclude that the ideas involved in our approach were quite applicable to a variety of settings and unique to no single area of pursuit. Coupled with application projects in Canada and Great Britain, we soon recognized that the concepts and methodology not only found congeniality in the American culture but held equal interest on a broader scale. In time, this took on an international scope as it led to projects in Japan, Indonesia, Saudi Arabia, Iran, western Europe, South Africa, Venezuela, Brazil, and Uruguay. All these influences were in the process of convergence, demonstrating to us the wisdom of founding Scientific Methods, Inc. and developing it as a worldwide company. The most recent additions are the Soviet Union, where this particular segment of writing is being composed, and in Korea, where an earlier section was in process some months ago. Most recently, a seminar was concluded in Thailand, the first in that nation, and, once again, the concepts were fully embraced. In fact, participants drew a number of parallels between the 9,9 Grid style and the Thai "ideal model" of living; itself heavily centered in Buddhism.

.From this widespread degree of generalization, we concluded that effectiveness in mobilizing human resources for productive outcomes is independent of the political system within which problems exist, the religion, the unique culture, national history, and other specialized factors. Fundamental effectiveness in any setting or among any people calls for the same insights into how to work with and through others, regardless of who the others are or what their specific life experiences have been.

Though I greatly enjoyed the application opportunities afforded by the founding of Scientific Methods, Inc., I readily acknowledge that I did not find great pleasure in being responsible for conducting the business. There is something of a contradiction here; that is, taking pleasure from helping others to be effective in conducting their own businesses while finding little personal pleasure in conducting my own. I can only account for such a discrepancy in one respect. It is that being responsible for application projects, which has afforded the opportunity over the years of gathering much data, has enabled me to write in order to crystallize the learnings as they developed, and has offered the possibility of rich and engaging discussions with those in the academic and business world alike. All this has provided full satisfaction for my research and development interest. On the other hand, preparing an annual tax report for the company or spending time in thinking through how it might best be structured or organized were not problems with which I cared to deal. In this sense, Scientific Methods, Inc. may have suffered over the years in terms of its own growth and development by my predilection for research, but I suspect there is a certain inevitability here. With so many opportunities, choice becomes necessary and, as choices reflect one's basic values, my choices clearly reveal mine.

THE ORIGIN OF THE MANAGERIAL GRID

Given our bent for theory-based formulation of hypotheses, predictions, and experimental tests, it is not surprising that Jane and I tried to create a conceptual framework within which to analyze concrete problems. This resulted in the development of the Managerial Grid.

It happened this way. In the beginning of the Bayway, New Jersey project in Exxon, I immediately attached myself to the top man in the company. Whenever his top team met, I met with it. Often I accompanied one of the members of this team back to his home department in order to see how he reported to his own people what had gone on in these top team meetings. For a period of some two or three months, I continued to attend these sessions, never participating, not even as a process facilitator, but merely being present as a silent observer. My goal was to learn as much as I could about the team and its individual members, its polarities, interpersonal conflicts, and operating difficulties. No experience could have been a richer source of raw material for our future work.

It seemed to me that the problem was rooted in how concepts of power and authority are employed as a means of integrating the available human resources in order to achieve productive outcomes. I was aware of the major leadership theories of the time. In my own estimation, Lewin's autocratic, democratic, and laissez-faire formulation was in the right direction but as yet it was too undeveloped to provide the precision and understanding necessary for really knowing what was going on. In my own work, the laissez-faire style appeared to be absent among this top group of managers, as did a "pure" autocratic style. Furthermore, the democratic approach did not seem to provide an effective characterization for the process as I observed it. Though McGregor's *The Human Side of Enterprise* had not yet been published, I was aware of Theory X and Theory Y from my many personal contacts with McGregor at

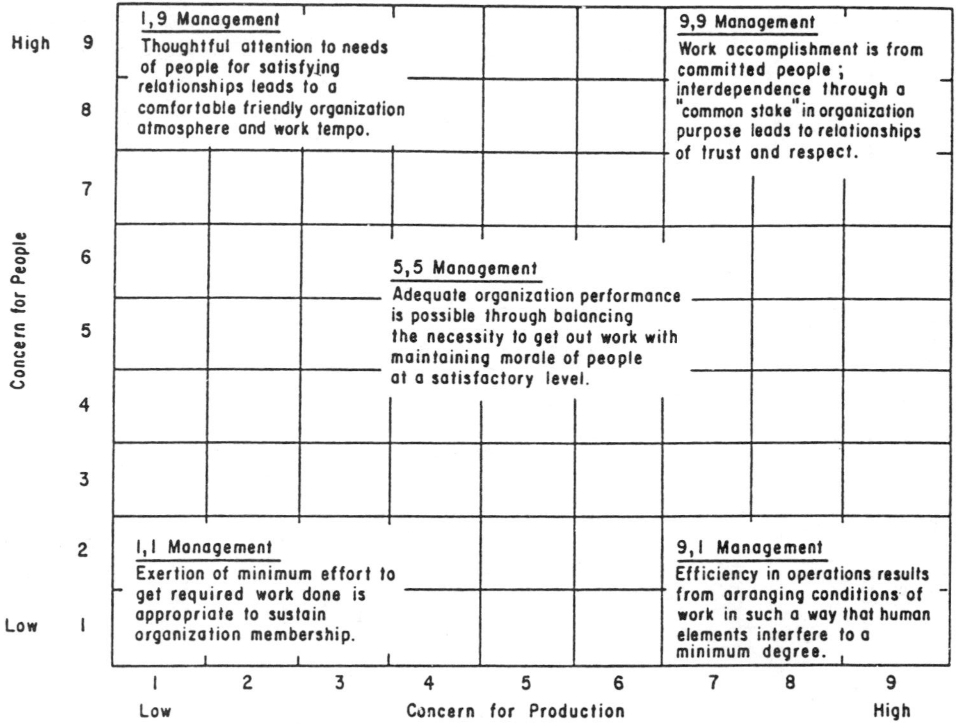

Figure 1. The Managerial Grid ®

High 9

1,9 Management
Thoughtful attention to needs of people for satisfying relationships leads to a comfortable friendly organization atmosphere and work tempo.

9,9 Management
Work accomplishment is from committed people ; interdependence through a "common stake" in organization purpose leads to relationships of trust and respect.

8

7

6

5

5,5 Management
Adequate organization performance is possible through balancing the necessity to get out work with maintaining morale of people at a satisfactory level.

4

3

2

1,1 Management
Exertion of minimum effort to get required work done is appropriate to sustain organization membership.

9,1 Management
Efficiency in operations results from arranging conditions of work in such a way that human elements interfere to a minimum degree.

Low 1

Concern for People

1   2   3   4   5   6   7   8   9
Low   Concern for Production   High

Source: R.R. Blake & J.S. Mouton. *The manageral grid* ®. Houston: Gulf Publishing Company, Copyright © 1964, p. 10. Reproduced by special permission of the authors.

129

NTL and elsewhere. X was too strong a formulation to characterize the give-and-take that occurred within this key group; yet Y was not strong enough. The lack of fit was not a matter of degree; it felt much more to have its origins in the hard extreme of X and the soft, non-conflict facing components of Y.

I was also aware of Fleishman's work on *structure* and *consideration*. I saw this theory as a more complex one which afforded a greater number of options. Therefore Jane and I made a concerted and determined effort to test its utility. As has been shown by the previously studied theories, the Fleishman approach, particularly when viewed from the perspective of the methods of quantification used, separates and isolates the two variables. Structure means just what the label designates: at the "high" extreme, it means telling a subordinate what to do, when to do it, how it should be done, and so forth—all extremely rational, logical, and one-way information. On the other hand, consideration at the high end indicates the giving of rewards to subordinates for doing what they have been instructed to do. This entire theory had all the hallmarks of paternalism. The high point of intersection (high structure-high consideration) constitutes a theory which in many respects is "destructive" of involvement, commitment, dedication, and particularly of creative or innovative thinking about how problems might be solved in a better way.

None of these "worked" in helping us to better understand at a conceptual level what was taking place in terms of group dynamics.

On the occasional weekend when I would return to Texas, Jane and I took the opportunity to review whatever dilemma I was presently confronting. In truth, this was a continuous review because, as already indicated, upon the completion of each work day, I dictated fully and comprehensively what had transpired. If the top team had a meeting, I provided a blow-by-blow account of the details. As a result, although Jane continued her work at the University, she was able to acquire vicariously something which directly paralleled my own participative experience.

As Jane and I persisted in our efforts, we slowly came to realize that the dimensions of the Fleishman graph were the problem. They were behavior dimensions, thus causing the reductionistic problem as described above, that is, the creation of two isolated variables followed by an effort to add some amount of each in order to gain an accurate picture of leadership.

As we pondered this problem, we came to realize that the dimensions needed for an effective description of operational conduct are attitudinal variables, not behavioral variables. Thus, we identified a horizontal axis, "Concern for Production," reflecting an underlying attitude toward achieving results. We designated the vertical axis as "Concern for People," meaning the character of thought and feeling one experiences in exercising leadership while working with and through others. We expressed differences in the magnitude of concern on a scale of 1 to 9. This enabled us to talk about the character of leadership that might be manifest when different degrees of the two concerns are observed to be operating in the leadership conduct of any individual.

Though we had pondered the dilemma of how to conceptualize leadership for many months, even years, the decisions that resulted in the Grid itself all took place in a very short span of time, perhaps some 30 minutes. These arrangements permitted us to say, "What would 9,1 leadership be like?" Immediately we could answer, "A boss who has a very high concern for getting results simultaneously present with a very low concern for people would certainly be expected to use people as tools of production rather than as human resources who themselves are capable of contributing to problem solving." The same could be done for 1,9, 1,1, 5,5, and 9,9, and a number of variations on these five basic styles. We had no difficulty in saying, "That style fits him to a T," or, of another person, "His basic thinking is in the 1,9 corner," or, "She constantly pushes for intermediate solutions, seeks a compromise, even though it's obvious that no one is ever truly satisfied."

This describes the origin of the Managerial Grid as it fell into place sometime late in 1957 or in 1958. We immediately started writing to crystallize our thinking, using this as the basis for further observation, which in turn led to greater refinement. By 1960, feeling ourselves on solid ground, we wrote the book that was published as *The Managerial Grid* in 1964. Seven years of intensive work had served to shape it, and we now felt assured that the theory had reached a point of stabilization.

Two later editions of the Grid have been published, one in 1978 and one in 1985. A new book was released in 1991, not as a fourth edition, but rather as a comprehensive rendition of the theory. This book is titled *Leadership Dilemmas-Grid Solutions.*

While this latest book is an entirely rewritten statement of the Managerial Grid, in no way does it alter the fundamental character of the original 1964 book. The dimensions as originally formulated continue to be sound. The use of a numerical system of expression has proven equally useful. Centering upon conflict in boss-subordinate relations remains fundamental. In fact, so central is this element of behavior that it has been elevated to a position of greater importance than in previous editions. In all other respects, though, the structure of thinking of the original book has stood the test of time.

What the new book does offer is some significant extensions of previous thinking. The most important is the expanded treatment of a third variable concerned with *motivation* as central to the core of thinking about leadership. This third dimension runs through each Grid style, from a plus end which characterizes what a person is striving to accomplish, through a neutral zone, which intersects with the Grid surface, to a negative pole, which designates what a person is seeking to avoid in his or her leadership conduct. As an illustration, 9,1+ is the "desire to control, master, and dominate the situation," and 9,1− is "fear of failure." The motivational dimension provides a further degree of clarification for the motivational situation being experienced by a person managing in a 9,1, 5,5, or 9,9 way, and so forth. It opens up new possibilities for research that hold great promise.

A second major change in *Leadership Dilemmas–Grid Solutions* is the introduction and expansion of paternalism and opportunism as two major Grid styles, making a total of seven. Paternalism and Opportunism were included in the original 1964 version of the book, but only alluded to in paragraph descriptions. As we have learned more and as the world has progressed, we have come to see these two theories as having far greater importance than previously thought. For this reason, they have been elevated to a comparable status with the original five Grid styles.

A third major shift lies in the means of illustration provided to the reader to aid in concretizing the concepts. The book is presented as a story which portrays each of the major Grid styles as it is characterized by one member of a work team, including its leader. This team and its members are introduced in the beginning of the book and carried through each of the chapters. The final chapters of the book provide a culmination of the story through a demonstration of Grid Organization Development as we would guide it through an organization.

There are some that say the Grid has become the unofficial leadership theory of the day. It is true that in the early years many attempts were made to pinpoint presumed weaknesses or limitations. As each of these appeared, we reexamined the underlying thinking of the Grid to determine in our own minds whether or not a fundamental limitation had been identified. Fortunately, we have never had to introduce a correction in what was presented in the 1964 edition by virtue of these ongoing efforts.

One frequently-alluded-to limitation, however, is worthy of comment. It is claimed that the Grid does not deal with situations that are different from one another. The argument is, "How might a person be 9,9 in two very different situations?" Our answer is illustrated by taking a 9,9 example. A 9,9 approach to exercising leadership, for instance, is applied in a far different way with a 50-year-old seasoned executive than it is with an 18-year-old new hire. The differences, however, are tactical in nature and relate to the situation itself. They are not differences in the style of exercising leadership—9,9 remains the constant strategy. The 50-year-old application is obviously different than the tactic most pertinent for dealing with an 18-year-old newcomer. For example, in the former case, goals may be set that extend over a year, or two, or five. With an 18-year-old, no shift is made in the manner in which goals are set; that stays the same. The time frame, however, varies; it may be a day, a week, or a month. In other words, the 9,9 principle remains constant; it is the 9,9 tactic that varies, depending on the specific situation. The 50-year-old has a wealth of experience and can engage in goal-setting over an extended period, whereas the 18-year-old has a very limited experience. If asked to set goals beyond one's time or range of experience, it would become a futile effort. Thus, the Grid is a strategic approach that fits all situations, but each of the applications are situationally unique. The situationalist criticism of the Grid claims that style should vary with the situation but this is simply not justified by the facts. Neither is it consistent with sound principles of human behavior.

The Grid formulation has enjoyed worldwide interest and continues to do so on an ever expanding basis. The importance of this from an autobiographical point of view is that it has enabled us to study and learn much about the exercise of power and authority across many different cultures, nationalities, religions, and economic systems.

Our conclusion is that human problem solving is not susceptible to distinctiveness based on any of the above factors. When two or more people are engaged in problem solving, the critical issue becomes that of relying upon effective human inquiry as to the nature of the problem and the facts surrounding it; open, clear, and candid advocacy of points of view between people who are engaged in collaboration; conflict solving by confrontation and resolution of differences rather than relying on other means of getting around the conflict problem; the full reliance on feedback and critique as a means for ensuring that interpersonal processes are healthy and sound and that progress toward resolution is being achieved. None of these can be characterized as American, European, or Japanese. Nor can they be called Christian, Jewish, Moslem, or Buddhist. They have no unique racial character. Nor do they belong to a single ideology—free enterprise, communism, or socialism.

These processes of human problem solving are deeper than any of the above considerations. They are inherent in solution seeking. They constitute the raw materials from which scientific methodology has been shaped.

It seemed to Jane and myself that the conclusion formulated here is truly of significant proportions because it leads to the implication that only when human problems of collaboration themselves are formulated in terms that permit their resolution is it possible for genuine progress to be experienced.

OTHER BOOK-LEVEL FORMULATIONS

Over the years Jane and I sought to create a comprehensive statement of what we see as important in the future unfolding of Organization Development. Apart from the Grid, I would include the following book-level formulations.

Synergogy

Synergogy is a statement of the learning methodology on which Grid OD is based. But Synergogy is much more than that. It is a way of rearranging learning conditions so that learners can be proactively engaged in their own learning while helping one another learn. It constitutes the single most radical formulation currently available in terms of providing an alternative to pedagogic training of children and adults alike.

When it is realized that pedagogy is a method of education premised upon paternalistic concepts, it can be seen how its use as a learning methodology creates dependent learners rather than people who are motivated to actively master the subjects being taught.

Synergogy has been resisted in educational circles, however, and a brief explanation is useful. Teachers have been extensively interviewed regarding their reactions to Synergogy. They are positive toward it as long as the teacher stays in charge of the learning process and is free to intervene at any point where clarification is needed or intervention seems appropriate. But it is just at these points that learners can learn the most by learning to overcome their own barriers to joint effectiveness by helping one another understand the concept or helping to diagnose the problem they as a team are facing which impedes progress. This places responsibility for learning in the students' hands, however, and removes that source of gratification from a pedagogically-minded teacher. It is a difficult transformation for any purveyor of knowledge or skill to make.

Change by Design

In earlier editions, this major change model has been called *Building a Dynamic Corporation Through Grid Organization Development* and *Corporate Excellence Through Grid Organization Development*. *Change by Design* is the latest edition of our work concerned with Organization Development. This book describes the principles, main phases, and probable outcomes available to any organization that engages in a full and comprehensive approach to Organization Development.

Consultation

Consultation represents the fullest treatment of consultation strategies and interventions yet available. It covers all recognizable units of change, focal issues involved in an intervention, and the dynamic aspect of behavior which is involved. This book has become a manual utilized by consultants who need the stimulation of seeing alternative ways of going about offering service to a client. Even more importantly, it confronts the issue of the consultant dealing with the inclusive unit of change rather than simply locking in on individuals as the inevitable recipients.

These four books present the main outlines of our thinking about human behavior in organized settings and how it might be strengthened and made more effective.

LANGUAGE AND EXPRESSION DEVELOPMENTS

At the beginning of Organization Development, there was a limited vocabulary for talking about organization phenomena. Jane and I found a number of words helpful in expressing what we saw to be important. None of these enjoyed currency at the time, but all are in use today.

Organization Development

Organization Development is, of course, the first term that comes to mind. During the decade of the Fifties, there was literally no conception of organization development as it is now understood. Restructuring was one means by which organizations might be reshaped, but this involved levels of hierarchy, reporting relationships, and so forth—the "mechanical" side of organization. In addition, there was some sense of individual development, that is, sending seasoned top executives and upper-level managers off to prestigious business schools. But here, too, the point of concentration was on the mechanics of thinking about business rather than the more vital consideration of mobilizing human resources and bringing them more fully to bear on productive purposes of an organization.

We coined Organization Development to express the "organization" culture point of emphasis. What we meant by this term was the development of an organization as a whole entity. We were not concerned with some isolated application, a piece of an organization as might be implied by "organizational." Rather, we were concerned with an organization as an intact and whole system, itself a primary entity that could be dealt with in its entirety, albeit through a sequence of development actions rather than some inclusive, simultaneously occurring event.

Organization Development seems now to have taken hold as standard language in the field.

Style

There was no ready shorthand when we began for clearly identifying the unique properties for how a person exercises leadership. Calling it "leadership behavior" did not solve the problem. Trait was unacceptable for a number of reasons. Finally, we settled on the word "style."

I have maintained some reservations about the use of this word that derive from its fashion industry usage. The word itself carries the notion of being "in" style or "out" of style, indicating that style is a preference that changes from time to time. We made no such assumption when we used this word in the context of leadership, as we see strong leadership, that is, the 9,9 style, enduring over time and place and not subject to the whims of change. The 9,9 leadership style is the single best approach to solving the leadership dilemma. It has demonstrated value in promoting productivity, creativity, satisfaction, and health and, in this sense, it can be regarded as unbounded by time.

Backup

An empirical observation is that even the strongest leaders may occasionally shift their style of leadership and fall back on another approach for solving a dilemma. The word "backup" provides a basis for understanding something of the unstable character of leadership, that is, when one preferred style fails to produce the needed consequences, then a person may shift to another approach. These shifts into a backup style provide a means for understanding why people are not rigidly consistent in their actions but rather seek to adapt to barriers and resistances which they seem incapable of overcoming in any other manner.

Win-Lose

One of the interesting terms that has had an enduring and expanded significance since we first introduced it is the concept of "win-lose." Win-lose became the shorthand phrase we used for characterizing the aftermath of interaction between two groups in the research experiments we conducted where one group was positioned to win at the expense of the other.

This afforded an opportunity to study the consequences associated with victory and defeat. This research has been published elsewhere and need not be commented upon further, except to point out that many applications and extensions of win-lose have been created since that time.

Team and Team Development

Another point of emphasis in the field of human resource development strategies is "Team," emphasizing the unifying communality of several engaged in common pursuit. Developing a team's capacity for mutual problem solving, that is, Team Development, as contrasted with aiding each individual isolated from the other to be more effective is another original contribution. The team is considered to be the least common denominator; seeming members on an isolated, one-by-one basis constitutes an unacceptable degree of reductionism.

Since the original use of these words, a number of others have served as substitutes, such as the phrase "Team Building." We have reservations about Team Building because of the mechanical implications in the word "building," that is, a block at a time, as contrasted with the more organic concept of integrated change contained within the word "development."

Conflict Solving

As we more and more centered our efforts upon conflict as the primary dynamic in human affairs, we felt the need to modify this word in a manner that might express what we were seeking to realize, that is, the solving of conflict. Thus, conflict solving became our way of expressing the important aspects that constitute the objective of studying such tensions in the first place.

Solution Selling

This same thinking was applied by us in trying to solve problems associated with the dynamics of selling. It seemed to us that what a person is actually buying in a sales relationship is a solution to his or her problem, whatever that problem might be. Therefore, if the salesperson is oriented to this aspect of the relationship, he or she can learn the skills of offering the customer solutions rather than simply describing various items or services for consideration.

Synergogy

As mentioned earlier, we attached great importance to the learning methodology that provides the delivery system enabling users to learn and use the various approaches that are embedded within Grid development. This methodology lies at the opposite end of the spectrum from traditional pedagogy and bypasses andragogic facilitation by placing the responsibility for learning in the hands of the learners themselves.

Synergogy came about in response to the need for a better and more acceptable educational delivery system than either pedagogy or andragogy could offer. Originally referred to as Instrumented Team Learning, this contrived word conveys the basic idea: "working together," from the Greek *synergos* and *agogus*, emphasizing "teacher." Synergogy thus refers to "working or learning together for shared understanding."

The need for a radical solution to the breakdown of education now confronting the nation goes far beyond simply helping teachers become better informed on their subject(s), or better communicators, or better disciplinarians. These are all symptoms of some deeper lying malaise in the classroom.

As Jane and I saw it, what has broken down is the concept of authority which is embedded within the classroom model. Adults and young people alike have repudiated authority in its many forms, yet the fundamental model of pedagogy and its variants rests on acceptance by students of the authority-obedience paradigm. Only by completely shifting the responsibility of learning onto themselves is it possible to arouse motivation to learn. This is done only partially by andragogy, when the expert maintains control of group process.

Synergogy approaches the educational setting from an entirely different perspective. The knowledge base is in books, instruments, and life experience. Learning the requisite model is through individual measurement followed by team testing *after* teams have reached agreement on best answers to set multiple-choice and other question formats. Keys are then distributed. Individual and team performances are assessed, with competition between teams for "best," "next best," and so forth, in terms of learning improvement based on initial individual prework understanding measured against ultimate team insight.

Responsibility is centered within the learning team since no teacher or andragogic facilitator "tells" or helps the teams in their pursuit of learning excellence. Rather, a post-scoring critique of team process, also instrument-guided, aids team members to evaluate what they need to do to strengthen team performance for greater or sustained success in the future.

Synergogy is uniformly embraced by learners as a more exhilarating activity than pedagogy, and one that stimulates more positive attitudes toward the learning itself. It has been applied all over the world with comparable enthusiasm. We saw it and I continue to see it as a fundamental solution to creating new and entirely different relations between the subject-matter to be learned, the learner and the "teacher." I have no reservations whatsoever to this conclusion, but I should point out that it tends to stimulate great reluctance and reservations on the part of teachers. The explanation for this is that it removes the teacher from the authority-obedience equation and *appears* to lessen teacher control. However, upon fuller examination, it frees the teacher to create learning materials which is a far more demanding and rewarding use of his or her knowledge and skills. Many more students can be educated and in a far more effective and enduring way.

POSTLUDE

This story is being completed, Christmas 1990, three years after Jane's tragedy, which also terminated almost four decades of my career. Since I had never worked alone for any substantial period, I seriously pondered my next move, which leads to the more recent part of this study.

Jane had an understudy during the last fifteen years, someone to whom she and we turned for help whenever we were dealing with a particularly complex or difficult project. This person is Anne McCanse who participated in many of our leading-edge projects, including membership in the UAL cockpit project and the nuclear control room design.

Anne stepped in to help me bring to a close some of the projects Jane and I had had underway. Rather than simply drawing these to conclusion, however, a new collaboration began to unfold with many unanticipated synergistic results.

Anne's teamwork differs in significant ways from the manner in which Jane and I worked together. Oftentimes Anne and I deliberate a course of action to verbal agreement, and then one of us creates a first draft. We then continue to work it through a conceptual and editorial phase, fine-tuning it until completion.

As members of a profit-making company, all of this must take place within the context of client work. This has involved extensive travel, taking us to Korea, Australia, the Philippines, Italy, Greece, Brazil, Venezuela, Thailand, the USSR, as well as to several locations in the United States during this same period. We have managed to write two more books during this time, several articles, and numerous projects still in the drafting stage.

The writing of this autobiography reflects this same model of our interdependence.

A main reason for writing a personal story of this sort is to learn from it. For me this lesson involves how human effectiveness emerges and how it might be enhanced. The learnings that seem of greater importance include the following.

1. Conceptual formulations, presented in written form to stimulate public scrutiny, constitute the main opportunity for making enduring contributions.
2. The synergies possible from effective teamwork provide access to much creativity that otherwise would be lost or not even recognized.
3. Intellectual teamwork based on openness and candor, confronting and resolving conflicts, and extensive reliance on feedback and critique can further the elimination of false assumptions, thereby increasing the quality of contributions.
4. Continuity of teamwork is possible even though memberships may shift.
5. Professional teamwork need not be limited to a few people working together over long periods of time. Much synergy is possible in terms of more limited collaborations, as is suggested in my work with Sherif, Helson, Bradford, and Moreno.
6. Similar gains are possible from "joining" with historical figures through taking their assumptions and testing them as the premise of one's own actions, as in my regard for Darwin, Lewin, Freud, and Korzybski.
7. Satisfaction from effort comes far more from the processes inherent in teamwork than in its products or its achievements.

PUBLICATIONS

1943

With W. Dennis. The development of stereotypes concerning the Negro. *Journal of Abnormal and Social Psychology, 38*(4), 525-531.

1944

With D.E. Super. The significance of participation in certain sports and hobbies as a predictor of success in pilot training. *AAF Psychology Program Research Bulletin*, 1-106.

1945

Measures of pilot proficiency at the training school level. In N.E. Miller (Ed.), *Measures of Pilot Proficiency in the Aviation Psychology Program.*

1947

With F.B. Davis & D.E. Super. Research on sports and hobbies participation tests. In J. P. Guilford (Ed.), *Army Air Forces Aviation Psychologyy Program Research Reports, Report No. 5, Printed Classification Tests* (pp. 359-361). Washington, DC: U.S. Government Printing Office.

With W.E. Galt, T.N. Ewing, I. Robbins, E. Ismael, & J.R. Rors. An investigation of data available at contact and instrument instruction schools. In N. E. Miller (Ed.), *Army Air Forces Aviation Psychology Program Reports, Report No. 8, Psychological Research on Pilot Training* (pp. 303-306). Washington, DC: U.S. Government Printing Office.

With N.E. Miller, R.P. Youtz, W.E. Galt, & I. Robbins. A study of returned combat pilots. In N. E. Miller (Ed.), *Army Air Forces Aviation Psychology Program Reports, Report No. 8, Psychological Research on Pilot Training* (pp. 294-299). Washington, DC: U.S. Government Printing Office.

With D.E. Super. Research on sports and hobbies participation tests. In J. P. Guilford (Ed.), *Army Air Forces Aviation Psychology Program Research Reports, Report No. 5, Printed Classification Tests* (pp. 341-359). Washington, DC: U.S. Government Printing Office.

With D.E. Super & J.L. Wallen. Extension of research on attitudes and interest inventories. In J. P. Guilford (Ed.), *Army Air Forces Aviation Psychology Program Research Reports, Report No. 5, Printed Classification Tests* (pp. 740-746). Washington, DC: U.S. Government Printing Office.

With D.E. Super & J.L. Wallen. Extension of research on attitude and interest inventories. In J.P. Guilford (Ed.), *Army Air Forces Aviation Psychology Program Research Reports, Report No. 5, Printed Classification Tests* (pp. 736-740). Washington, DC: U.S. Government Printing Office.

1948

Some quantitative aspects of Time Magazine's presentation of psychology. *American Psychologist, 3,* 124-126.
Ocular activity during administration of the Rorschach Test. *Journal of Clinical Psychology, 4,* 159-169.
With R.P. Falls. A quantitative analysis of the picture frustration study. *Journal of Personality, 16,* 320-325.
With B.S. McCarty. A comparative evaluation of the Bellevue-Wechsler Mental Deterioration Index Distributions of Allen's brain injured patients and of normal subjects. *Journal of Clinical Psychology, 4*(4), 415-418.

1949

The relationship between childhood environment and the scholastic aptitude and intelligence of adults. *Journal of Social Psychology, 29,* 37-41.
With J.M. Vanderplas. Selective sensitization in auditory perception. *Journal of Personality, 18*(2), 252-266.

1950

With J.M. Vanderplas. The effect of prerecognition hypotheses on veridical recognition thresholds in auditory perception. *Journal of Personality, 19*(1), 95-115.
With G.P. Wilson, Jr. Perceptual selectivity in Rorschach determinants as a function of depressive tendencies. *Journal of Abnormal and Social Psychology, 45*(3), 459-472.
With G.P. Wilson, Jr. A methodological problem in Beck's organizational concept. *Journal of Consulting Psychology, 14,* 20-24.

1951

With G.V. Ramsey. *Perception: An approach to personality.* New York: Ronald Press.
With G.V. Ramsey & L.J. Moran. Perceptual processes as basic to an understanding of complex behavior. In R. R. Blake & G. V. Ramsey (Eds.), *Perception* (pp. 3-24). Austin, TX: University of Texas Press.

1952

With L.J. Moran & F.A. Moran. An investigation of the vocabulary performance of schizophrenics: I. Quantitative level. *Journal of Genetic Psychology, 80,* 97-105.

With L.J. Moran, & F.A. Moran. An investigation of the vocabulary performance of schizophrenics: II. Conceptual level of definitions. *Journal of Genetic Psychology, 80,* 107-132.

With L.J. Moran & F.A. Moran. An investigation of the vocabulary performance of schizophrenics: III. Qualitative analysis of definitions. *Journal of Genetic Psychology, 80,* 141-150.

1953

The role of the social consultant in business and industry. In *Proceedings: Fifteenth Conference Texas Personnel and Management Association,* (pp. 55-61).

The interaction-feeling hypothesis applied to psychotherapy groups. *Sociometry, 16,* 253-265.

With J.V. McConnell. A methodological study of tape-recorded synthetic group atmospheres. *American Psychologist, 8,* 395.

With R. Tagiuri & J.S. Bruner. Some determinants of the perception of positive and negative feelings in others. *Journal of Abnormal and Social Psychology, 48,* 585-592.

1954

Social standards and individual conduct. *The Southwestern Social Science Quarterly, 35,* 11-24.

With J.W. Brehm. The use of tape recordings to simulate a group atmosphere. *Journal of Abnormal and Social Psychology, 49*(2), 311-313.

With D.H. Goodrich. Areas in occupational therapy that need to be explored by research: The evaluation of suggested topics. *American Journal of Occupational Therapy, 8,* 144-150.

With J.S. Mouton & B. Fruchter. The consistency of interpersonal behavior judgments made on the basis of short-term interactions in three-man groups. *Journal of Abnormal and Social Psychology, 49,* 573-578.

1955

Experimental psychodrama with children. *Group Psychotherapy, 8,* 347-350.

Transference and tele viewed from the standpoint of therapy and training. *Group Psychotherapy, 8,* 178-179.

The treatment of relational conflict by individual, group, and interpersonal methods. *Group Psychotherapy, 8,* 182-185.

With J.W. Brehm. The use of tape recordings to simulate a group atmosphere. In A.P. Hare, E.F. Borgatta, & R.F. Bales (Eds.), *Small Groups* (pp. 220-225). New York: Alfred A. Knopf.

With A.M. Freed, P.J. Chandler, & J.S. Mouton. Stimulus and background factors in sign violation. *Journal of Personality, 23*, 499.

With B. Fruchter & J.S. Mouton. Some dimensions of interpersonal relations in three-man airplane crews. *American Psychologist, 10*, 3-27.

With R.L. Kaiser. Aspiration and performance in a simulated group atmosphere. *Journal of Social Psychology, 42*, 193-202.

With M. Lefkowitz & J.S. Mouton. Status factors in pedestrian violation of traffic signals. *Journal of Abnormal and Social Psychology, 51*(3), 704-706.

With J.S. Mouton. Present and future implications of social psychology for law and lawyers. *Journal of Public Law, 3*(2), 352-369.

With J.S. Mouton. Conflicting careers. A short play by group and role playing methods. *Group Psychotherapy, 8*, 130-141.

With J.S. Mouton & B. Fruchter. The reliability of sociometric measures. *Sociometry, 18*, 7-48.

With J.S. Mouton & B. Fruchter. The validity of sociometric responses. *Sociometry, 18*(3), 181-206.

With J.A. Olmstead. The use of simulated groups to produce modifications in judgment. *Journal of Personality, 23*, 335-345.

With M. Rosenbaum. Volunteering as a function of field structure. *Journal of Abnormal and Social Psychology, 50*(2), 193-196.

With M. Rosenbaum & R.A. Duryea. Gift-giving as a function of group standards. *Human Relations, 8*, 61-73.

1956

Critique and discussion. In B. Schaffner (Ed.), *Group processes* (pp. 13-227). Madison, NJ: Madison Printing.

Group training versus group therapy. *Group Psychotherapy, 10*, 271-276.

With H. Berkowitz, R.Q. Bellamy, & J.S. Mouton. Volunteering as an avoidance act. *Journal of Abnormal and Social Psychology, 53*(2), 154-156.

With H. Helson & J.S. Mouton. An experimental investigation of the effectiveness of the 'big lie' in shifting attitudes. In R.R. Blake and H. Helson (Eds.), *Adaptability screening of flying personnel. Situational and personal factors in conforming behavior* (pp. 35-47). Randolph Air Force Base, TX: School of Aviation Medicine, United States Air Force.

With H. Helson & J.S. Mouton. The generality of conformity behavior as a function of factual anchorage, difficulty of task and amount of social pressure. In R. R. Blake & H. Helson (Eds.), *Adaptability screening of flying personnel. Situational and personal factors in conforming behavior* (pp. 27-34). Randolph Air Force Base, TX: School of Aviation Medicine, United States Air Force.

With H. Helson, & J.S. Mouton. Petition-signing as adjustment to situational and personal factors. In R. R. Blake & H. Helson (Eds.), *Adaptability screening of flying personnel. Situational and personal factors in conforming behavior* (pp. 57-61). Randolph Air Force Base, TX: School of Aviation Medicine, United States Air Force.

With H. Helson, J.S. Mouton, & J.A. Olmstead. Attitudes as adjustments to stimulus, background and residual factors. In R. R. Blake and H. Helson (Eds.), *Adaptability screening of flying personnel. Situational and personal factors in conforming behavior* (pp. 15-25). Randolph Air Force Base, TX: School of Aviation Medicine, United States Air Force.

With H. Helson, J.S. Mouton, & J.A. Olmstead. Attitudes as adjustments to stimulus, background, and residual factors. *Journal of Abnormal and Social Psychology, 52*(3), 314-322.

With J.S. Mouton. Personality factors associated with individual conduct in a training group situation. *Human Relations Training Laboratory Research Monograph, 1*(1), 1-30.

With J.S. Mouton. Evaluation of the simulated group technique for studying social behavior. In R. R. Blake & H. Helson (Eds.), *Adaptability screening of flying personnel. Situational and personal factors in conforming behavior* (pp. 5-14). Randolph Air Force Base, TX: School of Aviation Medicine, United States Air Force.

With J.S. Mouton. Human relations problem areas in work. *Group Psychotherapy, 9,* 253-264.

With J.S. Mouton & R.L. Bell, Jr.. Role playing skill and sociometric peer status. *Group Psychotherapy, 9*(1), 7-17.

With J.S. Mouton & J.D. Hain. Social forces in petition-signing. *The Southwestern Social Science Quarterly, 36,* 385-390.

With J.S. Mouton & J.A. Olmstead. The coercion dynamics of susceptibility to counter-norm attitude expressions in a small group situation. In R. R. Blake & H. Helson (Eds.), *Adaptability screening of flying personnel. Situational and personal factors in conforming behavior* (pp. 49-55). Randolph Air Force Base, TX: School of Aviation Medicine, United States Air Force.

With J.S. Mouton & J.A. Olmstead. The relationship between yielding, submissiveness, and the disclosure of personal identity. In R.R. Blake & H. Helson (Eds.), *Adaptability screening of flying personnel. Situational and personal factors in conforming behavior* (pp. 43-47). Randolph Air Force Base, TX: School of Aviation Medicine, United States Air Force.

With J.S. Mouton & J.A. Olmstead. The relationship between frequency of yielding and disclosure of personal identity. *Journal of Personality, 24,* 339-347.

With C.C. Rhead, B. Wedge, & J.S. Mouton. Housing architecture and social interaction. *Sociometry, 19*, 133-139.

1957

With H. Helson & J.S. Mouton. The generality of conformity behavior as a function of factual anchorage, difficulty of task and amount of social pressure. *Journal of Personality, 25*, 294-305.

With J.G. Kelly & C.E. Stromberg. The effect of role training on role reversal. *Group Psychotherapy, 10*, 95-104.

With J.S. Mouton. The study of social conduct within the framework of adaptation-level theory. In M. Sherif & M. O. Wilson (Eds.), *Emerging problems in social psychology* (pp. 143-180). Norman, OK: Institute of Group Relations.

With J.S. Mouton. The dynamics of influence and coercion. *International Journal of Social Psychiatry, 2*(4), 263-274.

With J.S. Mouton. Perspectives on housing architecture and social interaction. *International Journal of Sociometric Sociology, 1*, 95-98.

1958

I think TV teaching is a good idea, but.... In J.C. Adams, C.R. Carpenter, & P.R. Smith (Eds.), *College teaching by television* (pp. 92-97). Washington, DC: American Council on Education.

The other person in the situation. In R. Tagiuri & L. Petrullo (Eds.), *Person perception, and interpersonal behavior* (pp. 229-242). Stanford, CA: Stanford University Press.

Comments on "code of ethics of group psychotherapists." *Group Psychotherapy, 11*, 356-360.

Re-examination of performance appraisal. *Advanced Management, 7*, 19-20.

Group Training vs. Group Therapy. *Sociometry Monograph, 35*, 1-9.

With J.F. Coleman & J.S. Mouton. Task difficulty and conformity pressures. *Journal of Abnormal and Social Psychology, 57*(1), 120-122.

With B. Fruchter & J.S. Mouton. Some dimensions of interpersonal relations in three-man airplane crews. *Psychological Monograph, 71*(19), 1-19.

With H. Helson & J.S. Mouton. An experimental investigation of the effectiveness of the 'big lie' in shifting attitudes. *Journal of Social Psychology, 48*, 51-60.

With H. Helson, & J.S. Mouton. Petition-signing as adjustment to situational and personal factors. *Journal of Social Psychology, 48*, 3-10.

With D.L. Kimbrell. Motivational factors in the violation of a prohibition. *Journal of Abnormal and Social Psychology, 56*(1), 132-133.

With R. Tagiuri & J.S. Bruner. On the relation between feelings and perception of feelings among members of small groups. In E. E. Maccoby, T. M. Newcomb, & E. L. Hartley (Eds.), *Readings in social psychology* (3rd ed., pp. 110-116). New York: Henry Holt.

1959

Client-centered hypnosis. In S.W. Standal & R.J. Corsini (Eds.), *Critical incidents in psychotherapy* (pp. 148-149). Englewood Cliffs, NJ: Prentice-Hall.

The design of an industrial social science training laboratory. In *Proceedings, Fifteenth Annual Louisiana Personnel Management Conference*. Baton Rouge, LA: Esso Standard Oil Company.

The discovery of the spontaneous man with special emphasis upon the technique of role reversal. In J. L. Moreno (Ed.), *Psychodrama* (pp. 181-184). Beacon, NY: Beacon House.

Don't give me up. In S. W. Standal & R. J. Corsini (Eds.), *Critical incidents in psychotherapy* (pp. 6-8). Englewood Cliffs, NJ: Prentice-Hall.

Don't help Jim read. In S.W. Standal & R.J. Corsini (Eds.), *Critical incidents in psychotherapy* (pp. 105-106). Englewood Cliffs, NJ: Prentice-Hall.

Gaining acceptance of new ideas in the power structure of an organization. In *Proceedings, Twelfth Annual Industrial Engineer Institute* (pp. 1-5). Berkeley: University of California Press.

Go plumb to hell. In S.W. Standal & R.J. Corsini (Eds.), *Critical incidents in psychotherapy* (p. 240). Englewood Cliffs, NJ: Prentice-Hall.

Group dynamics and research aspects of management games. In *Proceedings, the National Symposium on Management Games* (p. 3). Lawrence, KS: Center for Research in Business.

Science and the soothsayer. In S.W. Standal & R.J. Corsini (Eds.), *Critical Incidents in psychotherapy* (pp. 196-197). Englewood Cliffs, NJ: Prentice-Hall.

The significance of the therapeutic format and the place of acting out in psychotherapy. In J.L. Moreno (Ed.), *Psychodrama* (pp. 116-120). Beacon, NY: Beacon House.

Psychology and the crisis of statesmanship. *The American Psychologist, 14*, 87-94.

With J.S. Mouton. Analyse concrete des problemes de relations humaines les situations de travail. *Psychosociologie Industrielle, 169*, 28-35.

With J.S. Mouton. Personality. *Annual Review of Psychology, 10*, 203-232.

1960

Typical laboratory procedures and experiments. In B. N. Peek (Ed.), *An Action Research Program for Organizational Improvement (in Esso Standard Oil Company)* (pp. 7-29). Ann Arbor, MI: Foundation for Research on Human Behavior.

Applied group dynamics training laboratories. *Journal of the American Society of Training Directors, 14*, 21-27.

Organizing a management development lab. *Petroleum Refiner, 39*, 227-230.

With J.S. Mouton & R.L. Bell, Jr. Role playing skill and sociometric peer status. In J. L. Moreno, with H.H. Jennings, J.H. Criswell, L. Katz, R.R. Blake, J.S. Mouton, M.E. Bonney, M.L. Northway, C.P. Loomis, C. Proctor, R. Tagiuri, & J. Nehnevajsa (Eds.), *The sociometry reader* (pp. 388-398). Glencoe, IL: Free Press.

With J.S. Mouton & B. Fruchter. The reliability of sociometric measures. In J.L. Moreno, with H.H. Jennings, J.H. Criswell, L. Katz, R.R. Blake, J.S. Mouton, M.E. Bonney, M.L. Northway, C.P. Loomis, C. Proctor, R. Tagiuri, & J. Nehnevajsa (Eds.), *The sociometry reader* (pp. 320-361). Glencoe, IL: Free Press.

With J.S. Mouton & B. Fruchter. The validity of sociometric responses. In J.L. Moreno, with H.H. Jennings, J.H. Criswell, L. Katz, R.R. Blake, J.S. Mouton, M.E. Bonney, M.L. Northway, C.P. Loomis, C. Proctor, R. Tagiuri, & J. Nehnevajsa (Eds.), *The sociometry reader* (pp. 362-387). Glencoe, IL: Free Press.

With J.S. Mouton. How power affects employee appraisal. *Petroleum Refiner, 39*, 141-144.

With J.S. Mouton. Power styles in the refinery organization. *Petroleum Refiner, 39*, 173-177.

With J.S. Mouton. How power affects human behavior. *Petroleum Refiner, 39*, 175-178.

With J.S. Mouton. The story behind intergroup conflict. *Petroleum Refiner, 39*, 181-185.

With J.S. Mouton. Group dynamics in decision making. *Petroleum Refiner, 39*, 253-260.

With J.S. Mouton. Why problem-solving between groups sometimes fails. *Petroleum Refiner, 39*, 269-273.

With J.S. Mouton. How to get better decisions from groups. *Petroleum Refiner, 39*, 323-326.

1961

Psychology and the crisis of statesmanship. In K.D. Benne, W.G. Bennis, & R. Chin (Eds.), *The planning of change* (pp. 466-477). New York: Holt, Rinehart, and Winston.

From industrial warfare to collaboration: A behavioral science approach. *General Semantics Bulletin, 28/29*, 49-60.

With A.C. Bidwell, & J.J. Farrel. Team job training—A new strategy for industry. *Journal of the American Society of Training Directors, 15*(10), 3-23.

With L.P. Bradford. Decisions...decisions...decisions. In L. Bradford (Ed.), *Group development* (pp. 69-72). Washington, DC: National Training Laboratories, National Educational Association.

With R.J. Corsini & M.E. Shaw. *Roleplaying in business and industry.* Glencoe, IL: Free Press.

With J.S. Mouton. *Group dynamics: Key to decision making.* Houston, TX: Gulf Publishing Company.

With J.S. Mouton. Competition, communication and conformity. In I. A. Berg & B. M. Bass (Eds.), *Conformity and deviation* (pp. 199-229). New York: Harper.

With J.S. Mouton. The experimental investigation of interpersonal influence. In A. Biderman & H. Zimmer (Eds.), *The manipulation of human behavior* (pp. 216-276). New York: Wiley.

With J.S. Mouton. How team training can help you. In B.F. White (Ed.), *Team Action Laboratory.* Dallas, TX: U. S. Treasury Department, Internal Revenue Service.

With J.S. Mouton. University training in human relations skills. In L. Bradford (Ed.), *Human forces in teaching and learning* (pp. 88-96). Washington, DC: National Training Laboratories, National Educational Association.

With J.S. Mouton. Comprehension of own and of outgroup positions under intergroup competition. *Journal of Conflict Resolution, 5*(3), 304-310.

With J.S. Mouton. Loyalty of representatives to ingroup positions during intergroup competition. *Sociometry, 24*(2), 177-183.

With J.S. Mouton. Perceived characteristics of elected representatives. *Journal of Abnormal and Social Psychology, 62*(3), 693-695.

With J.S. Mouton. Power, people, and performance reviews. *Advanced Management, 10*(4), 13-17.

With J.S. Mouton. Reactions to intergroup competition under win-lose conditions. *Management Science, 1*(4), 2-9.

With J.S. Mouton. Union-management relations: From conflict to collaboration. *Personnel, 38*(6), 38-51.

With J.S. Mouton. University training in human relations skills. *Group Psychotherapy, 14*(3 & 4), 140-153.

1962

Team management—A new approach. *YPO Enterprise* (April).

With J.S. Mouton. The instrumented training laboratory. In E. Wechsler & E. Schein (Eds.), *Issues of human relations training* (pp. 61-76). Washington, DC: National Training Laboratories, National Education Association.

With J.S. Mouton. The intergroup dynamics of win-lose conflict and problem-solving collaboration in union-management relations. In M. Sherif (Ed.), *Intergroup relations and leadership* (pp. 94-140). New York: Wiley.

With J.S. Mouton. Comprehension of points of commonality in competing solutions. *Sociometry, 25*(1), 56-63.

With J.S. Mouton. The developing revolution in management practices. *Journal of the American Society of Training Directors, 16*, 29-52.

With J.S. Mouton. Headquarters-field team training for organizational improvement. *Journal of the American Society of Training Directors, 16*(3), 3-11.

With J.S. Mouton. Intergroup therapy. *International Journal of Social Psychiatry, 8*(3), 196-198.

With J.S. Mouton. Overevaluation of own group's product in intergroup competition. *Journal of Abnormal and Social Psychology, 64*(3), 237-238.

With J.S. Mouton. The influence of competitively vested interests on judgments. *Journal of Conflict Resolution, 6*(2), 149-153.

With J.S. Mouton & A.C. Bidwell. The managerial grid. *Advanced Management-Office Executive, 1*(9), 12-15, 36.

With J.S. Mouton & M.G. Blansfield. How executive team training can help you. *Journal of the American Society of Training Directors, 16*(1), 3-11.

With J.S. Mouton & M.G. Blansfield. The logic of team training. In I. Wechsler & E. Schein (Eds.), *Issues in human relations training* (pp. 77-85). Washington, DC: National Training Laboratories, National Education Association.

With J.S. Mouton & B. Fruchter. A factor analysis of training group behavior. *Journal of Social Psychology, 58*, 121-130.

With H.A. Shepard. Changing behavior through cognitive change. *Human Organization, 21*, 88-96.

1963

With E.J. Hall & J.S. Mouton. Group problem solving effectiveness under conditions of pooling versus interaction. *Journal of Social Psychology, 59*, 147-157.

With J.S. Mouton. Loyalty of representatives to ingroup positions during intergroup competition. In W.E. Vinacke, W.R. Wilson, & G.M. Meredith (Eds.), *The character and scope of social psychology*. Chicago: Scott Foresman.

With J.S. Mouton. Improving organizational problem solving through increasing the flow and utilization of new ideas. *Training Directors Journal, 17*(9), 48-57.

With J.S. Mouton. Improving organizational problem solving through increasing the flow and utilization of new ideas. *Training Directors Journal,* *17*(10), 38-54.

With J.S. Mouton. Influence of partially vested interests on judgment. *Journal of Abnormal and Social Psychology, 66,* 276-278.

With E.W. Mumma, J.S. Mouton, & M.S. Williams. How does a manager manage? *Supervisory Management, 8*(6), 27-30.

1964

Studying group action. In L. Bradford, J. Gibb, & K. Benne (Eds.), *T-Group theory and laboratory method* (pp. 336-364). New York: Wiley.

With M.G. Blansfield & J.S. Mouton. The merger laboratory: A new strategy for bringing one corporation into another. *Training and Directors Journal, 18*(5), 2-10.

With J.S. Mouton. The managerial grid as a framework for inducing change in industrial organizations. In P. Worchel & D. Byrne (Eds.), *Personality change* (pp. 319-366). New York: Wiley.

With J.S. Mouton. *The managerial grid.* Houston, TX: Gulf Publishing Company.

With J.S. Mouton. Three strategies for exercising authority: One-alone, One-to-one, One-to-all. *Personnel Administration, 27*(40), 3-5, 18-21.

With J.S. Mouton, L.B. Barnes, & L.E. Greiner. Breakthrough in organization development. *Harvard Business Review, 42*(6), 133-155.

With H.A. Shepard, & J.S. Mouton. *Managing intergroup conflict in industry.* Houston, TX: Gulf Publishing Company.

1965

Managerial grid organization development. In *Proceedings: ANPA Thirty-Seventh Annual Rosecrest Institute in Production Management Conference* (pp. 1-3). Chicago: American Newspaper Publishers Association.

Managerial grid organization development: Applying the managerial grid. In *Proceedings, Annual Conference of Life Office Management Association* (pp. 12-21). Montreal: Life Office Management Association.

Managerial grid organization development: How to increase your ability to get more effective performance from people in your organization. In *Proceedings, General Management Division Conference of the Super Market Institute* (pp. 2-18). Chicago: Super Market Institute.

With L.G. Malouf & J.S. Mouton. A new look at the functions of managing people. *Personnel Administration, 28*(2), 28-32.

With J.S. Mouton. A 9,9 approach for increasing organization productivity. In E. H. Schein & W. G. Bennis (Eds.), *Personal and organizational change through group methods: The laboratory approach* (pp. 169-183). New York: Wiley.

With J.S. Mouton. Power, people, and performance review. In W.E. Schlender, W.G. Scott, & A.C. Filley (Eds.), *Management in perspective* (pp. 532-536). Boston, MA: Houghton-Mifflin.

With J.S. Mouton. Initiating organization development. *Training Directors Journal, 19*(10), 25-41.

With J.S. Mouton. International managerial grids. *Training Directors Journal, 19*(5), 8-23.

With J.S. Mouton. Managerial grid organization development. *Petroleum Management, 37*(12), 96-99.

With J.S. Mouton & R.L. Sloma. The union-management intergroup laboratory: Strategy for resolving intergroup conflict. *Journal of Applied Behavioral Science, 1*, 25-57.

1966

The managerial grid approach to integrating people and profit. In *Proceedings: NAWGA Annual Executive Conference* (pp. 29-34). New York: National American Wholesale Grocers' Association.

The managerial grid as a basis for organization development. In *Proceedings: Forty-Second Annual Meeting, American Society of Bakery Engineers* (pp. 40-46). Chicago: American Society of Bakery Engineers.

With W.E. Avis & J.S. Mouton. *Corporate Darwinism: An evolutionary perspective on organizing work in the dynamic corporation.* Houston, TX: Gulf Publishing Company.

With W.E. Avis & J.S. Mouton. Corporate Darwinism and the top man. *Personnel Administration, 29*(4), 6-12.

With J.S. Mouton. The grid way of managing. *Management Forum* (Volkswagen), *1*(2), 10-16.

With J.S. Mouton. Managerial facades. *Advanced Management Journal, 31*(3), 30-37.

With J.S. Mouton. The managerial grid—the pursuit of excellence. *The Management Review* (New Delhi, India), *6*(6), 20-23.

With J.S. Mouton. The rich grow richer. *Training and Development Journal, 20*(8), 2-5.

With J.S. Mouton. Some effects of managerial grid seminar training on union and management attitudes toward supervision. *Journal of Applied Behavioral Science, 2*(4), 387-400.

With J.S. Mouton. Using line instructors for organization development. *Training and Development Journal, 20*(3), 28-35.

With J.S. Mouton & E. Wallace. Use of the managerial grid to increase bank management effectiveness. *The Bankers Magazine, 194*(3), 9-14.

1967

With J.S. Mouton. Grid organization development. *Personnel Administration, 30*(1), 7-14.
With J.S. Mouton. The managerial grid in three dimensions. *Training and Development Journal, 21*(1), 2-5.
With J.S. Mouton. Organization excellence through effective management behavior. *Manage, 20*(2), 42-47.
With J.S. Mouton. There are clues to 'where' you are. *The Personnel Administrator, 12*(3), 28-35.
With J.S. Mouton. Training traps that tempt training directors. *Training and Development Journal, 21*(12), 2-8.

1968

With J. Chapiro. El desarrollo organizativo: Una nueva experiencia en la argentina. *Idea* (Buenos Aires), *20*, 1-10.
With J.S. Mouton. *Corporate excellence diagnosis.* Austin, TX: Scientific Methods, Inc.
With J.S. Mouton. *Corporate excellence through grid organization development.* Houston, TX: Gulf Publishing Company.
With J.S. Mouton. Managerial grid develops team action. *Industrial World, 182*(6), 21-23.
With J.S. Mouton. Work team development. *Training in Business and Industry, 5*(6), 33-35.
With J.S. Mouton, & E.D. Bryson. The military leadership grid. *Military Review, 48*(6), 3-18.
With J.S. Mouton & J.D. Hain. Social forces in petition signing. In P. G. Swingle (Ed.), *Experiments in social psychology* (pp. 44-49). New York: Academic Press.
With J.S. Mouton, R.L. Sloma, & B.P. Loftin. A second breakthrough in organization development. *California Management Review, 11*(1), 73-78.

1969

With J.S. Mouton. *Building a dynamic corporation through grid organization development.* Reading, MA: Addison-Wesley.
With J.S. Mouton. Military leadership in the post-seventies. In *Proceedings, Leadership in the Post Seventies* (pp. 63-78). West Point, NY: U. S. Army. U.S. Military Academy.

With J.S. Mouton. *Foundations of a science of organization development* (pp. 1-57). Austin, TX: Scientific Methods.

With J.S. Mouton. Use of the 'Rubric' for a corporate health checkup. *Training and Development Journal, 23*(6), 18-24.

With J.S. Mouton. Organization development in the free world. *Personnel Administration, 32*(4), 13-23.

With J.S. Mouton & A.C. Bidwell. The managerial grid. In W.B. Eddy, W.W. Burke, V.A. Dupre, & O. South (Eds.), *Behavioral science and the manager's role* (pp. 167-174). Washington, DC: National Training Laboratories.

With J.S. Mouton & E.D. Bryson. The military leadership grid. In J. H. Johns (Ed.), *Cadet guide* (pp. 4-30). New York: Office of Military Psychology and Leadership, United States Corps of Cadets.

With J.S. Mouton & R.L. Sloma. The union-management intergroup laboratory: Strategy for resolving intergroup conflict. In K. D. Benne, W. G. Bennis, & R. Chin (Eds.), *The planning of change* (2nd ed., pp. 176-191). New York: Holt, Rinehart, and Winston.

1970

With J.S. Mouton. *The grid for sales excellence: Benchmarks for effective salesmanship.* New York: McGraw-Hill.

With J.S. Mouton. The dilemma: Individual effectiveness or corporate excellence. In B.M. Bass, R.B. Cooper, & J.A. Haas (Eds.), *Managing for accomplishment* (pp. 152-166). Lexington, MA: D. C. Heath.

With J.S. Mouton. Issues in transnational development. In B.M. Bass, R.B. Cooper, & J.A. Haas (Eds.), *Managing for accomplishment* (pp. 208-224). Lexington, MA: D. C. Heath.

With J.S. Mouton. The fifth achievement. *Journal of Applied Behavioral Science, 6*(4), 413-426.

With J.S. Mouton. Grid models salesman's behavior. *Sales Meetings Magazine* (March), 52-53, 95-102.

With J.S. Mouton. 9,9 sales grid style produces results. *Training and Development Journal, 24*(10), 4-7.

With J.S. Mouton. OD—fad or fundamental? *Training and Development Journal, 24*(1), 9-17.

With J.S. Mouton. An overview of grid organization development. Austin, TX: Scientific Methods. pp. 1-74.

With J.S. Mouton. Sales grid: Foundation for a sound selling strategy. *Retail Overview, 3*(1), 51-60.

With J.S. Mouton, L.B. Barnes, & L.E. Greiner. Breakthrough in organization development. In G.W. Dalton, P.R. Lawrence, & L.E. Greiner (Eds.), *Organizational change and development* (pp. 281-314). Homewood, IL: Irwin-Dorsey.

With J.S. Mouton, L.B. Barnes, & L.E. Greiner. Breakthrough in organization development. In R. T. Golembiewski & A. Blumberg (Eds.), *Sensitivity training and the laboratory approach: Readings about concepts and applications* (pp. 390-413). Itasca, IL: E.E. Peacock.

With J.S. Mouton & E.D. Bryson. The military leadership grid. In *Artillery Journal* (pp. 52-68). New Delhi, India.

With J.S. Mouton & E.D. Bryson. The military leadership grid. In *Military Staff Notes* (pp. 1101-1200). Toronto: Canadian Forces Staff School.

With J.S. Mouton & B.M. McCann. International research on managerial behavior: Understanding and application of behavioral science concepts and value preferences by managers in 4 English-speaking cultures. *Interpersonal Development* (Basel, Switzerland), *1*(1), 48-53.

1971

The managerial grid approach. Organizational development: The state of the art. *Proceedings of the Western Organizational Development Conference* (April) pp. 5-23.

With J.S. Mouton. A behavioral science design for the development of society. *The Journal of Applied Behavioral Science, 7*(2), 146-163.

With J.S. Mouton. Complementarity of grid organization development and grid family development (pp. 1-58). Austin, TX: Scientific Methods.

With J.S. Mouton. *The marriage grid.* New York: McGraw-Hill.

With J.S. Mouton. Grid OD: A systems approach to corporate excellence. In H. A. Hornstein, B. B. Bunker, W. W. Burke, M. Gindes, & R. Lewicki (Eds.), *Social intervention: A behavioral science analysis* (pp. 401-420). Glencoe, IL: Free Press.

With J.S. Mouton. Comprehension of own and of outgroup positions under intergroup competition. In B. L. Hinton & H. J. Reitz (Eds.), *Groups and organizations: Integrated readings in the analysis of social behavior* (p. 373). Bloomington, IN: Indiana University Press.

With J.S. Mouton. Grid OD: A systems approach to corporate excellence. In D. A. Kolb, I. M. Rubin, & J. M. McIntyre (Eds.), *Introductory organizational psychology.* Englewood Cliffs, NJ: Prentice-Hall.

With J.S. Mouton. Loyalty of representatives to intergroup positions during intergroup conflict. In B.L. Hinton & H. J. Reitz (Eds.), *Groups and organizations: Integrated readings in the analysis of social behavior* (pp. 377-378). Bloomington, IN: Indiana University.

With J.S. Mouton. Overevaluation of own group's product in intergroup competition. In R.E. Overstreet, R.J. Burke, R.C. Joyner, V.V. Murray, W.H. Read, K.W.J.R. Funstall, & H.T. Wilson (Eds.), *Behavioral Problems and Issues in Organizations, Administration, 542, Selected Readings* (pp. 3465-1; 3465-2). New York: Simon and Schuster.

With J.S. Mouton. Overevaluation of own group's product in intergroup competition. In K. N. Wexley & G.A. Kukl (Eds.), *Readings in organizational and industrial psychology* (pp. 274-276). New York: Oxford University Press.

With J.S. Mouton. People—The wellsprings of corporate energy. In W. R. Lassey (Ed.), *Leadership and social change* (pp. 162-168). Iowa City, IA: University Associates Press.

With J.S. Mouton. Reactions to intergroup competition under win-lose conditions. In D. A. Kolb, I. M. Rubin, & J. M. McIntyre (Eds.), *Introductory organizational psychology*. Englewood Cliffs, NJ: Prentice-Hall.

With J.S. Mouton. Some effects of managerial grid seminar training on union and management attitudes toward supervision. In H.A. Hornstein, B.B. Bunker, W.W. Burke, M. Gindes, & R. Lewicki (Eds.), *Social intervention: A behavioral science analysis* (pp. 114-121). Glencoe, IL: Free Press.

With J.S. Mouton & E.D. Bryson. The military leadership grid. In D.E. Johnson (Ed.), *Concepts of air force leadership* (pp. 535-546). Maxwell Air Force Base, AL: U. S. Air Force.

With J.S. Mouton & E.D. Bryson. The military leadership grid. Leadership in the Air Force. Squadron Officer School. Air University, Maxwell Air Force Base, AL. July, pp. 5-39 to 5-48.

With J.S. Mouton & E.D. Bryson. The military leadership grid. *Naval Officer Training Center Educational Textbook*. Newport, RI: November.

With J.S. Mouton & E.D. Bryson. *The Military Leadership Grid. Readings in Management*. Fort Lee, VA: U. S. Army Logistics Management Center.

With J.S. Mouton & E.D. Bryson. *The Military Leadership Grid. Readings in Leadership*. Annapolis, MD: U. S. Marine Corps.

1972

With J.S. Mouton. *How to assess the strengths and weaknesses of a business enterprise: Vol. 1. Operations*. Austin, TX: Scientific Methods, Inc.

With J.S. Mouton. *How to assess the strengths and weaknesses of a business enterprise: Vol. 2: Marketing and sales*. Austin, TX: Scientific Methods, Inc.

With J.S. Mouton. *How to assess the strengths and weaknesses of a business enterprise: Vol. 3: Research and development*. Austin, TX: Scientific Methods, Inc.

With J.S. Mouton. *How to assess the strengths and weaknesses of a business enterprise: Vol. 4: Personnel management*. Austin, TX: Scientific Methods, Inc.

With J.S. Mouton. *How to assess the strengths and weaknesses of a business enterprise: Vol. 5: Financial management.* Austin, TX: Scientific Methods, Inc.

With J.S. Mouton. *How to assess the strengths and weaknesses of a business enterprise: Vol. 6: Corporate leadership.* Austin, TX: Scientific Methods, Inc.

With J.S. Mouton. Is the T-group consultant approach a method of organization development? In W. Dyer (Ed.), *Modern theory and method in group training* (pp. 197-220). New York: Van Nostrand Reinhold.

With J.S. Mouton. Organization and family viewed as open and interacting system in grid development. In W. W. Burke (Ed.), *Contemporary organization development: Conceptual orientations and interventions* (pp. 127-146). Washington, DC: NTL Institute for Applied Behavioral Science.

With J.S. Mouton. Organization excellence through effective management behavior. In D.R. Hampton (Ed.), *Behavioral concepts in management* (rev. ed., pp. 164-168). Encino, CA: Dickenson.

With J.S. Mouton. The American future (pp. 1-29). Austin, TX: Scientific Methods.

With J.S. Mouton. Behavioral science theories underlying organization development. *Journal of Contemporary Business, 1*(3), 9-22.

With J.S. Mouton. The D/D matrix (pp. 1-27). Austin, TX: Scientific Methods.

With J.S. Mouton. What is instrumented learning? (Part 1). *Industrial Training International, 7*(4), 113-116.

With J.S. Mouton. What is instrumented learning? (Part 2). *Industrial Training International, 7*(5), 149-151.

With J.S. Mouton. What is instrumented learning? *Training and Development Journal, 26*(1), 12-20.

With J.S. Mouton. What's your marriage I.Q.? *Family Circle, 80*(6), 76-78, 108.

With J.S. Mouton, L.B. Barnes, & L.E. Greiner. Breakthrough in organization development. In N. Margulies & A.P. Raia (Eds.), *Organizational development: Its theory and practice* (pp. 556-591). New York: McGraw-Hill.

With J.S. Mouton & M.G. Blansfield. How executive team training can help you. In N. Margulies & A. P. Raia (Eds.), *Organizational development: Its theory and practice* (pp. 363-372). New York: McGraw-Hill.

With J.S. Mouton & E.D. Bryson. The military leadership grid. In *Management news.* Hornell Heights, Ontario, Canada: Headquarters Air Defence Command.

With J.S. Mouton & R.L. Sloma. The union-management intergroup laboratory: Strategy for resolving intergroup conflict. In H. Hornstein & W. W. Burke (Eds.), *The social technology of organization development* (pp. 101-126). Washington, DC: NTL Learning Resources Corporation.

With J.S. Mouton, R.L. Sloma, & B.P. Loftin. A second breakthrough in organization development. In N. Margulies & A.P. Raia (Eds.), *Organizational development: Its theory and practice* (pp. 556-591). New York: McGraw-Hill.

1973

With M. Lefkowitz & J.S. Mouton. Status factors in pedestrian violation of traffic signals. In E. Aronson (Ed.), *Readings for the social animal* (pp. 13-18). San Francisco: W. H. Freeman.

With M. Lefkowitz & J.S. Mouton. In P.G. Swingle (Ed.), *Social psychology in natural settings: A reader in field experimentation* (pp. 48-52). Chicago: Aldine.

With J.S. Mouton. Interventions, strategies and styles for the OD-oriented manager. In T. H. Patten (Ed.), *OD-Emerging dimensions and concepts* (pp. 55-56). Houston, TX: American Society for Training and Development.

With J.S. Mouton. The fifth achievement. In F.E. Jandt (Ed.), *Conflict resolution through communication* (pp. 88-102). New York: Harper and Row.

With J.S. Mouton. The American future and the training and development profession. *Training and Development Journal, 27*(3), 3-12.

With J.S. Mouton. The D/D matrix. *Development Digest*, (Cassette).

With J.S. Mouton. Ist ihr unternehmen erstklassig? *Plus*, (February), pp. 21-24.

With J.S. Mouton. Organization development (OD) in a twenty-year perspective. *European Training, 2*(1), 4-7.

1974

With J.S. Mouton. The D/D matrix. In J.D. Adams (Ed.) *Theory and method in organization development: An evolutionary process* (pp. 1-36). Arlington, VA: NTL Institute for Applied Behavioral Science.

With J.S. Mouton. Designing change for educational institutions through the D/D matrix. *Education and Urban Society, 6*(2), 179-204.

With J.S. Mouton. Dilemma & decision. *International Management* (September), pp. 11-12.

1975

With J.S. Mouton. *The grid for supervisory effectiveness*. Austin, TX: Scientific Methods, Inc.
With J.S. Mouton. *Instrumented team learning: A behavioral approach to student-centered learning*. Austin, TX: Scientific Methods, Inc.
With J.S. Mouton. Group and organizational team building: A theoretical model for intervening. In C.L. Cooper (Ed.), *Theories of group processes* (pp. 103-129). Chichester, Sussex: John Wiley.
With J.S. Mouton. Managerial grid in practice. In B. Taylor & G. L. Lippitt (Eds.), *Management development and training handbook* (pp. 385-398). Maidenhead, England: McGraw-Hill.
With J.S. Mouton. An overview of the grid. *Training and Development Journal, 29*(5), 29-37.
With J.S. Mouton. Sommige verkopers hunkeren naar Bijval. *Tijdschrift voor effectief directiebelied, 5*, 119-124.

1976

With J.S. Mouton. *Consultation*. Reading, MA: Addison-Wesley.
With J.S. Mouton. *Diary of an OD man*. Houston, TX: Gulf Publishing Company.
With J.S. Mouton. Critiqube. *Training and Development Journal*, pp. 3-8.
With J.S. Mouton. Instrumented team learning. *Industrial Training International, 1*(2), 52-55.

1977

With J.S. Mouton. A comparison of spread and change strategies in two applied behavioral science movements. *Group & Organization Studies, 2*(1), 25-32.
With J.S. Mouton. Critica. Desenvolvimento de Executivos, 014, January 1977, pp. 5-22.

1978

With J.S. Mouton. *Making experience work: The grid approach to critique*. New York: McGraw-Hill.
With J.S. Mouton. *The new managerial grid* (2nd ed.). Houston, TX: Gulf Publishing Company.
With J.S. Mouton. Desenvoliemento de grupos e de equipes organizacionais Um modelo de intervencoes.
With J.S. Mouton. Interview. *Group & Organization Studies, 3*(4), 401-426.

With J.S. Mouton. Should you teach there's only one best way to manage? *Training* (April), pp. 24-25, 28-29.

With J.S. Mouton. Toward a general theory of consultation. *The Personnel and Guidance Journal, 56*(6), 328-330.

With J.S. Mouton. What's new with the grid? *Training and Development Journal, 32*(5), pp. 3-8.

1979

With J.S. Mouton. *The new grid for supervisory effectiveness* (2nd ed.). Austin, TX: Scientific Methods, Inc.

With J.S. Mouton. Intergroup problem solving in organizations: From theory to practice. In W. G. Austin and S. Worchel (Eds.) *The social psychology of intergroup relations* (pp. 19-32). Monterey, CA: Brooks/Cole.

With J.S. Mouton. Getting organization development moving again. *Managing Change: Keeping It Going: Building Blocks*, pp. 6-9.

With J.S. Mouton. Motivating human productivity in the People's Republic of China. *Group & Organization Studies, 4*(2), 159-169.

With J.S. Mouton. Why the OD movement is "stuck" and how to break it loose. *Training and Development Journal* (3 parts).

With J.S. Mouton, L. Tomaino, & S. Gutierrez. *The social worker grid.* Springfield, IL: Charles C. Thomas.

1980

With J.S. Mouton. *Grid approaches to managing stress.* Springfield, IL: Charles C. Thomas.

With J.S. Mouton. *The grid for sales excellence* (2nd ed.). New York: McGraw-Hill.

With J.S. Mouton. *The versatile manager: A grid profile.* Homewood, IL: Dow Jones-Irwin.

With J.S. Mouton. The board grid: An interview with Blake and Mouton. *Directors & Boards, 5*(2), 19-26.

With J.S. Mouton. HRD controversy: A la Blake and Mouton. *Training and Development Journal, 34*(5), 106-108.

With J.S. Mouton & D.E. Bryson. The military leadership grid. *Military Review, 60*(7), 13-26.

With J.S. Mouton, J. May, & W. May. *The real estate sales grid: Dealing effectively with the human side of selling real estate.* Englewood Cliffs, NJ: Prentice-Hall.

With J.S. Mouton, J. May, & W. May. The real estate sales grid. *Real Estate Today, 13*(7), 5-12.

With J.S. Mouton M.E. Shaw, & R.J. Corsini. *Role playing: A practical manual for group facilitators.* San Diego, CA: University Associates, Inc.

With J.S. Mouton, & W.R. Taggart. Grid management—How do you measure yourself? *Data Management* (August), 8-11.

1981

The grid. *The Berea Alumnus* (March-April), pp. 5-7.

With J.S. Mouton. *Productivity: The human side.* New York: AMACOM

With J.S. Mouton & M. Tapper. *Grid approaches for managerial leadership in nursing.* St. Louis, MO: C. V. Mosby.

With J.S. Mouton & M.S. Williams. *The academic administrator grid.* San Francisco, CA: Jossey-Bass.

With J.S. Mouton. *Synergogy: An instrumented team learning approach* (2nd ed.). Austin, TX: Scientific Methods, Inc.

With J.S. Mouton. *Desenvolvimento Organizacional: Equivicos, Fracassos e a Estrategia GRID.* INCISA, 1981.

With J.S. Mouton. Deeper truths about effective leadership. *BNAC Communicator, 2*(1), 1, 2, 4, 8.

With J.S. Mouton. The exercise of effective leadership. *Journal of Experiential Learning & Simulation, 3*(1), 13-16.

With J.S. Mouton. Increasing productivity through behavioral science. *Personnel, 58*(3), 59-67.

With J.S. Mouton. Management by grid principles or situationalism: Which? *Group & Organization Studies, 6*(4), 439-455.

With J.S. Mouton & D.E. Bryson. The military leadership grid. *An Cosantoir, 41*(9), 266-274.

1982

With J.S. Mouton. Catching up with multiple-solution realities. *Journal of Applied Behavioral Science, 18*(4), 473-476.

With J.S. Mouton. Comments on "A note on theory and research for developing a science of leadership." *Journal of Applied Behavioral Science, 18*(4), 539-541.

With J.S. Mouton. A comparative analysis of situationalism and the 9,9 approach of management by principle. *Organizational Dynamics, 10*(4), 20-43.

With J.S. Mouton. The grid concept of effective management. *Pakistan Management Review, 23*(4), 47-52.

With J.S. Mouton. Grid principles vs. situationalism: A final note. *Group & Organization Studies, 7*(2), 211-215.

With J.S. Mouton. How to choose a leadership style. *Training and Development Journal, 36*(2), 38-47.

With J.S. Mouton. Needless mistakes in consultation. *Academy of Management OD Newsletter* (Winter), pp. 2,5.
With J.S. Mouton. Sacred cows and silent structures. *Wharton Magazine, 6*(3), 9-10.
With J.S. Mouton. Theory and research for developing a science of leadership. *Journal of Applied Behavioral Science, 18*(3), 275-291.
With J.S. Mouton & Command/Leadership/Resource Management Steering Working Group [United Airlines]. *Grid cockpit resource management.* Austin, TX: Scientific Methods, Inc.
With J.S. Mouton & M.A. Ghani. The situationalism vs. one best style: A brief study of two controversial styles of managerial leadership in Pakistan and the U.S.A. *Pakistan Management Review, 23*(2&3), 70-91.

1983

With J.S. Mouton. *Consultation: A handbook for individual and organization effectiveness* (2nd ed.). Reading, MA: Addison-Wesley.
With J.S. Mouton. The conflict grid. In H.H. Blumberg, A.P. Hare, V. Kent, and M.F. Davies (Eds.), *Small groups and social interaction* (Vol. 2, pp. 101-104). Chichester, England: John Wiley.
With J.S. Mouton. The conflict grid update. In D.W. Cole (Ed.), *Conflict resolution technology* (pp. 116-119). Cleveland, OH: The Organization Development Institute.
With J.S. Mouton. Lateral conflict. In D. Tjosvold & D.W. Johnson (Eds.) *Productive conflict management: Perspectives for organizations* (pp. 82-134). New York: Irvington Publishers.
With J.S. Mouton. The new managerial grid in action. In B. Taylor and G. Lippitt (Eds.), *Management development and training handbook* (2nd ed., pp. 449-470). London: McGraw-Hill.
With J.S. Mouton. Developing a positive union-management relationship. *Personnel Administrator, 28*(6), 23-32, 140.
With J.S. Mouton. Effective crisis management. *The American Media Eagle, 6*, 14, 16.
With J.S. Mouton. Foundations for strengthening leadership. *General Semantics Bulletin, 50*, 93-139.
With J.S. Mouton. Improve the work flow between departments (Part 1). *Hydrocarbon Processing, 62*(10), 135-153.
With J.S. Mouton. Improve the work flow between departments (Part 2). *Hydrocarbon Processing, 62*(11), 227-260.
With J.S. Mouton. In search of transcultural OD. *Academy of Management OD Newsletter*, Summer 1983, pp. 3, 5.

With J.S. Mouton. Out of the past: How to use your organization's history to shape a better future. *Training and Development Journal, 37*(11), 58-65.

With J.S. Mouton. Participative management—It's not just a matter of routine. *BNAC Communicator* (Fall), pp. 8-9.

With J.S. Mouton. The urge to merge: Tying the knot successfully. *Training and Development Journal, 37*(1), 41-46.

With J.S. Mouton. Will the real theory Z please step forward? *Training, 20*(3), 26-27.

With J.S. Mouton & A. Stockton. *The secretary grid.* New York: AMACOM.

1984

With J.S. Mouton. *Solving costly organizational conflicts: achieving intergroup trust, cooperation, and teamwork.* San Francisco, CA: Jossey-Bass.

With J.S. Mouton. *Synergogy: A new strategy for education, training, and development* (3rd ed.). San Francisco, CA: Jossey-Bass.

With J.S. Mouton. Dos and don'ts of delegation. *GTD Manager* (December).

With J.S. Mouton. The grid: A standard for supervision. *Practical Supervision, 10*, 1, 3, 4.

With J.S. Mouton. Overcoming group warfare. *Harvard Business Review, 62*(6), 98-108.

With J.S. Mouton. Lots of theory: Not so much practice. *Financial Times* (January 30).

With J.S. Mouton. Principles and designs for enhancing learning. *Training and Development Journal, 38*(12), 60-63.

With J.S. Mouton. Surviving crises through participative management. *International Management, 39*(2), 9-10.

With J.S. Mouton. What's the focal issue? *Academy of Management OD Newsletter* (Winter), pp. 8-9.

With J.S. Mouton. The science of conflict management. *Administrative Radiology, 3*(6), 30-32.

With J.S. Mouton & A. Stockton. For secretaries only: Do you handle your position with style? *Real Estate Today, 17*(5), 17-18.

With J.S. Mouton & A. Stockton. What do you say after you say good morning? *The Secretary, 44*(2), 21-23.

With J.S. Mouton & A. Stockton. What do you say after you say good morning? *Journal of the Institute of Qualified Private Secretaries, 27,* 27-29.

With J.S. Mouton & I. Ueno. The productivity battle: A behavioral science analysis of Japan and the United States. *Journal of Applied Behavioral Science, 20*(1), 49-56.

1985

With J.S. Mouton. *The managerial grid III: The key to leadership excellence* (3rd ed.). Houston, TX: Gulf Publishing Company.

With J.S. Mouton. Establishing acceptable norms. In D.L. Kirkpatrick (Ed.), *How to manage change effectively* (pp. 40-44). San Francisco, CA: Jossey-Bass.

With J.S. Mouton. Getting more productivity from the last hour of work. In D.L. Kirkpatrick (Ed.), *How to manage change effectively* (pp. 217-223). San Francisco, CA: Jossey-Bass.

With J.S. Mouton. Organization development strategies for effective management of cockpit crises. In D.D. Warrick (Ed.) *Contemporary organization development: Current thinking and applications* (pp. 281-288). Glenview, IL: Scott, Foresman.

With J.S. Mouton. Don't let group norms stifle creativity. *Personnel, 62*(8), 28-33.

With J.S. Mouton. Effective crisis management. *New Management, 3*(1), 14-17.

With J.S. Mouton. How to achieve integration on the human side of the merger. *Organizational Dynamics, 13*(3), 41-56.

With J.S. Mouton. Presidential (grid) styles. *Training and Development Journal, 39*(3), 30-34.

With J.S. Mouton. The upcoming revolution in education & training (with a critique by Lana Au). *Performance, 2*(1), 6-10.

1986

With J.S. Mouton. *Executive achievement: Making it at the top.* New York: McGraw-Hill.

With J.S. Mouton. High-tech management: Back to the future? *SAM Advanced Management Journal, 51*(2), 4-8.

With J.S. Mouton. A rejoinder to "Comments on 'The productivity battle: A behavioral science analysis of Japan and the United States.'" *The Journal of Applied Behavioral Science, 22*(4), 507-508.

With J.S. Mouton. Vorteile und fallstricke der konflikt-moderation. *Congress & Seminar*, pp. 16-20.

With J.S. Mouton. From theory to practice in interface problem solving. In S. Worchel and W.G. Austin (Eds.), *Psychology of intergroup relations* (2nd ed., pp. 67-82). Chicago: Nelson-Hall.

With J.S. Mouton. Theory and research for developing a science of leadership. In T. Heller, J. Van Til, & L.A. Zurcher (Eds.), *Leaders and followers: Challenges for the future* (pp. 157-175). Greenwich, CT: JAI Press Inc.

1987

With J.S. Mouton. *GridWorks: An approach that increases employee participation and promotes esprit de corps.* Austin, TX: Scientific Methods, Inc.

With J.S. Mouton. Notings. *Indian Journal of Training and Development* (Bombay, India), *XVII*, (6), 46-48. (Interview conducted by Editor of IJTD.)

With J.S. Mouton. Organization interventions for productivity and transformation. *AMBIT: The Professional Management Magazine* (Bombay, India), *XVI*(10), 9-16.

With J.S. Mouton. Organization interventions for productivity and transformation. *Management Information Bulletin* (Bombay, India), *IX*, (1&2), 24-31.

With J.S. Mouton. Same problem—1,000 feet below or 35,000 feet above? *The Submarine Review*, 38-43.

With J.S. Mouton. Organization interventions for productivity and transformation. In *Proceedings, International Training & Development Conference*, (pp. 5-17).

With J.S. Mouton. Verhaltensgitter der Fuhrung (Managerial Grid). In A. Kieser, G. Reber, and R. Wunderer (Eds.), *Handworterbuch Der Fuhrung* (Enzyklopadie der Betriebswirtschaftslehre) (pp. 2015-2028). Stuttgart: C.E. Poeschel Verlag.

With J.S. Mouton & R.L. Allen. *Spectacular teamwork: How to develop the leadership skills for team success.* New York: Wiley.

1988

Organization development. In G. Dixon (Ed.), *What works at work: Lessons from the masters* (pp. 266-277). Minneapolis, MN: Lakewood Books.

Organisation transformation: Survival of the fittest corporations. In *Proceedings, 5th World Congress on Management Development* (pp. 4.1-4.10).

With J.S. Mouton. Besseres management fur den technischen Wandel. *io Management Zeitschrift, 57*(10), 452-455.

With J.S. Mouton. Follow-up with unique insights on program evaluation. *Group & Organization Studies, 13*(1), 33-35.

With J.S. Mouton. Comparing strategies for incremental and transformational change. In R.H. Kilmann, T.J. Covin, & Associates (Eds.), *Corporate transformation: Revitalizing organizations for a competitive world* (pp. 251-281). San Francisco, CA: Jossey-Bass.

With J.S. Mouton. The developing revolution in management practices. In J. Hall (Ed.), *Models for management: The structure of competence* (pp. 422-444). The Woodlands, TX: Woodstead Press.

With J.S. Mouton. How power affects employee appraisal. In J. Hall (Ed.), *Models for management: The structure of competence* (pp. 277-284). The Woodlands, TX: Woodstead Press.

With J.S. Mouton. How power affects human behavior. In J. Hall (Ed.), *Models for management: The structure of competence* (pp. 113-120). The Woodlands, TX: Woodstead Press.

With J.S. Mouton. Power styles within an organization. In J. Hall (Ed.) *Models for management: The structure of competence* (pp. 121-130). The Woodlands, TX: Woodstead Press.

1989

With D.A. Carroll. Ethical reasoning in business. *Training & Development Journal, 43*(6), 99-104.

With A.A. McCanse. The rediscovery of sociometry. *Journal of Psychotherapy, Psychodrama, & Sociometry, 42*(3), 148-165.

With J.S. Mouton. Lateral conflict. In D. Tjosvold and D.W. Johnson (Eds.), *Productive conflict management: Perspectives for organizations* (pp. 91-149). Edina, MN: Interaction Book Company.

With J.S. Mouton & A.A. McCanse. *Change by design.* Reading, MA: Addison-Wesley.

1990

With A.A. McCanse & P. McDonald. Intercultural comparisons of managerial effectiveness of Soviet with American executives. *OD Practitioner, 22*(4), 8-10.

With J.S. Mouton & Command/Leadership/Resource Management Working Group [United Airlines]. *Grid cockpit resource management* (2nd ed.). Austin, TX: Scientific Methods, Inc.

With S.E. Prather & J.S. Mouton. *Medical risk management.* Oradell, NJ: Medical Economics Books.

1991

With A.A. McCanse. *Leadership dilemmas–Grid solutions.* Houston, TX: Gulf Publishing Company.

In Preparation

With A.A. McCanse. *Organization diagnosis.*

With A.A. McCanse, J.J. Griffith, & K. Nascimento. *The Natural Resources Grid.*

With J.S. Mouton, A.A. McCanse, W. Avis, & B.M. Sack. *Survival of the fittest.*

Green Lights All the Way

ELWOOD SPENCER BUFFA

I spelled out my middle name to introduce the combination of my ethnic backgrounds. I daresay that my name is unique—there is no other person on earth with that name. My father was an Italian (Sicilian) immigrant, and my mother of English/German stock. Buffa means "funny" in Italian. Opera Buffa is comic opera, and a related word we know is Buffoon. No one ever charged me with being funny, though neither am I humorless. Spencer is my mother's maiden name, which is of English origin. I look like a Spencer, and when people have asked the ethnic origin of the name "Buffa," I have frequently had the response, "Oh, you don't *look* Italian." I have often wondered what that response really meant.

The Spencers were the "dispensators" of the realm in merry old England. They kept and dispensed the stores of materiel that were important in running a country, and particularly an army. I do not think that my interest in inventory systems stems from this medieval root of my name. My maternal grandmother's maiden name was Ruef, of German ancestry, migrating from Wirtenburg, Germany. Submerged in the German line is the French Huguenot name Phillippi—the Phillippis fled France and became thoroughly Germanized.

The given name "Elwood" results from a conflict between my mother and father about naming traditions. When my brother Frank was born my father stated that he must be named for his paternal grandfather, the Italian custom. The name, Francesco, was too foreign sounding for mother, so it was finally agreed that grandfather would be satisfied with the Anglicized version, Frank. With my birth on April 12, 1923 the Italian custom would have named me for my mother's father, Charles Warren Spencer. Charlie Spencer was an alcoholic, and mother would have none of it. She told me that she demanded the right to name me since my father had named the first born. Dad learned something about the independent spirit of American wives with this encounter. A relative whom she admired was a dentist named Elwood Hay and that name and her maiden name Spencer were the stamp she put on me. Elwood is an uncommon name; I have personally met only two other persons with that name. With the combination of three uncommon names, I am quite certain that no one else is blessed with the name, Elwood Spencer Buffa. The name has served me well. I am not confused with others.

As a youth my friends called me "Boof." The name Elwood drew some flak and I thought of changing it. At the lunch table one day I said, "I think I'll change my name to Spencer." The thought of being called Spence seemed inviting. Dad's deep brown eyes flashed in anger and he said, "If the name Buffa isn't good enough for you, you can get out now!" After I explained, his temper cooled. But that incident made me think about how families and family names are very important to Sicilians, and how affronted he felt at the seeming rejection.

Mother and dad met during World War I in Omaha, Nebraska where mother was born. Dad was in the army at Fort Omaha in the Balloon Corps, and they married immediately following the armistice. They moved a time or two and settled in Beloit, Wisconsin, where I was born. They chose Beloit because many of Dad's friends, relatives, and acquaintances from the village of Petrosino in Sicily had migrated there, attracted by economic opportunity offered by Fairbanks Morse & Co., the town's largest employer. Dad had few skills and only a third-grade education, so he became a factory worker at Fairbanks Morse to support his family. He was a core maker, paid by piecework rates. Dad's major asset was an outgoing personality and a great deal of personal drive, so he "moonlighted," selling insurance amongst his Sicilian friends during evenings and week ends.

The "mixed marriage" carried with it some benefits. Mother refused to live in the Sicilian ghetto, demanding a decent neighborhood where the average Beloiter lived. A result was that Dad learned to speak, read, and write English somewhat better than his friends in the ghetto; he did this by attending night school and having to speak English somewhat more than his friends. More important for me and my brother, however, was the fact that mother maintained a home with an American cultural heritage. English was spoken at home, but we had a window into the Sicilian culture. Because of the home setting we were Americanized, and we may have saved almost an entire generation in the American cultural absorption process. We still may have had some handicaps, but nothing approaching the constraints on the boys and girls we knew in the Sicilian ghetto. The disadvantage of being raised as we were was that we never learned to speak Italian at home, a fact that I have always regretted. Still, my ear became tuned to hearing the accents when dad's friends came to the house and when we attended some of the gay social events sponsored by the Italian American Club. When in 1958 I took my family to Italy for nearly a year the language and culture seemed somehow already familiar.

THE EARLY YEARS

Everything about my primary education seemed normal to me. The depression hit and Fairbanks Morse was an early casualty, being a manufacturer of heavy diesel engines. Dad was laid off and few among his clientele were able to buy insurance. In 1932 the family migrated back to Omaha where dad had found work.

It was there in Omaha that I had the first impression that I might have some academic potential, though I did not take it seriously. I was in the eighth grade and I now interpret the event as being the result of an enrollment bulge in the eighth grade. They needed to get rid of some students and the solution was to move a number into the high school system, where there was enough capacity. Examinations were given to all eighth graders and the lucky ones were double promoted to begin high school a year early.

Throughout the 1932-1937 period it was the depression that dominated our lives. Keeping a job was a big problem, and dad lost several in the process. The need to scrimp and the value of security were stamped into me with the force of a drop hammer. I cannot recall anything about my early years that made a bigger impression on me and shaped my values than the depression. I was a child of the depression and I was at least forty years old before I freed myself from the depression thought mold. I recall that once when dad was out of work again and spending a good deal of time sitting around the house, he acceded to my suggestion that we play checkers. We played several games which I won easily. Dad was nervous and uncertain. There was unusual tremor in his hands as he reached out to make moves. He could not concentrate and I understood why. So I let him win a few games. I guess I hoped that it would make him feel better and help him renew self confidence, which was certainly in short supply at the time. I had a paper route that earned $6.50 per week, and my brother also had a part-time job. When dad was out of work, we turned over our meager earnings for family support.

By 1937 the depression was slackening, Fairbanks Morse & Co. called back many of its former employees. Mother and dad decided to move back to Beloit after a five-year hiatus in Omaha. The last three years of high school were in Beloit. The highlights in school were Miss Thompson, a brilliant math teacher who got the best out of me, and Miss Owens, my senior English teacher. I thought that English was a bore until she introduced me to Othello and taught me the rudiments of writing essays. Little did I realize then that so much of my professional existence would depend on writing. Meanwhile I was learning a little about the world of work. I ushered in the local theaters in the evenings and weekends, and during the summers picked potatoes at some small piece rate beside Mexican migrant workers, and "tasseled" hybrid corn for $1.00 per day. I could never keep up with the migrant workers, and these summer jobs taught me respect for physical work that I have never forgotten.

Completion of high school was uneventful and undistinguished. Most of my friends were planning to go to the University of Wisconsin. Mr. Barens, the senior advisor suggested that higher education was an option, but certainly did not push the idea. I think that it was my peer group that was the most important force in shaping my desire to go to the university. When it came time to implement this plan, however, dad simply did not have the funds to send me the university. I remember so clearly that his response to my stated desire was, "That's fine, but how are you going to do it?" We decided that I would have to stay out a year to earn the necessary funds. Dad lined me up to talk with Mr. Burt McKenna, Superintendent of the Stores Department at Fairbanks Morse. Mr. McKenna was a crusty old guy with a soft interior; the latter fact made it possible for me to work summers and even Christmas vacations later. A job was offered at 40 cents per hour (minimum wage) to load and unload trucks, fill requisitions, fill bins with material, and so forth. I was a hard worker, perhaps being motivated by the university carrot. One day I was shovelling steel nuts into the appropriate bin, working so hard at it that one might have thought I was killing snakes. It made a great racket as I shoveled. I had striped to the waist and was sweating profusely because it was a hot summer day. Behind me someone said, "Elwood, don't overdo, it's a hot day." It was Burt McKenna, the boss, with a visitor whom he was showing around. A few days later Burt came to me to talk. I took off my gloves which he then took from me. "You won't need these, I have a new job for you." The job was in the office, maintaining inventory records, running errands, and generally doing whatever the boss wanted done. It was a break, for it was after that change in jobs that Burt told me that I had a job waiting for me during all vacation periods after I went to the university. Those extra funds were very important in continuing my education.

The new job required me to get around the huge machine shop. I was fascinated by what I saw. Metal was being cut! I had never thought about such a startling process. I saw huge marine diesels, six-feet high and ten-feet long, being assembled. I got to the engineering department and talked with the designers. Then there was the pump assembly line, where everything worked like clock work. That exposure sealed my decision about my university major—it had to be mechanical engineering.

As I neared the end of the year of work, it still did not seem clear that I could swing the costs. I had been unable to save as much as I had expected. Having pocket money for the first time was in part an infection. I had bought a secondhand car, and spent too much time and money at the resorts of Lake Geneva and Lake Delevan. The funds remaining in my bank account would not cover first-year costs. Dad finally threatened to charge me rent if I continued to squander my money. It was near this time that one of those chance events intervened to make the difference.

A friend, who was a violin student of the local high school music teacher, and I went to the home of the teacher, Frank Salerno. While my friend was engaged with the teacher, I talked with Mrs. Salerno. The topic soon centered on my frustrated desire to attend the university, except for the lack of support funds. She suggested that I work my way through. "Sure, but how do you do that." That naivete came from the fact that there was no one in my family with university experience to guide me to alternatives to accomplish that goal. She said, "Why not be a houseboy in a sorority. You would do odd jobs for your room and wait table for your meals." In 1940 room and board expenses constituted the major expenses of attending a state university. I did not know what a houseboy was, let alone a sorority. She suggested that I contact Mrs. Winnie, the housemother of the Alpha Phi sorority in Madison, Wisconsin. I got the job as houseboy and waiter. I credit Mrs. Salerno for making a very important difference in my life. The job ensured my attendance at the university. But in addition, I met my wife, Betty, at the sorority. We fell in love and have never fallen out again in forty-five years as of this writing. In April 1990 I looked up Mrs. Salerno through the Alpha Phi *Directory* and thanked her again for making a difference in my life.

THE UNIVERSITY OF WISCONSIN

I was not really looking for a wife at the sorority, but being houseboy and waiter provided an information base on thirty young women. Some were very nice but distant. Some looked down on the likes of me. Some came to breakfast looking like pigs, with uncombed hair and a pasty visage of face cream. Some had pleasant personalities, and some were bitches. For example, one girl came to breakfast one morning and sat down to be waited on. Our practice was to set a glass of the juice of the day before them and ask for their order. She picked up the juice and threw it at me saying, "I don't want tomato juice." She was physically attractive, but I crossed her off my list. My Betty was the perfect composite; she came to breakfast with her beautiful shoulder-length brown hair neatly combed, a pleasant personality, keen intelligence, and it turns out that we had common interests. Later she told me what one of my high school classmates whom she had met in one of her classes had said about me. I used to sit behind this girl in homeroom. She said, "I don't think that he's the type to go to college." That comment stung, and in fact gave me motivation.

As it turns out, she became one of those aging bleached blonds married to an airline pilot, and I became a university professor.

The study of mechanical engineering was in itself not very glamorous, but it gave me a good grounding in mathematics and science. There were no great teachers to comment on, but I took a number of other department electives on the advice of my future wife, Betty, and later the guidance of roommates, Buzz Harvey and Rollyn Rejahl. After a year and a half of being houseboy and waiter, I had found other ways to support myself, and thus had roommates. I took a courses in economics, psychology, and one or two in Business Administration. These outside courses provided a window into another world, but I had to wait until after World War II was over to follow the enticements they provided.

I had been deferred from military service for some time, but on the threat of being drafted I joined the Navy's Electronic Technicians Program in 1943. I was denied the opportunity for a commission because I had partial dentures. I learned something about electronics and repairing radar and sonar equipment, saw no action, but contracted spinal meningitis in Hawaii in 1945. Since my cousin had died of the disease a few years earlier my mother would not believe that I was not at least paralyzed in some way until I presented myself for physical inspection. Actually, the only residual effect may have been early baldness, presumably resulting from an extremely high fever.

The most important event of my service years was marriage to my sweetheart Betty on February 17, 1945, prior to being shipped to Hawaii for assignment. No honeymoon was possible since the Navy granted me a single Saturday night for the wedding. Meningitis intervened and I was discharged during the summer of 1945. The war was already over, but the battle for a B.S. degree was not.

Betty had planned a wonderful honeymoon at a Madison, Indiana resort, but when I realized that the fall semester at Wisconsin would start in one week, we canceled good times in favor of education. The first real honeymoon came with our twenty-fifth anniversary which we celebrated in Hawaii. Because I had taken overloads and attended summer session during the war, I had just one semester left to complete my B.S. degree. Therefore, the fall semester was also consumed with job hunting. I had been a good student and had collected keys from Tau Beta Pi (Honorary Engineering Fraternity), Pi Tau Sigma (Honorary Mechanical Engineering), and Pi Mu Epsilon (Honorary Mathematics), so I thought I had a reasonable chance in the job market. Dad was bursting with pride and put an announcement in the *Beloit Daily News* stating all the honors.

Career Decision

With a B.S. degree in mechanical engineering, the usual opportunities were in companies where mechanical design or power generation were important considerations. I interviewed with a number of company representatives in these areas, but there was one that was crucial in my decision making process. A representative from the Chicago area Edison company convinced me that I did not want any of these kinds of jobs. He was a kind, gentle, burned out, seedy character, and his crucial question was, "What was your favorite subject?" I thought about it and answered honestly, "thermodynamics." He responded, "Perfect, you're for us!" My immediate private reaction was that I did not want to be like this seedy character in thirty years, and while I had done well in my thermodynamics courses, I could not see a career of it. Later I shared my concerns with Betty and with friends. I was not prepared to do anything but the typical ME jobs, and they had no appeal for me.

Here is where the GI Bill provided an opportunity that I might not have had otherwise. Those elective courses in economics, business, and psychology had broadened my horizons. I decided on taking a two-year MBA program. I applied to Harvard and Wisconsin. At that time Harvard required a personal interview at the school site. We were living on a meager income from Betty's salary as a clerk-typist plus the small stipend from the GI Bill. We felt that we could not afford the expense of a trip to Boston and decided to stay on the banks of Lake Mendota at Wisconsin. There was also a minor factor in the decision. Among advisors I consulted there was controversy concerning the Harvard case method of instruction, a debate that has continued to this day.

The MBA program, even second rate as it was, was like a breath of fresh air to me. Every course opened up new horizons for me. I gravitated toward the industrial management and personnel management courses. Wisconsin was especially strong in labor economics because of the earlier work of John R. Commons. He was gone, but his legacy was still impressive. I took courses from such great scholars in the field as Elizabeth Brandeis, Don D. Lescohier, Selig Perlman, and Edwin E. Witte.

Without question, however, the faculty member who had the greatest impact on me was that infectious personality, Russell L. Moberly. Russ was not a great scholar, but he was a leader and had a considerable following amongst the students in his seminars. Russ was director of the Industrial Management Institutes, an organization that put on all kinds of extension short courses for Wisconsin company executives. He was the contact with the real world for the students. Russ did a lot of consulting work, to an extent that probably created waves within the school, but the politics went over my head. He got me involved with one of his consulting projects at the Weber Life-Like Fly Company in Stevens Point, Wisconsin. It was my first professional assignment as a consultant and I loved it. Russ also got me involved with my first research project, modest though it was. When I received the MBA degree, Dad again published an announcement in the Beloit paper.

Career Decision Number Two

When it came time for me to make the next career decision, Russ advised me to go on for the Ph.D. I thought that he was surely finally showing signs of senility; I was anxious to get out into the real world and help solve real problems. I wanted managerial responsibility. Again, I interviewed with a variety of companies. Those I remember were Crane Company, Eastman Kodak, and Procter & Gamble.

The chap from Crane was an accountant who was expanding his auditing function into areas of managerial control, and industrial engineering. He was interested in me because of my combined engineering/MBA background. During the interview he suddenly said, "Let me see your hands!" He wanted to know if I bit my fingernails, a characteristic that seemed important to him— I passed his test. We talked about what my duties would be in the general sense. Several months later near the time of graduation he called me, asking when I expected to arrive. I was shocked. We had never discussed salary or other conditions, indeed, he had never made an offer. I explained that I had accepted another position, and then he seemed shocked. Somehow he thought we had a deal, never suspecting that other companies might make offers.

Procter & Gamble had stability to offer, and as a child of the depression, that was still of great importance to me. Even in a depression, I thought people would want to be clean. But soap was not a very interesting product to me. Did I want to spend a career with soap? My answer was no.

Eastman Kodak seemed to offer stability, professionalism, and an interesting product technology. We also liked the location in Rochester, New York. Incidentally, I originally thought that the Kodak representative was talking about Rochester, Minnesota, showing my parochial orientation at that stage of my development. Kodak offered me $300 per month as a beginner in the Industrial Engineering Department. I was delighted. Again dad published an announcement.

EASTMAN KODAK

In 1948 the Kodak Park plant was a huge integrated plant employing about 20,000 people. It had facilities to make the plastic base, coat it with emulsion, slit it up into usable sizes, spool it, make the spools and cassettes. It had a paper mill to make photographic papers, emulsion coated it, and so forth. It had a machine shop to fabricate much of the process equipment used in the plant. In short, it was like a candy store to a young man interested in manufacturing.

The industrial Engineering Department provided staff functions to the plant through a professional staff of about 200; about half in an internal consulting capacity where I was located, and half in work measurement and standards. The department was filled with bright young men who had been recruited from universities all over the country. The internal consulting staff was further divided into functional groups, and I was in the Methods Group. The group worked on assignments from the line departments, or ones generated by the members of the group with departmental approval. The general objective was to improve the cost and quality of manufacturing operations. A typical assignment was, "Improve the Inspection and Gauging Procedures for 35mm Reels." The solution might involve new or redesigned equipment and procedures.

I did not find these assignments exhilarating, to say the least. The scope of the assignments seemed terribly narrow. And the products were not as glamorous as I thought, though more so than making soap at Procter & Gamble. True, I was learning about the overall process, but I was impatient. Part of the problem in my view looking back was simply "big company itus." A close friend of mine, Gordon Belshaw, solved his problem by taking the first opportunity to get into one of the manufacturing departments. He was successful and became Vice President and Assistant General Manager of the Kodak Park Works. I solved my problem in a different way.

One day a consultant from H. B. Maynard came with the latest panacea, Methods Time Measurement. It was a system for synthesizing the time required to perform any manual task. The consultant sold the boss on it, and I got the assignment to set up a training course and teach most of the professional staff how to use it. It was the first time I had taught and I found it thrilling. I had finally found a product that I could enjoy working on—educated people, at least more educated in some way than before they entered my classroom. My colleagues seemed to think I had done a good job, and even the boss sat in on one of the courses and complimented me. When the training assignment ended I went back to the boring assignments that turned me off. I felt trapped and did not know how to extricate myself. Then another door opened that again changed my direction.

Career Decision Number Three

Professor Everett Laitala from the Industrial Engineering Department of the University of Illinois visited the department, and the boss had arranged a series of presentations to illustrate the department's work. I was one of those making a presentation. Later I received a copy of a letter from Professor Laitala to the boss. The boss circulated it around the department. The essence of the letter was that he had been very impressed with what he had seen, and he would like very much to recruit someone with the kind of practical experience that one seemed to get at Kodak. If you read between the lines of the boss' covering note to his subordinate you could translate it as, "If there is anyone dumb enough to want this, let him go." I was dumb enough. I sent off my resume to Laitala and accepted an assistant professorship at a 9-month stipend of $5000, about what I was then making at Kodak in 12 months. I thought it was a great opportunity to give an academic career a try. Teachers in the field were in very short supply following the war, so non-Ph.D.s were tolerated. I knew that if I decided to stay in academic life that I would need the degree, but that could come later.

When I announced my decision, the boss was shocked. Apparently he valued my services. When I told him that I had enjoyed the training assignment, he responded that I could get involved with more training assignments if I wanted. I told him that teaching would never be valued at Kodak. If I were to teach I should go where it was truly valued, to a university. In the meantime, we had our first child, "the baby Carl," our quaint name for him. We packed up and moved to Urbana, Illinois. Dad published another announcement—he was really proud to have a professor in the family.

THE UNIVERSITY OF ILLINOIS

Following the war, the housing situation at Champaign/Urbana was atrocious. Everett and Grace Laitala actually put us up in their home for some substantial period of time. The extent of their kindness can only be understood by knowing them. Later we bought our first home, a new, very modest home at 602 West Vermont in Urbana, within walking distance of the campus.

Teaching proved to be the tonic I needed to pull me out of the doldrums that I had felt at Kodak. I enjoyed it thoroughly. During the first summer I did some more consulting work through Russ Moberly at the Allen Bradley Company in Milwaukee. I earned about $2,500, so I rationalized that the academic way of life was even more lucrative than Kodak anyway. However, people on the faculty were generally unhappy, largely I think because of the poor living conditions. At least that is the explanation I have for the bickering, and political infighting that I observed. That situation helped me to conclude early that, if I wanted to make a career in academia, I needed the Ph.D. to accomplish my ultimate goals.

I wrote to several schools and people, among them Professor Ralph Barnes at UCLA. Barnes was undoubtedly the best known and probably most outstanding academic in the industrial engineering field. I had met Barnes at a "Ten Company Conference" that he ran on a consulting basis—I made a presentation there, representing Kodak. I met him at the Chicago airport to discuss the situation. He had remembered me favorably, and we struck a deal very quickly. He could offer me a lectureship in the School of Business Administration at $5,100 per nine months, the top salary for an assistant professor. The teaching load was twelve classroom hours per week. They were also feeling the pinch for qualified instructors, or the terms would not have been that generous. Simultaneously I could work on the Ph.D. in the College of Engineering. Today, we do not allow full-time teaching in a Ph.D. program, but I was young and energetic and it never occurred to me that it was unreasonable. After all, I had family responsibilities and needed both a Ph.D. and a living. We sold the house, packed up and drove to Los Angeles, with the moving van a week behind us. We arrived, found a house to rent in the Pacific Palisades on one of those perfect days when the sky and the ocean were crystal clear blue. We loved it and never left the Pacific Palisades except for periods of a year or less.

UCLA, THE GOLDEN YEARS

The first task was to gear up to teach in the Business School. With the experiences of Illinois to back me, the teaching task was no major problem. I enjoyed it and it was a break from the rigors of the Ph.D. program. I wrote qualifying examinations in four fields, bio-technology, mathematical statistics, production engineering, and thermodynamics. Bio-technology at UCLA at that time meant "human engineering," rather than the genetic focus of today. Every Ph.D. student in engineering at that time had to have thermodynamics as a field, because it was Dean Boelter's conviction that it was truly fundamental to all knowledge. It was a much more rigorous version than I had been exposed to in mechanical engineering. To me, however, it was just a hurdle, for I knew that I had no future use for it with my interests.

I took after the Ph.D. program as if it were a footrace. In those days I had boundless energy and this remained true until about age 55 when my energy level began to fall off. I could work through the day and half the night, a 20-30 minute nap would refresh me. During the first year at UCLA we built a new house for $28,000 in the Palisades, doing a substantial portion of the work ourselves, including roofing the house with wood shingles, all the yard grading and landscaping, painting inside and out, and many other tasks. I should comment that Betty and I did all these tasks together, including the roofing. When we moved from Urbana, Illinois to the Palisades, we estimated that housing was slightly less expensive in the Palisades.

There were two or three others in a situation similar to mine, teaching in the business school and taking the degree in engineering. One had a two year head start on me, so I decided that I would privately pace myself by his progress. This pacing provided great motivation for me. He was startled to learn one day five years later that I had just completed my degree—his came six months later. I think he resented my eagerness.

The professors who supervised my four fields were, with one exception, outstanding from all points of view. John Lyman and Craig Taylor supervised my bio-tech field. John later supervised my research and dissertation. George Brown taught me statistics by a one-hour tutoring per week for a year, followed by the written examination. Ralph Barnes had a joint appointment in business and engineering and supervised the production engineering field. Interestingly, George Dantzig, then at Rand Corporation, offered a course in linear programming at night. It was not well taught, but I learned enough to teach myself the fundamentals. The fundamentals of management science were not well organized at that time, and most of what I know I learned on my own initiative.

Myron Tibus seemed to believe that doctoral students needed to suffer. Private sessions with him were like a cat and mouse game. When it came time for the written examination in thermodynamics his game reached its zenith. After grading the examination he explained that although most of the exam was ok, there was one important problem that I had not done "perfectly correctly." He was to be away for the summer and he said that I could work on it during the summer and present the results to him at the end of the summer. If I had solved the problem perfectly correctly at that time, he said that he would consider me to have passed. It was a trick problem and I indeed worked on it almost every day during the summer, presenting the results to Myron in the fall. He looked it over and said, "you are not perfectly correct." I became aggressive at that point, for I knew that I was not far from the mark, and I said so, reviewing my answer. In so doing, I gained a new insight. He backed off at that point and said that he thought I understood the key now, telling me to correct my work that evening. I did, and he passed me. I learned a great deal from Myron about how not to treat doctoral students. After my appointments with him I would go home and work on the house. Trenching with a mattox was my favorite way to work out the tensions he produced. I imagined each blow to be directed at his grinning head. It worked, I never lost my cool in his presence.

My dissertation, "The Additivity of Human Motor Response Elements," involved a statistical model, the construction of a new electronic instrument to measure the time of motor response elements accurately, and a series of experiments on human subjects. The hypothesis was that the times for elemental hand motions were additive, a controversial issue at the time. I knew they were, and the experiments proved it.

I published a paper concerning the instrument development, and two papers concerning the experiments and the results. I had also published two or three other papers by the time I was awarded the degree. The result was that when I made myself available in the academic job market I received some offers at the associate professor level, the most notable of which was from Stanford. The receipt of the degree, of course, made Dad burst with pride and produced another announcement in the *Beloit Daily News*.

At that point UCLA was awakened by Ralph Barnes' pressure and the School of Business Administration offered an associate professorship at a nine-month stipend of $8,500. Staying at UCLA had a considerable appeal. I had already learned how to exist in that environment, and our home in the Palisades was shaping up. However, the house was on a hillside with little space for the children. We now had two children, Jerry being born in 1954. There had been wet rain seasons for several years, and there was a great deal of publicity about houses that had slide down into the canyons in the Palisades. I was nervous about our location, which was exacerbated by watching a big chunk of our lot wash down the canyon in a heavy rain storm. I had been admiring a house three blocks down the street that had been for sale for quite some time. It was priced at $35,000, and its main attraction was a relatively flat half-acre lot with a beautiful view of the canyon in back, and a view of the Pacific to the south. The house was run down and the style and layout was not to Betty's liking. The lot had been overplanted with trees (over-planting is a common southern California error, not taking account of the fast and long growing season) and gave the appearance of a dense forest. I finally convinced Betty that the place had great potential—all we had to do was change everything, but what great possibilities! We offered $30,000 and it was snapped up. We sold the place up the street and moved into what would be a second career, fixing, expanding, and generally remodeling the house. Betty was tired of moving and made me promise to stay at least five years. By the last count we had stayed 34 years.

It was 1957, I was 34 years old, and I was really just starting my academic career. The free time generated by achieving the Ph.D. was channeled into the house, which became a sink for time and money. At the School of Business Administration I was free to concentrate on teaching and research, an atmosphere fostered by Dean Neil Jacoby who was deeply involved in research and writing even as dean. He set an example for the entire faculty.

IPSOA, An Italian Graduate School of Management

One day I was asked to see a visitor, Signor Enrico DeGenaro, who was recruiting faculty for a school in Torino, Italy called, IPSOA (Istituto Post Universitaro per lo Studio del Organizatione Aziendale, translated as Graduate School of Business Administration). He was looking for faculty to teach finance, personnel, and production. He had focused on Fred Case, Bob Tannenbaum, and me. The offer was $12,000 for six months work, plus travel expenses to and from Torino for me and family. Those terms seemed quite attractive at the time.

I came home that evening and asked Betty, "How would you like to spend next year in Italy?" After explaining, she was a mixture of enthusiasm and reticence. We were barely through phase I of adding to and remodeling the house, had two small children, and only a year away from receiving the Ph.D.

We agonized over the decision, but finally decided in favor of the adventure. It was an opportunity to reexamine my roots and gain some professional breadth.

We flew to Rome and on to Trapani, near my father's home in Sicily. We received the warmest welcome from relatives that can be imagined, though the only lingual link was the small amount of Italian that we had been able to learn before departing. They spoke mainly the Sicilian dialect which is heavily laced with Greek and Arabic, knowing only a little of the national language. Near the end of our stay in Italy we returned to Sicily to meet dad, who returned for the first time in 50 years. He was a mixture of emotions, objecting to some things that had changed ("Where is the shrine that used to be at this corner?"), but being very upset that little progress had been made in his 50-year absence (Heatedly, "Why don't you have screens at the windows to keep the flys out?").

Teaching at IPSOA had its problems because of the sequential translation required, but the Italian students were wonderful, being very receptive to us. We had entrees to industry through the sponsorship of the school. We were able to get into many plants and discuss problems with managers. The main impression that I took away was that Italian technology and productivity were sadly behind at that point, a not surprising observation. That impression led in part to a paper somewhat later that I wrote with Alexander Bogardy, "When Should a Company Manufacture Abroad." Product labor intensity and productivity were important factors in the analysis.

IPSOA had been started with the assistance of the Harvard Business School. Pearson Hunt, a finance professor at Harvard, had been the dean of the school, and he addressed a convocation of the current students and faculty. He decried what he saw as the shift, with our arrival, in pedagogical methods at the school away from the case method. This caused considerable controversy, and represented the second time that the case method had been the center of debate in my young academic career, but not the last. I did not understand why there should be an issue at that point, but then I confess that I did not understand the case method at that time.

The school director, a former Italian army colonel, having heard of participative management, tried to get the American faculty involved in running certain aspects of the school. Because of my interests and background, he suggested that I schedule the classes for the entire school, but he never imposed an objective function. After conferring with my colleagues, we concluded that since we had an unparalleled opportunity to see Italy, long weekends should be maximized. I constructed a schedule where four-day weekends were common, everyone had at least one seven-day weekend and one ten-day weekend. We all had FIAT 1100 cars that we had purchased at an advantage from FIAT, a school sponsor. The result was that each week end most of us planned trips to Venice, Florence, Rome, and so on, while some dutifully held the fort teaching. It does not take much imagination to see how to make up class schedules in a way that bunches classes in production, for example, followed by long periods with no classes.

The teaching loads were rather light by any standard, giving me time to think things through when not travelling around Italy. I used this time to plan the outlines of my first book in production management. This was the main scholarly product of the IPSOA adventure.

When we returned home I focused on the completion of the book. The basic books in the field were largely descriptive in nature at the time. With the post-war development of operations research, and so much of that work focused in the production function, I felt that a more analytical approach was needed throughout. I included an entire section on analytical methods in production management, including chapters on linear programming, waiting line models, simulation, and others. The manuscript received good reviews and John Wiley & Sons offered a publishing contract. At about this time I was being considered for promotion to the full professorship, and the book manuscript weighed in as part of the evidence. My colleagues felt that the book was innovative and was a highly positive element in my case. Therefore, in 1961, four years after receiving the Ph.D., two very important events occurred in my professional life; promotion to the professorship and publication of my first book.

The book, titled *Modern Production Management*, was extremely well received and within a relatively short time, it became the dominant book used in first courses around the country and abroad. The editor at Wiley said that he forecast that I would write another book within two years, and he was right.

I will have more to say about "the books." In the meantime, I must comment on the promotion process. Nine promotion cases from the school went to the Chancellor, and the Senate Budget Committee that year. The Budget Committee was the campus-wide Senate committee that reviewed all appointments and promotions, and their advice is taken seriously. Mine was the only case passed. You can imagine the uproar. Of course, I was happy about the outcome of my own case, but felt the bitterness of the other eight. The dean made special appeals for some, finally winning approval in several other cases. But the Budget Committee had served notice, the standards had been permanently raised.

Shortly after the promotion incidents, my first administrative duty was to intervene. The Dean, Neil Jacoby, was always going on leave for one reason or another, and this time it was to serve on President Eisenhower's Council of Economic Advisors. Associate Dean George Robbins was again appointed acting dean, as had just been announced in the faculty meeting I had attended. When I returned to my office, there was a message to call Dean Robbins; he asked me to come to his office to discuss a matter of some importance. George said that he wanted me to take the position for a year as Acting Associate Dean. He explained that to be effective, he needed someone who was trusted by the Academic Senate. My recent "clean" promotion was the event that convinced him that I was the right man. The associate dean was at that time handling all the promotion and appointment cases for the school, was chairman of the faculty, and was generally the number two man in the administrative hierarchy.

Administration was a new an exciting experience for me. George Robbins was not about to sit on his hands as acting dean. He had a Harvard MBA, and felt that we had no business in the undergraduate arena. He felt that we should concentrate on a two-year MBA program and get rid of the BS program. There were heated faculty meetings, and as faculty chairman I took the role as mediator between George Robbins and his most vehement detractors. Finally, we had a faculty meeting that had mainly other issues on the agenda, with dropping the BS program on the agenda for discussion but not an action item. I was in the chair when Professor John Clendenin, whom I had just calmed in his desire to remove Robbins from the acting deanship, moved to approve the elimination of the BS program. The motion was seconded, and after a relatively brief discussion, it was passed. I was shocked. The meeting ended and I went directly to George's office. He closed the door, we looked blankly at each other, and he asked, "What happened?" I will never know the answer, but I think it was a superb decision that allowed the school to concentrate its resources on the MBA and Ph.D. programs. It was an important step in making UCLA the outstanding Graduate School of Management that I believe it to be.

The one academic achievement during my administrative assignment was the publication of my second book, *Operations Management: Problems and Models.* That was the first use of the name "Operations Management" for the field. I was searching for a title that would embrace both manufacturing and service systems, and the name stuck on the field as a whole.

We had just completed the largest single addition to our home, adding about 1,200 square feet, and remodeling much of the adjacent space. Royalty checks were now funding our efforts. Betty had just bought white sectional sofas for the new living room when I came home with the announcement that I had an offer to spend the 1963-1964 year as a visiting professor at Harvard.

Jim McKenney, a former doctoral student at UCLA had urged Harvard to consider me, the new book having some effect too, I think. They had indicated that they were interested in acquiring my services permanently, but could not make a tenure appointment without a year's residence in a non-tenure appointment. Dean Baker had called Dean Robbins and told him that they intended to recruit me if possible. Betty was not enthused; our daughter, Linda, had just been born, and Betty loved the Palisades and wanted stability. We had stayed in the house for the five years I had promised, but barely. Our son Carl was 16 years old and did not want to leave his friends. On the other hand, I was "high" with anticipation. Harvard's outstanding reputation was a great attraction. Of course, I visited, and it would be difficult to be unimpressed. While I was using some Harvard cases in my teaching at UCLA, I could now go to Harvard and put the case debate to rest.

Harvard

I rented Professor C. Roland Christiensen's house in Lexington, Massachusetts sight unseen by Betty. Harvard was a puzzle. I was used to a more academic atmosphere, where the business school was more integrated with the rest of the university. As has often been said, the Charles river which divides the Harvard Business School from the rest of the university campus is very wide. One evening we were invited to dinner by someone we knew at UCLA in the political science department, who was visiting Harvard too. He also invited a prominent member of the faculty from the Government Department and his wife. When we were identified as visiting the business school, the wife said, "Dear, we do not know anyone from the business school, do we?" It was not only what she said, but the way she said it that convinced me that being on the wrong side of the river was comparable to being on the wrong side of the tracks, in spite of the reputation of the Harvard Business School.

Then there was the academic orientation toward teaching, rather than research, a fact that surprised me given the outstanding reputation of the university and the business school. On questioning a colleague at MIT about this, in an attempt to understand it, he said, "Yes, I have always maintained that HBS is anti-intellectual." At the same time, I must say that Dean George Baker and his Associate Dean Georges F. F. Lombard were trying to change the environment by bringing in research oriented new faculty. I also hasten to say that there is substantial important research going on in the production group currently; the situation has changed immeasurably in the 28-year period. I was assigned a rather average teaching load which I found to be oppressively heavy. My first-year production course had 99 students, to be taught by the case method. Even with the "picture book" help provided, I barely learned their names by the end of the term. I sat in on colleagues courses and was duly impressed by the effectiveness of the case method when used by an experienced professional. I wondered how long it would take me to achieve such levels of accomplishment.

My colleagues in the production group at Harvard, with the exception of Jim McKenney and Dick Rosenbloom, were cool toward me. I concluded that I was a threat to them. Finally, it was March, time to make a decision. My nine-month salary at UCLA was $13,600. Dean Baker offered $20,000 and when I seemed reticent he raised it to $22,000, a 38 percent increase over my UCLA salary. In fact, my reticence was not because of the salary offer. I agonized over the decision, rationalizing that I would learn to deal with the case method, large classes, the width of the Charles river, and the terrible weather. After a reasonable period to think, I accepted the offer; the attractions were simply too great to be resisted. It was difficult to dishearten me in those days, but here was an exception, I fell into a state of depression. Betty was unhappy with the decision. Only our sons Carl and Jerry seemed happy. Carl had found a girlfriend so the idea of staying seemed fine. Jerry was at a pliable age and would have been happy anywhere. Linda was a baby and home was where we were.

After about three weeks of agony, I concluded that I had made the wrong decision, at least it was wrong for me—the lack of a research oriented environment made me feel uneasy, and I was not sure about the case method as the sole teaching methodology. Of course, it was terribly embarrassing for I had already called Dean Robbins at UCLA to tell him that I would stay at Harvard. I called again to be sure that I could reverse my decision. They even raised my salary a notch, but it was still far below the Harvard offer. I then wrote a memo to Deans Baker and Lombard, and apologized as best I could. I explained that I felt that I would be a misfit at Harvard and that it was better to recognize that fact now, stating, "To thine own self be true." It did not go down well, especially with Dean Baker, and the balance of my stay was uncomfortable. In discussing the decision with Dick Rosenbloom, I stated that one of the reasons was that I would have to teach by the case method at Harvard. He said that it was not true, any appropriate teaching method was acceptable. I said, "No Dick, it's in the walls here," and I think he agreed.

Regarding teaching, the final debate about the case method was with myself. My observations about its effectiveness in professional MBA programs were penetrating, and after returning to UCLA I gradually introduced more cases into my teaching of such courses. Today, my organization and teaching of professional courses is closer to the Harvard model than the one that guided me in the 1960s. I must say that the entire Harvard experience had a profound influence on my thinking about professional education. Perhaps it shows that I could have adapted at Harvard with a little more time.

Leaving his lady love was difficult for Carl. We left Lexington before dawn, and had to drive to her house so that he could commune silently standing below her window. As a friend commented, "So it was a wrench going and a wrench coming back." Betty, on the other hand was joyful. When we came into the living room that we had remodeled before leaving a year earlier and she saw that the renters had treated her new white sofa with care, tears came to her and she said, "I never thought I would see this home again."

The Books

A big chapter in my life has to do with the books I wrote. There are fourteen books in the publications list. Some of them are what one might call "pot boilers," being a rehash of materials in another of my books, produced at the urging of an editor wanting to reach another market.[1] That leaves nine books which represent major efforts for which I am proud. There were 26 separate editions of all the books for which I prepared manuscript and went through the production process of reading galley and page proofs, and so forth.

I have already commented briefly on the first two. They were both major efforts on my part. The first book, *Modern Production Management* (1961), I grubbed out the old way, I wrote it out long hand, and Betty typed the manuscript when I thought I had it about right. After review, she typed it a second time. It went through eight editions[2] and the publisher wants a ninth. It was highly successful and changed the directions of the production and operations field. Many other books (too many) were cast in its image.

The second book, *Operations Management: Problems and Models* (1963), was written to emphasize the analytical techniques in the field. It gave its basic name to the field as it is now titled, operations management. It went through three editions,[3] and when it had run its course fourteen years later, Jim Dyer, now at the University of Texas at Austin and I wrote a broadly based book on management science methodology, *Management Science/Operations Research: Model Formulation and Solution Methods* (1977).[4] The differentiating part of the book was in its subtitle. We felt that for managers, the emphasis should not be algorithmic. Rather, they should be taught about the formulation of problems in quantitative terms, problem formulation being a uniquely managerial function. This kind of formulation should play a role that the analyst cannot adequately fill. The other function that we thought managers should emphasize was the interpretation of results. What goes on in between is of little interest to most managers. I think that we were a little early with this conceptual framework. In 1977, instructors were still hooked on the magic of the algorithmic approach.

I think that *Readings in Production and Operations Management* (1966), which I edited, served a purpose for seminars. Materials were available in the journals, but needed organization toward a specific educational goal.

Following the "readings" book, I finally yielded to that grand old man in business publishing, Dick Irwin. He and his cohorts, Burly Grimes and Bill Schoof were a trio to be reckoned with. Dick Irwin had wanted the contract for the first book, but I signed with Wiley. The three of them kept after me until I finally signed for *Production-Inventory Systems: Planning and Control* (1968). First, the book itself was well received, though the narrower subject matter resulted in a smaller audience. The book went through three editions.[5] Bill Taubert, a superb doctoral student of mine, joined me in the second edition, and Jeff Miller for the third edition. Second, however, it was the beginning of a long and excellent relationship with Dick Irwin and his outstanding colleagues. I became a member of the board of Directors in 1973. During the era of Dick's leadership, followed by the presidencies of Burly Grimes and Jack

Young, I think that the organization was the most finely tuned one I have observed. Morale was high and authors and customers were extremely well served.

By the middle to the end of the 1970s it was apparent that the field was demanding a stronger emphasis on service operations. While I had tried to adapt to these shifts, it was difficult to accommodate to them in the production orientation of *Modern Production Management*, renamed *Modern Production/Operations Management* with the sixth edition. I therefore decided to write an entirely new basic book with a broader framework, emphasizing the generality of operations management, as well as, the systems approach. The Wiley editor was enthusiastic, but the person occupying the editorship kept changing in that organization. A valiant effort was made in producing *Operations Management: The Management of Productive Systems* (1981), but it was somehow flawed and never gained acceptance.

Another flop occurred a year earlier in an attempt with Barbara Pletcher to write a broadly based introduction to business, *Understanding Business Today* (1980).

My last attempts at book writing were with two professional books, where the audience was the practicing manager. The first, *Meeting the Competitive Challenge: Manufacturing Strategy for U. S. Companies* (1984), I wrote with a passion. I was enraged to see what U.S. companies were doing to themselves in global competition. They were concentrating on "paper entrepreneurialism," trying to make a fast buck, ignoring the basic tenet of creating something of value, and ignoring manufacturing strategy where they were being run over rough shod by the Japanese, West Germans and others. Cost of production and quality were being ignored by top executives concerned with mergers and acquisitions, and their own golden parachutes. The second professional book, *Corporate Strategic Analysis* (1986), co-authored with Marc Bogue, brought together the results of consulting assignments into a rational analytical framework. It represented a culmination of my own broadening interests in manufacturing strategy.

There was another side to my interest in books and publishing. For fifteen years (1965-1980) I was consulting editor for the Wiley Series in Management and Administration. Jack Young, who was the Wiley Editor for many years until he returned to Irwin as President, set up the consulting editorship. By the time I resigned in 1980 from shear exhaustion from reading book proposals and manuscripts, there were 46 books in the series ranging over all subjects in the broad general field of management and administration. It was an education in itself.

My book publishing efforts were very rewarding over the years. First, the satisfaction of producing a book-length manuscript was very strong. I took great pride in these efforts and, of course, it gave my father great pride and more chances to put notices in the hometown paper. Second, book publication definitely carried my career forward—I was rewarded in many ways, including progress up the ladder here at UCLA. Finally, it has been remunerative financially, providing funds for the house financial sink, educating our children, and providing risk capital that on balance provided returns. The books often opened up consulting opportunities that provided financial returns. Financially, the book royalties made possible the marginal things.

Research and Doctoral Students

My research program was intimately intertwined with doctoral students who wrote their dissertations under my direction, as I think it should be. Good doctoral students are the key to any vibrant university research program. In publications that resulted from a dissertation, I was always careful to have the student's name listed first, with one exception. I felt that I would always get all the credit I needed, and it was the student who needed whatever extra credit that comes from being listed first. The exception was a paper written with Paul Ting. At that time Paul had a problem in expressing himself in English so I wrote the paper in its entirety and placed my name first. There are some secondary papers where my name is listed first.

While I worked with many doctoral students in both the Graduate School of Management, and the school of Engineering and Applied Sciences, there were seven for whom I was committee chairman. Their degree dates and current affiliations are:

- Gordon Armour, 1961, North American Aviation, Autonetics
- Arnold Reisman, 1963, Case Western Reserve University
- Thomas E. Vollmann, 1964, Boston University
- William H. Taubert, 1968, Vice President, Hunt Wesson Foods, Inc.
- Paul Ting, 1975, Vice President, ARCO
- Jaime Fensterseifer, 1980, University of Brazil
- Donald Rosin, 1985, Vanderbilt University

My research thrusts over time can divided into my own dissertation research on the additivity of human motor response elements, physical facilities and layout, general models of production systems, aggregate planning and scheduling, and finally in operations strategy. and policy. The broadening of interests over time seems entirely logical to me.

Concurrent with, and following my dissertation, I was interested in the functional layout problem, where no single sequence of operations dictates the relative location of departments. In 1955 I published a link-node analysis of the problem called Operation Sequence Analysis, that was effective conceptually, but could be applied to only small scale problems. Gordon Armour, my first doctoral student did the primary work in computerizing the graphic based analysis, and it was named CRAFT (Computerized Relative Allocation of Facilities Technique). The algorithm proved to be very robust, and CRAFT remains the standard, though many other computer solutions have been attempted. Tom Vollmann followed up on some of the research issues remaining in CRAFT, examining the conditions under which the technique work best, particularly defining flow dominance as a concept. The original work in this field sparked a great deal of other related work in other universities. One in particular was Roger Johnson, a former UCLA doctoral student, who developed a three-dimensional version called SpaceCRAFT.

In 1961, I had two brilliant engineering students in my graduate seminar, Jack Alcalay and Arnold Reisman. They had interests in systems engineering, and it was obvious to me that conceptual work on production systems might take advantage of systems concepts. Two different lines of work followed, one with each student. Jack Alcalay had other primary interests and wrote a dissertation in systems engineering, later becoming my neighbor two doors away and a life-long friend. Arnold Reisman, however, followed up on the primary work and wrote his dissertation in engineering, but under my direction. The working relationship with Arnold was very productive, also resulting in several papers in finance including Fred Weston, of our finance faculty, as a co-author.

In the meantime, I had become very interested in the general aggregate planning and scheduling problem, inspired by the pioneering work on the Linear Decision Rule (LDR) by Holt, Modigliani, Muth, and Simon. This coincided with the attendance in my research seminar by another brilliant student, Bill Taubert. The limitations on the practical use of the LDR were centered in the restrictive quadratic cost model, and the solution technique used. Bill had knowledge of computer search methods and suggested that they could be used to advantage. The advantages were that a highly realistic cost model for the firm could be used, instead of the constraining quadratic model used by the LDR, and the efficient solution technique for very complex models. It worked beautifully, and the Search Decision Rule (SDR) was born. It found solutions to the classic "paint company problem" that were virtually optimal, and performed extremely well on very complex realistic, as well as, real problems.

The original work on the SDR was followed by further work on the aggregate planning problem by Paul Ting and Don Rossin. Paul's work was on the fundamental search algorithms. The original SDR used the Hooke-Jeeves Pattern Search routine. Paul did fundamental work with many kinds of search algorithms with the objective of showing the limits of what they were good at and what they did poorly.

Finally, Don Rossin worked on the development of a manager interactive model for aggregate planning. The fundamental issue stemmed from the fact that formal models of aggregate planning were not used by practicing managers, in spite of the progress that had been made. On talking with managers, they said that current models did not deal with some of the really important issues. For example, a model might suggest that ten percent of the work force be laid off, the manager feeling that this was impractical, immoral, or whatever. A manager interactive model would take the final solution of the optimizing model as a starting point. The manager would state what he found wrong with the result and specify a new constraint on lay offs, inventories, or other parameters. The optimizing model would be run again to generate the best solution given the new constraints. The interactive process continues until the manager is satisfied with the solution.

Most of Jaime Fensterseifer's work was done under Don Erlenkotter's direction. I took over because Don was on leave, but the excellent research was not a part of my program. Some of the most enjoyable activities of my career I attribute to working, one-on-one, with doctoral students. It is sometimes said that they can keep one young.

My interest in strategy came too late in my professional life cycle to do more than the book defining some of the issues and associated papers that were general in nature. In 1980 I published a paper, "Research in Operations Management," in which I tried to chart a future course. The essence of it was that the management science/operations research thrust had run its course, or it should have. It had focused on smaller problems, often those that the researcher defined rather than the real problems. I pleaded for research on broader policy and strategic issues, rooted in dialogues with practicing managers, where the issues are usually messier and ill-defined.

Administration and the Academic Senate

When I returned from Harvard in 1964, one of the tasks I returned to was that of Assistant Dean for Graduate Programs. I had enjoyed the previous administrative assignment for one year as Acting Associate Dean and Chairman of the Faculty, and I enjoyed this assignment too. But after two years, the itch to spend more time on research, writing, and teaching was compelling. I was in the pattern of taking on heavy administrative or service assignments for a period of time, always stepping away from a permanent assignment. I seemed to alternate between administrative assignments and service assignments in the Academic Senate.

At the University of California on all its campuses, faculty self governance through the Academic Senate is taken quite seriously. I had taken on minor assignments in the past, but beginning in 1967 I was appointed to the Budget Committee, the most powerful and important committee of the Senate. The Budget Committee reviewed all promotions and appointments for the campus, making recommendations to the Chancellor, which were usually followed. Two to three full days per week were required for the committee's work. In 1969

I was appointed Chairman of the Committee. The Budget Committee was a wonderful place to learn about the university. The twelve members came from all parts of the campus. It was this kind of integration of the business school with the rest of the campus that I found lacking at Harvard. Most of my personal friends from the faculty whom we see socially are drawn from this wide spectrum.

In 1968-69, I chaired the search committee to find a new dean for our school. Some colleagues and committee members urged me to let my name stand, but that would have meant a permanent administrative career, and I refused. We found Harold Williams, then Chairman and CEO of Norton Simon, Inc. Then, Harold found me, asking me to be Associate Dean, a position I held from 1970 to 1974. It was a difficult but fascinating period to hold this position since Harold was shaking the school to its foundations, and I was absorbing much of the flak. Throughout the 1967 -1974 period I continued to publish new editions of my books, one new book and a few papers, but I was feeling that if I did not get back to full time teaching and research soon, it would be very difficult to make the transition. I had one year of liberty, but then I was asked to stand for election as Chairman of the UCLA Academic Senate for 1975-1976, and served in that post before a return to freedom.

By 1976, Harold Williams announced his acceptance of the chairmanship of the Securities and Exchange Commission. The Executive Vice Chancellor called me in and asked, "do you want to be a candidate, or shall I appoint you as chair the search committee." I asked him to do me a favor and make me chairman. This time we went all the way to the Letters and Science Economics Department to find Clay LaForce; he had been a fine Chairman of the Economics Department, and shown talents for fund raising.

I was free of heavy assignments until 1981. My son Jerry had completed a BS in Electronics Engineering, and after a few work years he had decided to take an MBA at UCLA. Not only that, he had selected Operations Management as a concentration field. There was no way he could avoid having me as an instructor, a fact that I thought intolerable; I could not fairly judge my own son. I ran for administrative cover. I had been on the committee to create our new Executive MBA Program, which now needed a director. It was the first time that I asked for an administrative assignment. The assignment as director of the Executive MBA Program took me out of the teaching schedule and solved my problem. I remained in the post for three years. During the last year as director I was appointed to the endowed *Times Mirror* Chair which entails honors, reduced teaching load, and ample research funds. Free at last!

The House

What does a house have to do with a professional career? In my case, I think it was important. Working on the house that Betty made me promise to inhabit for at least five years was a break from the rigors of the career, a therapy, my pride and joy, and as I mentioned, a sink for funds. We started with a beautiful lot with a view, but with a real "fixer upper." It had been built in 1941 with attendant shortages of material due to World War II. It was of a style that Betty did not particularly like, and the 1,400 square feet featured small rooms. The lot was over landscaped and had been poorly maintained.

The first remodeling and addition started before we even moved in—we tore into the tiny kitchen, ripped out the walls adjoining a bath and small bedroom, and removed the wall adjoining with the garage. The space was remodeled into a nice kitchen, half bath adjoining, and a family room, an adjoining carport built to replace the garage. There was plenty of lot space to accommodate the additions. When I say we tore into the project, I mean it literally, we were doing the work ourselves. I would come home from the university, put on work cloths, and we would work on the project. We soon realized that we were in over our heads, and obtained the services of an architect, Paul Sterling Hoag, AIA. Paul was to become very important in our lives, for in all the subsequent projects he did the design work, integrating the additions and modification into a sensible design. I maintain that the best money we have spent on the house has been for architectural design. Also, midway through that first project we realized that we needed an experienced carpenter, and hired Warren Harding—we were his helpers.

When the first project was completed, I went to work on the forest in the yard. I learned how to take out trees from a hard working Norwegian. You leave about four feet of stump above the ground for leverage, that will be needed later. Dig down around the stump as far as possible, chopping side roots close to the trunk. Then undermine the stump with a power nozzle on a hose, getting below the stump. Finally, allowing time for the water to saturate the soil, use the leverage of the four-foot stump to break loose the remaining roots. I took out over 30 small to medium sized trees that way.

In later projects we doubled the size of the living room and the dining room, adding a master bedroom and bath, and later added a large garden room as an entrance to the house. Book royalties fed the projects, which we now contracted out. Through five projects our 1600 square foot fixer upper became a wonderful home of 4000 square feet. It was all good therapy, completely different from the tension producing activities in which I was involved.

Our "final" project, constructed in 1989-1990, was a Japanese garden, mostly in the back. It involves a waterfall into two koi ponds, a Japanese bridge, and the careful arrangement of 60 tons of rock, overlooking the canyon with a view of the Pacific to the south. Takeo Uesugi, our Japanese landscape architect said that a Japanese garden is 40 percent rock and only 60 percent plant material. Japanese gardens are supposed to exude serenity, facilitate meditation, and promote longevity. Two large turtles, depicting longevity, are molded into the landscape with rocks representing the head, tail, and feet.

Admonitions for Academic Success

In 1987 or 1988, Ira Horowitz organized a panel for a doctoral consortium to discuss academic success and its parameters. The audience was filled with young men and women who were about to join the academic profession. In thinking about what to say, I looked at my own career, decided that I had been successful, and noted that I had done many things that I was advised against, but which had given me satisfaction and made me feel successful. In addressing the group, I said that I was talking about long-term success, not simply making tenure, and that good teaching and research were a prerequisite. Then I put tongue in cheek and commented on all the "don'ts, as follows with the brief rejoinders I provided:

- *Don't waste your time on administrative activities!*
  You may be able to accomplish something you think is really important. Some of the levers of power are here. The question is when in one's career to do it.
- *Don't waste your time writing textbooks!*
  It may give one pause to scan the list of successful academics to see if they have written textbooks.
- *Promotion committees and deans don't give weight to textbooks!*
  On the other hand, their existence cannot be denied. Again, the issue is when in one's career to do it. If a text is a carbon copy of a leading book, it shouldn't count for much.
- *Textbooks return only about $1 per hour anyway.*
  This is what most authors will tell you. Perhaps it is because they do not want colleagues to know just how much they have cleaned up, and they want to discourage potential competitors. I was a member of the Richard D. Irwin Company board for several years and got to see the returns, and believe me, my colleagues were doing very well.
- *Narrow your scope! Pick a research area that is the width of a hair and has no relevance, and model the hell out of it. No one will care about its relevance, only its elegance.*
  But you will have to live with yourself—relevance and breadth my provide a more satisfying career.
- *Recoil at the very thought of empirical or field research! Promotion committees will give it small weight.*
  Unfortunately it may be true. It is more time consuming, and seems not to be fully appreciated. However, it may be effective in generating relevant hypotheses.

- *Beware of time spent on campus-wide services! It's a time trap that will never count toward promotion, and what else is important?*
  On the other hand, Academic Senate or equivalent service helps one gain an understanding of the university as a whole, broadens your scope and network of colleagues and friends.
- *Consulting dollars can trap you into a living standard that must be maintained, ultimately destroying your academic career!*
  But, there is a value to consulting work. Our former dean, Neil Jacoby, engaged in consulting work if it met the following conditions: (1) It was of such character that it lead to some kind of publication, (2) fed back to useful classroom material, and (3) enriched him.

I had thoroughly enjoyed all these activities, and I believe I was rewarded for all of them. I felt that new Ph.D.s should be thinking about more than teaching and research for a full and satisfying career.

On May 6, 1990 (I noted the date), I met my colleague Dick Rumelt at a 3:00 p.m. meeting of the faculty to review a change in the new building plan. We were the first to arrive. He asked, "Are you all right? You don't look well. You don't have your usual ebullient look." While I feel well for my 67 years, I hope that the decay in my appearance is not symptomatic of a general decline. While I am of retirement age, I am in the cohort where there is no mandatory retirement age. On the other hand, if I retired my take home equivalent dollars would exceed my present salary take home—essentially I am working for nothing.

Still, there are some positives. I seem to have the support of an outstanding group of young scholars, a fact which touches me deeply. It is terribly gratifying to know that Reza Ahmadi, Sriram Dasu, Gordon Shirley, and Chris Tang are there to carry on. Showing some energy left in the old war horse, I organized and funded The Center for Technology Management in 1989 to focus external support for research and educational programs in the field. During the period of approximately 1960-1985, there was very little interest in Operations Management—finance and marketing were getting the resources. It was a real struggle to keep the operations faculty in existence and intact. There were moves to grab the resources and read us out of the MBA curriculum. It is gratifying to see the rebirth of the field, as attention focuses on some of the evils of paper entrepreneurship, and operations as the savior for U.S. competitiveness. Meanwhile, student interest in finance declines as the crooks on Wall Street are found, and opportunities for MBAs in finance declines. Also, over-staffing has occurred in the finance faculty.

Finally, there are many personal pleasures that I enjoy. A wonderful life-long partner, and a warm family relationship with our children and their families. We have enjoyed music throughout our lives. We support the Los Angeles Philharmonic and have concert series with friends. We support the new Los Angeles Music Center Opera Company, and attend all their productions. Opera has been an obsession all of our adult lives, and we go to the world's finest opera houses for performances whenever possible. Then, there is our home, and the Japanese garden which offers serenity and perhaps longevity.

Reflecting on what I have written about my personal and professional life, it all seemed so easy. I do not mean that I did not work hard, nor that there were no obstacles, but the obstacles were not insurmountable. However, it did not seem like work for I was enjoying every minute of it. The research and writing was not a distasteful task, but a thoroughly satisfying way to spend endless hours. Time spend on Academic Senate activities and administration was fascinating, even though I concluded that I did not want to be a career administrator. It seemed as though things worked for the best. At every junction a green light turned on to show the way and let me pass. It was "green lights all the way."

PUBLICATIONS

1947

With R.L. Moberly. *Job evaluation.* Madison, WI: Bureau of Business Research, University of Wisconsin.

1948

With R.L. Moberly. *Executive understudies.* Madison, WI: Bureau of Business Research, University of Wisconsin.

1955

Sequence analysis for functional layout. *Journal of Industrial Engineering, 6*(2).

1957

The additivity of universal standard data elements. *Journal of Industrial Engineering, 7*(5).
The additivity of universal standard data elements II. *Journal of Industrial Engineering, 8*(6).

1958

Analyse du deroulement des operations. *L'Etude du Travail, 83.*
The electronic time recorder—A new instrument for work measurement research. *Journal of Industrial Engineering, 9*(2).
L'additivite des temps de mouvements. *L'Etude du Travail, 85.*
With J. Lyman. The additivity of the times for human motor response elements in a simulated industrial assembly task. *Journal of Applied Psychology, 42*(2).

1959

With J. Boulden. The strategy of interdependent decisions. *California Management Review, 1*(4).

1960

Toward a unified concept of job design. *Journal of Industrial Engineering, 11*(4).
With A. Bogardy. When should a company manufacture abroad? *California Management Review, 2*(2).

1961

Modern production/operations management. New York: Wiley.
Pacing effects in production lines. *Journal of Industrial Engineering, 12*(6), 383-386.
Politique d'entretien preventif. *L'Etude du Travail, 117,* 33-38.

1962

With A. Reisman. A general model for investment policy. *Management Science, 8*(3), 304-310.

1963

Operations management: Problems and models. New York: Wiley.
With G.C. Armour. A heuristic algorithm and simulation approach to the relative location of facilities. *Management Science, 9*(2), 294-309.
With J.A. Alcalay. A proposal for a general model of a production system. *The International Journal of Production Research, 2*(1), 73-88.

1964

With A. Reisman & E. Harris. A general investment model and computer program. *L'Institute de Controle de Gestion.*
With G.C. Armour & T.E. Vollmann. Allocating facilities with craft. *Harvard Business Review, 42*(2), 136-149.
With A. Reisman. A general model for production and operations systems. *Management Science, 11*(1), 64-79.

1965

With G.C. Armour & T.E. Vollmann. Craft une: Nouvelle technique d'etude des implantations. *L'Etude du Travail, 158,* 33-43.

1966

Readings in production and operations management. New York: Wiley.
With T.E. Vollmann. The facilities layout problem in perspective. *Management Science, 12*(10), 450-468.
With A. Reisman & J.F. Weston. Beitrag zu einer theories der optimalen finanzstruktur. *Zeitschrift fur Betriebswirtschaft,36*(9), 568-577.
With G.C. Armour & T.E. Vollmann. Tecnia para el studio de las implantacioned de talleres. *Ingernieria E. Industria,*p. 6673.
With A. Reisman & A.B. Rosenstein. Resource allocation under uncertainty and demand interdependence. *Journal of Industrial Engineering, 17*(8), 402-409.

1967

Production inventory systems. *Rivista Internazionale di Scienze Economiche e Commerciali, 14*(2), 138-160.
Aggregate planning for production. *Business Horizons,* pp. 87-97.
With A. Reisman & J.F. Weston. A methodology for the evaluation of prospective mergers and acquisitions. *Mississippi Valley Journal of Business and Economics, 3*(1), 55-67.
With W.H. Taubert. Evaluation of direct computer search methods for the aggregate planning problem. *Industrial Management Review.*

1968

Production-inventory systems: Planning and control. Homewood, IL: Irwin.

1970

With J.B. Boulden. Corporate models: On-line, real-time systems. *Harvard Business Review*, pp. 65-83.

1971

Basic production management. New York: Wiley.

1975

A short course in managing day-to-day operations. New York: Wiley.
A short course in planning and designing productive systems. New York: Wiley.

1976

Operations management: The management of productive systems. New York: Wiley.
Communication to the editor on a paper by Scriabin and Vergin. *Management Science, 3*(1).
With M.J. Cosgrove & B.J. Luce. An integrated work-shift scheduling system. *Decision Sciences*, pp. 620-630.

1977

With J.S. Dyer. *Management science/operations research: Model formulation and solution methods.* New York: Wiley.
With J.S. Dyer. Managerial use of dynamic structural models. *Decision Sciences.*
With P.B. Ting. Empirical tests of constrained nonlinear optimization algorithms. *Decision Sciences.*

1978

With J.S. Dyer. *Essentials of management science/operations research.* New York: Wiley.

1980

Research in operations management. *Journal of Operations Management,* pp. 1-8.
With B.A. Pletcher. *Understanding business today.* Homewood, IL: Irwin.

1981

Elements of production/operations management. New York: Wiley.

1984

Meeting the competive challenge: Manufacturing strategy for U.S. companies. Homewood, IL: Dow Jones-Irwin.
Making U.S. manufacturing competitive. *California Management Review.*
Positioning the production system—Key element in manufacturing strategy. *Strategic Planning.*
Making operating decisions strategic. *Strategic Planning.*

1985

Meeting the competitive challenge with manufacturing strategy. *National Productivity Review.*
Manufacturing strategy for the eighties. *Manufacturing Engineering*, pp. 71-72.
With M.C. Bogue. Productivity and the exchange rate. *National Productivity Review*, pp. 32-36.

1986

With M.C. Bogue. *Corporate strategic analysis.* New York: The Free Press.

NOTES

1. *Basic Production Management* (First edition: 1971; International edition, 1971. Second edition: 1975; International edition, 1975; Turkish translation, 1981; Mainland Chinese translation, 1982). *A Short Course in Managing Day-to-Day Operations* (1975; Portuguese translation, 1977; Spanish translation, 1980). *A Short Course in Planning and Designing Productive Systems* (1975; Portuguese translation, 1977; Spanish translation, 1980). *Essentials of Management Science/Operations Research* (1978; International edition, 1978). *Elements of Production/Operations Management* (1981).
2. First edition: 1961; Far Eastern edition, Tokyo, 1962; Spanish translation, 1965. Second edition: 1965; International edition, 1966; Italian translation in three volumes (cloth and paper), 1967. Third edition: 1969; International edition, 1969; Far Eastern reprint, New Delhi, 1971; Italian translation, 1971; Portuguese translation, 1972, Romanian translation (3 vols.), 1973; Far Eastern reprint, New Delhi, 1975; Spanish translation, 1976. Fifth edition: 1977; International edition, 1977; Mainland Chinese translation, 1981. Sixth edition: 1980; International edition, 1980. Seventh edition: 1983; International edition, 1983; Mainland Chinese translation, 1985. Eighth edition (with R. Sarin): 1987; International edition, 1987.

3. First edition, 1963; Second edition, 1968; International edition, 1968; Russian translation, 1970; Spanish translation, 1973. Third edition: 1972; International edition, 1972.

4. First edition: 1977. Second edition: 1981; International edition, 1981; Mainland Chinese translation, 1982.

5. First edition: 1968; International edition, 1971. Second edition: 1972; International edition, 1975; Third edition: 1979; Turkish translation, 1981; Mainland Chinese translation, 1982.

Alfred D. Chandler Jr.

History and Management
Practice and Thought

ALFRED D. CHANDLER, JR.

I begin this sketch of my intellectual experience by reviewing how I, as a historian, came to write a book that in time qualified me as a "management thinker." I next indicate how this initial introduction into the practice and thought of business management had a profound impact on my academic and intellectual career as a historian. I then go on to show how I continued to place managers and management in their larger historical settings.

BECOMING A HISTORIAN

As a youngster history intrigued me. I read again and again Wilbur Fiske Gordy's *Elementary History of the United States*—a present my father gave me at the age of seven. As I grew older my interest in history was heightened when my father would read aloud in the evening to his five children from the historical novels of Sir Walter Scott, Robert Louis Stevenson, and others. At school in Wilmington, Delaware, and then at Exeter and Harvard history remained my favorite subject.

I particularly enjoyed my senior year at Harvard when I had to take only one course and could concentrate nearly all my time on writing an honors thesis on "The Gubernatorial Campaign of 1876 in South Carolina." That campaign marked the end of reconstruction in that state. In it a Confederate general, the aristocratic Wade Hampton, and a carpetbagger from Boston were the contestants. Surprisingly, the low country plantation owners preferred the carpetbagger; while the upcountry farmers were willing to use violence to assure the success of the aristocratic candidate. My research involved primarily reading newspapers and journals of the times and correspondence of the participants. The research and the writing up of the findings were done under the guidance of a master historian, Paul Buck, who had recently received a Pulitzer Prize in history. The thesis provided a fascinating introduction into the role of economic interests, demography, and race relations on politics. At Buck's suggestion I applied to do graduate work in history at the University of North Carolina, then the leading institution for the study of history, economics and sociology of the South.

The war intervened. Just as our class graduated in June 1940 with the Germans sweeping through France, President Roosevelt inaugurated the V-7 Program to train naval officers. A substantial number of classmates, including John F. Kennedy (we were fellow members of the Harvard sailing team) trooped down to the Charlestown Navy Yard to sign up.

Joining early, my war turned out to be a soft one. Before Pearl Harbor I had been assigned to the Atlantic Fleet Camera Party—a unit that was responsible for analyzing through photography the results of all gunnery exercises carried out by the ships of the Atlantic Fleet. Shortly after the Annapolis graduates in charge had moved on, I became second in command of the unit headquartered in Norfolk with branches at major Atlantic and Caribbean bases. That position provided me with an opportunity to witness one of history's most massive mobilizations of men and materials as well as to learn something about the mathematics of gunnery and photography.

Late in the war I attended photographic interpretation school and went out to the Pacific. The analysis of aerial photographs taken of steel, chemical, and other industrial plants and the evaluation of the success or failure of bombing runs on these targets gave me a valuable lesson not only about the organization of production facilities, but also about the way materials flowed into and out of these works. This lesson was reinforced by a continuing day to day study I made of weapons which the Japanese were bringing into a large beach in Kyushu, a site selected for a major United States landing in the Japanese homeland.

Because I had joined early, I was one of the first to be discharged at the war's end. By October 1945 I was enrolled at the University of North Carolina. After completing the course work required for an MA degree, I returned the next fall to Harvard. There three occurrences brought me to the study of economic and business history and introduced me for the first time to management thought and practice. The first of these was my selection of sociology as my nonhistorical field. Here my guide was Talcott Parsons, who introduced me for the first time to the value of explicit concepts, generalizations and theories in analyzing human behavior—an intellectual approach which my history mentors thoroughly distrusted. Through Parsons I made the intellectual acquaintance of Max Weber, Emile Durkheim, Werner Sombart, and Karl

Marx, and to Parson's own structural functional approach to the development and operations of human institutions. In his courses I read for the first time the works of Berle and Means and those of Chester Barnard, Elton Mayo, and other management thinkers.

Parson's sociological and institutional approach was reinforced when in 1949 I was invited to join Harvard's Research Center in Entrepreneurial History. After one of its co-founders, Joseph Schumpeter, died in 1950, the other, Arthur Cole, kept it going in a most admirable fashion. Cole, who had already made Harvard Business School's Baker Library the world's best for economic and business history, collected a group of senior scholars and a number of younger graduate students in economics, sociology, and history to carry out the research on and to meet regularly to discuss entrepreneurship, institutional change, business and economic thought, and other broad themes. The center became a seedbed for economic historians of my generation. These included Hugh Aitken, Bernard Bailyn, David Landes, Peter Mathias, Douglass North, Henry Rosovsky, and John Sawyer. For me the most valuable senior member was Fritz Redlich, a German scholar who had worked closely with leading German historians and economists before fleeing Hitler. Schumpeter and Cole had found him teaching in a girls' school in Georgia and brought him to Cambridge. Fritz's broad knowledge was central to enlarging the ideas and approaches to which Parsons had introduced me.

The third occurrence that turned my interest toward the history of business and management was my dissertation. I came upon my subject almost by accident. Shortly after I with my wife Fay and our 9-month-old daughter arrived in Cambridge, my great-aunt Lucy Poor died, leaving us an apartment in nearby Brookline. In its basement were the personal papers of her father, my great-grandfather, Henry Varnum Poor. Poor had been the editor of *The American Railroad Journal* from 1849 to 1861. After the Civil War he became editor of *Poor's Manual of Railroads*, published annually. His name is remembered today as one half of the Standard & Poor's Corporation, the provider of business information and bond ratings.

As editor of *The American Railroad Journal* in the 1850s, Poor wrote every week about current developments in what was to be the nation's first big business. In describing the construction of individual roads, he depicted the beginnings of the modern construction industry. In their financing he described the creation of modern Wall Street. For not only did the financing of railroads bring the rapid growth of the New York Stock Exchange, but it also led to the almost immediate invention of a rich variety of financial instruments including preferred stock, convertible stock (into bonds), convertible bonds (into stock), and second, third mortgages and debenture bonds. In addition his weekly articles chronicled the beginnings of modern management. They described the creation of the world's first, and for a long period of time the largest, managerial hierarchies in the business world and the formation of the statistical and control systems essential to manage them. Poor also told of the beginnings of modern labor relations and the coming of the most powerful of the nineteenth-century labor unions, the railroad Brotherhoods. He described the first modern oligopolistic competition between a small number of giant companies with huge fixed capital costs—competition which in turn led to the beginnings of modern government regulation of big business. After the Civil War Poor addressed himself to these same subjects in pamphlets, books, and in the introductions to the annual Poor's *Manual*.

Not only was the substance of Poor's writing of great significance for the historian, but so too was his approach. From the start he believed in a comparative analysis. From his own files and from questionnaires sent out to individual railroads he completed brief histories of all the major American roads. On this solid base rested his analyses of their performance and his generalizations about their construction, financing, and operations. Few young scholars have had this same opportunity to write a dissertation that dealt so thoroughly and intimately with so significant a set of economic and business developments.

MIT: THE LETTERS OF THEODORE ROOSEVELT and STRATEGY AND STRUCTURE

In 1950, even though the dissertation was unfinished, I accepted a much needed job. Our family now included two daughters. I was asked by Elting Morison to come to MIT to assist him and my close friend John Morton Blum in editing the letters of Theodore Roosevelt and to teach in the Institute's Department of English and History. The editing gave me a day to day acquaintance with T.R.—the youngest, most ebullient, and versatile of our Presidents. It introduced me into the complexities of high-level decision making and the intricacies of the political process. As important, I realized I was working with the basic sources on which all later historical analyses of Roosevelt, his administration and his times would be made. Interpretations change, but they must rest on the basic data—correspondence and internal memoranda and notes, published speeches, newspaper stories, articles, and books. I learned, too, that decisions, many with long-term consequences had to be made on insufficient information and with great uncertainty as to their outcomes.

At MIT my teaching soon involved organizing and managing one of the two humanities courses the sophomores were required to take—the one on American Civilization (the other was on the European story). I also offered a course of my own in American Economic and Business History—a course that I continued to give in numerous variations for the rest of my teaching career.

In 1954 I received an invitation to create and teach a course at the United States Naval War College on the basis of national strategy—a topic about which I knew almost nothing. Even so I found the invitation appealing because I had spent five years during the war in the lower ranks. At the War College I had the good fortune to meet William Reitzel of the Brookings Institution. Reitzel was as interested in government and military organization as I was in the structure of business. We soon made tentative plans to collaborate in writing a book that examined through detailed case studies major structural changes in large-scale organizations. He would focus on his concerns and I on mine.

On returning to Washington, Reitzel turned to other related topics. As I took up teaching again at MIT, I began a preliminary study of structural changes in large American corporations. From it I learned that the most fundamental change was that from a centralized, functionally departmentalized structure (the U-form, as economists later termed it) to a multidivisional one with a corporate office and a number of product or geographic divisions (the M-form). I learned too that the most important innovators of the new form were Du Pont, General Motors, Standard Oil (New Jersey)—it is now Exxon—and Sears Roebuck.

My next step was to get inside these companies so as to read their records and to talk to executives who had been involved. I was impressed when Du Pont's Walter Carpenter was able to have on his desk within half an hour the "Organization file" for the structural changes carried out between 1919 and 1921. On the other hand I was disappointed when the CEO at Sears reported that no such records existed. But I was delighted, when on a visit to Chicago, one of the executives who had participated in their reorganizations asked me if I wanted to see the records that were still in his office. They were indeed rich. At Standard Oil (New Jersey), I was distressed by the strong opposition of the Harvard historians who were then writing Jersey Standard's history, but pleased when the company gave me full access.

Just at this moment the real break came. I received a letter from Alfred P. Sloan Jr. saying he had read a piece I had recently written on management decentralization and invited me to assist him and Fortune editor John MacDonald in doing historical research and writing for the book that became *My Years with General Motors.*

Here was an opportunity indeed. When I first talked to Sloan he suggested that we sit down and he would tell me how he ran General Motors. I replied I would much prefer to review the documents (and after the Du Pont Company took control of GM those records became as complete and detailed as those at Du Pont) and then write up a rough draft of the manuscript which we would review together. This was a historian's dream—to have a full documentary record and then to review the findings from those records with the principal actor. When Sloan's memory disagreed, we checked the documents together. For example, he was under the impression that he had invented the annual model. I showed him the minutes of the Sales Committee in which he and his associates agreed that because of the cost, "We are all against yearly models." On the other hand, the minutes continued, Sloan and the other executives did not want to follow the Ford or Dodge strategy of producing just a single model. Their decision was to come up with "face-lifting" for two years and then incorporate product innovations during the third.

There was, however, one event that Sloan did not want to talk about. That was the failure of the air-cooled engine that Charles Kettering had developed in the early 1920s to revive the three weakest of the five car divisions. Once Sloan began to read the extensive documentation carefully, he realized how critical the part that the decisions in developing and then abandoning this impressive innovation played in the final rebuilding of the General Motors organization structure. That chapter on the "copper-cooled engine" became a central one in the book.

As I began to study my four companies (actually I completed two more case studies both on railroad reorganizations—those of the Burlington and of the Illinois Central—that were not included in the final work), I assumed, following the conventional wisdom of the day, that divisionalization was a response to the need to decentralize decision making, a need arising from the increasing enterprise size. Too many decisions were being made at the top and too few delegated to middle managers.

As the research progressed, I realized that the overload in decision making at the top was indeed the reason for creating the new structure. But the need did not result from the larger enterprise size per se. It came rather from the increasing diversity and complexity of decisions that senior managers had to make. It came when an enterprise began to operate in a number of geographic areas or in a number of related product markets. Decisions at Du Pont increased rapidly after its diversification into several new industries. Top-level decision making at General Motors differed from that at Ford precisely because Ford concentrated on the mass production and distribution of a single model, while General Motors made and sold many different lines of automobiles, trucks, parts, and accessories. Jersey Standard operated in many more foreign markets than did any other American oil company. At Sears the overload was sharply increased when under General Robert Wood's guidance Sears, the country's largest mail-order house, became one of its leading retail chains as well. Much the same was true for other leading industrial enterprises that adopted the multidivisional structure in the years before 1960.

Research in the records of these companies also revealed how existing management procedures, including the existing structure of the enterprise, shaped—usually holding back—changes in strategy. Just as basic reorganizations in structure came only after a sharp crisis (serious financial losses at Du Pont and General Motors; a series of smaller related crises over a much longer period of time at Standard Oil and Sears, Roebuck); so, too, the initial changes in strategy in these companies came only after a massive shift in their markets. At Du Pont the first try at diversification was a limited response to the loss of government orders for military propellants in 1908. The full-blown development of that strategy came from a search for peacetime uses for the vastly increased facilities and personnel required to meet the demands of the Allies, and then the U.S. government, for ammunition during World War I. For Jersey Standard, increasing concentration and expansion in overseas markets was a direct response to the Supreme Court's 1911 decision, which broke up the original Standard Oil Company into a number of large independent operating firms. By that decision the Court permitted its successor, Standard Oil (New Jersey), to sell in only a few northeastern states. At Sears the move into chain stores located in and near urban areas was a reaction to the diminution of the basic rural market for its mail-order business, as agricultural income declined sharply and agriculture became a minor sector in the American economy in terms of income and productivity. At General Motors, a new company in a new industry, the impetus was not from a shift in the market, but a collapse of the market.

Thus structure had as much impact on strategy as strategy had on structure. But because the changes in strategy came chronologically before those of structure, and perhaps also because an editor at The MIT Press talked me into changing the title from *Structure and Strategy* to *Strategy and Structure*, the book appears to concentrate more on how strategy defines structure than on how structure affects strategy. My goal from the start was to study the complex interconnections in a modern industrial enterprise between structure and strategy in an ever-changing external environment.

Although the pioneering firms I studied have had their ups and downs since they adopted the new structure, they still use it. Indeed by World War II most industrial enterprises that expanded into new geographic or related product markets adopted similar structures. The senior managers of area or product divisions had the responsibility for market share and profit. They were given full control of the functional activities—production, sales, purchasing, and research and development—essential to carrying out such responsibilities. Top managers in corporate offices monitored the operating divisions and, on the basis of the divisions' performances and estimates of changing markets and technologies, planned for future production and distribution and allocated resources to implement these plans.

The new institutional structure was no panacea. The firms I examined, as well as others, have had constant problems in defining the relationship between their corporate center and their operating divisions and among the divisions themselves. At Du Pont, for example, divisions became powerful baronies that often went their own way with too little oversight. At General Motors, on the other hand, the corporate office, particularly its financial executives and staff, exercised strong, probably too strong, authority over the divisions. In these and other diversified firms the introduction of profit centers within the divisions has confused responsibility and accountability. Nevertheless, a half-century after the restructuring described in this book, Du Pont is still the nation's largest chemical company, General Motors and Exxon the nation's largest automobile and oil companies, respectively, and Sears until very recently the nation's largest marketing enterprise. Their overall profit records for the sixty to seventy years since their initial reorganizations have been enviable.

The new structure had a significant impact on strategy. By reducing the overload at the top, it encouraged managers to adopt the long-term strategies of growth by moving into new geographic and product markets. Managers were much less reluctant to diversify or to go abroad when they could administer new business simply by creating a new division. Many soon realized that they had developed capabilities within their existing production, distribution, or research activities that gave them competitive advantage abroad and in related industries. Thus at Du Pont the capabilities created in the development and production of rayon permitted the company to become the nation's most efficient producer and to obtain a near-monopoly of moisture-proof cellophane, produced in much the same manner as rayon but sold to very different markets. In the same way, by the 1940s Du Pont's Textile Fiber Department had adopted a policy of developing new products that made their own existing lines, and therefore substantial existing facilities, obsolete. Nylon replaced rayon; Orlon took markets from Nylon, and Dacron from Orlon. Better to have the company use its own resources to improve product and process rather than leave this opportunity to competitors.

Similar strategies were developed by other divisions at Du Pont and by other chemical companies. Food, drug, and other producers of branded-packaged consumer products, makers of electrical and electronic equipment, and a wide variety of machinery companies were able to use internal capabilities to provide a competitive edge in related product markets. So, too, the expansion of oil, metal, and machinery companies overseas was facilitated by the adoption of a multidivisional area structure comparable to that of Jersey Standard. Indeed, the constant growth into new geographic and product markets based on existing functional capabilities became an even more dynamic force for the continuing growth of modern industrial firms in the years following World War II than it was before 1940.

Once *Strategy and Structure* was published I turned to the next project. Three members of the du Pont family still in top management asked me to write a biography of Pierre S. du Pont. Here again was an appealing opportunity. Pierre had been the person most responsible for the transformation of the Du Pont company from what it was in 1902—a family firm with only six stockholders operating from a tiny office—to what it was in 1917—the eighth largest industrial enterprise in the United States. Not only did Pierre du Pont create the modern Du Pont Company, but after he became president of General Motors at the end of 1920 following William Durant's financial disasters, he brought Alfred Sloan into top management. Together they turned General Motors into the world's largest and most profitable automobile company. I already knew that Pierre was an ardent recordkeeper and that the Du Pont Company and General Motors by following his example had superb archives. Here was a chance to observe the day-by-day creation and operation of two of the nation's most successful modern industrial corporations.

JOHNS HOPKINS: *THE EISENHOWER PAPERS* AND THE BIOGRAPHY OF PIERRE du PONT

Then, just as I was beginning to start work, I was asked by Milton Eisenhower, the president of Johns Hopkins to come to his university to teach modern American History and to edit the papers of his brother. A trip to Gettysburg where Dwight D. Eisenhower had retired on leaving the presidency convinced me that here was a chance to be first into a new period of history. Moreover, the opportunity to watch the day-by-day development of Allied strategy and the building of an organization to implement it during World War II was too good to miss. I decided, therefore, to do both projects, by recruiting an able young scholar, Stephen Ambrose, as associate editor of the papers and another, Stephen Salsbury, to be co-author of the du Pont biography. So our family moved from Brookline to Baltimore in the summer of 1963.

The years at Hopkins were busy ones. The du Pont records and the Eisenhower papers were all that I had anticipated. The initial decision on the Eisenhower project was to by-pass his early years and start when George Marshall brought Lieutenant Colonel Eisenhower to Washington immediately after Pearl Harbor to head War Plans for the Pacific. As with Sloan I suggested that I edit a six-month period of the General's papers and then bring them to Gettysburg for his review. In the case of Pierre du Pont we did begin at the beginning describing his early years on the Brandywine, at MIT, and his first business activities. His story did indeed inform in great detail the ways in which the two giant corporations were created and managed.

At Hopkins the teaching of both undergraduates and graduates went well. Good undergraduates and outstanding graduate students made the experience most rewarding. But four years as chairman of the History Department and the inauguration of a Center for the Study of Recent American History increased the pressure. Finally, in the fall of 1969 as the first five volumes of the Eisenhower papers—those on the war years—went to press and as the du Pont book reached completion, I realized that I could not edit the papers, continue to teach and also write the book I always wanted to on the rise of modern managerial enterprise in the United States. So I told Milton Eisenhower that I would have to turn the papers over to another editor.

At that moment I received an invitation to come to the Harvard Business School for a year with the thought of becoming Straus Professor of Business History on Ralph Hidy's retirement the following June. At Harvard I liked very much what I saw. I accepted the chair and then spent half of 1970 and 1971 turning over the Eisenhower papers to a most competent younger historian Louis Galambos. One regret I had on leaving that project was that I had not yet written the piece on Eisenhower as an organization builder. In creating a unified theater command that included not only the Army, Navy, and Air Forces of the United States, but also those of Britain and other allies, Eisenhower had a keen understanding of a need for and of problems involved in defining a clear-cut organization structure so essential to both the formulation and implementation of military strategy. I would have liked also to have compared more explicitly the differences in military and business structure and strategy. I was sorry to have unbeen able to utilize in my later work what I learned from the Eisenhower Papers in the way I did from the study of Pierre du Pont.

THE HARVARD BUSINESS SCHOOL AND
THE VISIBLE HAND

At the Business School I was able to concentrate on completing my major intellectual goal. I began by reorganizing the second year course in Business History around the theme of the coming of modern managerial capitalism. I wanted the course to do three things. One was to show how and why the American economy was transformed from a rural, agrarian and commercial one into its modern industrial and urban form. Another was to indicate the role played by salaried managers in this transformation; for in the first decades of the nineteenth century their number was tiny and those few were in charge of small mills or plantations. There were almost no middle managers; that is, managers to whom lower-level managers reported and who in turn reported to senior executives. Until mid-century owners managed and managers owned. By the end of the nineteenth century major industries had become dominated by large firms that were operated by scores of middle, lower, and top salaried managers who had little or no equity in the enterprises they administered. A third approach was to show when, where and how each of the processes and techniques that the students were studying at the School—those in production, marketing, accounting, control, and general management first came into being and how each generation of managers built on the achievements of earlier ones.

Thus the teaching of the course and the writing of the book went hand in hand. New research was incorporated into the course and the discussions and questions raised in class modified my analysis of the findings. As I developed the course, I had a chance to talk to colleagues—some of the most knowledgeable scholars in their fields—about current practices and techniques. As I have said many times, *The Visible Hand* would not have been the book it became had I not moved to the Harvard Business School.

The basic theme of *The Visible Hand* is that in the most vital sectors, but certainly no all sectors, of the economy *The Visible Hand* of managers replaced the invisible hand of market forces in coordinating flows and allocating resources. "The market remained the generator of demand for goods and services," as I say on page one of the book, "but modern business enterprise took over the function of coordinating the flow of goods through the existing processes of production and distribution, and that of allocating funds and personnel for future production and distribution." This statement was followed by a set of propositions about the growth and development of a new institution—the modern managerial enterprise—administered by a new subspecies of economic man—the salaried manager. As was the case with *Strategy and Structure*, these propositions were derived (induced) from the historical data. The data were not selected to illustrate or verify the propositions.

The Visible Hand begins with a description of American business institutions and processes as they existed in the first half of the nineteenth century. As late as the 1840s the traditional ways and organization of commerce had changed little since the commercial revival of trade in the Mediterranean six centuries earlier. Although the adoption of machinery and steam power in the making of metals and textiles was beginning to alter the ways of production, the movement of goods and messages through an economy still depended, as it had since ancient times, on the power of wind, water, animal or man. The small output of goods per unit of production and the slow and uncertain movement of goods and people meant that production and distribution were still easily handled by personally owned and managed enterprises.

The coming of the railroad (and its handmaiden the telegraph) in the two decades prior to the Civil War began to revolutionize transportation and communications. The demands of building and operating railroads forced their managers to pioneer in all ways and methods of modern big business. At the same time the railroad and telegraph, the steamship and cable, provided the transportation and communication infrastructure that made possible the unprecedented volume, speed and regularity in the movement of goods, messages and people that so swiftly transformed the processes of production and distribution. Here I enlarged on what I had learned from Henry Varnum Poor concerning the role of railroads in forcing innovations in construction, finance, competition, government regulation, labor relations, and above all, business management. The railroads required the building of hierarchies of lower, middle and top managers which were as large and whose tasks were as complex as the largest of the industrial enterprises in the mid-twentieth century. By the 1880s the Burlington, the Pennsylvania and other roads had created the multidivisional form of organization. By that time a single railroad, the Pennsylvania, had more full-time employees than did the Federal government including all the armed forces.

The book then describes the coming of mass distribution and mass production that became possible with the completion of the new transportation and communication systems. These changes came first in distribution with the appearance of the modern commodity dealers, the all-service wholesalers who made profits through markup rather than by commission as merchants had done from time immemorial. Then came the new mass retailers—the department stores, the mail-order houses and the chain stores. So revolutionary were the new institutions that by 1905 Sears, Roebuck's mail-order house in Chicago filled over 100,000 orders in a day, more than most merchants of the earlier years did in a lifetime. In production, factories powered by steam-driven machines grew swiftly in number and size in the oldest of American industries, those processing tobacco and grain. A variety of innovations transformed the refining and distilling industries as they did in metal making. American companies quickly acquired global dominance in the volume production of sewing, office and agricultural machinery mass produced through the fabrication and the assembling of standardized parts—a technique known worldwide as "the American system of manufacturers." And in the 1890s such mass production began to be systematized through the work of Frederick W. Taylor, the creator of "scientific management," and other consultants.

The next three chapters describe the swift rise of the modern industrial enterprise that integrated the processes of mass production with those of mass distribution, primarily wholesaling within a single business firm; thus combining the economies of high volume throughput with the advantages of high stockturn and generous cash flows. These firms came into being in two ways. Some single unit firms moved directly into building their own national and global marketing networks and extensive purchasing organizations. For others, mergers came first. The merged enterprises centralized the administration of their many production facilities, consolidated their marketing organizations and then integrated forward and backwards. Unless they rationalized their facilities in this manner they rarely remained competitive; and, even then, they were rarely successful in the long run unless they were in capital-intensive industries.

Then come chapters that outline the operations and the continuing growth of these new single product but often multinational enterprises. In describing and analyzing those firms that grew large by building their own marketing and purchasing organizations, I concentrate on examining the beginnings of middle management. I do so by looking at Duke's American Tobacco Company, Armour's meat-packing enterprise, the McCormick Harvester Works and Isaac Singer's and Edward Clark's sewing machine company. Here I examine the beginnings and operations of several functional departments— production, marketing and service, purchasing and finance. I use the history of another four companies—those which grew out of merger—to analyze the beginnings of top management in industrial corporations. Here I review the beginnings and operations of the corporate offices at the Standard Oil Trust, General Electric, U.S. Rubber and the Du Pont Company by observing the process of post-merger rationalization followed by department building (including a department for research and development), and then the creation of the internal control and accounting systems that became standard practice in American industry.

The last substantive chapter on the maturing of modern business enterprise tells of the perfecting of the new administrative organizations including a brief reference to the creation of the multidivisional structure in the 1920s and 1930s. It also reviews the increasing professionalization of management (including the coming of schools of business), the continuing growth of enterprises in capital-intensive industries where high volume production, complexity of product and process, and the growing importance of research and development, gave large U.S. enterprises with their lower, middle, and top managers competitive advantage in national and international markets. Such enterprises, I emphasize, did not come to dominate in the less capital-intensive industries where technology was relatively simple and where markets were less complex, requiring little in the way of specialized services and credit. Such industries as publishing and printing, textiles, apparel, lumber, furniture, and leather remain less concentrated and the enterprises in them less integrated. There the visible hand of management played a far less significant role in coordinating the flow of goods and in developing long-term strategies for investment in future production and distribution than was the case in capital-intensive industries.

It was only after I completed this history of where, when, and how, and, therefore, why modern managerial enterprise appeared and continued to grow in the second half of the nineteenth century and early twentieth century that I pulled together the general propositions with which I introduced the book. The first was that the modern multiunit enterprise replaced single unit ones (those that carried out a single function in a single geographical location) when administrative coordination permitted greater productivity, lower costs and higher profits than coordination by market mechanisms. Next, such advantages could only be realized by the creation of a managerial hierarchy of lower, middle, and top managers. Third, modern business enterprise appeared only after the volume of economic activity reached the level that made administrative coordination more efficient and profitable than market coordination. Once a managerial hierarchy was formed and carried out its functions of administrative coordination, the hierarchy itself became a source of permanence, power and continued growth. The careers of salaried managers became increasingly technical and professional. As these enterprises grew in size and diversity and as managers became more professional, the management of firms became separated from their ownership. In the making of administrative decisions, career managers preferred policies that favored long-term strategic growth to those that maximized current profits. Finally, as managerial enterprises grew and dominated many sectors of the economy, they altered the basic structure of those sectors and of the economy as a whole.

SCALE AND SCOPE

As I was finishing the research and writing for *The Visible Hand*, I began to think about the next project. I thought I might use these propositions to develop a theory or another set of propositions that would help to explain more broadly the rise of modern managerial enterprise worldwide and to understand better the role that that institution played in the transformation of the world's leading economies. One approach was to concentrate much more than I had in *The Visible Hand* on the historical growth of enterprises in the manufacturing sector (the core of modern economies), to carry their histories through World War II and, most important of all, to compare the historical experience of manufacturing enterprises in the United States with those of other leading industrial nations.

In 1975 I went to All Souls College at Oxford as a Visiting Fellow for two purposes. One was to get away from teaching and committee commitments in order to give the draft of *The Visible Hand* its final review and polish. The other was to begin work on the coming of large industrial enterprises in Britain. The latter I did by drafting a brief paper on what appeared to be obvious patterns of development, some quite different from those in the United States, and then presented that paper at a number of British universities. It also became the basis for a conference in London on Business History. The resulting papers edited by Leslie Hannah were published in 1976 as *Management Strategy and Business Development*. In this way I was able to get information and insights, as well as approaches to the subject, from leading British economic and business historians.

On returning to Harvard I decided that the new study should focus on the collective histories of the 200 largest industrial companies over an extended period of time in the United States and in at least two other industrial nations. The 200 provided an ample and a fairly neutral sample. I began by having lists made of the 200 largest in the United States, Britain, Germany, France and Japan at the time of World War I, at the end of the prosperity of the 1920s, at the beginning of the post-World War II period and then in 1973. This work was supplemented by a conference at the Business School in the fall of 1977 to celebrate the publication of *The Visible Hand*. Papers were presented on the growth of managerial enterprise in Britain, France, Germany, as well as the United States, and on related topics by informed economists and political and economic historians. These papers, edited by a young Belgium scholar, Herman Daems, and myself, were published in 1980 as *Managerial Hierarchies*.

After some further research and writing on the American story, I spent several months beginning in January, 1978 in Europe as a Visiting Professor at the European Institute for Advanced Studies in Management in Brussels. In doing this research in Europe I worked with Herman Daems. After visiting company archives and industrial libraries and completing and expanding our lists of the 200 largest, we decided to focus on the industrial and enterprise histories of three nations—Britain and Germany in addition to the United States. Not only did those three nations produce two-thirds of the world's industrial output before the 1930s, but also company archives and business and industrial libraries were more extensive in Germany and Britain than in France and other European nations. Moreover, the ways in which Germany had successfully challenged Britain's industrial power and competitive strength in the three decades before World War I had long been one of the best known and most discussed and debated events in modern economic history.

At the same time I decided on the format of the book. The collective histories of the 200 companies would be presented industry by industry, country by country, and time period by time period. The book would have three main parts—one for each country. Within each part the story would be told industry by industry up to World War I and then again industry by industry for the interwar years. My reasoning was that the managers within the same industry in the same country and in the same time period faced much the same challenges from changing technologies, markets and sources of supply. In addition in each country they operated in much the same basic institutional and cultural environment. To make this broader environment more explicit and understandable I decided to introduce each country's story with a chapter that provided a description of the size and nature of domestic and foreign markets, a review of the coming of modern transportation and communication, the resulting revolution in distribution and then in production, the size and nature of country's capital markets, and finally an even briefer review of its legal and educational systems as they directly affected the new industrial enterprises.

For the chapters on the United States the theme became that of the growth of competitive managerial capitalism. There in the industries that drove economic growth and transformed the economy a few large dominant managerial enterprises competed functionally and strategically for market share. The British story provided a counterpoint—an anthesis—of the American one. There few large managerial enterprises appeared. Industrial firms remained relatively small and personally managed. The story is one of continuing personal capitalism. Few founders and families did recruit teams of salaried management but even then owners continued to be senior executives. Nearly all of these personally managed enterprises had great difficulty in staving off German and American competitors. For Germany the theme became one of cooperative managerial capitalism. There families and founders built, as they did in the United States, impressive enterprises with extensive teams of managers. But these new firms worked together through banks and cartels and other cooperative contractual arrangements to a much greater degree than occurred in the United States.

This German story proved to be more complex, different and fascinating than I had anticipated. Indeed, I had expected to complete the manuscript in the summer of 1984. Instead, continuing research and writing largely on Germany meant that I did not deliver it to the Harvard University Press until the summer of 1988. At the same time the new German data helped to deepen and sharpen the work already done on the British and American stories. In carrying out this research and writing I had from close to the beginning of the project until the book was published the invaluable assistance of Takashi Hikino—a scholar with remarkable research skills and broad knowledge of economics and history.

Again teaching reinforced research. If the MBA course was invaluable in the creation of *The Visible Hand*, a seminar in business history was essential to the writing of *Scale and Scope*. In that seminar MBA students, including a number of foreign ones, compared patterns of enterprises and industry evolution in different nations; while the DBAs and PhDs wrote papers on comparative topics. When the seminar became more of a faculty-student one, and scholars were brought in from other universities both in the United States and abroad, it became an ideal place to try out early versions of individual chapters.

Recording and analyzing the experience of several hundred enterprises made clear that there were similarities in the collective histories of these companies despite major differences in different industries and in the three different national environments. Identifying and defining these similarities permitted me to develop a coherent generalized framework to help explain the beginnings and continued growth of private large-scale industrial enterprise and therefore the dynamics of modern industrial capitalism. In all three nations modern industrial enterprises made their first appearance suddenly in the last decades of the nineteenth century. They have continued to cluster ever since in capital-intensive, more technologically complex industries. And they were established and they grew in much the same manner.

The industries in which they appeared were those of what historians have correctly termed the Second Industrial Revolution. They came in the 1880s and 1890s in copper, aluminum and other nonferrous metals produced through a new electrolytic process, in steel, in oil, rubber, glass, chemicals, heavy machines (those that equipped and powered the new factories as well as the new transportation and communication systems), light machines (mass produced by the fabrication and assembling of standardized parts) including sewing, business and agricultural machines, elevators, pumps and the like, and finally in branded packaged food, tobacco, and drugs. In these industries large plants had powerful cost advantages over smaller ones, for cost per unit dropped as the volume of output rose at least until the minimum efficient scale determined by the nature of the new technologies and the size of existing markets was reached. Such economies of scale did not occur in the older more labor-intensive industries such as textile, apparel, leather, lumber, furniture, and printing and publishing. So too in many of the new industries, particularly chemicals and machinery, large plants could use the same raw and semifinished materials and production processes to produce a variety of end products. This exploitation of what has become called the economies of scope lowered unit costs of each of the individual goods produced.

But the potential cost advantages of the economies of scale and scope could only be fully realized if the flow of materials through a plant was kept at a constant level to maintain the use of existing capacity. For if throughput fell unit costs rose. Thus the economies of scale and scope could only be achieved after the completion of the new transportation and communication systems made possible for the first time in history a high volume, regularly scheduled, steady flow of materials in and out of large scale production facilities. Transportation that depended on the power of animals, wind and current was too slow and uncertain to reach the volume and assure the regularity of flow essential to achieve the cost advantages of scale and scope.

But in all these capital-intensive industries the new large plants were able to maintain the cost advantages of scale and scope only if the entrepreneurs who built them made two other sets of investments. They had to create national and then international marketing, distributing and purchasing organizations. They also had to recruit teams of lower and middle managers to coordinate the flow of products through the processes of production and distribution and top managers to coordinate and monitor current operations and to plan and allocate resources for future activities. The first to make such a three-pronged set of investments in manufacturing, marketing, and management essential to exploit fully the economies of scale and scope quickly dominated their industries and continued to do so for decades.

It is important here to distinguish between the *inventors* of a product or process, the *pioneers* who first commercialized such an innovation, and the *first movers* who made the three-pronged investment essential to exploit fully the economies of scale or scope. The triparte investment gave the first movers powerful advantages. To benefit from comparable costs challengers had to create distribution and selling organizations to capture markets where first movers were already established. They had to recruit management teams to compete with those already well down the learning curve in their specialized product-specific production, distribution, and (in technologically advanced industries) research and development. Challengers did appear, but they were only a few.

The three-pronged investment by the first movers created the modern industrial enterprises. It also transformed the structure of industries. The new capital-intensive industries were quickly dominated by a small number of large managerial enterprises which competed for market share and profit in a new oligopolistic manner. Price remained a significant competitive weapon, but these firms competed more forcefully through functional and strategic efficiency; that is, by performing more effectively the different processes of production, distribution, marketing, purchasing, product development, and the like and by entering into expanding markets and exiting out of declining ones more quickly. The test of such competition was changing market share. In the new oligopolistic industries market share and profits changed constantly.

Such oligopolistic competition sharpened the product-specific capabilities of workers and managers. These capabilities plus retained earnings from profits of the new capital-intensive technologies became the basis for the continuing growth of these managerial enterprises. Firms did grow by combining with competitors (horizontal combination) or by moving backward to control materials and forward to control outlets (vertical integration), but they made these moves usually in response to specific situations.

For most the continuing long-term strategy of growth was to expand into new markets—either into new geographical areas or into related product markets. The move into geographically distant markets was normally based on competitive advantages resulting from organizational capabilities developed from exploiting economies of scale. Moves into related industries rested more on those advantages developed from the exploitation of the economies of scope. Such organizational capabilities honed by oligopolistic competition provided the dynamic for the continuing growth of such firms, of the industries which they dominated, and of the national economies in which they operated.

The idea of organizational capabilities is an essential explanatory concept in *Scale and Scope*. The creation of such capabilities and their maintenance and growth permitted American and German enterprises to drive British firms not only out of international markets but even Britain's own domestic market, and to do so in most of the industries of the Second Industrial Revolution. But they did so largely because British entrepreneurs failed to make the essential three-pronged investment in the new core industries—metals (steel, copper, aluminum), heavy machinery, light machinery, electrical equipment, chemicals, and pharmaceuticals. Even where British family firms did make the three-pronged investment as occurred in rayon and glass, they often failed to recruit and train a strong managerial staff. So in the interwar years they lost market share rapidly until they began to concentrate on building managerial hierarchies and developing their own organizational capabilities. So too German enterprises with their highly developed organizational skills were able o quickly retrieve their place in international markets after a decade of war, defeat, and inflation between 1914 and 1924. Again in the 1950s they came back after a far more disastrous and devastating war. So, too, organizational learning permitted Japanese enterprises, first, to carry out a massive transfer of technology from the West to Japan. Then once their domestic market had become large enough to permit the construction of plants to exploit fully the economies of scale and scope, they created organizational capabilities necessary to give them competitive advantage in global markets. Moreover, the nations that followed the Soviet model and relied on central planning to allocate resources (Gosplan in the Soviet Union) and to coordinate flows of goods through the processes of production and distribution (Gossnap) failed to develop echelons of top and middle managers with the product-specific experience and skills so essential to improve product and process and so to create goods that could compete internationally.

The most critical of these organizational capabilities have been the experience and skills of salaried managers. As I wrote in the concluding chapter of *Scale and Scope*, at the core of the dynamics of industrial capitalism were the organizational capabilities of the enterprise as a unified whole. These capabilities were the collective physical facilities and human skills as they were organized within the enterprise. They included the physical facilities of each of the many operating units—the factories, the selling and other offices, the research laboratories and the like—and the skills of employees working in such units.

But only if these facilities and skills were carefully coordinated and integrated could an enterprise achieve the economies of scale and scope that were needed to compete in national and international markets and to continue to grow. Thus even more important to the maintenance of market share than the capabilities of the lower-level managers in charge of operating units were those of the middle managers responsible for the performance of the lower-level executives. These middle managers not only had to develop and apply functional-specific and product-specific skills, but they also had to train and motivate lower-level managers and to coordinate, integrate, and evaluate their work. And most critical to the long-term health and growth of the industrial enterprise were the abilities of senior executives—the top operating managers in the product or regional divisions and those in the corporate office—who recruited and motivated middle managers, defined and allocated their responsibilities, and monitored and coordinated their activities; and who, in addition, planned and allocated the resources for an enterprise as a whole.

Such managerial skills were based on learning that had begun with the three-pronged investment that established an enterprise as an effective competitor. Such learning within operating units, functional departments, divisional headquarters, and corporate offices was a process of trial, feedback, and evaluation. It was more organizational than individual. Even the value of the individual skills depended on the organizational setting in which they were developed and used. Such capabilities—both in facilities and skills—provided the competitive advantage that permitted enterprises to move into new geographical and related product markets. Thus past investments in facilities and learning determined a firm's current competitive strength and set the direction for continued growth. They also placed constraints on the course of that growth, for moves into markets where existing skills and to a lesser extent existing facilities did not provide competitive advantage proved to be risky indeed.

Organizational capabilities are then heritage on which continuing competitive strength and profitability of enterprises and industries rest. Once created they have to be maintained. Their maintenance is as great a challenge as their creation, for facilities depreciate and skills atrophy. They can be destroyed far more quickly than they can be created and maintained. Moreover, changing technologies and markets constantly make both existing facilities and skills obsolete. This is why improvement of such capabilities demand a long-term view and constant reinvestment in physical facilitie and skills.

In the past quarter of a century many leaders in American industry and finance appear to have ignored this heritage. They have failed to understand the need to maintain their core strengths. In the 1960s managers moved into markets where their companies' existing organizational capabilities provided little in the way of competitive advantages. As they pulled back in the 1970s by divesting themselves of recent acquisitions, the buying and selling of companies became a highly profitable business for investment bankers, other financiers, and for the managers themselves. In such buying and selling the worth of an enterprise was often seen in terms of the value of existing facilities and the costs of wages and salaries, as the very language of the financial community suggests. Such terms as "bust-up takeovers," "putting companies into play," and "break-up value" indicate that short-term profits from such transactions overrode long-term considerations for maintaining the organizational capabilities of the enterprises being bought and sold.

As the market for corporate control expanded and these transactions increased, some American firms took themselves apart. Financial raiders dismantled others. Still others by increasing debt or expanding dividends to protect themselves from takeovers were unable to make the continuing investment in facilities and personnel essential to maintain competitive strength. Almost inevitably these firms had great difficulty in competing in international markets with rivals from Europe and Japan where such market for corporate control had not yet appeared. There managers and financiers remained committed to maintaining the organizational capabilities of the companies in which they were involved.

MY CURRENT PROJECT

This apparent disregard of industrial and financial executives for the industrial heritage of the enterprises they managed or help to finance turned me to taking up my current project. I am now bringing the history told in *Scale and Scope* down to the present with a sharp focus on American competitive capabilities. I have made a list of the 200 largest companies in the United States and in Europe for 1988 and have begun to describe and evaluate the changes that occurred between 1973 and 1988.

On the whole the results of my initial review are more encouraging than I anticipated. American firms have indeed lost competitive strength in industries, particularly light mass-produced machinery including automobiles, where as late as the 1960s they dominated international markets. But even in these industries some companies have avoided the pitfalls engendered by the market for corporate control and have maintained their organizational capabilities and their competitive position worldwide. Of even more significance in the science-based industries—those most critical to the nation's long-term industrial health and competitive strength including aerospace, chemicals, pharmaceuticals, computers, and much electorial equipment—U.S. firms remain world leaders. Of the high-tech industries U.S. companies have lost out the most in consumer electronics and semiconductors. Here they did so because they failed to make the long-term investment in facilities and personnel essential to create and maintain their organizational capabilities at the very moment that Japanese firms (nearly all long established enterprises) did so. Why then have some American companies and some American industries been able to maintain their industrial heritage and competitive strength and others have not?

Attempting to answer this and related questions makes my current project as fascinating and challenging to me as my earlier ones. Now that I am retired I may have more time in meeting this next challenge. But I will miss one important tie that was so essential to the writing of my earlier books. I no longer have the continuing opportunity to test ideas and get essential feedback from students and colleagues that goes with the teaching of courses. Even so I will continue to benefit from participating in the Harvard Business School's Business History Seminar.

PUBLICATIONS

1946

The expansion of Barbados. *Journal of the Barbados Museum and Historical Society, 13*(May/November), 106-136.

1949

Du Pont, Dahlgren, and the Civil War nitre shortage. *Military Affairs, 13*(Fall), 142-149.

1950

Henry Varnum Poor: Business analyst. *Explorations in Entrepreneurial History, 2*(May 15), 180-202.

1951

Theodore Roosevelt and the Panama Canal: A study in administration. *Explorations in Entrepreneurial History, 4*(December), 103-111. [Apppeared in slightly different form in E.E. Morison (Ed.), *The letters of Theodore Roosevelt*(Vol. 6, Appendix I, pp. 1547-1557). Cambridge, MA: Harvard University Press, 1952.]

1952

[Assistant Editor] *The letters of Theodore Roosevelt* (Vols. 5-8). Cambridge, MA: Harvard University Press.
Henry Varnum Poor: Philosopher of management. In W. Miller (Ed.), *Men in business: Essays in the history of entrepreneurship* (pp. 254-285). Cambridge, MA: Harvard University Press.

1954

The origins of progressive leadership. In E.E. Morison (Ed.), *The letters of Theodore Roosevelt* (Vol. 8, Appendix 3, pp. 1462-1465). Cambridge, MA: Harvard University Press.
Patterns of American railroad finance, 1830-1850. *Business History Review, 28*(September), 248-263.

1955

[Review of *Gulf to Rockies: The heritage of the Fort Worth and Denver-Colorado and Southern Railways, 1861-1889*]. *Journal of Economic History, 15*(April), 165-167.
[Review of *The regulation of businessmen: Social conditions of governments economic control*]. In *Exploratons in Entrepreneurial History, 8*(December), 111-112.

1956

Henry Varnum Poor: Business editor, analyst and reformer. Cambridge, MA: Harvard University Press.

Management decentralization: An historical analysis. *Business History Review, 30*(June), 11-174. [Reprinted in J.P. Baughman (Ed.), *The history of American management: Selections from the "Business history review"* (pp. 187-243). Englewood Cliffs, NJ: Prentice-Hall, 1969.]

[Review of *Management Sucession: The recruitment, selection, training and promotion of managers*]. *Explorations in Entrepreneurial History, 9*(December), 110-112.

1957

[Review of *Dream and thought in the business community, 1860-1900*]. *Journal of Economic History, 17*(September), 456-458.

[Review of *The industrial worker in Pennsylvania, 1800-1840.*] *Economic History Review, 9*(2nd ser., April), 513-514.

1958

George Bruce Cortelyou. In *Dictionary of American Biography* (Vol. 22, Suppl. 2, pp. 122-123). New York; Scribner's.

1959

The beginnings of 'big business' in American industry. *Business History Review, 33*(Spring), 1-31.

[Review of *Swope of G.E.: The story of Gerard Swope and General Electric in American business.*] *Economic History Review, 11*(2nd. ser., April), 545-546.

[Review of *Altgeld's America, 1892-1905: The Lincoln ideal versus changing realities.*] *Business History Review, 33*(Autumn), 467-468.

1960

Development, diversification and decentralization. In R.E. Freeman (Ed.), *Postwar economic trends in the United States* (pp. 237-288). New York: Harper and Brothers.

[Review of *The American petroleum industry: The age of illumination, 1859-1899.*] *Mississippi Valley Historical Review, 47*(June), 153-155.

[Review of *Administrative vitality: The conflict with bureaucracy.*] *Business History Review, 34*(Winter), 501-503.

1961

With F. Redlich. Recent developments in American business and their conceptualization. *Weltwirtschaftliches Archiv, 86,*103-130. [Reprinted in *Business History Review, 35*(Fall), 429-444.]

[Review of *The American civil engineer: Origins and conflict.*] *American Historical Review, 66*(January), 536-537.

[Review of *Right-hand man: The life of George W. Perkins.*] *Mississippi Valley Historical Review, 48*(June), 142-144.

1962

Strategy and structure: Chapters in the history of the industrial enterprise. Cambridge, MA:: MIT Press.

Jacksonian democracy and the Bank War: The crisis of 1830-1834. In L.W. Levy & M.D. Peterson (Eds.), *Major crises in American history: Documentary problems:* Vol. 1. *1689-1861* (pp. 332-342). New York: Harcourt, Brace & World.

The Depression crisis and the emergence of the welfare state, 1932-1935. In M.D. Peterson & L.W. Levy (Eds.), *Major crises in American history: Documentary problems:*Vol. 2. *1865-1953*)(pp. 328-338). New York: Harcourt, Brace & World.

[Review of *For the years to come: A story of International Nickel of Canada.*] *Journal of Economic History,22*(March), 142-143.

[Review of *Gantt on management: Guidelines for today's executives.*] *Business History Review, 36*(Winter), 479-480.

1963

Entrepreneurial opportunity in nineteenth-century America. *Explorations in Entrepreneurial History, 1*(2nd. ser., Fall), 106-124.

[Review of *Insull.*] *Mississippi Valley Historical Review, 50*(June), 144-147.

[Review of *The age of the manager: A treasury of our times.*] *Economic History Review, 15*(2nd. ser., April), 578-579.

[Review of *Changes in the location of manufacturing in the United States since 1929.*] *Economic History Review, 15*(2nd. ser., April), 578-579.

1964

[Editor and Compiler] *Giant enterprise: Ford, General Motors, and the automobile industry.* New York: Harcourt, Brace & World.

With S. Salsbury. Le rôle de la firme dans l'économie américaine. *Économie Appliquée, 17*(April/September), 303-352.

[Review of *The automobile under the blue eagle: Labor, management, and automobile manufacturing code.*] *Business History Review, 38*(Summer), 280-281.

1965

[Editor and Compiler] *The railroads: The nation's first big business.* New York; Harcourt, Brace & World.

The railroads: Pioneers in modern corporate management. *Business History Review, 39*(Spring), 16-40.

The organization of manufacturing and transportation. In D.T. Gilchrist & W.D. Lewis (Eds.), *Economic change in the Civil war era* (pp. 137-151). Greenville, DE: Eleutherian Mills-Hagley Foundation.

[Review of *Efficiency and uplift: Scientific management in the progressive era, 1890-1920.*] *Journal of American History, 51*(March), 734-735.

With S. Salsbury. The railroads: Innovators in modern business administration. In B. Mazlish (Ed.), *The railroad and the space program: An exploration in historical analogy* (pp. 127-162). Cambridge, MA: MIT Press.

1966

[Review of *Explorations in enterprise.*] *Technology and Culture, 7*(Summer), 434-436.

1967

The large indutstrial corporation and the making of the modern American economy. In S.E. Ambrose (Ed.), *Institutions in modern America; Innovations in structure and process* (pp. 71-101). Baltimore, MD: The Johns Hopkins University Press.

[Review of *The papers of Woodrow Wilson.* Vols. 1 and 2.] *New England Quarterly, 40*(December), 592-597.

1968

The coming of big business. In C.V. Woodward (Ed.), *The comparative approach to American history* (pp. 220-237). New York; Basic Books.

Comment [on Alfred Conrad, 'Econometrics and Southern History']. *Explorations in Entrepreneurial History, 6*(2nd. ser., Fall), 66-74. [Reprinted in R.L. Andreano (Ed.), *The new economic history: Recent papers on methodology* (pp. 143-150). New York: Wiley, 1970.]

[Editor] With S. Bruchey & L. Galambos. *The changing economic order: Readings in American business and economic history.* New York: Harcourt, Brace & World.

1969

Henry Varnum Poor: The American Geographical Society and the Pacific Railroad. In W. Webster (Ed.), *The golden spike: A Centennial remembrance* (pp. 1-5). New York: American Geographical Society.

L'economia americana e i suoi capi. *Mercurio, 12*(September), 13-17.

The structure of American industry in the twentieth century: A historical overview. *Business History Review, 43*(Autummn), 255-298.

The role of business in the United States: A historical survey. *Daedalus, 98*(Winter), 23-40.

[Review of *American railroads and the transformation of the ante-bellum economy.*] *Journal of Economic History, 29*(September), 562-566.

1970

[Editor] With S.E. Ambrose (Associate Editor), J.P. Hobbs (Assistant Editor), E.A. Thomson (Research Editor), & E.F. Smith (Editorial Assistant). *The papers of Dwight David Eisenhower* (Vols. 1-5). Baltimore, MD: The Johns Hopkins University Press.

With L. Galambos. The development of large-scale economic organizations in modern America. *Journal of Economic History, 30*(March), 201-217.

Introduction. In A.D. Chandler (Ed.), *The papers of Dwight David Eisenhower: The war years* (Vol. 1, pp. xiii-xxxiv). Baltimore, MD: The Johns Hopkins University Press.

Dwight D. Eisesnhower: The training and the tasks. In R.H. Lucas (Ed.), *Outstanding American statesmen* (pp. 57-884). Cambridge, MA: Schenkman.

1971

Business history as institutional history. In G.R. Taylor & L.F. Ellsworth (Eds.), *Approaches to American economic history* (pp. 17-24). Charlottesville, VA: University Press of Virginia for the Eleutherian Mills-Hagley Foundation.

With S. Salsbury. *Pierre S. du Pont and the making of the modern corporation.* New York: Harper & Row. [Audio cassettee edition, Englewood, CO: Newstrack, 1987.]

[Review of *The emergence of multinational enterprise: American business abroad from the Colonial era to 1914.*] *Business History Review, 45*(Summer), 223-224.

1972

Anthracite coal and the beginnings of the Industrial Revolution in the United States. *Business History Review, 46*(Summer), 141-181. [Critique by T.R. Winpenny and reply by Chandler in *Business History Review, 53*(Summer 1979), 247-258.]
Introduction. In T.C. Cochran (Ed.), *The new American state papers: Manufacturers* (Vol. 1, pp. 15-30). Wilmington, DE: Scholarly Resources.

1973

Decision making and modern institutional change [Presidential address to the Economic History Association]. *Journal of Economic History, 33*(March), 1-15.
[Review of *The coming of age in American business: Three centuries of enterprise, 1600-1900.*] *American Historical Review, 78*(February), 142-143.
[Review of *The evolution of management thought.*] *Business History Review, 47*(Autumn), 393-395.

1974

Strucutre and investment decisions in the United States. In H. Daems & H. van der Wee (Eds.), *The rise of managerial capitalism* (pp. 35-53). Louvain, The Netherlands: Leuven University Press.
John Jakob Raskob. In *Dictionary of American Biography*: Suppl. 4. *1946-1950* (pp. 681-683). New York: Scribner's.
[Editor] *Harvard studies in business history* (Vols. 27-40). Cambridge, MA: Harvard University Press (1964-1989).

1975

Beikoku Keieishi no Saikin no Dōkō [Recent trends in American business history]. *Keiei Shigaku, 9*(June), 55-57.
Lo sviluppo della macroimpresa e l'avvento dell'economia dualistica. In R. Artioli (Ed.), *Il dualismo nelle economie industriali* (pp. 37-48). Turin: Editoriale Valentino.
The multi-unit enterprise: A historical and international comparative analysis and summary. In H.F. Williamson (Ed.), *Evolution of international management structure* (pp. 225-254). Newark, DE: University of Delaware Press.

1976

The chief executive's office in historical perspective. In J.D. Glover & G.A. Simon (Eds.), *Chief executive's handbook* (pp. 38-49). Homewood, IL: Dow Jones-Irwin.
Institutional integration: An approach to comparative studies in the history of large-scale business enterprise. In. K. Nakagawa (Ed.), *Strategy and structure of big busines: Proceedings of the First Fuji Conference* (pp. 121-147). Tokyo: University of Tokyo Press. [Comments by Chandler on other papers presented on pp. 39-41, 198-200, 214-216.]
The development of modern management structure in the US and UK. In L. Hannah (Ed.), *Management strategy and business development: An historical and comparative study* (pp. 23-51). London: Macmillan.
Divestiture in historical perspective. In G.A. Reigeluth & D. Thompson (Eds.), *Capitalism and competition: Oil divestiture and the public interest* (pp. 1-11). Baltimore, MD: The Johns Hopkins Center for Metropolitan Planning and Research.

1977

The visible hand: The managerial revolution in American business. Cambridge, MA: Belknap Press of Harvard University Press.
Pierre Samuel du Pont. In *Dictionary of American Biography*: Suppl. 5. *1951-1955* (pp. 192-194). New York: Scribner's.
The United States: Evolution of enterprise. In P. Mathias & M.M. Postan (Eds.), *The Cambridge economic history of Europe:* Vol. 7. *The idustrial economies: Capital, labour, and enterprise:* Part 2. *The United States, Japan, and Russia* (pp. 70-133, 503-504, 561-564). Cambridge: Cambridge University Press.
[Review of *Images and enterprises: Technology and the American photographic industry, 1839-1925.*] *Technology and Culture, 18*(January), 107-110.
[Review of *Managers and workers: Origins of the new factory system in the United States, 1880-1920.*] *Journal of Economic History, 37*(June), 543-544.

1978

[Editor] With L. Galambos (Editor), S.E. Ambrose, J.P. Hobbs, E.F. Smith (Associate Editors), D. Van Ee & E.S. Hughes (Assistant Editors). *The papers of Dwight David Eisenhower:* Vol. 6. *Occupation 1945.* Baltimore, MD: The Johns Hopkins University Press.

[Consulting Editor] *The papers of Dwight David Eisenhower:* Vols. 7-9. *The Chief of Staff.* Baltimore, MD: The Johns Hopkins University Press.

History and the professional school. *Harvard Business School Bulletin,* *54*(July/August), 34.

Business history—A personal experience [Presidential address at the Business History Conference]. *Business and Economic History, 7*(2nd. ser.), 1-8.

[Review of *200 years of American business.*] *American Historical Review,* *83*(February), 264-265.

[Review of *America by design: Science, technology, and the rise of corporate capitalism.*] *Technology and Culture, 19*(July), 569-572.

[Review of *Essays in British business history.*] *Journal of Economic History,* *38*(December), 1048-1050.

1979

With H. Daems. Administrative coordination, allocation and monitoring: Concepts and comparisons. In N. Horn & J. Kocha (Eds.), *Law and the formation of th big enterprises in the 19th and early 20th centuries: Studies in the history of industrialization in Germany, France, Great Britain and the United States* (pp. 28-54). Göttingen: Vandenhoeck & Ruprecht.

Historical perspectives and political protest. In E.M. Fox & J.T. Halverson (Eds.), *Industrial concentration and the market system; Legal, economic, social and political perspectives* (pp. 214-215). New York: American Bar Association.

Government versus business: An American phenomenon. *Harvard Business Review, 57*(November/December), 88-92.

With K.E. Carpenter. Fritz Redlich: Scholar and friend. *Journal of Economic History, 39*(December), 1003-1007.

1980

[Editor] With H. Daems. *Managerial hierarchies: Comparative perspectives on the rise of modern industrial enterprise.* Cambridge, MA: Harvard University Press.

Industrial revolutions and institutional arrangements. *Bulletin of the American Academy of Arts and Sceinces, 33*(May), 33-50.

The growth of the transnational industrial frim in the United states and the United Kingdom: A comparative analysis. *Economic History Review,* *33*(2nd ser., August), 396-410.

Rise and evolution of big business. In G. Porter (Ed.), *Encyclopedia of American economic history: Studies of the principal movements and ideas* (Vol. 2, pp. 619-638). New York: Scribner's.

Amerika Igirisu ni okeru Daikigyo. no Seiritsu to Hatten [Rise and development of big business in the U.S. and U.K.]. *Hosei, 7*(December), 2-13.

The United States: Seedbed of managerial capitalism. In A.D. Chandler, Jr. & H. Daems (Eds.), *Managerial hierarchies: Comparative perspectives on the rise of the modern industrial enterprise* (pp. 9-40). Cambridge, MA; Harvard University Press.

With H. Daems. Introduction. In A.D. Chandler, Jr. & H. Daems (Eds.), *Managerial hierarchies: Comparative perspectives on the rise of the modern industrial enterprise* (pp. 1-8). Cambridge, MA: Harvard University Press.

1981

[Editor] With K.E. Carpenter (Advisory Editor) & S. Bruchey (Consulting Editor). *History of management thought and practice* (32 vols.). New York: Arno Press.

Managerial enterprise: Past and present [Special issue]. *Keiei Shirin*(March), 11-19.

'Keieisha Kigyo.' no Seich. Senryaku [Growth strategies of 'managerial enterprises']. *Chu. Karon: Keiei Mondai, 20*(Spring), 62-77.

Historical determinants of managerial hierarchies: A response to Perrow. In A.H. Van de Ven & W.F. Joyce (Eds.), *Perspectives on organization design and behavior* (pp. 319-402). New York: Wiley.

The American system and modern management. In O. Mayr & R.C. Post (Eds.), *Yankee enterprise: The rise of the American system of manufactures* (pp. 153-170). Washington, DC: Smithsonian Institution Press.

Irénée du Pont. In *Dictionary of American biography:* Suppl. 7. *1961-1965*(pp. 2209-211). New York: Scribner's.

Coming of oligopoly and its meaning for antitrust. In *National competition policy: Historians' perspectives on antitrust and government-business relationships in the United States* (pp. 62-95). Washington, DC: Federal Trade Commission.

Business history: What is it about? *Journal of Contemporary Business, 10*(Fall), 47-66.

1982

Sekaiteki Kyodaikig.: Kokusai Hikaku Bunseki [Global enterprise: International comparison]. *Keiei Shigaku, 16*(January), 1-25.

The M-Form: Industrial groups, American style. *European Economic Review, 19*(September), 3-23.

Evolution of the large industrial corporation: An evaluation of the transaction cost approach. *Business and Economic History, 11*(2nd ser.), 116-134.

1983

The place of modern industrial enterprise in three economies. In A. Teichova & P.L. Cottrell (Eds.), *International business and central Europe, 1918-1939* (pp. 3-29). New York: St. Martin's.

1984

The emergence of managerial capitalism. *Business History Review,, 58*(Winter), 478-503.

Comparative business history. In D. Coleman & P. Mathias (Eds.), *Enterprise and history: Essays in honour of Charles Wilson* (pp. 3-26). Cambridge: Cambridge University Press.

1985

With R.S. Tedlow. *The coming of managerial capitalism: A casebook in the history of American economic institutions.* Homewood, IL: Irwin.

Commentary [on N. Rosenberg, 'The commercial exploitation of science by American industry']: From industrial laboratories to departments of research and development. In K.B. Clark, R.H. Hayes, & C. Lorenz (Eds.), *The uneasy alliance: Managing the productivity-technology dilemma* (pp. 53-61). Boston, MA: Harvard Business School Press.

1986

Technological and organizational underpinnings of modern industrial multinational enterprise: The dynamics of competitive advantage. In A. Teichova, M. Lévy-Leboyer, & H. Nussbaum (Eds.), *Multinational enterprise in historical perspective* (pp. 30-54). Cambridge: Cambridge University Press.

The evolution of modern global competition. In M.E. Porter (Ed.), *Competition in global industries* (pp. 405-448). Boston, MA: Harvard Business School Press.

Managers, families and financiers. In K. Kobayashi & H. Morikawa (Eds.), *The development of managerial enterprise: Proceedings of the Fuji Conference* (pp. 35-70). Tokyo: University of Tokyo Press.

1987

The beginnings of the modern industrial corporation. *Proceedings of the American Philosophical Society, 130*(December), 382-389.

A framework for analyzing modern multinational enterprise and competitive advantages. *Business and Economic History, 16*(2nd ser.), 1-15.

Technology and the transformation of industrial organization. In J. Colton & S. Bruchey (Eds.), *Technology, the economy and society: The American experience* (pp. 56-82). New York: Columbia Univeristy Press.

1988

Alfred P. Sloan, Jr. In *Dictionary of American biography:*Suppl. 8. *1966-1970*(pp. 598-600). New York: Charles Scribner and Sons.

Une Response Des Firms Americanaines Aux Nouvelle Norms de Concurrence. *Revuee Française de Gestation, 70*(September-Octobre), 10-21.

1990

With the assistance of T. Hikino. *Scale and scope: The dynamics of industrial capitalism.* Cambridge, MA: Belknap Press.

Fin de Siecle: Industrial transformation. In M. Teich & R. Porter (Eds.), *Fin de Siecle and its legacy* (pp. 10-27). Cambridge, England: Cambridge University Press.

The enduring logic of industrial success. *Harvard Business Review, 90*(March/April), 130-140.

Integration and diversification as business strategies—A historical analysis. *Business and Economic History: The Journal of the Business History Conference, 19*, 65-73.

1991

Creating competitive capability: Innovation and investment in the United States, Great Britain and Germany from the 1870s to World War I. In H. Rosovsky & P. Higonnet (Eds.), *Favorites of fortune* (pp. 432-458). Cambridge, MA: Harvard University Press.

The functions of the HQ unit in the multibusiness firm [Special issue]. *Strategic Management Journal, 12*(Winter), 31-50.

Larry L. Cummings

Calling, Disciplines, and Attempts at Listening

LARRY L. CUMMINGS

This essay is dedicated to the other two directors of "The Institute"–Jon L. Pierce and Chris J. Berger–and to all "The Institute"'s friends.

PROFESSIONAL ACADEMIC DEVELOPMENT AND ACHIEVEMENTS

This autobiography is divided into two sections. These represent two streams of my life, if you like. The first section will be devoted to my professional academic development and achievements. I will unfold these by periods of learning and stages of my work, reflecting on those who helped and guided me, and on what I have learned. The second will focus on the personal and spiritual highs and lows that have paralleled the first set of events. This section is a much more personal, less intellectual account of my development over time.

I firmly believe that these two streams are interconnected and interdependent— both in their causes and consequences. I have never been able to isolate one stream from the other. At times these interdependencies brought great joy to me and those I love; at other times the connections have produced severe pain, struggle, and even depression. I will try to reflect the positive, encouraging lessons I have learned as I have attempted to integrate both streams.

THE EARLY YEARS

I was born at 5:30 a.m. October 28, 1937 in Indianapolis. I have been blessed with excellent, robust health, and generalizable preparation for achievement and responsibility. Both my father and mother provided very traditional

239

midwestern models of the 1940s and the 1950s. My father's gift to me was a model of achievement, discipline, and hard work. My mother's gift was a model of playfulness, loving, caring, and giving of self.

While I was born in what we now refer to as "Indy," a major metropolitan area in the 1940s and 1950s, most of my early socialization and learning was in a small, mid-Indiana school located in the nearby suburb of Camby. The quality of the student body and expectations of teachers were such that I could be seen, in a relative sense, as good at everything. I was good in academics, in sports, in speech, and in class leadership. I starred in all three major sports—football, baseball (my best), basketball—and I was brighter and worked harder than most students.

But I was unaware of the levels of preparation or sophistication I was soon to face upon graduation. I graduated from high school with letters in sports, with all-county and all-city-wide honors in baseball, as starting quarterback in football, and as class valedictorian. I mention these things not merely to brag but because they provide a setting for what was to happen in the next four years as I entered college.

I attended Wabash College in Crawfordsville, Indiana from 1955 to 1959. Wabash was and is a small, liberal arts, all-men's school. It is a fiercely competitive environment. It is an environment in which people work hard and play hard. One's first introduction to Wabash is to be invited to take the so-called "Honor Scholar Exams." If successful in these exams one has a free ride at a very good school, including all tuition and expenses for four years. As you might expect, I entered the exams with full expectations of receiving such a scholarship given my high-school achievements. I was soon to learn that in fact my high-school achievements were not what I thought they were. Reflecting back upon it today, my years of high school from 1951 to 1955 were in an environment in which eventually only five persons out of my class of sixty-three went to college—four of those graduated. I fully believe now that perhaps twenty percent of my high school class was functionally illiterate. It was a rural community. People worked hard. As long as you behaved yourself and did not cause trouble you were passed through high school from one grade to the next. So being class valedictorian was not that great an honor.

Of course I did not realize this until I failed to win a Wabash honor scholarship, and yet my father and mother were willing to support me at a private school for four years. I entered Wabash never having received anything other than an A except in Citizenship, where I got a B for dipping Artensia Dixon's pigtails into an inkwell. Other than that I had a perfect record. At the end of my first semester at Wabash I had earned three Bs and two As. One of those Bs was almost a C. I was in utter shock. I had also pledged Sigma Chi fraternity in that first year and the hazing process was intense. It engaged in things which are no longer allowed in most environments, if any college environments. Those hazing experiences left very mixed dents on me. One, they were very aggressive acts reminding me very much of the aggression I felt from my father and the controlling techniques he used while I was growing up. On the other hand, they were in one sense well-intended, in the same sense the Marine Corps intends when it socializes people intensely, or the Society of Jesus intends as it socializes novices. They taught my pledge class of sixteen to operate as a group and to help one another to take the consequences, good or bad, for our individual actions.

As time drew on at Wabash things improved. I began to find my place in the fraternity. I enjoyed the small community life of Crawfordsville. I also enjoyed participating in extracurricular activities. My grades began to move up. My second semester I earned three As and two Bs, and from that point onward discovered my love for psychology.

The discovery of my affection for the topic of psychology is an interesting story in and of itself. I was taking a beginning psychology course the first semester of my sophomore year. The course met at 7:30 a.m. and I was continually falling asleep in class. Dr. Lovell, the instructor, who later became my advisor and my mentor, called me into his office and questioned me concerning my study habits and nightlife. I explained that in fact my study habits were fine and that the fraternity was reasonably quiet and I was not having any difficulty studying. Of course he queried, "Why in the world then are you falling asleep in class?" I explained that I was not going to bed until two or three in the morning. Then he very politely and gently inquired, "What are you doing with your time at that hour of night?" (He knew that I was somewhat of an expert pool player). I explained to him, not expecting him to believe it, that in fact I was going to the library at about ten each night and reading journals which had been footnoted in our beginning psychology textbook. I fully expected him to not call me a liar, but at least smile, puff on his pipe, roll his eyes, look out the window, and say, "My God, how creative an excuse can one find?" On the other hand he said, "Do you know what that means, Larry?" And I looked at him and said, "No, I'm not quite sure what you're driving at." He said, "Well, I think you've discovered your interest." And he was absolutely right.

From that day on I decided I was going to major in psychology, mathematics, and economics, and had a quite successful and enjoyable intellectual experience at Wabash, eventually graduating with full honors, number two in my class, summa cum laude, and Phi Beta Kappa.

So I had weathered the first major storm of my life. Wabash was reaching for the stars for me compared to my background. I had much loving support from Dr. Lovell and from many of my fraternity brothers and I ended up with a fierce loyalty which lasts until this day.[1]

The Graduate Years

I graduated from Wabash in June 1959. Exactly two weeks later I was married to Suzanne Jay. I had earned a Woodrow Wilson Fellowship in psychology and had decided to attend the University of California at Berkeley. This was the second major shock of my life. Not only did the level of competition again move dramatically upward, but during that time the Berkeley campus was not an easy environment in which it to study. I had been raised in a conservative Indiana community by a conservative family and I really did not understand why everyone was in fact so upset by the events of the late 50s and early 60s. What I wanted to do was to study, take care of my wife, and prepare for our expected daughter, Lee Anne, who was eventually born in May 1960.

I resented our classes being interrupted. I resented the campus distractions, and this resentment spilled over to affect my academic life. I enjoyed the social psychology and the personality psychology that I learned, but I did not particularly enjoy the requirements in physiological and experimental psychology, although I did learn a great deal in those courses. I went to Berkeley largely to study with two individuals, Professor Mason Haire, and a young assistant professor by the name of Lyman W. Porter. When I reached the Berkeley campus I could find neither. I eventually found Porter, but he was busy doing what most assistant professors do, that is, working on his own research. I eventually located one other graduate student interested in industrial and organizational psychology. His name was Stan Nealy. And I also found another by the name of Edward E. Lawler III. We interacted upon occasion, but not to any great extent, and I felt very isolated from a mainstream community interested in organizational behavior. By the end of my first year I was sufficiently frustrated with both the social and political situation as well as the academic environment at Berkeley that I decided to move.

I was very fortunate to learn of a new program in organizational behavior being started at Indiana University in Bloomington. It was being started with Ford Foundation money. The money had been used to recruit James D. Thompson in a business school chair. I was also fortunate to be introduced to William E. Scott, who had recently graduated from Purdue University. It ended up that Thompson and Scott were my primary intellectual mentors during my doctoral program at IU. It also ended up that I was extremely fortunate to be introduced to Professor Edgar G. Williams. Ed was probably the major influence at this stage in my life. He represented hard work, complete honesty (to the point of bluntness at times), an excellent role model for achievement, and expressed complete faith in my ability to do good work. Ed was also willing to share his tutelage with Bill and Jim from whom I learned a great deal. I was privileged during those years to be a part of a doctoral seminar in which Jim's *Organizations in Action* was actually written. It was a privilege to work through the various versions of the book and watch a very great mind at work. From Bill I got reinforcement for my experimental training, my methodological training, and for rigorous thinking. I was also introduced, in a rather heavy dose, to behavioralism, which to this day still impacts my work.

It is important to note that up until this time in my intellectual development I had not heard of, let alone taken, a course in management. I was introduced to management as a discipline by John F. Mee, a master at teaching doctoral seminars by the Socratic method. He did his work under Ralph C. Davis at Ohio State University. Both are important figures in the history of management thought, each being Dean of the Academy of Management Fellows Group.[2] John taught us in a management history doctoral seminar to appreciate the thinking of such early European and American management scholars as Babbage, Fayol, Taylor, the Gilbreths, as well some of the more traditional theorists. John had a way of presenting their works as representing an intellectual discipline which might have practical relevance but should be appreciated for its own genre and its own internal logic and structure. I like that combination of intellectual stimulation with possible practical utility. I had not seen that, except in the possibility of clinical psychology, in my earlier Berkeley training. I also appreciated the insight John provided in terms of the importance of clear thinking and writing. John was always both a friendly critic of his doctoral students and one to teach more by parable than by direct lecture. I later realized, in relatively recent years, the importance of that form of teaching for the development of strong doctoral students, and I owe a great debt to John for my first exposure to this pedagogical form.

My Years at Indiana

I completed my doctoral degree at IU in May 1964. In that same year our son Glenn Cummings was born in Bloomington. My IU career was to continue as an assistant professor from 1964 to 1967. These were good years and brought much joy to me professionally and our family seemed to be happy as well. Bloomington was a very compatible place for both academic work and for raising a young family. I was very fortunate that Sue was committed to both our children and to working, initially part-time and then full-time, as a teacher in the Bedford, Indiana school system. This meant that the economic pressures on our family were minimal and because she worked while I was in graduate school, I entered the profession relatively free of debt and with good spirits.

My academic development during my IU student years was very strong. I continued to work with Thompson for awhile and then Scott. I also began a stream of work with Professor Donald Harnett which was to prove to be particularly productive. It focused on bargaining and negotiation behaviors, and many of the things that we did in the late 60s and early 70s predated much of the work that is being done now in the negotiations field. Our efforts eventually culminated in a co-authored book, *Bargaining Behavior: An International Study*. Don Harnett and I remain good friends to this day although our academic collaboration has largely ceased.

It was also during this period that I began to feel as if *while* I had learned a great deal at IU and was treated extremely well by the administration and by my colleagues there, I was also becoming a bit stale and inbred. When an opportunity arose to take a visiting associate professorship at Columbia University in 1967/68, we as a family decided to go. We moved to Long Island where Anne went to a very progressive, competitive school as a second grader, and I commuted each day into Manhattan. Moving from Bloomington to the New York City area was another major cultural shock for the family. We enjoyed that, particularly Sue and I. We enjoyed the city, we enjoyed the entertainment, we enjoyed the dining, and our tastes became much more sophisticated, and I think our attitudes changed slightly in a liberal direction by an exposure to its cultural differences. Columbia offered me an opportunity to stay as a faculty member. We decided that in fact we wanted to return to the Midwest.

I had always been attracted to the North Woods and the lakes of Wisconsin, where I had spent several summers earlier in my life. So when the University of Wisconsin at Madison offered me a tenured position as associate professor beginning in 1968, we readily accepted and moved to Madison.

My Wisconsin Years

Joining the University of Wisconsin faculty was to lead to several major differences in my life. At the time, Wisconsin was building a strong organizational studies group. Not only was this occurring in the Business School but it was also occurring very dramatically in Sociology. Jerry Hage, Michael Aiken, and Charles Perrow were all on the campus at the same time. It was a powerhouse group and many good students came to Wisconsin during this period to study organizations and organizational behavior. I was very active professionally during this time and my activities became a major outlet for professional development and leadership.

My competitive and aggressive instincts grew during my years at Wisconsin. They were largely rewarded by my colleagues both locally and nationally. However, I am certain there were times in which my competitive instincts were played out in less than completely constructive ways. My major collaboration during my Wisconsin years was with Professor Donald Schwab and with many very good graduate students. It was during these years that I was fortunate to have worked very closely with such graduate students as Tom Kochan, Chris Berger, Kim Boal, Dick Blackburn, Mike O'Connell, Stuart Schmidt, Art Brief, and Jon Pierce. This exposure to outstanding doctoral students, each of whom has gone on to make significant advances in the fields of organizational behavior and human resources, was a real treasure. My work with Don Schwab has been to this day a major source of intellectual stimulation. I have always admired Don's brilliance. I have also admired his intellectual integrity, honesty, and forthrightness regarding appropriately developing both constructs and theory. I learned a great deal from Don in terms of the empiricism which he brought with him to Wisconsin from his Ph.D. training at Minnesota.

I was also privileged to have the opportunity to work with colleagues in other departments through my association with the University of Wisconsin Graduate School. I eventually became Associate Dean for the Social Sciences for a three-year period. These years were like going back to a liberal arts education at Wabash. I interacted almost daily with colleagues from sociology, psychology, geography, history, the classics, romance languages—nearly all parts of the campus having to do with the social sciences and the humanities. I was very much influenced by Wisconsin's strong and exciting intellectual environment. Of course these were also years of great turmoil on the Madison campus and my Berkeley experiences began to be remembered. At this point in time I was, of course, more anchored in my family and I was more anchored in a secure position having earned tenure. But nevertheless I once again found that campus disruptions were major influences on my resentment with regard to my ability to carry out my academic and professional life. I never really became identified with the constructive part of the social and political debates. To this day I regret that I was not a greater participant in that discourse.

Much to my subsequent regret, I devoted most of my years from 1968 until 1981 (when I left Wisconsin) to my professional development, neglecting my family. I rose quickly through the ranks in the Academy of Management, serving in various capacities, including chairman of the Organizational Behavior Division, editor of the *Academy of Management Journal*, and eventually President. Wisconsin provided an ideal environment for that type of professional development. I was affirmed and rewarded for those kinds of contributions, and I found that I truly enjoyed getting involved in building a professional organization and attempting to build upon what others had done in the interests of providing a larger platform for more junior colleagues.

I was also able during these years to develop close personal friendships that have lasted until this day, particularly not only with Don Schwab, but also with Gil Churchill and George Huber. Gil Churchill and I have spent many, many hours on the water fishing, my major hobby, and have maintained a close personal friendship, having shared both great joy and suffering through the years.

There was a real sense of community at Wisconsin between the faculty and most of the students. I worked with students both in the Management Department and the Industrial Relations Research Institute. Both groups of students were good, but they were different in terms of their interests and their background. These were the years in which I began to develop a real sense of my ability to collaborate with doctoral students as the best venue for the expression of my own intellectual development. My resume reflects this and of course my later development from 1981 until the present also reflects a strong tendency toward doctoral student co-authorship. I have always believed that doctoral students deserved first authorship on the work we have done together, but I also feel that in several cases I have been able to make a significant contribution to their intellectual and personal development.

1978 brought what was to be a major beginning of change in my life. My daughter Anne graduated from high school that year and headed off to Stanford University for her undergraduate work. Also in the summer of 1978 my wife Sue and my son Glenn left Madison and moved to Colorado Springs where Glenn was invited to train as an ice dancer. Glenn had developed skating and dance skills to the point where he was beginning to be viewed as a potential national figure in ice dancing. So in 1978 I found myself living alone in Madison and spending a great deal of time travelling back and forth to Colorado Springs. I had also, over the previous four years, grown very close as a friend and what I thought as a mentor for my daughter Anne. She had excelled in every way in high school, reminding me of my earlier days back in Camby where everything seemed to go right. Of course she was faced with much different competition than I had ever known. She chose Stanford, over my wishes, but that is where she wanted to go, and for the first two years she did very well. Beginning at about age 20 Anne began to develop behaviors which in fact were very aggravating to me but which I did not understand until much later. My wife Sue blamed me for many of these difficulties that Anne had developed. Looking back, that indictment was probably true. I had placed too much pressure on Anne during her high school years, and she had in fact never gone through her adolescence and was then doing so. I was a very aggressive, intense, high-pressured individual, and I brought those professional attributes home. It eventually became clear that the relationship between myself and Sue had deteriorated to the point that by 1984 we were eventually divorced, after having lived apart for about six years. In 1979 I was invited to visit Northwestern University's Kellogg Graduate School of Management as a faculty member. So I took a leave of absence from Wisconsin and served a year as a visiting professor at Northwestern. At the end of that year I returned to Wisconsin as Slichter Research Professor thinking I would spend the rest of my career there. During that academic year Northwestern recruited me for a permanent endowed chair, the Kellogg Chair in Organizational Behavior. The attraction to the status of the Kellogg School, the attraction to the big city, the attraction of the change in environment, all led me to resign my position at Wisconsin and go to Northwestern.

In many ways my best intellectual work was done during my thirteen years at Wisconsin. I grew strong as an individual, a scholar, but also as a collaborator. I learned many different kinds of methodologies from people in economics and those in psychology as well as trained in industrial relations. I truly enjoyed the intellectual stimulation. I was also leading, up until the last few years, a very integrated life—that is, I was able to live on a lake and do my fishing, which I dearly love, and have my friends enjoy the same sorts of sports, and to also have a challenging intellectual life.

The Northwestern Years (1981-1988)

My Northwestern years represent in many ways the highs and the lows of my professional career. My move back to Northwestern from Wisconsin was largely driven by the opportunities for a high-status position, a very attractive salary, a good opportunity for consulting income, and a power position within the profession. During my Northwestern years I was very, very fortunate to be able to develop two or three new research programs in the general areas of feedback-seeking behavior, citizenship behavior, and some continued work with Randall Dunham, Donald Gardner, and Jon Pierce.

The work on citizenship behavior and on feedback-seeking behavior were initiated by two very fine graduate students, the first by Jill Graham, the second by Susan Ashford. I mention Jill and Susan in particular because they are good examples of what I will later in this autobiography refer to as my "intellectual heroes;" that is, they stimulated me to develop new ideas, they defended their ideas with vigor and perseverance, and developed their ideas to the place where they have both made significant contributions to the literature. My role was primarily one of facilitation, behind-the-scenes directing, and sort of a general quality control—although they, by-and-large, needed little of that. During my Northwestern years I was also blessed to work with a number of other very important doctoral students. Among them I would like to especially note Rekha Karambayya, Ralph Stablein, Marc Siegall, Anne Reilly, Lauri Ruttenberg Weingart, Elizabeth Wolfe Morrison, Becky Beggs Bennett, and Father Ron Anton, SJ. Each of these individuals contributed significantly to my intellectual stimulation. They represented the highlights of my Northwestern career.

At Northwestern I became increasingly involved in teaching practicing executives at the Allen Center and MBAs in Kellogg's outstanding graduate program. For four or five of the eight years I spent at Northwestern these MBA and executive education opportunities were very stimulating. They provided a perfect arena for testing out the applicability and relevance of my ideas for managers. Increasingly, however, toward my latter years at Northwestern, that emphasis upon MBA training and executive training began to interfere with the sense of balance that I had begun to work hard to attain in my life. That is, I was spending an increasing amount of time in what I considered to be a performance circus, entertaining students in the classroom in pursuit of teaching evaluations. I do not in any way mean to be critical of the high-calibre students at Northwestern or the high-calibre teaching that many of my colleagues exhibited. But to me personally it became a bit of a conflict between scholarly stimulation and intellectual environment on the one hand, and the production of daily classroom performances for MBAs on the other. Many of those MBAs were very intolerant of in-depth thinking or theoretically developing ideas and were primarily interested in the immediate application of whatever material was being presented.

By 1985 I had begun to be really frustrated with this and began to think about possible alternative career lines. It was impossible at Northwestern to negotiate a change in the allocation of my effort toward more doctoral work. I continued to enjoy my interaction with doctoral students, but increasingly began to think about in what arenas I might find a more fulfilling and balanced academic life.

It was also true that by 1983 it was clear that my marriage with Sue was breaking up. I became very depressed by this, and in May 1983 was hospitalized for depression for a short time period and was then under therapy and medication for about six months. This was a painful period, but was also blessed by two other resources which became available to aid my thinking.

The first of these resources was Father Paul Clifford, SJ, who was the leader of novice training for Loyola University of Chicago's Jesuit community. I was very fortunate to make contact with Father Clifford (through Father Ron Anton, one of our doctoral students at Northwestern). He and I worked together for nearly two years on the Ignatian Exercises that the Jesuits use for introducing novices to the vocation of being a Jesuit. While I had no intention of ever becoming a Jesuit, Father Clifford was sensitive enough to the transitions I was going through, both personally and professionally, that he took the time to meet with me once a week for two years to work on the Ignatian Exercises. These exercises, and the thought and contemplation that went into them, were later to influence major decisions in my life.

I have mentioned Father Ron Anton. Ron and I are now good friends. He graduated from Northwestern and now is a Jesuit professor and dean at Loyola College in Maryland. Ron and I spent many hours together talking about theories of education, the stress of intellectual pressures that MBA students face, the kinds of performance criteria that are applied to professors, and whether this leads to a balanced life and a wholesome existence. Ron was very helpful in encouraging me to consider a wide range of alternatives during the period from 1983 to 1985.

By January 1987 I had decided to take a leave from Northwestern to consider what I wanted to do for the next few years of my life. I further decided, after much exploration, to spend the 1987/88 academic year at St. Benedict's Monastery near Madison, Wisconsin. The monastery had recently established a residence program for approximately fifteen persons who were willing and enthusiastic about living the Benedictine tradition for anywhere from three months to nine months. I chose to take an unpaid leave of absence so that I would not be obligated to return to Northwestern and committed myself to live at the monastery for the academic year. The Benedictine tradition emphasizes balance in life. The balance seemed to be one of a mixture of physical labor, intellectual study, prayer and worship, and silence. I practiced these four components on a daily and weekly basis at the monastery for nine months. I gained a great deal of insight into my real desires and about what I wanted to do in my career from there on out. I discovered that my primary strengths and my primary callings were to work one-on-one or in small groups with doctoral students and with colleagues in a collaborative mode. In a sense I had burned myself out teaching MBA students in a high-pressure teaching environment. That environment had become toxic for me.

I was also influenced during this period by the writings and the personal friendship of Parker Palmer. Parker introduced me to a new way of thinking about the spirituality of education. It is best represented in his book titled *To Know as We are Known* (1983). He has also written a more recent book which expresses those same themes in other areas of life called *The Active Life* (1990). Parker and I spent many hours together during that 1987/88 academic year talking about educational philosophies and pedagogical approaches that were more closely attuned to some of my early beliefs in Quakerism.

When I was 17 years old I joined the Quaker church (some of us may know that as The Society of Friends). The Society is primarily known for its activism with regard to the peace movement and its nonviolent stance on almost all issues. To me, the important contribution Quakerism has made over the years has been what I call "The Three Ss." They stand for a life based on simplicity, silence, and serenity. The simplicity and silence themes I was able to practice very well at St. Benedict's Monastery during that academic year, and have become an important part of my life since. I am still working on the serenity side, and given my early background of hard-hitting aggressiveness, competitiveness, and even the occasional use (or threat of use) of violence, it may take years before the serenity theme really sinks in. But the opportunity to live, in a sense, out of the world for part of a year allowed me to reflect upon what kind of an environment I wanted to enter next.

I considered a full range of opportunities, including joining a religious order, moving to the North Woods to my home in northern Wisconsin (which has been affectionately called "The Institute"), becoming a fishing guide (perhaps in Alaska), but also including reentering academics in a different setting.

After much deliberation, thought, consultation with many of my friends, and prayer, I decided to accept a job as Carlson Professor at the University of Minnesota in the Carlson School of Management. I also married Diane Bailiff in July 1988, and we moved to the Twin Cities in August 1988, starting a new life for both of us.

The Minnesota Years (1988-present)

Minnesota life has been a good one, but it has also been one filled with surprises. The first surprise was that five months after our marriage, Diane decided to return to Madison, Wisconsin from whence she had come, and file for divorce, which was immediate. The basis for the split-up has never been completely clear to me. In some ways the metaphor that comes to mind is the famous movie "The Sting." In other ways that is probably unfair. Diane did not fit well into the Twin Cities environment because everything was new. She had removed herself from her support group, she had removed herself from finishing her Ph.D., and she had removed herself from a very attractive job. In any event, by early 1989 I was again severely depressed. This time it required hospitalization for a month, and to this day requires occasional medication and continuing therapy. Progress has been excellent since early 1989 and I owe a particular thanks to Dr. Donald Mayberg and to Mr. Gary Turnwall, for their excellent professional care and love. I also have great gratitude to several of my colleagues at Minnesota who have been with me during this recovery period and have made it a joyful experience. In particular I would like to thank Hal Angle, Rich Arvey, Mike Houston, and Linn Van Dyne. Each in their own way have provided love and care and support and encouragement as I have regained my intellectual excitement and as I have reentered the stimulating world of working with excellent doctoral students.

My work at Minnesota has continued on the themes of citizenship behavior and feedback-seeking, but it has also extended into goal-setting and principles of timing. My colleagues here are excellent. In particular I am blessed by having colleagues such as Chris Earley, Jack Hughes, Mary Nichols, Andy Van de Ven, Phil Bromiley, Stuart Albert, and John Dickhout.

Living in Minnesota is like being in God's country. It is close to the North Woods, it is close to the Great Lakes, it is close to "The Institute," and I also enjoy the excitement of the Twin Cities. I find myself moving back and forth between the Minneapolis metropolitan environment where I live downtown and my North Woods cabin in north central Wisconsin, which has provided a place of simplicity, silence, and peace when needed.

I have found the intellectual environment at Minnesota to be outstanding. Compared to Northwestern, I find myself spending much more time working on research ideas in a setting with a much greater sense of community among colleagues. There is constructive competition and there certainly is debate among us with regard to intellectual issues. But there is not the devastating and destructive political behavior which can dominate a school which is bound and determined to be "Number One" on some list at the sacrifice of a balance of humanity, a balance of constructive intellectual input, and a balance of humane concern for students.

Conclusions

As I reflect back upon my professional development since 1959, there have been a few people who have been of extremely great importance and influence on my life, and whose friendship I treasure and whom in some cases I have collaborated with. Most important among these people would be Barry Staw, my fellow editor of the *Research in Organizational Behavior Series*. Another would be Peter Frost at the University of British Columbia. Peter and I published a book in 1985 called *Publishing in the Organizational Sciences* which helped me to summarize my some 20 years of experience as a review editor, as an associate editor, and as a journal editor. It also allowed me for the first time to express in writing some of the emotional and affective dimensions that I have always felt about the writing process and about interpreting and judging other persons' writings. Peter was a major input into giving me the courage and the insight and the skill to do that. I also learned a lot from the late Bill Glueck. Bill was the President of the Academy of Management while I was President-Elect. He died while in office. I took over the reins from Bill. That was an easy task to do professionally because Bill was an excellent organizer. It was a painful and emotional task because in Bill's last days I learned of the many values that he had hoped to articulate for the Academy and to carry forth. I have tried to do that since Bill's death. I also want to mention two other persons who, while I have not directly collaborated with either of them except for an occasional article, have had a major impact on my thinking and whom I consider to be close personal friends. One is George Huber, now at the University of Texas at Austin, and the second is John Slocum, now at Southern Methodist University. Both of them are lasting friends who have provided strong support and encouragement, and in the case of George, a great fishing buddy.

It is noteworthy that I have not discussed very many of the specific publications that I have produced over the past twenty-seven years. A complete list follows and I leave it to others to judge whether any of them have had a significant impact. I have seen my role primarily as one of an integrator, as an introducer of concepts, and as a facilitator who has attempted to help others bring forth knowledge and ideas which were already within them. I found this a particularly joyful experience in working with doctoral students and working with junior colleagues. I love to work with individuals who are having trouble formulating their ideas but who believe firmly in a concept or in a vision that they have for a research project or a piece of writing. I like to help them and see ideas develop, both in terms of intellectual stimulation, but also in terms of the support during the tough, difficult times. I see that as my most important contribution to the management discipline.

I also believe that it is possible to make an important contribution to the management discipline through one's institutional roles. I have taken seriously my involvement in the Academy of Management over the years, and in the American Psychological Association's Division 14, now referred to as The Society of Industrial and Organizational Psychology. I have intentionally remained active in both organizations because I believe that it is possible to exert more impact on a profession, and on its development and values operating through organizational venues, than it is by purely personal efforts.

PERSONAL AND SPIRITUAL DEVELOPMENT

As I noted in my opening comments, I deeply believe that there is a basic interconnection between the professional and academic development of an individual and the personal and spiritual development of that person. In this section I will attempt to articulate more clearly what I have chosen as the title of my autobiography, that is, the relationship between callings and disciplines and attempts at listening. First let me say that when I refer to callings, I am not necessarily referring to a calling from a higher spiritual being. I do believe in my personal case that this has happened and continues to happen. But I do believe there can be such things as a calling to career because of an appropriate match of career requirements and skills and abilities. It can be both secular and sacred. For me, it has both components.

I have felt since my early teens a very strong calling to a combination of teaching, sharing, giving, and compassion. I have found the academic route to be an excellent avenue for expressing this combination of callings. I have learned over the years that I can identify or at least I can approximate when I feel I am being called to do or not to do something by using the following criterion. If I feel both peaceful and productive I have the sense of knowing I am on the right track. There have been times in my life, in both my personal and professional lives, in which I felt I have been productive but have not been peaceful. There have also been times when I have been peaceful in the sense of contentment but my mind was not productive. I look for and search for, and in a sense wait for, those opportunities where the productivity of my mind and the peacefulness of my soul meet. It is under those conditions that I seem to make my greatest contribution to others and perhaps to the management profession as well.

The disciplines that have been helpful to me over the years have changed. As I mentioned early on I was taught primarily by my father the disciplines of obedience, achievement, perseverance, aggression, and a vigorous pursuit of what one believed in, in the face of whatever odds might be presented. I have developed in the last twenty years disciplines that focus upon intellectual integrity, compassion, sharing, giving, and empathy. This combination of disciplines, which I have certainly not mastered, are in fact life-long journeys. I continue to be amazed at the new lessons that these disciplines can bring.

With regard to both calling and disciplines, there are five books that have been major influences on my life and to which I continually refer for thought and meditation. Two of them I have already mentioned. Those are the books by Parker Palmer, *To Know as We are Known: A Spirituality of Education* (Harper & Row, 1983), and *The Active Life: A Spirituality of Work, Creativity, and Caring* (Harper & Row, 1990). Two other books are by Richard J. Foster. The first is titled *Celebration of Discipline: The Path to Spiritual Growth* (Harper & Row, 1978), and the second is titled *Freedom of Simplicity* (Harper & Row, 1981). Both of these books have helped me to provide a basis for integration and balance between my professional, my personal, and my spiritual life. The fifth book is titled *The Rule of St. Benedict: In Latin and English with Notes* (Liturgical Press, 1981). It is in fact the book that guides the system of living in Benedictine monasteries and has done so for the past 1,500 years. While the language is ancient, and the examples are out-of-date, the basic principles of life that are laid out by St. Benedict in that book serve as a useful daily guide for my living.

I do not claim that I live up to what Palmer, Foster, or St. Benedict claim as the ideal life. But I do attempt to use these disciplines and these attempts at interpreting callings as guides to daily decisions and as guides to daily meditation.

Finally, I have attempted to listen to different lessons along the way. As I have mentioned, my early lessons were around the focus of obedience, achievement, and hard work. I was taught early in my life that one earns play via working, that one learns to earn fun via planning, that planning and work are the antecedents to play and fun. To do it the old-fashioned way. That is, to earn it. If it is not earned, then do not dare enjoy it. I also learned early on that the *gifts* of peace and grace and joy are not to be trusted. The best insurance policies are preparation and effort.

Much of my subsequent learning, particularly in the past fifteen years, has been to try to balance those early lessons with a softer side, and with in fact a more charitable, graceful side of living. In many ways, it has required an active attempt to discard some of those early lessons. That has been an ever-present struggle. The listening for prestige, professional power, material possessions, has softened. I have found it has been more profitable, more peaceful, and gives me greater serenity, to listen to the silence within me learned from The Society of Friends, from the Jesuits, from Father Paul Clifford and Father Ron Anton. I have also paid attention to the Benedictine emphases on balance among work, physical labor, study, prayer, intellectual development, recreation, play—in other words—all parts of life. I owe a great debt to Sister Joanne Kollasch, O.S.B., and to Sister Mary David Walgenbach, O.S.B., for those lessons and for the opportunity to live in their Benedictine community for almost a year. I have also learned to listen to Parker Palmer and other Quakers on silence and the importance of periods of solitude in one's life. And lastly I have listened to my students and colleagues. Particularly, I have found my junior colleagues and my students to be my real heroes in terms of my intellectual and personal development. In this regard I think I can do no better in closing this autobiography than to quote from an essay that I wrote for the *Organizational Behavior Teaching Review* (1986) a few years ago:

> Recently I was a participant in a symposium on 'Intellectual Heroes in Organizational Behavior.' My fellow participants and I were asked to reflect back on our careers with an eye to identifying our intellectual heroes and explicating why those persons seemed heroic to us. On the surface this appeared to be a straightforward assignment—name and rationalize the importance of one's key mentors. Giving this task some thought, however, has led me to conclude that my heroes and mentors are not the same people. In what follows, I will elaborate on the position I have taken and outline my arguments for holding it— as one example of the creative interactions that do occur among educators, and students, and the development and learning within our discipline.
>
> My heroes are my best graduate students, not my first teachers and collaborators, nor my now aging, retired or dead mentors. How are heroes and mentors to be distinguished?
>
> My heroes are emerging and pushy, models of enthusiasm with new ideas and approaches. They bring new vigor, sometimes with rigor (but in its absence, that can be taught), and light to established topics. Some even bring new topics to the field. They encourage me, some even force me (otherwise I lose face) to consider new topics and to defend my reasons for requesting (even forcing) them to go through dated literature on established topics. My heroes stimulate, start, ignite my intellectual curiosity and critical capacities. Occasionally, but not often, and even then primarily on methodological issues, do they teach me anything. That contribution would be less significant. It is to these heroes that I turn when I need new food for thought, controversy, questioning and encouragement (usually through their behaviors rather than words) to undertake yet another new research topic. To me, they are heroic because:
>
> 1. they start things in me;
> 2. they are pleasant when I am active, alert, intellectually exciting; yet, they can be distant, even punishing, when my mind seems dead and my thinking and expression unimpressive;
> 3. they ask so little of me in return, and
> 4. they frequently are not aware of these extremely beneficial consequences of their acts; i.e., they go about the task of keeping a mid-career scholar interesting, stimulated and as pleasant as possible without expectation of direct reward for those acts.
>
> I suppose most think of mentors, early influences, intellectual guides and historically significant others when contemplating the construct 'hero.' To me, that's too abstract to represent a hero. Oh yes, George Lovell (my undergraduate advisor and professor of psychology at Wabash College), Mason Haire (my graduate advisor and professor of psychology at Berkeley), John Mee and Ed Williams (my graduate advisors and professors of management at Indiana), William E. Scott, Jr. and Jim Thompson (my intellectual guides in psychology and sociology at Indiana), Don Schwab and Gil Churchill at Wisconsin and Bob Duncan at Northwestern have each been important influences in three respects:
>
> 1. they have taught me content I did not know but wanted to grasp;
> 2. they have exhibited styles and moods of extremely great range, allowing me to quietly absorb their best and reject their worst while not so humbly feeling smug by contrast, and

3. they have read my papers, listened to my ideas, and helped me through these processes to fine-tune my contributions.

They have not, however, generally stimulated me with new ideas, provoked me to defend mine or pushed me to be something new, something better. Rather, they have generally supported me in becoming what I was already on track toward being. They were/are important, do not misunderstand. But, no doubt, they have been or are becoming too close at hand to be heroes. Teachers, colleagues, and collaborators, indeed, but heroes—not quite. Can students really be heroes to established scholars? Not if they try. That is, it is largely, by necessity, a natural process or it does not occur at all. Why do I take this position? The barriers between students and professors can be many and high. So, for my supply of heroes to continue, there are implications for my behavior, for the selection of students, and for the infrastructure of education and rewards within graduate training. Hero breeding and nurturing from above is a subtle and fragile process. It requires:

1. the reduction of status barriers between established scholar and the potential hero;
2. the willingness and ability to take risks by the potential hero, risks associated with asking what may appear to be naive questions, requesting clarification from a more senior professional whose thoughts seem unclear or nonsensical;
3. a sense of playfulness by both the established and the emerging, playfulness with ideas, concepts, and even data; and
4. looking for heroic acts (i.e., those acts possessing the qualities of novelty, risk, boldness, imagination, substance, and social and/or organizational significance) in uncommon places within the institutional and professional framework of our discipline. That is, this perspective suggests looking to the newly entered (not the established), to those in the early stages of socialization into organizational behavior (not to the priests and gurus), to those with substance on the fringes of our field (not to those at the center of sometimes too tightly structured networks).

The natural processes of professionalism and institutionalization will uncover, label and honor the mentors, the protectors of the discipline, the gatekeepers, and the stars. Our processes to perform this function are well established and frequently practiced.

It is the nurturance of the heroes which requires our conscious attention and vigilance for, all too often, heroes in the making become the casualties of rigidification of paradigms and excessively narrow and authoritarian training. Our processes to breed and nurture my heroes are much less securely anchored in our disciplinary traditions and institutional practices. I believe that the vitality and attractiveness of the management and organizational behavior disciplines as scholarly arenas depend, to a significant extent, on the continual identification, recognition and renewal of my heroes. Without that, these fields become less exciting to me and allow me the comforts of complacency, privilege and status without accountability for reproduction.

Oh, yes, my two favorite heroes are doing very well. Glenn is spending the summer (1991) at "The Institute" studying for his Ph.D. prelim examinations in American Literature at the University of Virginia.[3] Anne is spending the summer as a fishing guide on the Anvik and Yukon Rivers in Alaska.[4] In September (1991) she entered the Ph.D. program in Organizational Behavior at the University of Illinois.

Management is first, and most important, a human endeavor. This account of my life and career has emphasized the human side of my life—both the joys and triumphs and the times of utter distress and pain. My lifestyle, my scholarship, and my approach to teaching and mentoring, have been influenced by this basic assumption.

PUBLICATIONS

1964

With E.G. Williams. *Personnel Management, A Bibliography*. Washington, D.C.: Small Business Administration.

1965

The impact of the technology of automation on the art of management. *Personnel Administration, 28*(3), 46-47.

Foundations for a longitudinal study of managerial effectiveness. In *Proceedings of the Midwest Division of the Academy of Management.* (pp. 55-68).

Organizational climates for creativity. *Academy of Management Journal, 8*(3), 222-227.

Trends in education for manpower administration. *Business Horizons, 8*(4), 113-126.

With W.E. Scott. Academic and leadership performance of graduate business students. *Business Perspectives, 1*(3), 11-20.

1966

Managerial effectiveness I: Formulating a research strategy. *Academy of Management Journal, 9*(1), 29-42.

The manager as a leader. *The Personnel Administrator, 10*(5), 32-38.

With F.A. Schull. Enforcing the rules: How do managers differ? *Personnel, 43*(2), 33-40.

1967

Managerial effectiveness II: Performance at the graduate level. *Academy of Management Journal, 10*(2), 145-160. (Reprinted in *Organizational Behavior,* 1968).

With J. Galbraith. An empirical investigation of the motivational determinants of task performance: Interactive effects between instrumentality-valence and motivation-ability. *Organizational Behavior and Human Performance, 2*(3), 237-257.

1968

With D.L. Harnett & G.D. Hughes. The influence of risk-taking propensity on bargaining behavior. *Behavioral Science, 13*(2), 91-101.

With D.L. Harnett & G.D. Hughes. Bilateral monopolistic bargaining through an intermediary. *The Journal of Business, 42*(2), 251-259.

With G.L. Mize. Risk taking and organizational creativity. *Personnel Administration, 31,* 38-41.

With A.M. ElSalmi. Empirical research on the bases and correlates of managerial motivation: A review of the literature. *Psychological Bulletin, 70*(2), 127-144.

With A.M. ElSalmi. Managers' perceptions of needs and need satisfaction as a function of interactions among organizational variables. *Personnel Psychology, 21*(4), 465-477.

With D.L. Harnett. Managerial problems and the experimental method: A frontier for professional development. *Business Horizons, 9*(2), 41-48.

With A.M. ElSalmi. Managerial motivation: The impact of role diversity, job level and organization size. In *Proceedings of the Midwest Division of the Academy of Management* (pp. 123-134).

With D.L. Harnett. Bargaining behavior in an asymmetric triad: The role of information, communication, and risk-taking propensity. In B. Lieberman (Ed.), *Social Choice* (pp. 163-183). New York: Gordon and Breach.

1969

With D.L. Harnett. Bargaining behavior in a symmetric triad: The role of information, communication, and risk-taking propensity. *Review of Economic Studies, 35*(4), 485-501.

With G.W. Mize. Risk-Taking and Cognitive Set. *Journal of Social Psychology, 79,* 277-278.

With W.E. Scott (Eds.). *Readings in organizational behavior and human performance.* Homewoood, IL; Irwin.

1970

With E.A. Cecil & J. Chertkoff. Risk-taking in groups as a function of group pressure. *Journal of Social Psychology, 81,* 273-274.

With A.M. ElSalmi. The impact of role diversity, job level, and organizational size on managerial satisfaction. *Administrative Science Quarterly, 15*(1), 1-12.

With D.P. Schwab. Theories of performance and satisfaction: A review. *Industrial Relations, 9*(4), 408-430.

With D.P. Schwab. An evaluation of theories linking employee satisfaction and performance. *American Psychologist, 25*(12), 1125.

With F.A. Shull and A.L. Delbecq. *Organizational decision making.* New York: McGraw-Hill.

1971

With D.L. Harnett & O.J. Stevens. Risk, fate, conciliation and trust: An international study of attitudinal differences among executives. *Academy of Management Journal, 14*(3), 285-304.

With A.C. Johnson and S. Sloan. What's new in personnel theory and practice? *The Personnel Administrator, 16*(1), 9-16.

With D.P. Schwab and H. Wm. DeVitt. A test of the adequacy of the two-factor theory as a predictor of self report performance effects. *Personnel Psychology, 24*(2), 293-304.

With D.P. Schwab & M. Rosen. Performance and knowledge of results as determinants of goal-setting. *Journal of Applied Psychology, 55*(6), 526-530.

1972

With R.L. Winkler. On the choice of a consensus distribution in Bayesian analysis. *Organizational Behavior and Human Performance, 7*(1), 63-76.

With S.M. Schmidt. Managerial attitudes of Greeks: The role of culture and industrialization. *Administrative Science Quarterly, 17*(2), 265-272.

With D.L. Harnett. *Bilateral monopoly bargaining: An international study.* Paper presented at the Conference on Experimental Economics, Kronberg, West Germany, September.

With D.L. Harnett & S.M. Schmidt. Cross-cultural and cross-language stability of personality: An analysis of the Shure-Meeker personality-attitude schedule. *Journal of Psychology, 82*, 67-84.

1973

A field experimental study of the effects of two performance appraisal systems. *Personnel Psychology, 26*(4), 489-502.

Managerial motivation: Models and applications (Studies of Sources of Employee Satisfaction). *UIR/Research Newsletter, 8*(1), 13.

Motivation, productivity, and individual performance. In W.T. Stanbury and M. Thompson (Eds.), *People, productivity, and technological change* (pp. 157-177). Vancouver: Versatile Publishing Company, Ltd.

With D.L. Harnett & S.M. Schmidt. Factor similarity of personality across private and military samples: Analysis of the personality-attitude

schedule. *Journal of Psychology, 83,* 215-226.
With E. Cecil & J.M. Chertkoff. Group composition and choice shift: Implications for administration. *Academy of Management Journal, 16*(3), 412-422.

With T.A. De Cotiis. Organizational correlates of perceived stress in a professional organization. *Public Personnel Management, 2*(4), 275-282.
With D.L. Harnett & W.C. Hamner. Personality, bargaining style and payoff in bilateral monopoly bargaining among European managers. *Sociometry, 36*(3), 325-345.
With D.L. Harnett. Personality and bargaining among Thai managers. *Thai Management Association Information Bulletin* (October) [complete issue].
With D.L. Harnett. Personality and bargaining behavior of private and public enterprise managers. In *Proceedings of the American Institute for Decision Sciences.*
With C.R. Forrest & A.C. Johnson. Turnover theory and research: A suggested new direction. In *Academy of Management Proceedings* [33rd Annual Meeting], pp. 338-343.

1974

Behavioral science contributions to the decision sciences, I. *Decision Sciences, 3,* 428-429.
Behavioral science contributions to the decision sciences, II. *Decision Sciences* (October).
Analysis of power cage protest. In J. Champion & J.H. James (Eds.), *Critical incidents in management* (3rd ed.). New York: Irwin. (Revised for 4th [1979], 5th [1984], and 6th]1988] editions).
Comparative management and organization theory: Who needs whom? *Organization and Administrative Sciences, 5*(4), 125-128.
With K. Hayashi & D.L. Harnett. Personality and behavior in negotiations: An American-Japanese empirical comparison. *Organizational Science, 8*(3), 50-60.
With G.P. Huber & E. Arendt. Effects of size and spatial arrangements in group decision making. *Academy of Management Journal, 17*(3), 460-475.

1975

Extensions of current approaches, A critical appraisal: Assessing the Graen-Cashman Model and comparing it with other appoaches. *Organization and Administrative Sciences, 6*(2/3), 181-186.
Strategies for improving human productivity. *The Personnel Administrator, 20*(4), 40-44. (Reprinted in *Perspectives in Business, 2,* 20-23.)

With T.A. Kochan & G.P. Huber. Determinants of intraorganizational conflict in collective bargaining in the public sector. *Administrative Science Quarterly, 20*(1), 10-23.

With C.J. Berger. Organization structure, attitudes and behavior: Where are we now? In *Proceedings of the Academy of Management*, (pp. 176-187).

With B.L. Hinton & B.C. Gobdell. Creative behavior as a function of task environment: Impact of objectives, procedures, and controls. *Academy of Management Journal, 18*(3), 489-499.

With C.J. Berger & H.G. Heneman, III. Expectancy theory and operant conditioning predictions of performance under variable ratio and continuous schedules of reinforcement. *Organization Behavior and Human Performance, 14*(2), 223-243.

With S.M. Schmidt. Organizational environment, differentiation and perceived environmental uncertainty. In *Proceedings of the Decision Sciences Institutes*, (pp. 275-277).

With G.P. Huber & M.J. O'Connell. Perceived environmental uncertainty: Effects of information and structure. *Academy of Management Journal, 18*(4), 725-740.

1976

Reinforcement analysis in management: An overview. *Organization and Administrative Sciences, 6*(4), 41-43. (Part of L.L. Cummings, O. Behling, F. Luthans, W.R. Nord, & T.R. Mitchell. Symposium— Reinforcement analysis in management: Concepts, issues, and controversies. *Organization and Administrative Sciences, 6*(4), 39-84).

With D.P. Schwab. A theoretical analysis of the impact of task scope on employee performance. *Academy of Management Review, 1*(2), 23-35.

With C.J. Berger. Organization structure: How does it influence attitudes and performance? *Organizational Dynamics, 5*(2), 34-49.

With D.L. Harnett & W.C. Hamner. Managerial decision making under intransitive conditions: An international study of the voter's paradox. *Decision Sciences, 7*(3), 510-523.

With M.J. O'Connell. The moderating effects of environment and structure on the satisfaction-tension-influence network. *Organizational Behavior and Human Performance, 17*(2), 351-366.

With S.M. Schmidt. Organizational environment, differentiation and perceived environmental uncertainty. *Decision Sciences, 7*(3), 447-467.

With T.A. Kochan & G.P. Huber. Operationalizing the concepts of goals and goal incompatibilities in organizational behavior research. *Human Relations, 29*(6), 527-544.

With M.J. O'Connell & G.P. Huber. The effects of environmental information and decision unit structure on felt tension. *Journal of Applied Psychology, 61*(4), 493-500.

With E. Schmikl & R. Blackburn. The attitudes of White South African executives: Is South Africa really that different? In R.L. Taylor, M.J. O'Connell, R.A. Zawacki, and D.D. Warrick (Eds.), *Proceedings of the 36th Annual Convention of the Academy of Management* (pp. 332-335).

1977

The basis for evaluation in performance appraisal systems: The importance of congruence. In J.B. Stolen and J.J. Conway (Eds.), *Proceedings of the 9th Annual Conference of the Decision Sciences Institute* (pp. 417-418).

Needed research in production/operation management: A behavioral perspective. *Academy of Management Review, 2*(3), 500-504.

Emergence of the instrumental organization. In P.S. Goodman & J.M. Pennings (Eds.), *New perspectives on organizational effectiveness*, (pp. 56-62).

With C.J. Berger. History, schedules, and anticipations: A comparison of operant and valence-instrumentality-expectancy positions. In T.H. Hammer and S.B. Bachrach (Eds.), *Reward systems and power distribution* (pp. 8-32). Cornell University Press.

With B. Paramita. Organizational performance as a function of organizational size and structure: A comparative analysis of Indonesian industry. In R.L. Taylor, M.J. O'Connell, R.A. Zawacki, and D.D. Warrick (Eds.), *Proceedings of 37th Annual Meeting of the Academy of Management*, 317-321.

With E. Schmikl & R. Blackburn. White South African managers: How different are they? *Business Management* [Journal of the South African Association of Business Management] *8*(1), 3-10.

With C.R. Forrest & A.C. Johnson. Organizational participation; A critique and model. *Academy of Management Review, 2*(4), 586-601.

1978

Themes and issues on work and organizational design. In A.R. Negandhi & B. Wilpert (Eds.), *Work organization research: American and european perspectives*. Kent, OH: Kent State University Press.

Toward organizational behavior. *Academy of Management Review, 3*(1), 90-98.

With M.J. O'Connell. Organizational Innovation: A Model and Needed Research. *Journal of Business Research, 6*(1), 33-50.

With M.J. O'Connell, & G.P. Huber. Informational and structural determinants of decision-maker satisfaction. In B. King, S. Streufert & F.E. Fiedler (Eds.), *Managerial control and organizational democracy*, (pp. 231-249). Washington, D.C.: V.H. Winston and Sons.

With D.P. Schwab. Designing appraisal systems for information yield. *California Management Review, 20*(4), 18-25.

1979

Task design: Resolved: Individual differences add explained variance in predicting task design outcomes—The negative position. In B.M. Karmel (Ed.), *Point and Counterpoint in Organizational Behavior*. W.B. Saunders.

Disturbing trends in the organizational behavior teaching society. *Exchange: The Organizational Behavior Teaching Journal, 4*(2), 6-7.

With C.J. Berger. Organization structure, attitudes, and behavior. In B.J. Staw (Ed.), *Research in organizational behavior* (Vol. 1, pp. 169-208). Greenwich, CT: JAI Press.

1980

The case of the disrupted design. *Exchange: The Organizational Behavior Teaching Journal, 5*(2), 42-43.

Information, individuals, and organizations. *A Review of a Theory of Behavior in Organizations* In J.C. Naylor, R.D. Pritchard, & D.R. Ilgen (Eds.), *A review of a theory of behavior in organizations.* New York: Academic Press.

With D.L. Harnett. *Bargaining behavior: An international study.* Houston, TX: Dame Publications.

With R.B. Dunham. *Introduction to organizational behavior.* Homewood, IL: Irwin.

With B.M. Staw (Eds.). *Research in organizational behavior* (Vol. 2). Greenwich CT: JAI Press.

1981

Organizational behavior in the 1980's. *Decision Sciences Journal, 12*(3), 365-377.

With S. Ashford. Strategies for knowing: When and from where do individuals seek feedback? In *Academy of Management Proceedings.*

With K.B. Boal. Cognitive evaluation theory: An experimental test of processes and outcomes. *Organizational Behavior and Human Performance, 28*(3), pp. 289-310.

With G. Latham & T.R. Mitchell. Behavioral strategies to improve productivity. *Organizational Dynamics* (Winter), 5-23.
With B.M. Staw (Eds.). *Research in organizational behavior* (Vol. 3). Greenwich CT: JAI Press.

1982

Organizational behavior. In M. Rozenzweig & L. Porter (Eds.), *Annual review of psychology* (Vol. 33, pp. 541-579). Annual Reviews.
An analysis of the contribution of collective bargaining and industrial relations by Thomas Kochan. *Industrial Relations, 21*(1), 79-83.
With R.S. Blackburn. Cognitions of work unit structure. *Academy of Management Journal, 25*(4), 836-854.
With B.M. Staw (Eds.). *Research in organizational behavior* (Vol. 4). Greenwich CT: JAI Press.

1983

Organizational effectiveness and organizational behavior: A critical perspective. In K. Cameron & D. Whetton (Eds.), *Organizational effectiveness: A comparison of multiple models* (pp. 189-204). New York: Academic Press.
Performance evaluation in the context of individual trust and commitment. In F. Landy & S. Zedeck (Eds.), *Frontiers in Performance Evaluation.* Erlbaum.
A framework for decision analysis and critique. In G. Ungson & D. Braunstein (Eds.), *Decision making: An interdisciplinary inquiry* (pp. 298-308). West.
The logics of management. *Academy of Management Review, 8*(4), 532-538.
An editor's perspective on being published. In V. Mitchell (Chair), *The 1983 Proceedings of the National Academy of Management Convention.*
Improving human resource effectiveness: An annotated bibliography of behavioral science contributions. American Society for Personnel Administration.
With S. Ashford. Feedback as an individual resource: Personal strategies for creating information. *Organizational Behavior and Human Performance, 32*, 370-398.
With B.M. Staw (Eds.). *Research in organizational behavior* (Vol. 5). Greenwich CT: JAI Press.

1984

On the relation between theory and practice. In R. Dunham (Ed.), *Introduction to organizational behavior.* Homewood, IL: Irwin.

Compensation, culture, and motivation: A systems perspective. *Organizational Dynamics*, (Winter), pp. 33-44.

With J. Pierce & R.B. Dunham. Sources of environmental structuring and participant responses. *Organizational Behavior and Human Performance, 33*(2), 214-242.

The case of the changing power cage. In J. Champion & J. James (Eds.), *Critical incidents in management* (5th ed.) Homewood, IL: Irwin.

A review of C. Perrow's *Normal Accidents. Adminstrative Science Quarterly* (December).

With B.M. Staw (Eds.). *Research in organizational behavior* (Vol. 6). Greenwich CT: JAI Press.

1985

With S.J. Ashford. Proactive feedback seeking: The instrumental use of the information environment. *Journal of Occupational Psychology* (British Psychological Society), *58*, 67-79.

With P.J. Frost. Reflections on the experiences in an editor's chair: An analysis of reported experiences of journal editors in the organizational sciences. Chapter 26 in Cummings and Frost, *Publishing in the Organizational Sciences*, Homewood, IL, Richard D. Irwin, Inc., 1985, 379-468.

With P.J. Frost & T.F. Vakil. The manuscript review process: A view from the inside on coaches, critics and special cases. In Cummings and Frost, *Publishing in the Organizational Sciences* (pp. 469-508). Homewood, IL: Irwin.

With P.J. Frost. Two case studies of author/journal interactions: An acceptance and a rejection. In Cummings and Frost, *Publishing in the Organizational Sciences* (pp. 509-765). Homewood, IL: Irwin.

Spinning on symbolism: Creating and using the threads of our minds. *Journal of Management, 11*(2), 81-82.

Reflections on the relevance of organizational behavior literature from an academic administration position. *Proceedings of the Western Academy of Management.*

With R.B. Dunham, D.G. Gardner, & J.L. Pierce. The direct and interactive effects of focus of attention and work-unit structure on worker effectiveness. *Proceedings for the American Institute for Decision Sciences* (pp. 646-648).

With P. Frost. *Publishing in the organizational sciences.* Homewood, IL: Irwin.

With B.M. Staw (Eds.). *Research in organizational behavior* (Vol. 7). Greenwich CT: JAI Press.

1986

Heroes, mentors and the development of teaching and scholarship. *Organizational Behavior Teaching Review, 10*(3), 60-63.

Reexamining our thoughts concerning groups in organizations. In P. Goodman and Associates (Eds.), *Designing effective work groups* (pp. 350-361). San Francisco, CA: Jossey Bass.

With S. Gupta. Perceived speed of time and task affect. *Perceptual and Motor Skills, 63,* 971-980.

With M. Siegall. Task role ambiguity, satisfaction, and the moderating effect of task instruction source. *Human Relations, 39*(1), 1017-1032.

With M. Siegall. Changes in perception of personal role networks as a means of role stress coping. *International Journal of Small Group Research, 2*(2), 232-234.

With B.M. Staw (Eds.). *Research in organizational behavior* (Vol. 8). Greenwich CT: JAI Press.

1987

With D.G. Gardner, R.B. Dunham, & J.L. Pierce. Employee focus of attention and reactions to organizational change. *Journal of Applied Behavioral Science, 23*(3), 351-370.

With B.M. Staw (Eds.). *Research in organizational behavior* (Vol. 9). Greenwich CT: JAI Press.

1988

Caution in interpreting popular management literature. In J.L. Pierce & J.W. Newstrom (Eds.), Epilogue to *The Manager's Bookshelf* (pp. 337-342). New York: Harper and Row.

Organizational decline from the individual perspective. In K. Cameron, R. Sutton, & D. Whetten (Eds.), *Readings in Organizational Decline* (pp. 417-424). Ballinger.

With D.G. Gardner. Activation theory and job design. In B.M. Staw & L.L. Cummings (Eds.), *Research in Organizational Behavior* (Vol. 10, pp. 81-122). Greenwich, CT: JAI Press.

With R.J. Bies & D.L. Shapiro. Causal accounts and managing organizational conflict: Is it enough to say it's not my fault. *Communication Research, 15*(4), 381-399.

With B.M. Staw (Eds.). *Research in organizational behavior* (Vol. 10). Greenwich CT: JAI Press.

1989

With D. Gardner, R.B. Dunham, & J.L. Pierce. Focus of attention at work: Construct definition and empirical validation. *Journal of Occupational Psychology, 62,* 61-77.

With D. Greenberger, S. Strasser, & R.B. Dunham. The impact of personal control on performance and satisfaction. *Organizational Behavior and Human Decision Processes, 43*(1), 29-51.

With J.L. Pierce, D.L. Gardner, & R.B. Dunham. Organization-based self-esteem: Construct definition, operationalization and validation. *Academy of Management Journal, 32*(3), 622-648.

With B.M. Staw (Eds.). *Research in organizational behavior* (Vol. 11). Greenwich CT: JAI Press.

1990

With B.M. Staw (Eds.). *Research in organizational behavior* (Vol. 12). Greenwich CT: JAI Press.

1991

With P.C. Earley. Commentary on resolving scientific disputes by the joint design of crucial experiments by the antagonistic. In P. Frost & R. Stablien (eds.), *Doing Exemplary Organizational Research*. Beverly Hills, CA: Sage.

[Review of *Management education and development: Drift or thrust into the 21st century.*] *Academy of Management Review*, October, *14*(4), 694-696.

Management education drifts into the 21st century. *Academy of Management Executive, 4*(3).

With R.J. Bennett. The effects of schedule and intensity of aversive outcomes on performance: A multi-theoretical perspective. *Human Performance, 4*(2), 155-169.

With B.M. Staw (Eds.). *Research in organizational behavior* (Vol. 13). Greenwich CT: JAI Press.

1992

With E.W. Morrison. The impact of feedback diagnosticity and performance expectations on feedback seeking behavior. *Human Performance.*

With B.M. Staw (Eds.). *Research in Organizational Behavior* (Vol. 14). Greenwich, CT: JAI Press.

NOTES

1. Effective October 1992, I will serve as an elected member of the Wabash College Board of Trustees.
2. I was elected Dean of the Fellows in 1991 for a three-year term.
3. He passed!
4. A long-time fantasy!

Keith Davis

A Journey Through
Management in Transition

KEITH DAVIS

ROOTS

To understand someone, it is desirable to know that person's roots, because they give insights into a person's interests, experiences, values, and other attitudes toward life. Perhaps most important of all, the values that a person learns in the first 20 years of life probably have a significant influence on how one thinks and what one does later in life.

My family came from humble beginnings in central Texas; neither of my parents ever attended college. When my father, Charles A. Davis, graduated from high school, he remained at home and took an apprenticeship in a bank, working full time and receiving no pay for one full year. After working a few more years with pay, in about 1900 he moved to the nearby town of Thorndale (population about 1,000) to take a job as the cashier of a new bank. He worked there as a respected community leader until he died in 1932. His first wife died from appendicitis, and he later married Grace M. Fulcher, daughter of a rural mail carrier who later became postmaster. I was born to that union on July 3, 1918. The local physician delivered me in our home, where my mother still lives. My brother, Neil, was born five years later, and is an engineering Program Manager. My mother's grandparents came from Holland, and my father's ancestors came from the British Isles.

CHILDHOOD

A number of experiences in my early years may have influenced my values and choices later in life. For example, my father always brought me a book when he returned from occasional out-of-town business trips. I accepted the books enthusiastically, because I seemed to like books. Even when I was too young to read, I enjoyed having someone read them to me. The result was that I learned to read and spell at an early age. Perhaps these experiences encouraged my interest in academia and writing books later in life. Inheritance also may be a factor here, because my mother has been a successful news reporter during the latter half of her life, and she writes well. Today at age 91 she still works two days a week as a newspaper editor-reporter.

In addition, I was taught the value of work as a necessary contribution to one's family, community, or to any organization to which one belonged. Work was necessary to give almost any person a favorable self-image and feeling of usefulness. Work was a public good that helped both us and our neighbors, and it was a necessary part of being a member of a group. It was also the way that civilization advanced with every generation. Therefore, work took the role of an ethical-moral good that rose above being just an economic good. Work was part of our reason for being on earth. Consequently, my parents gave me a number of chores to do, such as working in the garden, berry picking, shucking corn, and feeding chickens. My father also wanted me to learn about the work of others, so he arranged with friends for me to work a few days packing corn for shipping to the table market and picking cotton along with the regular field workers. I also was encouraged to sell *The Literary Digest*, a news magazine, on the downtown streets. If I made thirty cents a week selling the magazine, it was a good week.

During my entire youth I was active in a local church, so I had a solid foundation in religious values to guide me throughout my life. During my last two high school years I was chosen to be Superintendent of the Sunday morning church school, which added to my speaking and perhaps leadership experience. I remember that the gift of luggage the church gave me when I departed for college was one of the most appreciated and meaningful gifts I ever received.

My father died in 1932 in the middle of the Great Depression when I was 14. After his death our living conditions were difficult, because we had no money and no job, so we had to live mostly off the land. During this period I had many more home chores, such as milking cows and splitting firewood for our home fireplaces. Perhaps it was a stroke of good fortune that my mother felt it necessary to take in three to four boarders at $20 a month in order to help provide our meals. The boarders were mostly public school teachers. I made friends with them, and we talked about many semi-academic things; so from that time forward I always knew that I was going to college and lack of money would not stop me.

PUBLIC SCHOOL

Public school was relatively easy because I viewed it as a challenging opportunity, not a problem, so I skipped third grade and graduated as valedictorian in 1935. Interscholastic competitions were especially enjoyable in debate, English composition, drama, softball, and tennis. These competitions gave me self-confidence, and the debate probably helped prepare me for university classroom discussions and community speeches.

One viewpoint that I learned in public school undoubtedly influenced my later philosophy in the area of social issues in business. Since I lived in a small, cohesive town, school discipline was strict and had the support of the community. One absolute rule was, "If you caused the mess, you will clean it up." Accordingly, if we threw paper airplanes and paper balls around the room when the teacher was out, we (not the janitor) stayed after school to clean the room. If I alone threw the paper or trash, then I stayed to pick it up; and I did so on several occasions. The same view applied if we threw trash on the schoolground. In time I came to support this philosophy, because it seemed to be the rational approach: that is, "If you cause damage, you correct it." When I wrote later on social power, responsibility, and the environment, a viewpoint similar to the school one was evident: "If you pollute the environment, you are responsible for cleaning it up. This is your social responsibility."

Another viewpoint from public school was "Whatever you do, always do your very best. Learn from experience and constantly improve yourself." This philosophy influenced both my professional and personal life during my entire career. For example, I kept serving the Academy of Management and eventually became president, and my books kept improving until they became very successful in their market areas. Also most of my consulting with clients was long-run, because I was able to adapt and grow with their needs. A somewhat unusual personal result of this philosophy was my work with citrus trees in Arizona. After moving there in 1958 we planted about 25 citrus trees in our yard because they are evergreen and bear delicious fruit. As the trees grew, I also grew to become a semi-expert on citrus growing. Faculty members and townspeople regularly sought my help with their citrus problems, and I appeared on a television program about citrus growing. After entering my fruit in Arizona State Fair competition, I won in ten years over 50 first prizes for different types of citrus and six grand prizes for the "Best and Most Complete" annual citrus exhibit. Soon this hobby became widely known in the Academy of Management and helped me make many new friends there. All this was done with 25 citrus trees, even though my competitors included commercial growers with large citrus groves.

UNIVERSITY EDUCATION

In the fall of 1935, I entered the University of Texas at Austin. Since I was a high school valedictorian, I was able, with my mother's help, to secure a job as a library page. The job was half-time (20 hours a week) and paid $15 a month. This was not enough to pay my tuition, books, and room and board, so I also worked as a waiter in campus restaurants and boarding houses. These jobs provided free or discount food during breaks, so they helped my very tight food budget. Since this was during the Great Depression of the 1930s every penny saved was important. I have retained an accounting record of every penny that I spent during one month, and it shows that I spent an average of less than thirty cents a day for food! My college persistence was tested these first two years, but I did make it with top grades.

At the beginning of the third year, the library promoted me to supervisor of reserve reading room, a full-time job in the line-item State Budget with a salary of $67 a month. I continued in this job for three years, all the while attending the university full-time for 12 months each year. The schedule of two full-time activities was quite difficult, but I did manage to make it and graduate in 1939 with a nearly straight-A record, receiving a Bachelor of Business Administration degree with high honors and with an accounting major. In my senior year I decided to choose management as a major; so I stayed another year in order to seek an MBA in management. I chose management because both my experience and education convinced me that current management was rather undeveloped in theory and practice, and much improvement was needed. Management also offered more opportunity to study and interact with people.

During my graduate year I found time to run for Graduate Representative on the Student Council, and I won the election. As a representative, I gained some valuable leadership and negotiating experience. For example, I accepted an assignment to make a management audit of the student-owned cooperative bookstore, and I gained notoriety for the thoroughness of the audit and some of the unusual practices that I uncovered.

WORK AND MILITARY EXPERIENCE

In the fall of 1940 I completed all work but the thesis, so I sought employment. (The thesis on work scheduling was completed and the MBA received in 1941.) I had a campus interview with Hughes Tool Company which was the world's largest manufacturer of oilfield drilling equipment at that time, and they rejected me. I still wanted the job, so, with some impudence, I wrote them telling them that I was the person for the job, and they were missing an opportunity. Apparently they liked my persistence, so I received a job as a personnel assistant. I truly did like the factory environment, because it was a chance to study the application of university theory, and I needed a balance of these two environments. During my next two years I had much useful experience, some of it under wartime emergency conditions, at Hughes Tool Co., the Hughes Aircraft Company, and the Hughes Dickson Gun Plant, all near Houston, Texas. On a few occasions I even had an opportunity to observe the famous Howard Hughes in action. He undoubtedly was brilliant.

Shortly after arriving at Hughes the personnel director told me that, because of the defence emergency and my MBA degree, he had agreed that I would teach a noncredit night course on supervision for the Federal ESMDT (Engineering, Science, Management Defense Training) program in Houston. I did this for over one and one-half years and gained much valuable teaching experience.

With the beginning of World War II on December 7, 1941, I felt a personal obligation to join the military, so in October of 1942, I joined the Army Air Force in Houston and was assigned locally to Ellington Field. Since I had an MBA, which was rare in those days, I eventually was assigned as a pre-flight classroom instructor of Air Tactics and Weather. While I was assigned to Ellington Field I met Mary Sue Moore, a beautiful brunette with sparkling eyes. Although I met her in Houston, she was from Gause, Texas, in the same county where I grew up. She had graduated from Sam Houston State University and was working in the laboratory of a Houston chemical plant. We were married January 1, 1944.

In early 1944 I was assigned because of my experience to First Air Force as a Civilian Personnel Officer. My office had the responsibility for handling records, rules, and payroll for all civil service employees on an air base, usually 800 to 1,500 people. This job provided much leadership and negotiating experience. I served at Richmond Army Air Base in Virginia, Godman Field at Fort Knox in Kentucky, Selfridge Field near Detroit, and Shaw Field in South Carolina. In my last year I gained excellent crisis experience as a troubleshooter for difficult civilian problems. In one instance, when a base was restructured I had to lay off over 300 employees with only one day's notice and then help them find employment elsewhere within 60 days. In another instance I had to clean up a situation in which the paperwork for two weeks was stuffed into a desk drawer and unanswered. In summary, all of these Hughes and military experiences were wonderful preparation for enhancing the theories in my courses with interesting applied ideas.

BEGINNING A TEACHING CAREER

After the war, I was released from the Air Force in the spring of 1946. We drove to the home of my wife's parents, since we were expecting our first shild in a few weeks. Our son, Charles Terry Davis was born March 19, 1946, in Hearne, Texas; and on August 5, 1950, our twin daughters, Jean Susan and June Sharon were born in Austin, Texas, but June Sharon died three days later.

Since my former civilian job with Hughes was protected by law, I planned to return to that job the week after we arrived in Texas. However, through a series of unusual events that I believe were more than a coincidence, I found myself in the office of the Dean of the School of Business at the University of Texas. He did not invite me; I simply arrived there after a series of events relating to efforts to visit friends. The Dean stated that yesterday he had been told that the person hired to teach spring semester management classes would not be released from the army. Since I had a proven record, based on my teaching ESMDT earlier, he asked me to teach temporarily for a semester, but I refused because of my Hughes obligation. He stated that he would get me an extension of leave so that my job would be protected, and after discussion with my wife and several faculty, I accepted and began teaching two days later. It seemed that my destiny was teaching, because I had been moved into it, sometimes reluctantly, at Hughes, in the military, and now at the University of Texas.

In the spring I faced the same decision again and finally decided to enter teaching as a profession. By this time I deeply believed that management was very essential in the world and that better management was necessary for world progress, so I welcomed the opportunity to teach it. University teaching required a Ph.D., so the following summer I entered the doctoral program at Ohio State University. The University of Texas required that I return in September, but the following year I took a leave for 15 months in order to complete my course work with only one "B" at Ohio State. I majored in general management with R.C. Davis, especially the human side with Jucius, and minored in industrial management, labor economics, and economic theory and history, with additional courses or audits in psychology under Shartle and Burt, marketing under Beckman, the Spanish language, and other subjects. To provide 100% of my doctoral expenses, my wife and I leased a rooming house and kept 11 roomers, and I had a teaching assistantship and received government aid through the "GI Bill" for education of former wartime military. Upon my return to the University of Texas in 1949 I was made the first Chairperson of the Department of Management.

It seemed that I was also destined to do research and write, since I published eight articles and two small monographs during my 1946-1951 years at Texas. Six of these were studies that gave me field research experience. Also during this period John Mee, a widely known contributor to management, asked me to write a chapter on "Employee Communication" for his forthcoming *Personnel Handbook*. This was a major item with about 80 text pages, including a variety of illustrations. I still view this chapter as well done and useful, and it undoubtedly influenced John to invite me to join his staff at Indiana University, and I accepted in 1951.

Before leaving for Indiana I felt that I must complete my dissertation research, so I spent the spring and summer of 1951 on it. Since my early days at Hughes, I had been interested in employee communication, especially the grapevine, because I saw its importance as an influence on all employee relations; so I determined to research the grapevine. I found very little material on this subject, which meant that I needed to develop a research method that was "original and creative" as the dissertation instructions said. This I did primarily through discussions with Wilfred Watson, another professor in management. Finally I developed a grapevine study method that later was called ECCO analysis derived from the initials of "Episodic Communication Channels in Organization" to be discussed later.

I knew C.C. Welhausen, President of Tex-Tan, a leather company in Yoakum, Texas, because I had worked with him in the Texas Personnel Association; so I contacted him, and he agreed to let me conduct my research at his company. I carefully developed the research plan, even covering minor details, and then refined it with two on-site "dry runs"; so the actual research moved very smoothly without any major problem during about 20 trips to Tex-Tan. These results taught me a lesson that was very useful in later research, namely, that careful planning prior to research makes the research easier. Perhaps this is one of the reasons I felt at ease with field research during my career and usually enjoyed it. My dissertation was finished a year later, and I received my Ph.D. at Ohio State University in 1952, at age 33. At this point in my career, I finally felt that I was free of many work and financial burdens and able to be more-or-less a full-time faculty member. The years of 1932 to 1952 were quite difficult for me in financial and other ways, and several times I felt I was not going to make it, but I persisted and finally did.

A TEACHING CAREER

Before discussing my various areas of specialty and interest, it seems appropriate to summarize my teaching career. I taught at Indiana University from 1951 to 1958. The first year I taught graduate classes, and after receiving my degree in 1952, I worked two-thirds of the time for three years supervising doctoral dissertations, because the department was temporarily short of faculty with doctorates. My chairman was John F. Mee, and he was a truly remarkable, supportive person. He undoubtedly helped me more than any other person in my career. He gave me a very good start with supervision of doctoral dissertations, guided me through my first major consulting job, and supported me with the faculty. He also gave me my start in the Academy of Management and helped me arrange to coauthor my first book, *Cases in Management* (1954). The book was successful, going through three editions and a Spanish translation.

In 1957 I became somewhat restless, and sought a job at Florida and UCLA. The Florida job was my first offer, but I developed severe hay fever while visiting there, and a local allergist advised me against taking the job. The faculty screening committee kept delaying my offer at UCLA, and during this time an Indiana graduate, Dean Glenn Overman of Arizona State, invited me to visit his school. I did so and finally accepted a job there as the first Chair of the Department of Management. *Three hours* after I accepted the Arizona State job, the UCLA offer finally was confirmed, but I declined because I now felt obligated to Arizona State. Furthermore, I believed that the growth situation at Arizona State would give me more opportunity to do a variety of tasks that I liked. Subsequently, I have been quite satisfied with that decision, even though it probably led to reduced research activities. I remained at Arizona State until my retirement.

In 1978 my wife and I had just arrived in San Francisco for the national Academy of Management meeting, when suddenly I had a serious heart attack in the lobby of the hotel. Through a set of remarkable coincidences I was able to reach a hospital in 5-6 minutes and get my heart restarted twice. During the next few days many friends came by to encourage my recovery. However, the effects of the heart attack eventually required me to lighten my load by giving up either teaching or book writing. Because of my current success as an author, I reluctantly gave up teaching, and kept the more sedentary work of book authorship. I retired in 1980 as Professor Emeritus of Management, although I continue some activities in academic affairs and professional meetings. Retirement was a painful choice, but 12 years later I continue to believe my decision was the right one. My retirement from consulting followed in 1983. I was university professor for 34 years from 1946 to 1980, and a frequent consultant for 34 years from 1949 to 1983.

During my years at Arizona State University I participated in a number of community service activities. I served on the governing board of two local professional groups, the American Society for Training and Development and the Society for Advancement of Management. Also I served on the boards of the Phoenix Executives Club, Grand Canyon University, a state committee to award state and Federal grants, and Scottsdale Memorial Hospital. In addition, I gave public service speeches to various groups in Arizona and around the United States.

As I look back on my career in management, my advice to anyone considering it as a teaching career is as follows:

1. Be sure you understand the social role of management and that you will feel favorable toward studying, teaching, and writing about it.
2. Be sure you are willing to make the sacrifices necessary to secure a doctorate and work your way into teaching.
3. Be sure you expect quality work of yourself and feel internally rewarded by it.
4. Be sure you will enjoy teaching and its allied activities.

ACADEMIC HONORS AND VISITING PROFESSORSHIPS

During my teaching career I earned quite a few academic honors and visiting professorships. My first major honor was my election as a Fellow in the Academy of Management in 1956, which I greatly appreciated because it was from my peers. My second honor developed from my study of the role of project managers in engineering management, in which I interviewed and surveyed managers in one company, and in another company I observed individual managers for one-half day each in order to record and classify their actual tasks. From this research I wrote several articles, and one of them won me an award in 1963 for the best article of the year from the Institute of Electrical and Electronic Engineers. A cash award accompanied the honor.

Another award that was especially appreciated was the Faculty Achievement Award from Arizona State University in 1964. Then in 1966, I received one of five awards given by the Academy of Management for the Best Management Book of the Year. This book was the first edition of my coauthored book in the area of social issues in management, *Business and Its Environment*. The awards were determined by a panel of five distinguished business leaders.

Also in 1966 I received the National Human Relations Award from the Society for Advancement of Management. Then in 1975 I was elected a National Beta Gamma Sigma Distinguished Scholar; and in 1978, with the recommendation of Dalton McFarland, Harold Koontz, Stanley Vance, and others, I was elected as a Fellow in the International Academy of Management. This was an appropriate cap for my career since there were relatively few Fellows in the United States, and about half of them were business leaders.

In connection with my academic activities I also accepted several visiting professorships. These include a visiting chaired professorship at Georgia Tech, and regular professorships at the University of Hawaii, the University of Western Australia (to be discussed under international activities), University of Colorado, and twice at the University of Central Florida. I viewed all of these as opportunities to work with peers and students in different environments and to expand my own horizons.

Another academic activity that I truly enjoyed was lecture-discussions with students and/or faculty at various universities. I was quite active in this area, taking about five trips a year for this purpose. During any summer lecture trip my wife and children usually accompanied me, so our children had seen much of the United States by the time they graduated from high school. At that time my wife could accompany me anytime, so she soon knew many of my professional friends and their families. We viewed these trips as a type of minivacation that gave us a break from our daily routine. During many years I lectured in this manner from New Hampshire to California, and Florida to Washington, and many places in between. Sometimes I would visit three to four universities on one trip. Often I received some travel aid and a small honorarium, but this was a labor of love rather than a moneymaking activity. These trips were some of the most enjoyable experiences of my career.

CONSULTING

During my entire career I was active in consulting. It provided some additional income, but I also enjoyed it because it was an opportunity to exchange ideas with people who were practicing the subjects I taught in the University, so they kept me from straying too far from reality in the classroom. My first consulting job was in 1949 while I was at the University of Texas. A large furniture retailer and interior designer with 110 employees was having personnel problems, and he asked my help. I took a one-day trip to visit him, and fortunately I was able to help, for which I received $25. Though the amount was small, the success of this first venture was a strong encouragement for me to want to continue consulting.

My next opportunity, and first major consulting, was at Indiana with John Mee. He asked me to aid him with some management training materials for the Marketing Department of Texaco, Inc., of New York City. I prepared a 32-page manual on "Employee Communication" which was my specialty at the time. John guided the company in introducing the training that went with the manuals, and the program was successful. When the manuals were revised several years later I was selected to revise three of them, and from that time forward I revised all seven manuals along with the conference leader's seven guidebooks that accompanied them. My last revision was 1977, so this consulting relationship lasted 25 years. In the Texaco project and in most of my other consulting I often used reprints or summaries from my articles and books, and the participants seemed to like this connection with published material. It also provided them many handouts to take home.

Some of my other consulting also tended to be longer term, including Mobil Oil, Motorola, and Pepsi Cola. One long-term consulting project that I especially enjoyed was working with the Department of Education, State of

Hawaii, to create and serve as conference leader of their management training program. They seemed to be especially pleased with the program and required almost all of their local and state supervisors to take the program during the five years that I handled it. The job required over 20 trips of one week or more to Hawaii, and the program was given on four of Hawaii's islands. Subsequently I gave a similar program for the county of Maui and the State Department of Justice. My wife accompanied me over 50 percent of the time, and on weekends we enjoyed sightseeing throughout the islands.

For 5-6 years I also taught in a management training program for U.S. Internal Revenue Service district and regional managers. The district programs were taught throughout the west, and regional programs were in Baltimore and in Arlington, Virginia. Another long-term relationship was with Pitman-Moore Pharmaceuticals (now a Dow Chemical subsidiary) in Indianapolis. During about 7 years, I aided them with job evaluation, top-management development, and opinion surveys.

As might be expected, university executive and supervisory training programs were an active area for me. For several years I taught in the Pacific Coast Banking School at the University of Washington, and during this period I was able to see the planning, building, and operation of the Seattle World's Fair. I still think that the restaurant on top of the Fair's Space Needle has the most beautiful dining view in the world, and the restaurant is still open. Some additional executive programs where I taught were the University of California at Los Angeles, San Diego, Santa Barbara, Davis, and Irvine; University of Houston, Indiana University, Georgia State, Arizona State, Oregon, Oklahoma State, Northeast Louisiana, Florida State, Wake Forest, Utah State, Louisiana State, and Georgia Institute of Technology.

My most unique consulting occurred shortly after I moved to Arizona State. It was with Salt River Project, an irrigation utility in the Phoenix area. The company was having a dispute with its union about work loads for workers who operated the field irrigation system. It contacted a computer firm, and the firm said it might be able to do the job for $125,000 but was not sure. The company asked my advice, and I recommended a human approach that would have union-management meetings using the point system of job evaluation, which I explained to them. I said that this approach should give more satisfaction and be much cheaper (under $5,000). Both management and union agreed, and in about fifteen meetings of two hours each, we (union, management, and consultant) developed a satisfactory program that cost less than $5,000 and lasted the next 20 years.

Additional organizations where I did consulting included Firestone Tire, General Motors, International Nickel, Quaker Oats, Arvin Industries, Mead-Johnson, General Electric, and others. My most interesting and educational project was consulting for the Cape Kennedy Space Center, because the work allowed me to get an inside look at the entire space program. I was much impressed by the quality of the people and by the space hardware. In general, it is evident that I liked consulting, have been active in it most of my career, and have been reasonably successful with it.

ACADEMY OF MANAGEMENT

Since 1951 when John Mee introduced me to the Academy of Management, I have been active in it. That is a time period of approximately 40 years, and I have enjoyed every minute of it. It gave me a chance to meet my professional colleagues, exchange ideas with them, make friends, and participate in professional leadership. Since the beginning I have believed quite strongly in the objectives of the Academy because I am confident that they will aid our discipline. In my first years with the Academy it was much smaller than now, so rather early I became active in committee work and soon knew nearly every member.

As an example of the committee work, I was a member of the committee that recommended starting the *Academy of Management Journal*. The first year our committee recommended the *Journal*, and I presented our report to the Academy, but we were rebuffed for two years because of the per capita cost for our small group. Finally in the third year, 1956, our proposal was accepted, and we were asked to proceed on a trial basis. Fortunately Paul Dauten of the University of Illinois accepted the role as editor, and he persuaded his dean to bear most of the cost. Consequently, the *Journal* finished its first year within budget, and was continued by the Academy on a permanent basis. I also served on the editorial board of the *Journal* for over 10 years.

In 1961 I was selected to be Secretary-Treasurer of the Academy, and served for two years. In 1963 I was elected to be Vice President and Program Chairman, and the following year I became President of the Academy. One of my major responsibilities during my presidency was to direct the process that made Sigma Iota Epsilon, the honorary and professional management society for students, an affiliate of the Academy of Management. At that time there were two different management student honoraries, and they had chosen earlier not to merge, so there was some member pressure to have only one in order to unify the management field. The board recommended to the membership that we accept the larger one as our affiliate, and the Academy members accepted by mail ballot. At the end of my term my presidential address to the Academy in its Chicago meeting was on "The Public Role of Management," which essentially encouraged more social response and responsibility on the part of management. The address was well received, although some felt I was going too far. This was the first Academy presidential address that concerned social issues in management.

After my presidency I served on the Board of Directors for three years, and on several other committees during later years. Also I participated in a founding meeting of the Social Issues Division and served on its governing board. In addition, I served on the National Executive Board of Sigma Iota Epsilon for ten years, and after my retirement they established an annual Keith Davis Graduate Scholarship Award in honor of my service as President and then as board member during a period of more than 20 years. Another organization that I helped establish along with Harold Koontz and others, was the Foundation for Administrative Research, an organization for receiving tax-deductible contributions in order to give Academy of Management awards, and I later served on its governing board for about 10 years. As of this date the Foundation continues as the tax-deductible foundation serving the Academy.

Regional Academy meetings were not my idea, but when Bill Wolf proposed them, I strongly supported the idea from the beginning. It was my good fortune to participate in the organizing meetings of both the Midwestern Academy and the Western Academy, and in 1964 I was president of the Western Academy. Now that the national Academy is very large, the divisions offer a wonderful opportunity for more members to present papers, visit professionally, form friendships, and learn new developments. Even today, 1990, I continue to be active in regionals, most recently serving on a committee and attending the Southern Academy two months ago. Truly my participation in the national and regional Academies has been one of the most rewarding experiences of my life.

THE GRAPEVINE

When I joined Hughes Tool in 1940, I quickly discovered the practical importance of the grapevine; so I learned as much as I could about it. Then when I joined the University of Texas faculty, I was introduced to Roethlisberger and Dickson's *Management and the Worker* and Mayo's *Social Problems of an Industrial Civilization*. The ideas in these books seemed so impressive that even today I consider these books to be two of the most influential ones that I ever read. They affected my entire career and were one of the reasons that I selected grapevine communication as my dissertation subject.

Somewhat to my surprise the grapevine research proved to be more significant than I expected. Shortly after my dissertation was accepted, *Harvard Business Review* editors contacted me about writing an article on my research results. (I don't know how they learned about the dissertation.) The article was accepted, and it proved to be one of the best known and most influential articles that I ever published. Other management and communication colleagues noted it; there was newspaper publicity of it; and it was reprinted in books, the most recent being in 1988, more than 35 years after its publication. Also in later years I was invited to teach management communication and the grapevine in a number of management development programs. As a result of all this interest in employee communication, I continued to do research, including studies in two electronics plants, several public utilities, and a bank. These studies confirmed both the method and the earlier results. The most significant replication of the research was by Harold Sutton and Lyman Porter in *Personnel Psychology* (Summer 1968); it generally supported both the method and the original research results.

In 1973 one of my articles was picked up by the news wire and given much publicity in newspapers in the United States and Europe and on radio and TV, and this publicity reawakened interest in employee communication. In summary, my grapevine research proved to be a useful beginning for later research, writing, teaching, and consulting. It also appeared to be a significant contribution to grapevine study and the field of management in general.

ORGANIZATIONAL BEHAVIOR (OB)

I had been teaching OB since the beginning of my academic career, and I continued teaching it, both graduate and undergraduate, at Indiana University. In 1954, after teaching the course for eight years and writing several articles in the field, I felt that I was both motivated and professionally prepared to write an undergraduate textbook in OB. I discussed this with John Mee, and he gave me support. He said that he wanted the book for the Irwin Series in Management, which he edited, and I agreed to submit the finished manuscript first to Irwin. I needed a quiet writing place, and none was available at the university; so with my own hands I built an office in the basement of our 800-square-foot prefabricated home. When that was completed, along with basement finishing and lighting, I began work on the book. Because of my other duties and my inexperience, the work went slowly, and I did not complete the manuscript until December of 1956. In my usual manner I kept a record of my hours invested in writing the manuscript and they totaled nearly 4,000, for which I expected to earn $12,000 to $15,000 in this rather small market with a book price of $5.95. The expected "wages" seemed small, but this was a labor of love. It was something I wanted to do.

Regrettably Irwin sent the book to a reviewer who apparently expected a more theoretical text, so the reviewer report was relatively negative and included several recommendations for significant changes. Since I had taught the course several years, I felt that I had the right formula, so I refused to make the changes and finally submitted the book to McGraw-Hill Book Company because it had a friendly sales representative and appeared to be a good marketer. McGraw-Hill received good reviews, so I accepted its publication contract.

From the beginning the book was a success, since the competitive situation with OB books was favorable. When monographs, readings books, and research books such as Roethlisberger were excluded, there was only one textbook competitor, Gardner and Moore, *Human Relations in Industry*, published by Irwin. That is, my book was the second basic OB textbook ever published. In this environment, my book received many favorable comments about its content, real-life examples to illustrate practice, readability, appropriate coverage, and thorough references; consequently, the financial reward was more than the expected $15,000.

Partly because of the success of the OB book, McGraw-Hill invited me in 1958, to become Consulting Editor of its planned new series of management textbooks. I accepted and became the single consulting editor of the Series in Management. This role was one of considerable influence in management, because no book could be included in the Series without my approval. Fortunately the Series had several successful books in the first five years, so it became a major success. Since the editing load was heavy, Fred Luthans was added as co-editor in the 1970s. My career as editor lasted about 25 years, and during that period I personnally edited over 130 textbooks for the Series. The job meant that, along with manuscript acceptance, I also had to reject other manuscripts. This process alienated a few friends; but as a whole, the editing role was a wonderful experience that gave me some influence on the development of management thought and practice during a quarter century.

With regard to later editions of my OB book, I often substantially revised each edition to keep up with the market, so sales nearly doubled for each of the next three editions, which indicated strong acceptance in an expanding OB market. Sales continued to be excellent through the 7th edition in 1985, even though at that time the book had over one hundred competitors. Also for the 7th edition John Newstrom joined me as coauthor. Strong international acceptance led to translations into other languages, and to international editions published in Japan, India, and Singapore. Feedback from readers has been favorable since the first edition. For example, within the last two weeks I received feedback from a manager in a large international corporation who said, "Your book changed my career at "X" Company. After reading your book, I completely changed my way of looking at problems, and I started moving upward in management. I've talked about your book so much that it now is widely used in our company." Naturally this kind of feedback is quite rewarding to an author.

In the 1940s and 1950s, OB was typically known as human relations. There were few teachers and researchers in this field at that time, so most of us knew each other through visits to professional meetings and exchange of correspondence. We were a friendly group, perhaps because we felt the field offered many opportunities for all of us. Generally we shared and helped each other without competition.

During this period the name of the field was gradually changed to organizational behavior, and by 1970 it had become the more common term for the field. Therefore, in 1967 for the third edition of my book, I adopted a subtitle having *Organizational Behavior* in order to reflect the new term. Meanwhile Dan Wren had written the first edition of his *The Evolution of Management Thought* (1972). His work referred to me as "Mr. Human Relations" because I had widely popularized the field with regard to both its theories and their application. With the name change to OB, there was a renewed emphasis on OB theory, but by the late 1980s the emphasis on theory had gone so far that there was a need to give more attention to practice. I hope that the next few decades will see a better balance of theory and its application in operating situations. With regard to all of management, I feel that we have merely uncovered the tip of the iceberg in management research, and that we will learn much, much more during the next fifty years.

My research and writing in OB continued until retirement. The main thrust of these activities was both formal and informal communication along with occasional other areas such as Herzberg's motivational and maintenance factors. I published about 50 articles in OB, and I continue to be interested in it. Other than my grapevine articles, my most widely noticed and reprinted articles were the theory articles: "Evolving Models of Organizational Behavior" (*Journal of the Academy of Management,* March 1968), and "The Case for Participative Management" (*Business Horizons,* Fall 1963).

HUMAN RESOURCES AND PERSONNEL MANAGEMENT

Nearly all of my experience prior to entering the academic world was in human resources management (HRM; formerly "personnel management). Since this field is closely related to OB, I found it comfortable to do research, writing, and consulting in it. I studied and wrote about wage surveys, collective bargaining contracts, personnel practices, staff-line relationships, the supervisor's personnel role, and similar subjects. Among these items was what I think was the first published opinion survey of a regional labor union group in the *Journal of Applied Psychology* (October 1952). In addition I made a nationwide longitudinal study of the readability of employee handbooks. After the first study I made a second study of the same companies fifteen years later. Both articles about the studies were published in *Personnel Psychology.* I also achieved ranking as an Accredited Senior Professional in Human Resources.

Later in my career I coauthored an HRM textbook with William B. Werther, now a chaired professor at the University of Miami. This book was especially well received in the international market, earning translations into French,

Spanish, and Portuguese, along with international editions published in Tokyo and Singapore, and a Canadian adaptation for the Canadian market.

SOCIAL ISSUES IN MANAGEMENT (SIM)

Concurrently with my interest in the human side of business, I maintained a strong interest in the social issues that involved management. My view from the beginning has been that management has social obligations that accompany its power, and that its acceptance of these obligations will enhance its role in the long run. As mentioned before, my background emphasized responsibility, that is, "If you mess it up, you clean it up." More generally stated, "If you assume power, you also have the responsibility that goes with it." Responsibility is the reciprocal of power. Furthermore, my management education supported the idea that responsibility goes with power in an organizational context. The book that crystallized my thinking on the subject was Howard Bowen's *Social Responsibilities of the Businessman* (Harper & Row, 1953), which he prepared for the National Council of Churches. After I read this book in the 1950s, I was ready to teach and write in SIM.

An opportunity came when the University of California at Los Angeles, knowing of my interest and preparation, asked me to teach the subject in the UCLA Executive Program in the summer of 1959. In those early days, the executives received the subject with little interest. Nevertheless, I used the framework of my presentation to write an article titled "Can Business Afford to Ignore Social Responsibilities?" (1960), which was well received by both business and academic people. Shortly thereafter the staff at Arizona State became interested in teaching SIM; in 1962 we became one of the earlier universities to teach a course in SIM. Faculty interest was so strong that Bill Greenwood published probably the first or second readings book on the subject, *Issues in Business and Society* (Houghton Mifflin, 1964). Also, as mentioned earlier, in 1964 I gave my Academy Presidential Address on social issues. Then I joined with Bob Blomstrom of our staff to publish *Business and Its Environment* (McGraw-Hill, 1966), which I think was the second regular textbook in SIM. As I write this autobiography in 1990, the book (with Bill Frederick and Jim Post as coauthors) is said to be the leader in its field.

I enjoy speaking and writing about SIM. Like OB, it is a subject dear to my values. Gradually the business environment changed, and my presentations were well received. In fact, the change during the 1960s and 1970s was remarkable and much more to the favorable side than I ever expected. It was exciting to be a part of this great change in business history. In addition to the book, I wrote about 15 articles in the field. Several of them emphasized theory, and one of these, "The Case for and against Business Assumption of

Social Responsibilities" (1973), was widely referenced and reprinted in both college textbooks and the business world.

One speech that I gave during much of my career was a combination of SIM with other business subjects and economics. It was "Some Basic Trends Affecting Management in the Next Decade," and I regularly updated it to fit the appropriate decade. Business people seemed to like it, but it was not printed until 1976 when I gave it in the Alumni Lecture Series of the University of Minnesota in Minneapolis. The key points at that time were a trend toward a service economy, a knowledge society, a socially concerned humanistic society, and a fast-changing unstable society.

INTERNATIONAL BUSINESS

My interest in international business developed at an early stage of my career, probably when I took my first college course in the subject. Also I had two years of high school Spanish, and it was the additional language chosen for my doctorate. The cultures of other parts of the world were quite interesting to me; and, as I moved into teaching and writing, there was a job purpose for my learning about other cultures.

My first opportunity for teaching outside the United States came in 1956 when I was invited to discuss *What You Should Know about Administrative Communication* (1954) with the Executives' Club of Havana, Cuba. After my first week of daily lectures, the Club asked me to stay another week to present the program to another group, and I did. My family accompanied me, and we all had a wonderful experience with these friendly hosts.

My second international opportunity was an invitation from the United States Agency for International Development to join a team to teach a six-week executive program in Chile in the summer of 1960. The team was led by James Healey, a former professor at Ohio State University, and the managers who attended were top executives in government and business. There was simultaneous translation for the few who were not fluent in English. Both students and faculty seemed to enjoy this opportunity to exchange ideas, and I learned much from this experience. During my trip to and from Chile I was able to visit for a week in Peru with my half-sister, whose husband was working there, and also to visit Argentina, Brazil, and several Caribbean islands. The following year I was invited to return to Chile but was unable to do so because of book commitments.

These favorable international experiences encouraged me to do further international teaching and travel, all of which I enjoyed. During my career I have traveled to six continents and 35 nations, including much of the Caribbean and South Pacific. Often I have visited factories in these locations in order to learn more about the business culture as well as the social culture.

These visits gave me examples that I could use in my books in order to enhance their breadth and international appeal, so I was prepared for the international interest that arose in business schools in the late 1960s and 1970s. To the best of my knowledge I had the first international chapter in an SIM textbook (1st edition, 1966) and in an OB textbook (3rd edition, 1967). In the beginning the publisher's book surveys revealed some faculty objections to including an international chapter, but these viewpoints rather quickly died as business school pressure for international coverage increased. Perhaps my international coverage is one of the reasons my textbooks currently sell tens of thousands of copies annually in the international market. I also wrote a number of international articles mostly related to improving productivity.

One especially helpful international visit was a three-week tour of Japanese business that was sponsored by the Academy of Management in 1972. The Japanese generously arranged for us to visit and interview top management, including the Chairman or President, in major companies such as Sony. Discussions were primarily at the strategy level and in depth (2-3 hours). Usually we also visited production facilities. I returned with two strong convictions that I discussed with students and faculty: (1) the remarkable capacity of Japanese management to think strategically, and (2) the probability that Japanese factory productivity would become competitive with the United States in one to two decades. My views largely fell on deaf ears until there was better American understanding of Japanese progress. (Regretfully, about one year later the Academy sponsored trips ceased, because liability insurance issues arose that caused the Academy to back off.)

Another wonderful learning experience was my visit to Australia to teach one quarter at the University of Western Australia in Perth in 1974. In addition I lectured at three other universities and in two management development programs. During the trip to and from Australia, I took an additional four months to spend several days in each of 13 other nations. My wife accompanied me on both the Australian and the Japanese trip, so we learned together about international cultures.

As I look back on my international viewpoints and teaching, this activity was primarily to help my understanding, teaching, and writing, rather than to qualify me as an academic authority on the subject. However, in retrospect it seems that most of my views were accurate and somewhat ahead of their time, so I feel that I helped my students understand the world and prepare for its future.

CONCLUSION

In conclusion, I wanted my career to make a positive contribution to this world. When I was directed into teaching, I soon discovered that there was a good match between its requirements and my interests; so I was strongly motivated. Rather than choosing a narrow emphasis, such as teaching or research, my interests were broadly into all facets of academic life, such as teaching, research, writing, consulting, and community relations. My motivation was to do high quality work, because I felt that it would benefit people and be inwardly rewarding to me. Fortunately, book writing proved also to be economically rewarding, for which I am thankful. But the quality work and the public benefit were consistently the motivating drives, not the money. My philosophy of life always has been, "Contribute to society and do it in a quality way."

At this stage in my career, do I feel that I have succeeded in my goals? In general, I do. My textbooks in three fields have been quite successful worldwide: *Business and Society* (6th edition, 1988); *Organizational Behavior* (8th edition, 1989); and *Human Resources* (3rd edition, 1989). Assuming a standard estimate that about two and one-half students read each textbook sold, I have reached a few million students with human and social ideas that I hope will help build a better world. These books are what I especially want to be remembered for, because I believe they have been an influence for learning and progress. Also I have reached thousands through my articles, consulting, teaching, and other activities. My goal has been to encourage people to work together, rather than in conflict; that is, to improve cooperation and responsible behavior in both the organizational and societal contexts. We are all in this one world together, so we must learn to share it cooperatively. This view has sustained my intellectual efforts throughout my career. Toward this end I have primarily worked in organizational behavior, human resources, social issues in management, and international management. Since these fields have grown in favor during my career, my assumption is that maybe I helped in some way. At least I have tried, and that is what inwardly counts.

PUBLICATIONS

1942

A tailor-made schedule for seven-day operations. *Texas Personnel Review,* *1*(2).

1946

Summary of the conference. *Texas Personnel Review, 5*(3).
The need for research in industrial relations and personnel management. *Texas Personnel Review, 5*(2), 5-10.

1947

A summary of labor and employment conditions in Texas in 1946. *Texas Personnel Review, 6*(1), 8-13.

A selected and annotated bibliography of recent literature on personnel administration and industrial relations (Bibliography No. 1). Austin: Bureau of Business Research, College of Business Administration, The University of Texas.

1950

Points to remember in making a wage survey. *Management Review, 39*(7), 397-399.

Is personnel a profession? *Personnel Journal, 28*(11), 420-421.

Wage survey method illustrated by a wage survey of Austin, Texas. Austin, TX: Bureau of Business Research, College of Business Administration, The University of Texas.

With J.O. Hopkins, Readability of employee handbooks. *Personnel Psychology, 3*(3), 317-326.

1951

With G. Gillett, Jr. *Personnel policies and practices of public accounting firms in Texas.* Austin, TX: Bureau of Business Research, University of Texas.

Interpreting personnel ideas to operating officials. *Personnel Administration, 14*(5), 9-13, 17.

With H.W. Nash. *Indiana collective bargaining contract analyses.* Indianapolis, IN: Indiana State Chamber of Commerce, October 1951 to January 1955. (Monthly series, mimeographed. Second author is William G. Scott beginning October 14, 1953).

Learning to live with informal groups. *Advanced Management, XVI*(10), 17-19.

Employee communication. In J.F. Mee (Ed.), *Personnel handbook* (pp. 755-834). New York: Ronald Press.

1952

Suggestion programs and productivity. *Personnel Journal, 30*(9), 339-341.

With C.A. Smith. Survey of 75 Texas firms shows wide variation in accounting personnel practices. *The Journal of Accountancy, 93*(5), 584-588.

With E.E. St. Germain. An opinion survey of a regional union group. *Journal of Applied Psychology, 36*(5), 285-290.

1953

The supervisor's job in communications. *Manage,* 5(8), 6-7, 21.
How supervisors can communicate better. *Personnel Journal 31*(11), 417-420.
Management communication and the grapevine. *Harvard Business Review,* 31(5), 43-49.
A method of studying communication patterns in organizations. *Personnel Psychology,* 6(3), 301-312.
With W.G. Broehl, Jr. Let the foreman in on induction. *Personnel, 29*(5), 408-411.
With W.G. Broehl, Jr. Die rolle des vorgesetzten bei des einfuhrung des neven mitarbeiters [Let the foreman in on induction]. *Arbeitswissenschaftlicher Auslandsdienst* (Berlin, Germany, February 1), pp. 15-16.
With E.G. Williams. Desirable characteristics for personnel directors. *Personnel Journal, 32*(7), 258-262.

1954

What you should know about administrative communication (Business Information Bulletin No. 20). Bloomington, IN: School of Business, Indiana University.
Communication *within* management. *Personnel,* pp. 212-218.
Que sabe usted sobre "Communication administrativa." Translated by Santos Villar Saavedra. Habana, Cuba: Laboratories Gravi.
With H.M. Cruickshank. *Cases in management. Chicago: Irwin.*

1955

With R.E. Parker. *Collective bargaining contract provision in Indiana, 1949 to 1954.* Indianapolis, IN: Indiana State Chamber of Commerce.
Dilemma of stenographic pool. *Office Execitive* (May), pp. 37-39. (Reprinted as, The Dilemma of the stenographic pool. *Management Review* [June], pp. 415-416.)

1956

Grapevines need tender care. *The Advertiser's Digest, 21*(12), 14-15.
Making constructive use of the office grapevine. *Office Management Series, 142,* 25-35.
Frictions in human relations: A study of staff-line relationships. *Business Horizons* (December), pp. 44-48.
Management by Participation: Its place in today's business world. *The Management Review, XLVI*(2), 69-79.

Management looks to the future. *The Manager's Key* (February), pp. 5-6.
Human Relations in Business. New York: McGraw-Hill.
New angles on getting your story. *Factory Management and Maintenance,*
115(9), 98-100. (Reprinted in *Management Review*, November 1957, pp.
66-68, "Making Communications count"; Abstracted in *Weekly News*
Review Digest [Insurance Research and Review Service Indianapolis],
April 26, 1958, pp. 15-16).
Human relations as a basis for business education. In *Education for Business*
beyond High School (pp. 136-149). New York: New York University
Bookstore.
Sputnik and the new management era. *The Manager's Key* (February), pp.
304.
Understanding your management role. *The Manager's Key* (April), pp. 1-3.
A faith for modern management (Symposium). *The Atlanta Economic Review*
(September), pp. 2-3.
With H.M. Cruickshank. *Cases in management* (rev. ed.). Homewood, IL:
Irwin.

1959

People are our opportunity, not our problem. *The Manager' Key* (Summer),
p. 3.
Role of Management in the industial world. *The Manager' Key* (Fall), pp.
3-4.
A management teacher by any other name. *Journal of the Academy of*
Management (December), pp. 197-199.
With W.G. Scott (Eds.). *Readings in human relations*. New York: McGraw
Hill.

1960

Can business afford to ignore social responsibilities? *California Management*
Review, II(3), 70-76.
Management needs for the 1970's. *Arizona Business Bulletin, VII*(4), 10-12.
Management in perspective: Management brainpower needs for the 1970's.
Journal of the Academy of Management (August), pp. 125-127.
The changing climate of business social responsibilities. *The Manager's Key*
(December), pp. 3-4.

1961

Togetherness: The informal variety. *Arizona Business Bulletin* (March), pp.
1-9.

Steps twoard a more flexible disciplinary policy. *Personnel* (May-June), pp. 52-56.

The organization that's not on the chart. *Supervisory Management, 6*(7), 2-7.

When can you be flexible? *Supervisory Management, 6*(9), 4-7.

Technical managers and human relations. In *Proceedings of the Thirteenth Annual Industrial Engineering Institute* (pp. 29-32). Berkeley, CA: University of California Press.

Chances are—You'll be a manager. *Petroleum Refiner, 40*(9), 271-273.

A preliminary study of management patterns of research project managers in manufacturing in the Phoenix area. Tempe: Arizona State University Press.

United Mutual Insurance Company. Boston: Intercollegiate Case Clearing House, Harvard Graduate School of Business Administration.

Bountiful Grain Company. Boston: Intercollegiate Case Clearing House, Harvard Graduate School of Business Administration.

Northern States Insurance Company. Boston: Intercollegiate Case Clearing House, Harvard Graduate School of Business Administration.

Development of participation. [Sound Tape]. Executapes.

Increasing Productivity in International Management [Sound Tape]. New York: Executapes.

The Grapevine in Work Groups [Sound Tape]. New York: Executapes.

The role of project management in scientific manufacturing. *IRE Transactions on Engineering Management, EM-9[3] 109-113.* [Award winner as best article of the year in this journal.]

Group behavior and the organization chart. *Advanced Management-Office Executive, 1*(6), 14-18. (Abstracted in *Public Management* [August 1962], p. 191).

Mainsprings of motivation. *Supervision,* Part I (July), 4-6, 24-25.

Mainsprings of motivation. *Supervision,* Part II (August), 10-12.

With H.M. Cruickshank. *Cases in management* (3rd ed.). Homewood, IL: Irwin.

Human relations at work (2nd ed.). Tokyo: Kogakusha Company, Ltd. (International Student Edition)

Human relations at work (2nd ed.). New York: McGraw-Hill.

1963

Group behavior and the organization chart. *Manage, 15*(9), 25-32.

Good listener, good nurse. *RN* (October), p. 113.

The case for participative management. *Business Horizons* (Fall), 55-60. (Reprinted in *Notes & Quotes*, January 1964)

Individual needs and automation. *Journal of the Academy of Management* (December), 278-283.

1964

Human adjustment to automation. *Advanced Management Journal* (January), 20-27.
Managing productivity in developing economies. *Management International,* *4*(2), 65-85. (Published in French, German, and English).
With W.G. Scott. *Readings in human relations* (2nd ed.). New York: McGraw-Hill.
With R.L. Blomstrom. *Business and its environment.* New York: McGraw-Hill.

1965

How to increase productivity. *International Management, 20*(3), 81-83.
Automation is coming your way. *The Credit Union Executive, 4*(2), 9-124.
Human relations trends. *The Management Review* (Delhi, India), *5*(4), 5-8.
Mutuality in understanding of the program manger's management role. *IEEE* *Transactions on Engineering Management, EM-12*(4), 117-122.
The public role of management (Academy Presidential Address). In E.B. Flippo (Ed.), *Proceedings, 1964 Meeting of the Academy of Management* (pp. 3-9). University Park, PA: The Academy of Management, Department of Management, Pennsylvania State University.
Encouraging productivity in international management. In K.E. Ettinger (Ed.), *International handbook of mangement* (pp. 334-341). New York: McGraw-Hill.

1966

Management to encourage productivity in developing countries. *Development* *Digest* (National Planning Association), *3*(4), 91-97.
The management of science. *Medical Group Management, 13*(6), 4-5.
Organization for policy formulation and orderly decision making in the bank— concepts. In W.H. Baughn & C.E. Walker (Eds.), *The banker's handbook* (pp. 23-26). Homewood, IL: Dow Jones-Irwin.

1967

Developing employees to fill 400,000 bank job openings. *Bank PRMA Journal,* *52*(3), 143-144.
The banker's role in human relations. *Mid-Continent Banker, 63*(4), 33, 54-55.
Evolution of ideas in organizational behavior. *The Southern Journal of* *Business, 2*(2), 147-154.

Management must emphasize social responsibility. *The Georgia Tech Alumnus, 45*(8), 14-17.

In the spotlight: The supportive manger. *Arizona Business Bulletin, XIV, [10],* 252-256.

Human relations at work: The dynamics of organizational behavior (3rd ed.). New York: McGraw-Hill.

Human relations at work: The dynamics of organizational behavior. Bombay, India: Tata McGraw-Hill.

With H.M. Cruickshank. *Casos practicos de direction de empresas.* Madrid: Ediciones Railp, S.A. (Spanish translation)

1968

Evolving models of organizational behavior. *Academy of Management Journal, 11*(1), 27-38. (Reprinted in *The Internal Auditor*, November-December 1968, pp. 25-35).

Attitudes toward the legitimacy of management efforts to influence employees. *Academy of Management Journal, 11*(2), 153-162.

New concepts in human relations. In *1967 Report, Pacific Newspaper Mechanical Conference* (pp. 1, 8-9). Van Nuys, CA: Van Nuys Publishing company.

Understanding the grapevine and controlling rumor [Sound Tape]. New York: McGraw Hill, Sound Seminars.

Evolving models of organizational behavior [Sound Tape]. New York: McGraw HIll, Sound Seminars.

Understanding social responsibility in business [Sound Tape]. New York: McGraw Hill, Sound Seminars.

Readability changes in employee handbooks of identical companies during a fifteen-year period. *The Journal of Business Communication, 6*(1), 33-40.

Success of chain-of-command oral communication in a manufacturing management group. *Academy of Management Journal, 11*(4), 379-387.

Comment on "Technology and organizational government: A speculative inquiry into the functionality of management creeds," by W.G. Scott. *Academy of Management Journal, 11*(4), 443-445.

Readability changes in employee handbooks of identical companies during a fifteen-year period. *Personnel Psychology, 21*(4), 413-420.

Are you a forceful communicator? *The Credit Union Executive, 7*(4), 19-24.

Making sense of the social responsibility puzzle. In *Proceedings of the 10th Annual Academy of Management Conference, Midwest Division* (pp. 133-141). Carbondale, IL: Business Research Bureau, Southern Illinois University.

1969

How do you motivate your engineers and scientists? *Arizona Business Bulletin,* *XVI*(2), 27-32.
Grapevine communication among lower and middle managers. *Personnel Journal, 48*(4), 269-272.
With F.H. Besnette. Management's obligation to public service activities. *Advanced Management Journal, 34*(2), 33-39.
The effective manager is supportive with his people. *The Credit Union Executive, 8*(1), 24-29.
Understanding the social responsibility puzzle. *Business Horizons, 10*(4), 45-50. (Abstracted in *The Social Science Reporter, XVII*(3) 1-2, as "Social Responsibility Puzzle.")
With W.G. Scott. *Human relations and organizational behavior: Readings and comments* (3rd ed.). New York: McGraw-Hill.

1970

With G.R. Allen. Length of time that feelings persist for Herzberg's motivational and maintenance factors. *Personnel Psychology, 23*(1), 67-76.

1971

Modern business value systems. *Arizona Business Bulletin, XVIII*(2), 9-13.
Social involvement by business: The risks and potential gains. *University of Washington Business Review, XXX*(3), 5-13.
Grapevine analysis for organizational communication. *Arizona Business Bulletin, XVIII*(7), 10-14.
Pluralism's role in defining business's social responsibility. In T.J. Atchinson & J.V. Ghorpade (Eds.), *The future of management: Practice and teaching* (pp. 87-105). Bowling Green, OH: Academy of Management.
With R.L. Blomstrom. *Business, society, and environment* (2nd ed.). New York: McGraw-Hill.

1972

Managers of change: A rogue's gallery. *Management Review, 61*(7), 41. (Reprinted in: *Welfare News,* Department of Public Welfare, Halifax, Nova Scotia, Summer 1972, p.44; *Supervisory Management,* August 1972, pp. 25-26, as "The Management of Change: A Rogue's Gallery.")
Using human relations ideas in less developed nations. *Quarterly Journal of Management Development* (India), *3* (Part 1, No. 7), 1-8.

Human behavior at work: Human relations and organizational behavior (4th ed.). New York: McGraw-Hill.

1973

The case for and against business assumption of social responsibilities. *Academy of Management Journal, 16*(2), 312-322.

The care and cultivation of the corporate grapevine. *Dun's, 102*(1), 44-47. (Reprinted in: *IABC Journal* [International Association of Business Communicators], Fall 1973, pp. 105; *Management Review,* October 1973, pp. 53-55 [Edited form]; *Dialogue,* November 1973, pp. 1-4.

Trends in organizational design. *Arizona Business, XX*(9), 3-7.

1974

Let's study the grapevine. *Shoptalk, 22*(5), 12-14.

Organizational behavior: A book of readings (4th ed.). New York: McGraw-Hill.

Trends in organizational design. In T.B. Green & D.F. Ray (Eds.), *Academy of Management Proceedings: Thirty-third Annual Meeting* (pp. 1-6). Boston, MA: Academy of Management.

With R.L. Blomstrom. Observations on ecology and business responsibility. *Arizona Business, XXI*[*3*]*, 19-26.*

1975

The interpersonal approach is not enough. *The Teaching of Organization Behavior, 1*(2), 4-6.

Five propositions for social responsibility. *Business Horizons, XVIII*(3), 19-24. (Reprinted in *The Brewers Digest,* August 1975, pp. 20-26).

Cut those rumors down to size. *Supervisory Management, 20*(6), 2-6.

A law of diminishing returns in organizational behavior? *Personnel Journal* (December), pp. 616-619.

The challenge of business. New York: McGraw-HIll. (Edited volume)

Human behavior at work (4th ed.). New Delhi, India: Tata McGraw-Hill.

With R.L. Blomstrom. Adapting the organization for social response. *Arizona Business, XXIII*(6), 12-16.

With R.L. Blomstrom. Implementing the social audit in an organization. *Business and Society, 16*(1), 13-18.

With R.L. Blomstrom. *Business and Society: Environment and Responsibility* (3rd ed.). New York: McGraw Hill.

1976

Some basic trends affecting management in the 1980's (pp. 1-8). Minneapolis, MN: University of Minnesota Graduate School of Business Administration, Alumni Lecture Series. (Reprinted in: *The Brewers Digest, 51*[9], 16, 18, 22, 70; *Arizona Business, XXIII*[9], 18-22.)

Human behavior at work. Cairo, Egypt: Franklin Press Books. (Arabic translation)

Understanding the organizational grapevine. *Business and Public Affairs, 2*(2), 5-10.

Social responsibility is inevitable. *California Management Review, XIX*(1), 14-20.

With R.L. Blomstrom. *Responsabilidad de la nueva empresa.* Buenos Aires: Ediciones Marymar. (Spanish translation)

1977

Human behavior at work: Organizational behavior (5th ed.). New York: McGraw-Hill.

Organizational behavior: A book of readings (5th ed.). New York: McGraw Hill. (Edited volume)

1978

Methods of studying informal communication. *Journal of Communication, 28*(1), 112-116.

Some fundamental trends affecting management in the future. In L. Benton (Ed.), *Management for the future* (pp. 63-76). New York: McGraw-Hill.

1979

The office grapevine: Social responses in business, *Arizona Statesman* (Winter), pp. 6-7.

Equifinality model [of management] needed. In G.W. England, A.R. Negandhi, & B. Wilpert (Eds.), *Organizational functioning in a cross-cultural perspective* (pp. 128-310). Kent, OH: Kent State University Press.

With R.L. Blomstrom. *Business and Society: Environment and Responsibility* (3rd ed.). Tokyo: McGraw-Hill Kogakusha, Ltd. (International Student Edition)

1980

An interview with Keith Davis [Color Tape, Video]. Ft. Collins, CO: Videodocumentary Clearinghouse, Colorado State University.

A Dialogue between Keith Davis and Rensis Likert [Color Tape, Video]. Ft. Collins, CO: Videodocumentary Clearinghouse, Colorado State University.
Low productivity? Try improving the social environment. *Business Horizons, 23*(3), 27-29. (Reprinted in *The Harvest,* Ocotober 1980, pp. 4, 9 [Productivity Institute, College of Business Administration, Arizona State University]).
With W.C. Frederick & R.L. Blomstrom. *Business and society, concepts and policy issues* (4th ed.). New York: McGraw-Hill.

1981

Human behavior at work: Organizational behavior (6th ed). New York: McGraw-Hill.
With J.W. Newstrom. *Organizational behavior: Readings and exercises* (6th ed.). New York: McGraw-Hill.
With W.B. Werther, Jr. *Personnel management and human resources.* New York: McGraw-Hill.

1982

With W.B. Werther, Jr. *Dirección de personal y recursos humanos.* Translation by A. Contin. Mexico City: Libros McGraw-Hill de Mexico. (Spanish translation)
With W.B. Werther, Jr. *Personnel management and human resources.* Tokyo: McGraw-Hill Kogakusha, Ltd. (International Student Edition)
With W.B. Werther, Jr., H.F. Schwind, T.P. Hari Das, & F.C. Miner, Jr. *Canadian personnel management and human resources.* Toronto: McGraw-Hill Ryerson Limited.
With W.C. Frederick & R.L. Blomstrom. *Business and society: Concepts and policy issues* (4th ed.). Tokyo: McGraw-Hill Kogakusha, Ltd. (International Student Edition)

1983

Isletmede insan davranisi: Orgutsel davranis [*Human behavior at work: Organizational behavior*]. Istanbul, Turkey: University of Istanbul. (Turkish translation)
El comportamiento humano en el trabajo (6th ed.). Translation by H.C. de Contin. Mexico City: Libros McGraw-Hill de Mexico. (Spanish translation)
With W.B. Werther, Jr. *Administracao de pessoal e recursos humanos.* Translation by A.B. Simoes. Sao Paulo, Brazil: McGraw-Hill do Brazil.

1984

With W.C. Frederick. *Business and society: Management, public policy, ethics* (5th ed.). New York: McGraw-Hill.
With W.C. Frederick. *Business and society: Management, public policy, ethics* (5th ed.). Singapore: McGraw-Hill. (McGraw-Hill International Edition)

1985

With J.W. Newstrom. *Human behavior at work: Organizational behavior* (7th ed.). New York: McGraw-Hill.
With J.W. Newstrom. *Organizational behavior: Reading and exercises* (7th ed.). New York: McGraw-Hill.
With W.B. Werther, Jr. *Personnel management and human resources* (2nd ed.). New York: McGraw-Hill.
With W.B. Werther, Jr. *Personnel management and human resources* (2nd ed.). Singapore: McGraw-Hill Book Company-Singapore. (International Student Edition)
With W.B. Werther, Jr., & H. Lee-Gosselin. *La gestion des ressources humaines* [*Personnel management and human resources*]. Montreal, Canada: McGraw-Hill Editeurs. (French translation)
With W.B. Werther, Jr., H.F. Schwind, H. Das, & F.C. Miner, Jr. *Canadian personnel management and human resources* (2nd ed.). Toronto: McGraw-Hill Ryerson Limited.

1986

With S.A. Adams. Academy of Management journal: The first decade. In D.A. Wren & J.A. Pearce, II (Eds.), *Papers dedicated to the development of modern management* (Management Centennial Issue) (pp. 89-94). Academy of Management, Mississippi State University.

1987

Human behavior at work: Organizational behavior. Grolier Business Library Edition. Fort Washington, PA: Grolier.
With W.B. Werther, Jr. *Administracion de personal y recursos humanos* [*Personnel management and human resources*] (2nd ed.). Translation and adaptation by J.M. Gomez; technical revision by A.N. Mendoza. Mexico City: Libros McGraw-Hill de Mexico. (Spanish adaptation and translation)

1988

With W.C. Frederick, & J.E. Post. *Business and society: Corporate strategy, public policy, ethics* (6th ed.). New York: McGraw-Hill.

With J.W. Newstrom. *El comportamiento humano in el trabajo: Comportamiento organizational* [*Human behavior at work: Organizational behavior*] (7th ed.). Translation by A.E. Agea; technical revision by A.N. Ostrowiak and J.F. de Miguel. Mexico City: Libros McGraw-Hill de Mexico. (Spanish adaptation and translation)

1989

With W.C. Frederick & J.E. Post. *Business and society: Corporate strategy, public policy, ethics* (6th ed.). Singapore: McGraw-Hill. (McGraw-Hill International Edition)

With J.W. Newstrom. *Human behavior at work: Organizational behavior* (8th ed.). New York: McGraw-Hill.

With J.W. Newstrom. *Organizational behavior: Readings and exercises* (8th ed.). New York: McGraw-Hill.

With J.W. Newstrom. *Human behavior at work: Organizational behavior* (8th ed.). Singapore: McGraw-Hill. (McGraw-Hill International Edition)

With J.W. Newstrom. *Organizational behavior: Readings and exercises* (8th ed.). Singapore: McGraw-Hill. (McGraw-Hill International Edition)

With W.B. Werther, Jr. *Human resources and personnel management* (3rd ed.). New York: McGraw-Hill.

With W.B. Werther, Jr. *Human resources and personnel management* (3rd ed.). Singapore: McGraw-Hill. (McGraw-Hill International Edition)

1990

With W.B. Werther, H.F. Schwind, & H. Das. *Canadian human resource management* (3rd ed.). Toronto: McGraw-Hill Ryerson Limited.

1991

Popular American Colloquialisms: Their Meaning and Origin. Tempe, AZ: Author.

Life in a
Pretzel-Shaped Universe

FRED E. FIEDLER

Lee Cronbach once remarked that we live in a pretzel-shaped universe rather than a linear one, and that it takes pretzel-shaped hypotheses to account for pretzel-shaped data. Most of my life as a researcher has been devoted to hypotheses of this type, although it did not start out in this way.

PERSONAL BACKGROUND

Post-World War I Vienna, where I was born and raised, was alive with ideas. Not only did Freud, Adler, Jung, and their followers live and work there, but so did such philosophical luminaries as the members of the Wittgenstein Circle, musicians such as Gustav Mahler, Franz Lehar and Richard Strauss, writers such as Franz Werfel, architects such as Walter Gropius, and painters such as Klee and Kokoschka.

I started out wanting to be a detective, an explorer, or a writer, but by age 11 or 12 I had decided to become a psychologist. I knew that psychology had to do with studying people and their behavior which intrigued me, and I had read a number of books about psychology we had around the house.

My father had a business that sold tailoring supplies and manufactured textiles, but he was also a competent amateur painter and had worked on a historical novel. I read the novel when I was about 14 and thought it was pretty good, though it never saw the light of day. My parents were avid readers with varied intellectual interests, but business was clearly the center of their lives, as it was for all other members of my father's family. My great-

303

uncles on my mother's side were prominent architects (one built Vienna's famous Hotels Bristol and Imperial) but my contact with them was minimal.

Being the only child, I was expected to go into the family business. This idea never excited me. On the other hand, I certainly did not seem cut out for intellectual pursuits and was a poor student in my elementary school. Being the smallest kid in my class and Jewish meant being beaten up on an almost daily basis, and this may well have dampened my enthusiasm for school. At age 10, to everyone's surprise, I passed the stiff examination to the State Real-Gymnasium, the academic track of the 8-year secondary school, where I became an even worse student.

My half-yearly and yearly report cards in Real-Gymnasium registered a proud A for physical education, and grades between C and D for everything else. I even got an F in free-hand drawing—a first in the many years the school had been in existence. In my third year I managed to fail three of my courses and had to repeat the year. At that point, my parents decided to send me to a private school, and either because the school made me do my homework or because I was older and no longer the smallest boy in the class, my grades suddenly became quite respectable. I finished the first four grades of the 8-year Gymnasium in good order. In a fit of misplaced nostalgia for the bad old times, I visited my State Real-Gymnasium a few years ago. One of the faculty members, duly impressed by the academic title on my business card, pulled my grade record, blanched and silently shook her head, no doubt wondering what kind of people become professors in American universities.

By the time I was 15, I had finished the first four years of Real-Gymnasium which was not a bad education for that time. However, in view of Austria's deteriorating political situation, there did not seem much future in continuing in school. I reluctantly became an apprentice in my father's business, but decided to leave as soon as possible. I started to write to various distant relatives in the United States in hopes of eventually going there. This turned out to be a timely move, and when Hitler invaded Austria in March 1938, I was ready to concede Vienna to his army and left just three months later. Just short of 16, I was ready to make my fame and fortune in America. I still vividly recall running up the gangplank of the SS Manhattan in Hamburg while a couple of German storm troopers mockingly laughed at my eagerness to get aboard. My parents subsequently went to Shanghai, one of the few places which did not require entry visas, and I did not see them again for 10 years.

I was taken in by distant relatives in South Bend, Indiana, but was not too thrilled when I was informed that I had to go to school until I was 18. Nevertheless, when my relatives moved to Florida for health reasons one year later and I began to live by myself, I faithfully attended classes and found a part-time job. I must have learned more in my four years in school in Vienna than my grades had indicated, because I was able to finish the four years of South Bend's senior high school in just two years.

After graduation in 1940, I held a number of low-level jobs—21 in fact—and learned that I did not, among other things, like bill collecting, auto repair, bookkeeping, selling men's shirts, hawking popcorn, and driving or repairing trucks. I finally ended up as a hydro-electric operator in Buchanan, Michigan. After working there the better part of a year, I enrolled for the 1942 summer session at Western Michigan College of Education (now Western Michigan University) in Kalamazoo. I racked up 28 credit hours during that summer without too much trouble. This seemed too easy, and with the draft breathing down my neck, I applied to the University of Chicago with the notion that I could then get back into the University when the war was over. As expected, I was drafted during my first quarter.

After basic training in the Army's medical department and the infantry, and one term in the Army's Turkish Language and Area Program, I ended up in the Civil Affairs/Military Government Branch in Germany. I may not have been a happy soldier, but I was a reasonably good one. Unfortunately, my unit's adjutant did not appreciate my sense of humor, and I retired from military service with the exalted rank of Technician Grade V, a half notch below corporal.

University of Chicago

When I was discharged in November 1945, with four years of GI Bill in my pocket, I lost no time in heading back to the University of Chicago. Chicago gave credit by comprehensive examinations, and by reading the various syllabi and assigned books, I managed to pass the six required six-hour comprehensive exams. This enabled me to be admitted into the graduate program in Psychology and revived my earlier hopes of becoming an industrial psychologist.

I started courses in January 1946 and resurrected a broken engagement to Judith Joseph whom I had met at the University of Chicago before my military service; we got married in April of that year. While taking classes, I also completed a two-year Veterans Administration traineeship in clinical psychology, was active in campus politics (I drafted the first student government constitution and ran the first student government election), and worked as a janitor for the Great Books Program at Chicago. By December 1949, in just four years and a summer session, I had finished my Ph.D. in record time—my only scholarly distinction. A touch of being manic will do wonders for speeding one's career! My wife has since confided that living with me at that time was on the stressful side.

While at the University of Chicago, Carl Rogers took me on for my master's thesis—"An Experimental Approach to Preventative Psychotherapy" (1949)—which addressed the efficacy of preventative nondirective therapy for alleviating examination anxiety. In addition to working with Carl Rogers and doing some client centered therapy, I also went through two years of psychoanalysis which I probably needed more for personal than professional reasons.

I thought I knew something about different types of therapy and decided to test whether the client-centered relationship was really as different from a psychoanalytic relationship and Adlerian relationship as Rogers then believed. My doctoral committee—James G. Miller (chair), Jack Butler, Donald Fiske, Elias Porter, Carl Rogers, and William Stephenson—gave me somewhat reluctant consent. I compared the therapeutic relationship of two expert psychoanalysts—Jules Masserman and Walter Adams—two nondirective therapists—Carl Rogers and Jack Butler—and one Adlerian—Rudolph Dreikurs—with an equal number of nonexperts with each of these schools.[1] I recorded their therapy sessions and then had each of them rated by Q-technique. As it turned out, the experts were more similar to other experts than to nonexperts of their own orientation. The dissertation shook up clinical psychology by focusing on the therapeutic relationship rather than the different techniques, and the articles based on the dissertation are still my most cited papers.

While I was working on my dissertation and during my first post doctoral year, Lowell Kelly and Don Fiske asked me to join their Veterans Administration Project[2] on predicting the competence of clinical psychologists. Here I was able to combine my training in clinical and organizational psychology. The two years I spent on the VA project under Don Fiske's tutelage had a major influence on my professional life.

Don and I, along with Kenneth Isaacs, worked on developing criteria for assessing the performance of diagnosticians and therapists. We had the notion that you could objectively measure diagnostic competence by seeing how well the diagnostician understood the patient, that is how well he or she could predict the patient's self-concept. Self-concept, in this case was a Q-technique rating of one's self on various personality statements, and the diagnostician's task was "simply" to predict how the patient had described himself or herself. Lee Cronbach was one of our consultants.

As it turned out, most clinicians could not predict the patient's self-concept much better than chance, either with or without seeing the patient and all psychological tests. However, one result did show up loud and clear: The reputedly better therapists saw considerably more similarity between their own and their patient's self-concepts than did therapists who were rated as less experienced and less competent.[3]

This measure, called the Unwarranted Assumed Similarity correlated with reputed therapeutic competence .59 ($n = 22$, $p = <.01$), and suggested that the measure tapped "feeling close." This hypothesis was supported in a study of a fraternity—"Unconscious Attitudes as Correlates of Sociometric Choice in a Social Group" (1952)—in which we obtained each fraternity man's Q-technique rating for himself, for his best and for his least liked fellow member. As predicted, the assumed similarity to the best liked person was substantially greater than the similarity to the least liked fraternity brother. The Assumed Similarity measures were the forerunners of the Least Preferred Coworker (LPC) score.

The University of Illinois

In 1951, Lee Cronbach invited me to work with him at the University of Illinois as Research Assistant Professor of Education. He and I had applied for a big research contract ($20,000!) which supported me, a research associate, a secretary, a couple of research assistants, and part of Lee Cronbach's salary. For 1951, it was Big Money.

Before going to Illinois in October 1951, I spent four hot, sweaty summer months at the Combat Crew Research Laboratory at Randolph Field with Robert L. French, who directed the laboratory. Among my coworkers were Leonard Berkowitz, Donald Forgays, Williams Haythorn, Thornton Roby, and several others who later made a name for themselves. I learned a lot about B-29 bomber crews, military research, and hot Texas summers. When we finally got to autumn weather in Urbana, Illinois, it seemed like heaven.

If working with Don Fiske was my research internship, my two years with Lee Cronbach was my residency where I got my first taste in directing a research program. Lee and I were quite different in our approach to research, and to his everlasting credit let it be said that he had more faith in my judgment than I would have had. Our extended research group included Nathaniel Gage, William Warrington, Irving Lazar, Elizabeth Ehart, and consultants such as Goldine Gleser and the mathematician Franz Hohn, as well as several research assistants. It was a heady time.

Two years later, I was invited to join the Psychology Department at Illinois where I established the Group Effectiveness Research Laboratory. This grew into a fairly large and successful operation in which Harry Triandis later joined me as Associate Director. I worked closely with Harry for over eight years, and I cannot recall a single major argument.

Among the faculty who were associated with the laboratory at one time or another were Sheldon Alexander, Martin Fishbein, Uriel Foa, Charles Hulin, Lloyd Humphreys, Stanly Nealey, Joseph McGrath, Charles Osgood, and Lawrence Stolurow. Some of the students and research associates who later became well known were Lynn Anderson, Allan Bass, Anthony Biglan, Duangduen Bhanthumnavin, Milton Blood, Martin Chemers, Peter Dachler, David DeVries, Jack Feldman, Richard Hackman, J.G. Hunt, Edwin Hutchins, Daniel Ilgen, James Julian, Melvin Manis, Bilha Mannheim, Terence Mitchell, Anthony Morris, Gordon O'Brien, and Alexander Wearing. Mitchell, Hunt, Ilgen, Hackman, and Chemers eventually earned named professorship chairs, and a number were department chairs at one time or another. These included Wearing (Melbourne), Chemers (Utah), Julian (Buffalo), Mannheim (Dean of the Technion in Haifa, Israel), and Feldman (Florida). Joseph McGrath later chaired the Psychology Department at the University of Illinois and Sheldon Alexander did the same at Wayne State.

The University of Washington

In 1969 I moved to the University of Washington as Professor of Psychology and Adjunct Professor of Management and Organization. Terence Mitchell who moved with me to Washington obtained an appointment at the business school.

Seattle turned out to be a good choice. The Organizational Research Group I established at the University of Washington continued and extended the work at Illinois, but on a blessedly smaller scale. My colleagues at Washington included Gary Latham and Terence Mitchell in the business school and Lee Beach and myself in the Department of Psychology. With the recent departures of Gary Latham and of Lee Beach, who was my closest professional colleague at Washington, as well as my own imminent retirement in 1992, the future of organizational research at the University of Washington is in doubt.

I have had excellent students at Washington who have begun very distinguished careers even though most are, of course, still at a relatively early stage in their professional life. Among the already better known of my Ph.D.s are Delbert Nebeker and Renate Mai-Dalton, and James Larson, Dennis Dossett, and Robert Hansson who worked with me on their masters' degree.

Shortly after my arrival in Washington, West Point began to send me military officers for their graduate training. Eight army officers, one Coast Guard, and one Air Force officer earned their Ph.D. under my tutelage, and five more left with an M.S. degree with all requirements completed except the dissertation. A number of these students ended up in teaching and research at such military schools as West Point, the National Defense University, the Command and General Staff College, the Coast Guard Academy, and the Air Force Academy. Some of these students also held major research and staff positions in the Department of Defense.

RESEARCH

Four major contributions seem worth noting. The first, as already discussed, was my dissertation study on therapeutic relations which had considerable influence on psychotherapy research. It was later extended into research on quasi-therapeutic relations. A second was a research program to develop culture training programs. Third, and most important from my perspective, was my research and development of the Contingency Model,[4] and the fourth contribution is my current projects related to the development of Cognitive Resource Theory.

Therapeutic Relationships

This research peaked during my graduate years at the University of Chicago. Later, in collaboration with Joan Dodge, Edwin Hutchins, and Robert Jones, I directed a project on "quasi-therapeutic relations" under a contract with the Office of the Surgeon General. The purpose of the project was to identify the types of interpersonal relations among individuals in various organizations, and especially in military units, which would facilitate and enhance personal adjustment. We conducted a series of studies that showed the value of inter-group competition as a means to making groups more cohesive. The thinking was that a more cohesive group would increase the individual's value to coworkers, provide more social support, and therefore raise his or her self-esteem and reduce psychological problems.[5] Although this project produced quite respectable results, it did not have much direct impact on the field.

Culture Assimilators

The second contribution was in the area of cross-cultural research and training. The research was conducted as part of a large project developed by a group at Illinois consisting of Charles Osgood, Harry Triandis, Lawrence Stolurow and myself, as principal investigator. It was funded by the Advanced Research Projects Agency of the Defense Department for the purpose of developing culture training programs for the military services.

Among the other senior investigators were Uriel Foa, Gordon O'Brien, Martin Fishbein, anthropologist William Archer, and a number of graduate students, including Martin Chemers, Terence Mitchell, Duagnduen Lekhiananda Bhanthumnavin, and Samuel Shiflett. My own part, aside from administering the project, was to conduct field validation studies.

The project produced a method and theory of culture training, and self-paced culture training programs for Iran, Honduras and Central America, Thailand and Greece as well as numerous papers.[6] These programs were empirically tested and several have since then been used by the military services and private organizations. Triandis later adapted the method for developing training programs for improving relations between African-Americans and whites, and the programmed instruction method, developed for this project by Lawrence Stolurow, has been used by other researchers since then.

The Contingency Model

My best known contribution is the development of the contingency model.[7] It was really then that I had my first eyeball-to-eyeball confrontations with the pretzel shape of life in leadership research. The first foray into leadership studies luckily turned out to be a highly successful study of high school basketball teams.[8] We had expected to find that sociometrically chosen leaders would, like effective psychotherapists, see a lot of similarity between themselves and their most preferred coworkers.

Exactly the opposite was the case: The informal leaders of the teams who won most of their league games, perceived more "distance" between themselves and their coworkers than did leaders of less successful teams. In fact, the best results were obtained when we computed the difference between a leader's description of his most and least preferred coworkers, dubbed the "Assumed Similarity between Opposites" (ASo) score.

In other words, the leaders who described their least preferred coworkers in very negative and rejecting terms, as compared to preferred coworkers, had the best teams. Since everyone tended to describe the most preferred coworker in very favorable terms, the score depended mostly on how the leader described the person with whom he or she could work least well. A simpler and more reliable measure was therefore developed somewhat later by asking the leader only to describe the one person with whom he or she could work least well. This score, the esteem for the *least preferred coworker* (LPC), has been used ever since with only slight modifications.

To everyone's surprise, the results of the first basketball study were validated in a second basketball study, and subsequently, in studies of surveying parties and open hearth steel crews.[9] At that point, I thought that I had discovered the TRUE leadership trait in the LPC score. This fantasy did not last long. I quickly learned in my next study of 72 B-29 Air Force bomber crews[10] that it is wise to quit while you're ahead. The B-29 bomber study bombed abominably.

During the summer that followed, my wife and I must have run well over 1,000 rank-order correlations on a "coffee-mill" Facit hand calculator, trying to find out why the bomber crew data gave such disappointing results. I saw many more zero correlations than could have been predicted by chance. My friends and colleagues, relieved that they could now forget about my funny findings, shrugged and washed their hands of the problem. Being tenacious (or obsessive), I did not. I had faith that the same results obtained in these studies could not be due to chance.

What finally emerged was a set of rather complex findings. We obtained very high negative correlation ($-.81$) between the leader's LPC score and crew performance, but only when the aircraft commander was sociometrically accepted by his crew and also had a good relationship with his "keymen" (crew members who performed the simulated radar or visual bombing on which the crew's performance was based). In crews in which the aircraft commander did not choose his navigator or bombardier (his keymen), the correlations were significantly positive.

This same finding also showed up in a sample of army tank crews. Again, when a tank commander was accepted by his crew and sociometrically chose his gunner, the correlation between tank commander LPC and crew performance was −.60; when he did not choose his gunner, the correlation was +.60.[11] All this was very exciting but highly mysterious, and generated several very creative hypotheses of dubious validity.

In 1958-59 I went to the Municipal University of Amsterdam as a Fulbright Fellow. The Department of Psychology, then chaired by Hubert Duijker, extended its hospitality. I had the assistance of Nico Frijda, now Professor at Amsterdam, and two students with whom I conducted a complex laboratory experiment in which groups were given creative tasks.[12] We studied groups which were homogeneous or heterogeneous in religious background, that is consisting of either Catholics or Calvinists and groups composed of two Catholics and two Calvinists. Leaders were appointed in one-half of the groups while the other groups had informal leaders. The results showed that leader LPC scores correlated positively with performance in the homogeneous groups with appointed leaders, but negatively in heterogeneous groups with emergent leaders. I went around for months trying to figure out what all this could mean. Finally after extended discussions with students and colleagues, I began to look at these groups as falling on a continuum of how much power and influence the situation gave to the leader. This study really constituted the inception of the contingency model.

A year after I got back from Holland, I had a fairly good idea of what was going on in my research. My students and I had been conducting a number of different studies in my laboratory at the University of Illinois, and we spent the following year collecting more data. The Office of Naval Research still supported me rather handsomely, and by 1962 I had amassed and analyzed data from 13 different studies, and milked the data until they bled.

At that time, Leonard Berkowitz, my erstwhile colleague from Randolph Field and then editor of the *Recent Advances in Experimental Social Psychology* series, asked me to write a chapter for his first volume, and the contingency model had found a home. In 1963-64 I was able to work at the University of Louvain in Belgium with Jozef Nuttin and his students, and we conducted a major validation study with personnel from the Belgian naval forces.[13]

After some further validation studies, I published *A Theory of Leadership Effectiveness* in 1967. It was clearly a landmark. The contingency model was the first leadership theory which operationally measured the interaction between leadership personality and the leader's situational control in the prediction of leadership performance. The paper in the Berkowitz volume and the 1967 book created a great deal of interest and, at least according to some, were responsible for a paradigmatic shift in thinking about leadership.

The contingency model also offered a field day for critics. The theory was almost immediately attacked (a) for difficulties in interpreting the LPC score, (b) because not every study confirmed the theory in all respects, and (c) because it was a black box which did not explain the reason for the results. Many of the criticisms were justified: the interpretation of the LPC score and the reason why the contingency model predicted performance was far from clear. However, some critiques were almost unbelievably emotional and impassioned, and by the time many of the attacks on the theory were published, many problems under attack, though certainly not all, had been resolved. As is usually the case, some criticisms successfully slew nonexistent dragons.

There are now some 400 or more studies that deal with the contingency model in one way or another. Not all of them support the model, but R.W. Rice's[14] reviews of the literature show the LPC measure to be reliable, stable and valid, and two meta-analyses have found substantial support for the contingency model.[15] The model has had a relatively long and prominent place in the leadership literature. It has probably served its purpose. It still has warts.

Leader-Match Training.   One practical outcome of the contingency model was a self-paced leadership training program called Leader-Match.[16] This training method differs most markedly from others by stating that effective leadership depends on the leader's personality (measured by LPC) as well as the leadership situation (i.e., situational control). It is based on the assumption that it is easier to change one's leadership situation (relations with subordinates, task structure, and position power) than to change one's personality. For this reason, Leader-Match trains leaders to modify situational control to fit their personality.

This program requires only about 6 to 8 hours of time, and has been successfully validated in 18 of 19 empirical studies. Leader Match is one of the few programs that actually has been validated with appropriate control groups and carefully matched groups.[17] In the discussion of their meta-analysis of leadership training programs, Burke and Day summarize, "The results suggest that the effectiveness of the Leader-Match training method with respect to subjective behavior criteria generalize across situations.... On the basis of these results as well as the cost-effectiveness of Leader-Match training and compared with that of other leadership training programs, this method of leadership training is encouraged."[18] Although the training manual— *Improving Leadership Effectiveness: The Leader Match Concept* (co-authored by Martin Chemers and Linda Mahar)—has sold over 45,000 copies, the training is more complex than others on the market, and Leader-Match has not become a household word in the business community.

It is of interest to note that Leader-Match, despite the short training time it requires, has long-lasting results. The Leader-Match training, along with behavior modeling, was used in a large field experiment to test its effectiveness in increasing safety and productivity in underground mining operations. The training was administered in a large soda-ash mine and the effects were compared with all other soda-ash mines being used as controls. A three-year study showed a decline of about 50 percent in accidents and injuries and an increase in productivity (tons per man-day) of 13 percent above that of the other mines in the industry.[19] A five-year follow-up study showed that the improvement in safety and productivity had continued throughout the five year period.[20] Management credits the improved organizational performance to the training which the managers and supervisors received.

Cognitive Resource Theory

Fourth and probably last, is the continuing development of the cognitive resource theory[21] which again takes us out of a linear world and into a pretzel-shaped universe. The theory seeks to identify the conditions under which leaders and group members make effective use of their intellectual resources, skills and knowledge. This problem is of interest for several reasons.

Practically all who are able to attain to and hold leadership and managerial positions must have the minimum skills, knowledge and abilities to handle the job. However, within this otherwise qualified group, it is generally taken for granted that bright and experienced leaders will perform better than leaders who are intellectually less well endowed. This assumption is not supported. More intelligent leaders are only slightly more effective than less intelligent leaders, and more experienced leaders do not perform better on the whole than do those with less experience.[22] Nevertheless, most organizations choose their managers, in large part, for their intellectual abilities and their track record in previous jobs.

Even more puzzling was the finding of high negative correlations between leader intelligence and performance in a number of studies. These counter-intuitive results usually occurred when the leader was nondirective or reported high interpersonal stress.[23] Moreover, a dissertation by Jon Blades titled "The Influence of Intelligence, Task Ability, and Motivation on Group Performance" (University of Washington, Seattle) showed that leader intelligence and task ability correlate with performance only if (a) leaders are directive and (b) group members are motivated or support the leader.

Since the inner dynamics of the contingency model remained a black box, I had hoped to find an explanation by identifying the conditions in which high and low LPC leaders were able to make effective use of their intellectual abilities and experience. Cognitive resource theory[24] began, therefore, as an attempt to explain the contingency model. Up to now, this attempt to relate the two theories has been only partly successful. It did, however, uncover a number of highly interesting and potentially important phenomena which throws new light on the leadership process.

Our research shows, for example, that a relatively stress-free relationship with the immediate boss permits leaders to make effective use of their intelligence, but not of their experience. In contrast, stress with the boss causes leaders to use their experience but not their intellectual abilities. In fact, as mentioned earlier, leader intelligence and performance tends to correlate negatively under these stressful conditions. The studies also show that leader intelligence tends to correlate very highly in situations in which the leader is directive and has a motivated or supportive group, but again negatively when the leader is nondirective.[25]

These findings have major implications for selection and training. Our selection tests measure capacity to perform certain jobs, and our training is designed to teach individuals skills and knowledge that will improve their performance. However, we also must make sure that the people we select and train are placed into situations in which they are able to make effective use of what they learned, if the selection and training efforts are not to be wasted. *New Approaches to Effective Leadership: Cognitive Resources and Organizational Performance* (1987) which describes cognitive resource theory and supporting research spells out these conditions in detail. Unfortunately this book (co-authored by Joseph Garcia) seems to have been published as a classified document or not widely advertised for other reasons. Nevertheless, it seems to me that the integration of cognitive variables into the mainstream of leadership theory is highly important and long overdue.

SOME FINAL REFLECTIONS

In my 40 years of academic life, research on leadership performance has not only been my major occupation but an abiding passion. I have been, and still am, a happy workaholic whose addiction has turned out to be professionally very rewarding. I have always preferred research to other hobbies. So much for the well-balanced life! Like other surviving species, I seem to have found the ecological niche in which I could thrive. As the Leader-Match program points out, "If you learn to avoid situations in which you are likely to fail, you're bound to be a success."[27] I have not, for this reason, become a psychotherapist, but have left this professional activity to two of my more able daughters. Nor have I ever tackled the job of writing a text, become an entrepreneur, a leadership trainer, or department chair. While I firmly believe that it is better to be rich and healthy than sick and poor, I am certain that it would have been a less rewarding experience for me as well as everyone else even if I had managed to become a successful consultant, entrepreneur, trainer, or administrator.

Along with my research, my most rewarding accomplishment has been my contribution to the development of the many young psychologists with whom I have had the privilege to work. Practically all of my former students, whether or not I supervised their theses and dissertations, have told me that the time they spent in my research group was one of the most important periods in their professional development.

For better or worse, I have believed in throwing people into research projects as soon as they got into my lab, and having them work with "older" graduate students. I think that I have given them a great deal of leeway in what they did, and I've pushed them to go as fast as they could. While some did not like this regime, most have enjoyed the experience. The latter also benefitted from being in my research groups.

I also firmly believe (based on my own experience no doubt) that those who take a long time in getting their degree are likely to forget that jobs, whether in business, research organizations or university departments, require getting things done with dispatch. There are deadlines to meet wherever we are, even after being tenured, and students need to learn this lesson in graduate school.

I have tried to imbue students with my firm conviction that a clean and elegant experiment may be a thing of beauty and a joy forever, but building a sound theory is more like trying to solve a picture puzzle in which half the pieces are missing, or like a mystery story which does not give you all the clues. And to round out this mess of mixed metaphors, I am convinced that data are adversaries that have to be beaten into submission or milked dry. I have been struck time and again by the realization that I did not really begin to understand some of our research results until many years and studies later. Research to me is more like an archaeological dig than a mathematical game. It takes a lot of shoveling and sifting, at least in the area of leadership, before you really begin to hit pay dirt.

Living in the state of Washington also gave me the chance to do things which most other psychologists never experience. Almost immediately after coming to Seattle, I became a consultant to the County Executive, and for 10 years I was able to work closely with his office, and practically every department in county government. It was quite an education in local government and politics. I later served on the transition team on personnel and on technology transfer, and worked with some of the state agencies when the County Executive became governor. I also served for four years as the Consumer Member of Washington State's Medical Disciplinary Board. It was a fascinating, if often disturbing, experience. It would be hard to find a place to live and work that compared with the Seattle area and the Pacific Northwest which my family and I love. My major regret in recent years has been the paucity of colleagues in the Psychology Department at Washington who shared my interests.

Would I recommend my type of life to my students? Without question. I would not trade it for any other way of making a living. I have had sabbaticals and leaves which took me to the Universities of Amsterdam, Louvain, Oxford, and the Technion in Israel, and I spent the better part of a year as holder of the Marshall Chair in the Army Institute of Research in the Behavioral and Social Sciences. In my opinion, the life of the academic is the best racket going. It gave me intrinsic satisfaction as well as unusual assignments in politics, law, the military and business organizations. I certainly would not trade my career as a psychologist and educator for any other way of life even if I had another chance.

PUBLICATIONS

1947

Some client reactions to substitution of group leaders. *The Personal Counselor, 2*(3), 164-166.

1949

An experimental approach to preventative psychotherapy. *Journal of Abnormal and Social Psychology, 44*(3), 389-393.

With S.M. Siegel. The free drawing test as a predictor of nonimprovement in psychotherapy. *Journal of Clinical Psychology, 5*(4), 386-389.

1950

The concept of an ideal therapeutic relationship. *Journal of Consulting Psychology, 14*(4), 239-245.

A comparison of therapeutic relationships in psychoanalytic, nondirective and Adlerian therapy. *Journal of Consulting Psychology, 14*(6), 436-445.

1951

Factor analyses of psychoanalytic, nondirective and Adlerian therapeutic relationships. *Journal of Consulting Psychology, 15*(1), 32-38.

A method of objective quantification of certain counter-transference attitudes. *Journal of Clinical Psychology, 7*(2), 101-107.

With J.M. Wepman. An exploratory investigation of the self-concept of stutterers. *Journal of Speech and Hearing Disorders, 16*, 110-114.

1952

With K. Senior. An exploratory study of unconscious feeling reactions in fifteen patient-therapist pairs. *Journal of Abnormal and Social Psychology, 47*(2), 446-453.

With W.G. Warrington & F.J. Blaisdell. Unconscious attitudes as correlates of sociometric choice in a social group. *Journal of Abnormal and Social Psychology, 47*(4), 790-796.

With W. Hartmann & S.A. Rudin. *Interpersonal perception in the prediction of effectiveness of basketball teams.* Urbana: University of Illinois, Group Effectiveness Research Laboratory.

1953

Personality and situational determinants of leadership effectiveness. In D. Cartwright & A. Zander (Eds.), *Group Dynamics Research and Theory* (pp. 742-775). New York: Harper & Row.

Quantitative studies on the role of therapists' feelings toward their patients. In O. H. Mowrer (Ed.), *Psychotherapy-Theory and Research* (pp. 296-315). New York: Ronald Press.

The psychological-distance dimension in interpersonal relations. *Journal of Personality, 22*(1) 142-150.

1954

Assumed similarity measures as predictors of team effectiveness. *Journal of Abnormal and Social Psychology, 49*(3), 381-388.

Good leadership: Nature or nurture. *Contact* (Journal of the U.S. Naval School of Aviation Medicine), *12*(1), 22-24.

1955

The influence of leader-keyman relations on combat crew effectiveness. *Journal of Abnormal and Social Psychology, 51*(2), 227-235.

With E.F. Golb. *A note on psychological attributes related to the score assumed similarity between opposites (ASo).* Urbana: University of Illinois, Group Effectiveness Research Laboratory.

With E.B. Hutchins & E.R. Ostrander. Comments on training conditions by instructors. *Special Report No. 55-8.* Pensacola, FL: U.S. Naval School of Aviation Medicine.

1956

With R.E. Jones. *The relation of interpersonal perception to personality adjustment among members of small face-to-face groups.* Urbana: University of Illinois, Group Effectiveness Research Laboratory.
With W.A. Cleven. Interpersonal perceptions of open-hearth foremen and steel production. *Journal of Applied Psychology, 40*(5), 312-314.

1957

A note on leadership theory: The effect of social barriers between leaders and followers. *Sociometry, 20*(2), 87-94.

1958

Leader attitudes and group effectiveness. Urbana: University of Illinois Press.
With J.S. Dodge, R.E. Jones, & E.B. Hutchins. Interrelations among measures of personality adjustment in nonclinical populations. *Journal of Abnormal and Social Psychology, 56*, 345-351.
Interpersonal perception and group effectiveness. In R. Talgiuri & L. Petrullo (Eds.), *Person Perception and Interpersonal Behavior* (pp. 243-257). Stanford, CA: Stanford University Press.
Psychological distance and team effectiveness. *Personnel Administration, 21*(6), 21-23.
Non-fraternization between leaders and followers and its effects on group productivity and psychological adjustment. Walter Reed Institute for Research, Washington, DC, *Symposium on Preventive and Social Psychiatry* (pp. 337-343). Washington, DC: Supt. of Public Documents.
With J.S. Terwilliger. An investigation of determinants inducing individuals to seek personal counseling. *Journal of Consulting Psychology, 22*(4), 288.
With E.G. Potter. Physical disability and interpersonal perception. *Perceptual and Motor Skills, 8*, 241-242.
With F.W. Uhlmann. Choices of fraternity presidents for leadership and maintenance roles. *Psychological Reports, 4*, 498.

1959

With E. Godfrey & D.M. Hall. *Boards, Management, and Company Success.* Danville, IL: Interstate Press.
With E.B. Hutchins & J.S. Dodge. Quasi-therapeutic relations in small college and military groups. *Psychological Monographs: General and Applied, 72*(3), 1-28.

A review of R. Stogdill's individual behavior and group achievement theory: The experimental evidence. *American Journal of Sociology, 65*, 214-215.
With A.R. Bass. *Delinquency, confinement, and interpersonal perception.* Urbana: University of Illinois, Group Effectiveness Research Laboratory.
With A.R. Bass. *Interpersonal perception scores: A comparison of D scores and their components.* Urbana: University of Illinois, Group Effectiveness Research Laboratory.

1960

With E.B. Hutchins. Task-oriented and quasi-therapeutic role functions of the leader in small military groups. *Sociometry, 23*(4), 393-406.
The leader's psychological distance and group effectiveness. In D. Cartwright & A. Zander (Eds.), *Group Dynamics Research and Theory* (2nd ed., pp. 586-606). New York: Harper & Row.
With J.M. Fiedler. A review of Liveright's *Strategies of Leadership*, Miles' *Learning to Work in Groups*, and Hoffman and Plutchik's *Small Group Discussion in Orientation and Teaching. American Sociological Review, 25*, 591-592.

1961

Leadership and leadership effectiveness traits: A reconceptualization of the leadership trait problem. In L. Petrullo & B.M. Bass (Eds.), *Leadership and Interpersonal Behavior* (pp. 179-186). New York: Holt, Rinehart & Winston.
With W. Meuwese & S. Oonk. An exploratory study of group creativity in laboratory tasks. *Acta Psychologica, 18*(2), 100-119.
The ubiquity of leadership. A review of Bernard M. Bass' *Leadership, Psychology and Organizational Behavior. Contemporary Psychology, 6*, 178-180.
With A.R. Bass & J.M. Fiedler. *The leader's perception of coworkers, group climate and group creativity: A cross-validation.* Urbana: University of Illinois, Group Effectiveness Research Laboratory.
With A.R. Bass. Interpersonal perception scores and their components as predictors of personal adjustment. *Journal of Abnormal and Social Psychology, 62*(2), 442-445.
With A.R. Kohn. Age and sex differences in the perception of persons. *Sociometry, 24*(2), 157-164.
With P. London & R.S. Nemo. *Hypnotically induced leader attitudes and group creativity.* Urbana: University of Illinois, Group Effectiveness Research Laboratory.

1962

The nature of teamwork. *Discovery, 23,* 36-41.
With E.L. Hoffman. Age, sex, and religious background as determinants of interpersonal perception among Dutch children: A cross-cultural validation. *Acta Psychologica, 20*(3), 185-195.
Leader attitudes, group climate, and group creativity. *Journal of Abnormal and Social Psychology, 65*(5), 308-318.
With J.C. Naidoo. Perceptions of self and significant others by Indian and American students. *Indian Journal of Psychology, 37,* 115-126.

1963

With W.A.T. Meuwese. Leader's contribution to task performance in cohesive and uncohesive groups. *Journal of Abnormal and Social Psychology, 67*(1), 83-87.
Leadership and leadership effectiveness traits: A reconceptualization of the leadership trait problem. In E. P. Hollander & R.G. Hunt (Eds.), *Current Perspectives in Social Psychology* (pp. 480-485). New York: Oxford.

1964

With L.R. Anderson. The effect of participatory and supervisory leadership on group creativity. *Journal of Applied Psychology, 48*(4), 227-236.
With A.R. Bass & S. Krueger. *Personality correlates of assumed similarity (ASo) and related scores.* Urbana: University of Illinois, Group Effectiveness Research Laboratory.
With C.G. Morris. *Application of a new system of interaction analysis to the relationships between leader attitudes and behavior in problem-solving groups.* Urbana: University of Illinois, Group Effectiveness Research Laboratory.
Industrious adjustment. A review of H. Levinson, C. R. Price, K. J. Munden, H. J. Mandl, & C. M. Solley (Eds.), *Men, management, and mental health. Contemporary Psychology, 9,* 227-228.
Factors operative in shaping the concept of the ideal therapeutic relationship. In H. Ito (Ed.), *Readings in Counseling Psychology* (Vol. 3). Tokyo: Seishin Shobo Co., Ltd.
The effect of group climate on the leader's influence on creative group performance. In C. W. Taylor & F. Barron (Eds.), *Widening Horizons in Creativity* (pp. 401-409). New York: Wiley.

1965

With W. Meuwese. *Leadership and group creativity under varying conditions of stress.* Urbana: University of Illinois, Group Effectiveness Research Laboratory.

The contingency model: A theory of leadership effectiveness. In H. Proshansky & B. Seidenberg (Eds.), *Basic Studies in Social Psychology* (pp. 389-396). New York: Holt, Rinehart & Winston.

The nature of teamwork. In R.S. Daniel (Ed.), *Contemporary Readings in General Psychology* (pp. 336-340). Boston: Houghton Mifflin Co.

With W.A.T. Meuwese. Leader's contribution to task performance in cohesive and uncohesive groups. In I. D. Steiner & M. Fishbein (Eds.), *Current Studies in Social Psychology* (pp. 389-396). New York: Holt, Rinehart & Winston.

Leadership—a new model. *Discovery, 26,* 12-17.

Engineer the job to fit the manager. *Harvard Business Review, 43,* 116-122.

A model for the organizational management of leadership effectiveness. *Rivista di Psicologia del Lavoro,* 9-22.

Un modele de l'efficience du commandement. *Bulletin du C.E.R.P., XIV,* 179-202.

1966

With W.A.T. Meuwese. *The effect of stress on the contribution of member intelligence to group creativity.* Urbana: University of Illinois, Group Effectiveness Research Laboratory.

With S.M. Nealey. *Second-level management: A review and analysis.* U.S. Civil Service Commission, Office of Career Development, Washington, D.C.

A review of research on ASO and LPC scores as measures of leadership style. Urbana: University of Illinois, Group Effectiveness Research Laboratory.

Leadership style and the performance of co-acting. Urbana: University of Illinois, Group Effectiveness Research Laboratory.

The contingency model: A theory of leadership effectiveness. In C.W. Backman & P.F. Secord (Eds.), *Problems in Social Psychology* (pp. 278-289). New York: McGraw-Hill.

Leadership style and managerial effectiveness. In *Management Services' First Annual Personnel Conference Summary Report* (pp. 64-72). National Rural Electric Cooperative Association.

The effect of leadership and cultural heterogeneity on group performance: A test of the contingency model. *Journal of Experimental Social Psychology, 2,* 237-264.

With D. Bishop & J.M. Alsobrook. *The effects of intergroup competition in quasi-therapeutic leaders on the adjustment of small military groups.* Urbana: University of Illinois, Group Effectiveness Research Laboratory.

With M.M. Chemers, D. Lekhyananda, & L.M. Stolurow. Some effects of cultural training on leadership in heterocultural task groups. *International Journal of Psychology, 1*, 301-314.
With J.W. Julian & D.W. Bishop. Quasi-therapeutic effects of intergroup competition. *Journal of Personality and Social Psychology, 3*, 321-327.
With A.E. Myers. Theories and probleme der Fuhrung. In G. Luschen (Ed.), *Kleingruppenforschung und Gruppe im Sport* (pp. 92-106). Cologne, Germany: Westdeutscher Verlag.

1967

A Theory of Leadership Effectiveness. New York: McGraw-Hill.
The effect of intergroup competition on group member adjustment. *Personnel Psychology, 20*, 33-44.
Styles of leadership. In E. P. Hollander & R. G. Hunt (Eds.), *Current Perspectives in Social Psychology* (2nd ed., pp 498-504). New York: Oxford University Press.
Fuhrungsstil and leistung koagierender gruppen [Leadership style and performance of co-acting groups]. *Zeitschrift fur Experimentelle und Angewandte Psychologie, 14*, 200-217.
Situational factors related to leadership effectiveness. In E.A. Fleishman (Ed.), *Studies in Personnel and Industrial Psychology* (pp. 349-360). Homewood, IL: Dorsey Press.
With N.M. Barron. *The effect of leadership style and leader behavior on group creativity under stress.* Urbana: University of Illinois, Group Effectiveness Research Laboratory.

1968

Personality and situational determinants of leadership effectiveness. In D. Cartwright & A. Zander (Eds.), *Group Dynamics: Research and Theory* (3rd ed., pp. 362-380). New York: Harper.
The effect of culture training on leadership, organizational performance, and adjustment. *Naval Research Reviews, 21*, 7-13.
With S.M. Nealey. Leadership functions of middle managers. *Psychological Bulletin, 70*, 313-329.
With M.M. Chemers. *Group performance under experienced and inexperienced leaders: A validation experiment.* Urbana: University of Illinois, Group Effectiveness Research Laboratory.

1969

Style or circumstance: The leadership enigma. *Psychology Today* (March).

With A. Biglan. *The first job after graduation as a measure of departmental performance.* Urbana: University of Illinois, Group Effectiveness Research Laboratory.

With G.E. O'Brien. Leadership and organizational performance. In S. Seashore & R. McNeill (Eds.), *The Management of Crises: Metropolitan Government and the Behavioral Sciences.* New York: Free Press, MacMillan Co.

With G.E. O'Brien and D.R. Ilgen. The effect of leadership style upon the performance and adjustment of volunteer teams operating in a stressful foreign environment. *Human Relations, 22,* 503-514.

Organizational engineering—a new approach to effective leadership. In S.W. Koster (Ed.), *Leadership in the post-70's* (pp. 79-93). West Point, NY: U.S. Military Academy.

Culture training and performance in multi-cultural situations. *NATO Conference Publication–Special Training for Multilateral Forces* (July), 42-52.

Leadership style and organizational performance. In N. A. B. Wilson (Ed.), *Manpower Research* (pp. 376-388). London: English University Press.

Leadership determinants of organizational performance. *Proceedings of the 12th Annual Midwest Management Conference, Academy of Management.* Des Moines, IA: Drake University Press.

With S.M. Nealey & M.T. West. The effects of training on performance of post office supervisors (Final report).

1970

Leadership experience and leader performance—Another hypothesis shot to hell. *Organizational Behavior and Human Performance, 5,* 1-14.

With P. Ninane. Member reactions to success and failure of task groups. *Human Relations, 23,* 3-13.

With T.R. Mitchell, A. Biglan, & G. Oncken. The contingency model: Criticisms and suggestions. *Academy of Management Journal* (September).

Organizational engineering—A new approach to leadership. In *Concepts of Air Force Leadership.* Air Force ROTC, Air University.

With T.R. Mitchell. The effect of culture training on task group effectiveness. In Bass, Cooper, & Haas (Eds.), *Managing for Accomplishment* (pp. 195-206). Lexington, MA: D.C. Heath.

1971

With T.R. Mitchell & H. Triandis. The culture assimilator: An approach to cross-cultural training. *Journal of Applied Psychology, 55,* 95-103.

Personality & situational determinants of leader behavior (Techn. Rep. No. 71-18). Seattle: University of Washington, Organizational Research.

A note on the methodology of the Graen, Orris, and Alvares studies testing the contingency model. *Journal of Applied Psychology, 55,* 202-204.

Validation and extension of the contingency model of leadership effectiveness: A review of empirical findings. *Psychological Bulletin, 76,* 128-148.

With R. Smith. The measurement of scholarly work in academic institutions: A critical review of the literature. *Educational Record* (Summer), 225-232.

With U.G. Foa & T.R. Mitchell. Differentiation matching. *Behavioral Science, 16,* 130-142.

With G.E. O'Brien & T. Hewett. The effects of programmed culture training upon the performance of volunteer medical teams in Central America. *Human Relations, 24,* 209-231.

Leadership. New York: General Learning Press.

Do leaders really learn leadership? In *The Perceived Role of the Military* (pp. 191-211). Rotterdam: Rotterdam University Press.

With A. Biglan & G.R. Oncken. *Convergence among academic outputs as a function of academic area* (Technical Report No. 71-26). Seattle: University of Washington, Organizational Research.

With M. Wood, S. Nealey, & P. Bates. *Informal leadership preference and managerial effectiveness in a complex government organization.* Mimeographed report, University of Washington.

Note on Zimmer and Pepyne's study comparing counselor responses. *Journal of Counseling Psychology, 18,* 123-124.

With J. Fiedler & S. Campf. Who speaks for the community? *Journal of Applied Social Psychology, 1,* 324-333.

1972

Research on quasi-therapeutic relations in small task groups. In S.R. Brown & D.J. Brenner (Eds.), *Science, Psychology, and Communication: Essays Honoring William Stephenson.* New York: Teachers College Press.

Predicting the effects of leadership training and experience from the contingency model. *Journal of Applied Psychology, 56*(2), 114-119.

Personality, motivation systems, and behavior of high and low LPC persons. *Human Relations, 25,* 391-412.

How do you make leaders more effective? New answers to an old puzzle. *Organization Dynamics, 1,* 3-18.

The effects of leadership training and experience: A contingency model interpretation. *Administrative Science Quarterly, 17,* 453-470.

With T.R. Mitchell, D. Dossett, & H. Triandis. Culture training: Validation evidence for the culture assimilator. *International Journal of Psychology, 7,* 97-104.

With L.S. Csoka. The effect of military leadership training: A test of the contingency model. *Organizational Behavior and Human Performance, 8,* 395-407.

With T.R. Mitchell. Leadership theory, management training: New developments. *Management Quarterly, 13,* 29-34.

1973

Stimulus/response: The trouble with leadership training is that it doesn't train leaders. *Psychology Today, 6,* 23-92.

The contingency model—A reply to Ashour. *Organizational Behavior and Human Performance, 9,* 356-368.

Predicting the effects of leadership training and experience from the contingency model: A clarification. *Journal of Applied Psychology, 57,* 110-113.

Toward a comprehensive system of leadership utilization (Technical Report No. 73-50). Seattle: University of Washington, Organizational Research.

With P.M. Bons & L.L. Hastings. New strategies for leadership utilization. In W.T. Singleton & P. Spurgeon (Eds.), *Measurement of Human Resources* (233-244). London: Taylor and Francis.

With R.O. Hansson. Perceived similarity, personality and attraction to large organizations. *Journal of Applied Social Psychology, 3,* 258-266.

With J. Blades. *Participative management, member intelligence, and group performance* (Technical Report No. 73-40). Seattle: University of Washington, Organizational Research.

1974

Personality and situational determinants of leader behavior. In J.G. Hunt & E.A. Fleishman (Eds.), *Current Developments in the Study of Leadership* (pp. 41-61). Carbondale, IL: Southern Illinois University Press.

The contingency model—New directions for leadership utilization. *Journal of Contemporary Business* (Autumn), 65-79.

New concepts for the management of managers. Paper presented at the Hawthorne Studies Commemorative Symposium (November).

With M.M. Chemers. *Leadership and effective management.* New York: Scott Foresman.

With M.M. Chemers. Leadership and management. In *Contemporary Management: Issues and Viewpoints* (pp. 362-390). Englewood Cliff, NJ: Prentice-Hall.

With L.S. Csoka. The contingency model and the effect of leadership training and experience. In K. W. Tilley (Ed.), *Leadership and Management Appraisal* (pp. 215-231). London: English University Press.

With M. Gillo. Correlates of performance in community college. *Journal of Higher Education* (December).

With T.R. Mitchell. Review of Stodgill's Handbook of Leadership: *A Survey of Theory and Research. Wall Street Journal Review of Books, 3*, 183-187.

With J. Prothero. *The effect of situational change on individual behavior and performance: An extension of the contingency model* (Tech. Rep. No. 74-59). Seattle: University of Washington, Organizational Research.

With P.M. Bons. Change in command and the behaviour of subordinate leaders. In P. B. Warr (Ed.), *Personal Goals and Work Design* (pp. 199-208). Sussex, England: John Wiley.

1975

With M.M. Chemers & L. Mahar. *Leader match.* Seattle: University of Washington, Organizational Research.

With J. Fiedler. Port noise complaints: Verbal and behavioral reactions to airport-related noise. *Journal of Applied Psychology, 60*, 498-506.

With I. Gochman. *The effect of situational favorableness on leader and member perceptions of leader behavior* (Technical Report No. 75-64). Seattle: University of Washington, Organizational Research.

New concepts for the management of managers. In E. Cass & F. Zimmer (Eds.), *Man and Work in Society* (pp. 207-220). New York: Van Nostrand Reinhold Co.

1976

With P.M. Bons. Changes in organizational leadership and the behavior of relationship- and task-motivated leaders. *Administrative Science Quarterly, 21*, 453-473.

Validation and extension of the contingency model of leadership effectiveness. A review of empirical findings. In N.S. Endler & D. Magnusson (Eds.), *Interactional Psychology and Personality* (pp. 308-338). New York: Wiley.

The leadership game: Matching the man to the situation. *Organizational Dynamics* (Winter), 6-17.

With D.E. Schmidt. *The contingency model and leader behavior: An instrumentality approach* (Tech. Rep. No. 76-82). Seattle: University of Washington, Organizational Research.

With M.M. Chemers & L. Mahar. *Improving leadership effectiveness: The leader match concept.* New York: Wiley.

With D.F. Borden. *The effects of leadership style on leader supervisor and leader subordinate interpersonal relations* (Tech. Rep. No. 76-84). Seattle: University of Washington, Organizational Research.
Intelligence and group performance: A multiple screen model (Tech. Rep. No. 76-79). Seattle: University of Washington, Organizational Research.

1977

With A.F. Leister. Leader intelligence and task performance. A test of a multiple screen model. *Organizational Behavior and Human Performance, 20,* 1-14.
With P. Scontrino & J. Larson. *Perceived leader behavior and control in racially homogeneous and heterogeneous dyads.* (Tech. Rep. No. 55-69). Seattle: University of Washington, Organizational Research.
With A.F. Leister & D.F. Borden. Validation of contingency model leadership training: Leader match. *Academy of Management Journal, 20,* 464-470.

1978

Situational control and a dynamic theory of leadership. In B. King, S. Streufert, & F. Fiedler (Eds.), *Coordination and control of group and organizational performance* (pp. 107-131). Washington, D.C.: Winston.
With B. King & S. Streufert. *Managerial control and organizational democracy.* Washington, D.C.: V. H. Winston & Sons.
With P.M. Bons. Leadership. In L. Bittel (Ed.), *Encyclopedia of professional management* (pp. 468-477). New York: McGraw-Hill.
With R. Mai-Dalton & G.P. Latham. Selection, management and performance of food service personnel: A survey of the literature. *The Cornell HRA Quarterly, 19*(2), 40-45.
The contingency model and the dynamics of the leadership process. In L. Berkowitz (Ed.), *Advances in experimental social psychology* (Vol. 11). New York: Academic Press.
With M.M. Chemers. The effectiveness of leadership training: A reply to Argyris. *American Psychologist Journal, 33,* 391-393.
Recent developments in research on the contingency model. In L. Berkowitz (Ed.), *Group processes.* New York: Academic Press.
A contingency model of leadership effectiveness. In L. Berkowitz (Ed.), *Group processes.* New York: Academic Press.

1979

Responses to Sergiovanni. *Educational Journal of Leadership, 36*(6), 394-396.
Organizational determinants of managerial incompetence. In J. G. Hunt & L. L. Larsen (Eds.), *Cross currents in leadership research.* Carbondale: Southern Illinois University Press.

With L. Mahar. The effectivenesss of contingency model training: A review of the validation of leader match. *Personnel Psychology, 32*, 45-62.
With L. Mahar. A field experiment validating contingency model leadership training. *Journal of Applied Psychology, 64*(3), 247-254.
With E.H. Potter, III, M.M. Zais, & W. Knowlton, Jr. Organizational stress and the use and misuse of managerial intelligence and experience. *Journal of Applied Psychology, 64*(6), 635-647.

1980

With R. Mai-Dalton. Contingency model leadership training: A new approach. *Die Betriebwirtschaft* (German Journal), *40*, 45-51.
Organizational psychology in Thailand. *Special Monograph of the Behavioral Science Research Institute*, pp. 131-135.
With F.E. Sepic & L. Mahar. Match the manager and the milieu: Testing the Contingency Model. *The Cornell Quarterly, 21*(1), 19-22.
A report on the health of the Contingency Model. *IAAP Newsletter, 4*(2), 8-11.
With C.H. Bell & M.M. Chemers. Organizational development methods for increasing mine safety. *Bureau of Mines Circular No. 8858* (pp. 71-76).

1981

With E.H. Potter. The utilization of staff member intelligence and experience under high and low stress. *Academy of Management Journal, 24*(2), 361-376.
Leadership effectiveness. In E.F. Borgatta (Ed.), *American Behavioral Scientist, 24*(5).
With D.E. Frost & R.L. Swartout. Use of experience under stress. *Fire Chief Magazine, 25*(9), 49-51.
With C.H. Bell & M.M. Chemers. Review of organizational development programs for mine safety. *Ergonomics-Human Factors in Mining*, December, Bureau of Mines Information Circular No. 8866, 106-115.

1982

Why your boss makes you feel stupid. *Industry Week, 212*(1).
The contribution of intellectual ability and organizational experience to leadership performance. *Psychology in the Department of Defense*, (April), pp. 282-290.
Effective use of managerial ability and knowledge—Beyond selection and training. Colloquium on *Selected Topics in Behavioral Science Basic Research* (pp. 103-106). Alexandria, VA: U.S. Army Research Institute for the Behavioral and Social Sciences.

1983

With D.E. Frost & J.W. Anderson. The role of personal risk-taking in effective leadership. *Human Relations, 36*(2), 185-202.

With E.H. Potter, III. Dynamics of leadership effectiveness. In H.H. Blumberg, A.P. Hare, V. Kent, & M. Davies (Eds.), *Small groups and social interaction* (Vol. 1). New York: John Wiley.

With V.E. Barnes & E.H. Potter, III. The effect of interpersonal stress on the prediction of academic performance. *Journal of Applied Psychology, 68*(4), 686-697.

Hari Kari, kamikaze and other indications of commitment. *Commitment in the Miliary Professions: Report of a Leadership Symposium* (pp. 107-133). Royal Roads Military College, Canada.

Tailoring the leadership situation to fill your style: Leader match training. *Concepts for Air Force Leadership.* Air University, Maxwell Air Force Base, AL.

New tools for new times. In *Proceedings: Air University Leadership and Management Symposium* (pp. 203-234). Leadership and Management Center, Maxwell Air Force Base, AL.

1984

Leadership. *The Encyclopedic Dictionary of Psychology.* Oxford: Basil Blackwell.

With C.H. Bell, Jr., M.M. Chemers, & D. Patrick. Increasing mine productivity and safety through management training and organization development: A comparative study. *Basic and Applied Social Psychology, 5*(1), 1-18.

With M.M. Chemers & L. Mahar. *Improving leadership effectiveness: The leader match concept* (2nd. ed.). New York: Wiley.

With M.M. Chemers. Leadership. *Wiley Encyclopedia of Psychology.* New York: John Wiley.

Cognitive resource utilization and leadership performance: A preliminary model (Tech. Rep. No. 84-1). Seattle: University of Washington, Organizational Research.

With S.M. Jobs & D.F. Borden. *Downward transmission of stress and its effect on the performance of motivated and unmotivated leaders* (Tech. Rep. No. 84-2). Seattle: University of Washington, Organizational Research.

The contribution of cognitive resources and leader behavior to organizational performance (Tech. Rep. No. 84-4). Presented at APA Convention, Toronto.

With P.J. Bettin. *The effects of leadership experience on organizational performance: A review* (Tech. Rep. No. 84-5). Seattle: University of Washington, Organizational Research.

FRED E. FIEDLER

1985

With J.E. Garcia. Comparing organization development and management training. *The Personnel Administrator, 30*(3), 35-47.

1986

The contribution of cognitive resources and behavior to leadership performance. In C. F. Graumann & S. Moscovici (Eds.), *Changing conceptions of leadership*. New York: Springer-Verlag.
The contribution of cognitive resources and leader behavior to organizational performance. *Journal of Applied Social Psychology, 16*(6), 532-548.
With M.M. Chemers. The trouble with assumption: A reply to Jago and Ragan. *Journal of Applied Psychology*.
With J.E. Garcia & C.T. Lewis. *People management, and productivity*. Boston: Allyn & Bacon.

1987

With J.E. Garcia. *New approaches to effective leadership: Cognitive resources and organizational performance*. New York: John Wiley. (Translated into Chinese, 1988)
When to lead, when to stand back. *Psychology Today, 21*(9), 26-27.
With W.A. Wheeler, M.M. Chemers, & D.P. Patrick. Managing for mine safety. *Training and Development Journal, 41*(9), 40-43.
With M.A. McGuire. *Cognitive resource theory and the question of participative management*. Proceedings of the Army Leadership Conference, Kansas City, Missouri.
Structured management training in underground mining—five years later. *Technology Transfer Seminar* (July, Bureau of Mines Information Circular No. 9145), pp. 149-153.
Fuehrungstheorien-Kontingenztheorie [Theories of leadership-contingency theories]. In A. Kieser, G. Reber, & R. Wunderer (Eds.) *Handwoerterbuch der Fuehrung*. Stuttgart: C. E. Poeschel Verlag.

1988

With R.J. House. Leadership theory and research: A report of progress. In C. L. Cooper & I. Robertson (Eds.), *International review of industrial and organizational psychology*. New York: John Wiley and Sons.
With E.H. Potter, III & M.A. McGuire. *Stress and Effective Leadership Decisions*. Proceedings of The XXIV International Congress of Psychology, Sydney, Australia.

When to lead: Autocratic versus participative management. *Small Business Reports, 13*(8), 14-16.

1989

With M.A. McGuire & M. Richardson. The role of intelligence and experience in successful group performance. *Journal of Applied Sport Psychology, 1*(2), 132-149.

The effective utilization of intellectual abilities, competence and job-relevant knowledge: Cognitive resource theory and an agenda for the future. *Applied Psychology: An International Review, 38*(3), 289-304.

1990

With F.W. Gibson. Determinants of effective utilization of leader abilities. In *Concepts for Air Force Leadership.* Air University, Maxwell Air Force Base, AL.

With S.M. Jobs & C.T. Lewis. Impact of moderate alcohol consumption on business decision-making. In S.W. Gust & J.M. Walsh, (Eds.) *Drugs in the workplace: Research and evaluation data* (NIDA Research Monograph, Vol. 92). Rockville, MD: NIDA.

With F.W. Gibson & K. Daniels. *Stress, babble, and utilization of leader intellectual abilities* (Tech. Rep. No. 90-1). Seattle: University of Washington, Organizational Research.

With S.E. Murphy & D. Blyth. *Cognitive resource theory and the utilization of the leader's and group members' technical competence* (Tech. Rep. No. 90-2). Seattle: University of Washington, Organizational Research.

The Role of Situational Factors in Current Leadership Theory. In J. van Andel & M. van Vonderen (Ed.), *Liber Samicorum voor W.A.T. Meuwese.* Tilburg, Netherlands: University of Tilburg Press.

1991

[Review of *A Theory of Leadership Effectiveness*]. *Journal of Management, 17*(2), 489-509.

With S.E. & D. Blyth. Cognitive resource theory and the utilization of the leader's and group member's technical competence. *Leadership Quarterly.*

Time-based measures of leadership experience. In K.E. Clark, M.B. Clark, & D.P. Campbell (Eds.), *Impact of leadership.* Greensboro, NC: Center for Creative Leadership.

The leadership situation and the black box. In M.M. Chember (Ed.), *Leadership and organizattional effectiveness.* New York: Academic Press.

With T.G. Link. Leader intelligence, interpersonal stress and task performance. In R.J. Sternberg & R.K. Wagner (Eds.), *Mind in context: Interactionist perspectives on human intelligence.* Cambridge: Cambridge University Press.

1992

With E.H. Potter, III & M.A. McGuire. Stress and effective leadership decisions. In F.A. Heller (Ed.), *Decision making and leadership.* Cambridge, England: Cambridge University Press.
The role and meaning of leadership experience. In K.E. Clark, M.B. Clark, & D.P. Campbell (Eds.), *Impact of leadership.* Greensboro, NC: Center for Creative Leadership.
With S.E. Murphy & F.W. Gibson. Inaccurate reporting and inappropriate variables: A reply to Vecchio's (1990) examination of cognitive resource theory. *Journal of Applied Psychology, 77*(3), 372-374.

NOTES

1. "The Concept of an Ideal Therapeutic Relationship" (1950); "A Comparison of Therapeutic Relationships in Psychoanalytic Relationships" (1950).
2. E.L. Keey & D.W. Fiske, *The Prediction of Performance in Clinical Psychology* (Ann Arbor, MI: University of Michigan Press, 1951).
3. "A Method of Objective Quantification of Certain Counter-transference Attitudes" (1951).
4. *A Theory of Leadership Effectiveness* (1967).
5. "Task-Oriented and Quasi-Therapeutic Role Functions of the Leader in Small Military Groups" (1960); *A Theory of Leadership Effectiveness* (1967); "Interrelations Among Measures of Personality Adjustment in Nonclinical Populations" (1958); "Quasi-Therapeutic Relations in Small College and Military Groups" (1959); A.E. Meyers. (1962). Team competition, success, and adjustment of group members. *Journal of Abnormal and Social Psychology, 65*, 325-332.
6. "The Effect of Leadership Style Upon the Performance and Adjustment of Volunteer Teams Operating in a Stressful Foreign Environment" (1969); "The Effect of Culture Training on Task Group Effectiveness" (1970); "The Culture Assimilator: An Approach to Cross-Cultural Training" (1971); "The Effects of Programmed Culture Training Upon the Performance of Volunteer Medical Teams in Central America" (1971); "Culture Training: Validation Evidence for the Culture Assimilator" (1972).
7. "A Contingency Model of Leadership" (1964); *A Theory of Leadership Effectiveness* (1967); *New Approaches to Effective Leadership: Cognitive Resources and Organizational Performance* (1987).
8. "Assumed Similarity Measures as Predictors of Team Effectiveness" (1954).
9. "Interpersonal Perceptions of Open-Hearth Foremen and Steel Production" (1956).
10. "The Influence of Leader-Keyman Relations on Combat Crew Effectiveness" (1955).
11. Ibid.
12. "An Exploratory Study of Group Creativity in Laboratory Tasks" (1961).
13. "The Effect of Leadership and Cultural Heterogeneity on Group Performance: A Test of the Contingency Model" (1966).

14. R.W. Rice. (1978). Psychometric properties of the esteem for least preferred coworker (LPC scale). *Academy of Management Review, 3,* 106-118; Construct validity of the least preferred coworker. *Psychological Bulletin, 85,* 1199-1237.

15. M.J. Strube & J.E. Garcia. (1981). A meta-analytical investigation of Fiedler's Contingency Model of leadership effectiveness. *Psychological Bulletin, 90,* 307-321; L.H. Peters, D.D. Hartke, & J.T. Pohlmann. (1985). Fiedler's contingency theory of leadership: An application of the meta-analysis procedure of Schmidt and Hunter. *Psychological Bulletin, 97,* 274-285.

16. *Improving Leadership Effectiveness: The Leader Match Concept* (1976, 1984).

17. K.N. Wexley & F.P. Latham. (1981). *Developing and training human resources in organizations.* Glenview, IL: Scott, Foresman.

18. M.J. Burke & R.R. Day. (1986). A cumulative study of training. *Journal of Applied Psychology, 71*(2), 242.

19. "Increasing Mine Productivity and Safety Through Management Training and Organization Development: A Comparative Study" (1984); "Comparing Organization Development and Management Training" (1985).

20. "Structured Management Training in Underground Mining—Five Years Later" (1987).

21. "The Contribution of Cognitive Resources and Behavior to Leadership Performance" (1986); "The Contribution of Cognitive Resources and Leader Behavior to Organizational Performance" (1986); *New Approaches to Effective Leadership: Cognitive Resources and Organizational Performance* (1987).

22. Ibid, pp. 31-41.

23. "An Exploratory Study of Group Creativity in Laboratory Tasks" (1961); *Leadership and Group Creativity Under Varying Conditions of Stress* (1965).

24. "The Contribution of Cognitive Resources and Behavior to Leadership Performance" (1986); "The Contribution of Cognitive Resources and Leader Behavior to Organizational Behavior" (1986); *New Approaches to Effective Leadership: Cognitive Resources and Organizational Performance* (1987).

25. "Stress and Effective Leadership Decisions" (1990); "The Utilization of Staff Member Intelligence and Experience Under High and Low Stress" (1981).

26. "Leadership" (1984).

27. *Improving Leadership Effectiveness: The Leader Match Concept* (1984, p. 4).

Jay W. Forrester

From the Ranch to System Dynamics

Jay W. Forrester

Since 1956 I have had the exciting and challenging opportunity to found and develop the new field of system dynamics. System dynamics deals with how the structure of a system and its information flows determine behavior—the control of growth, stability, decay, success, and failure. The field focuses on the way internal feedback-loop relationships cause a system to change through time. Understanding why a system behaves as it does permits redesign of structure and policies to improve behavior. The ideas and methods of system dynamics are applicable to natural, human, and technical systems. The field combines theory and computer simulation with a very practical application to real-world problems.

As I look back, I see that my career evolved through several critical changes in direction. When opportunities knocked, I was willing to give up the past and turn in new directions. Each change led to pioneering in new and more challenging arenas. With the succession of experiences came the growing realization that new ideas will naturally be met with skepticism. One must have the courage and persistence to sustain a long-term vision against oppositions that arise along the way. Everything that I have done converged to make the development of system dynamics possible.

THE BEGINNING

My childhood experiences came from a cattle ranch in the Nebraska Sandhills located in the middle of the United States. My father and mother were the original homesteaders in about 1910 on that late-developing part of the American frontier.[1] Shopping was 18 miles away by horse and wagon.

Although we lived in a concrete block house with running water, most of our first neighbors built sod houses from the top layer of the grass land. It was a community of pioneers settling under the Kinkaid Homestead Act, which allowed a square mile of land per family. When early attempts to farm the thin top soil failed, and most settlers left, those who stayed turned to cattle ranching.

My parents were the only people in the community with a college education. Dad graduated from Hastings College in Nebraska where he was a football player, on the track team, glee club, and debating society, while also working as a newspaper reporter. Mother attended Hastings College three years and then worked in libraries in Springfield, Massachusetts and Jacksonville, Florida. In later years, the superintendent of the Anselmo, Nebraska, high school, which I attended, described his first visit to our home as the discovery of a cultural oasis in the intellectual wilderness.

When they first settled on the ranch, both my parents taught in one-room country schools. After she gave up her position as public school teacher, my mother taught me at home during my first two years of school. Later, I rode a horse a mile and a half to third and fourth grades at a one-room school taught by my father. Women who had been my father's students taught me in grades five through eight at the same school. It was there that my interest in electricity started with experiments on batteries, doorbells, and telegraphs. Inspiration came from the Nebraska "traveling library" that sent a box of books on loan to the school each year.

A ranch is a cross-roads of economic forces. Supply and demand, changing prices and costs, and economic pressures of agriculture become a very personal, powerful, and dominating part of life. Furthermore, in an agricultural setting, activities must be very practical. One works to get results. It is full-time immersion in the real world. Children have their regular chores as part of the family business. In such closely knit activities, my parents guided learning and character development. Although ranch obligations were demanding, I was fortunate in being allowed time to develop interests that were not immediately related to the daily needs.

While a senior in the Anselmo, Nebraska, high school, I built a 12-volt wind-driven electric plant that provided the first electricity on our ranch. It powered the radio, lights in the house, and motors for shop work. Building an electrical system from discarded automobile parts was a very practical undertaking and another step in learning how to succeed in uncharted territory.

On finishing high school, I had received a scholarship to go to the University of Nebraska Agricultural College, when one of those important turning points intervened. Three weeks before enrolling in agriculture, I decided it wasn't for me. Caring for sick cattle and herding them in Nebraska winter blizzards never had captured my enthusiasm. I had preferred the tractors, machinery, and shop work. My parents had never tried to limit my interests or direct my future vocation. So, I enrolled in the Engineering College at the University of Nebraska. Electrical engineering, as it turns out, was the only academic field with a solid, central core of theoretical dynamics. The road began toward my work in the behavior of systems.

Finishing at the University brought another turning point. I came to the Massachusetts Institute of Technology for two reasons. First, they offered me a $100 per month research assistantship, which was more money than any other university had offered. Second, my mother, from her library experience in Springfield, Massachusetts, knew about MIT. In the high plains of the United States at that time, "M.I.T." more often implied salesmen for a financial institution, the Massachusetts Investors Trust, than an engineering school.

MY INTRODUCTION TO FEEDBACK SYSTEMS

In my first year at MIT came another of the decisive branches in my career. I was employed in 1940 as a research assistant by Gordon S. Brown when he founded the Servomechanisms Laboratory and began to pioneer "feedback control systems" at MIT for military equipment. During World War II with Brown, I developed servomechanisms for the control of radar antennas and gun mounts. Departing from my training in electrical engineering, the work focused on designing mechanical hydraulic variable-speed pumps, motors, and high-gain hydraulic amplifiers because at that time the military mistrusted vacuum tubes in anything except radios.[2]

Again, it was research toward an extremely practical goal that ran from mathematical theory of control and stability to the military operating field, and I do mean the operating field. At one stage, we built experimental hydraulic controls for a radar designed at the MIT Radiation Laboratory. After redesign, the radar was intended for aircraft carriers to direct fighter planes against enemy targets. The captain of the carrier U.S.S. Lexington visited MIT and saw this experimental unit, which was planned for production a year or so later. He said, "I want that; I mean that very one; we can't wait for the production equipment." He got it.

In the following nine months the experimental laboratory radar had directed fighters in shooting down some 20 enemy planes before they came close enough to see the Lexington. But then, the experimental control units stopped working. In November 1943, I volunteered to go to Pearl Harbor to find the reason and repair the hydraulic controls.

Having discovered the problem, but not having time to fix it, I was approached by the executive officer of the Lexington who said they were about to leave Pearl Harbor. He asked me to come with them to finish my job. I agreed, having no idea where that might lead.

We were offshore during the invasion of Tarawa and then took a turn down between the Ratak and Ralik chains of the Marshall Islands. The islands on both sides held enemy air bases, and the Japanese didn't like having a U.S. Navy Task Force wrecking their airports. They kept trying to sink our ships. Finally, twelve hours later and after dark they dropped flares along one side of the task force and came in with torpedo planes from the other side. About 11:00 PM, they succeeded in hitting the Lexington, cutting through one of the four propeller shafts and setting the rudder in a hard turn. Again, the experience gave a very concentrated immersion in how research and theory are related to practical end uses.

PIONEERING IN DIGITAL COMPUTERS

At the end of World War II came yet another turning point for which I am indebted to Gordon Brown. I had about decided either to get a job or start a company in feedback control systems when Brown, who was my mentor for many years at MIT, again intervened. He offered a list of projects that he thought might be of interest. I picked the building of an aircraft flight simulator. It was to be rather like an elaborate aircraft pilot trainer. However, it was to be precise enough to take wind tunnel data from a model of a proposed plane and predict the behavior of the full-scale airplane before construction.

The aircraft analyzer project was promoted by Admiral Louis deFlorez of the U.S. Navy. deFlorez was a flamboyant individual with a pointed waxed mustache. He was apparently the only person who had somehow acquired standing permission to land a seaplane on the sailing basin in front of MIT. He came to MIT on Alumni Day and the Metropolitan District Police cleared the basin of sailboats so he could land his seaplane. He attended part of the program and, when the speeches became boring, would rev up the seaplane engines and take-off with the noise drowning out the program he was leaving behind.

The admiral taught me a number of helpful insights about dealing with government bureaucracies. Later, when we were building a digital computer, we needed another hundred thousand dollars to continue. The response from deFlorez was "Impossible! That is above my approval authority and too little to justify going to the Secretary of the Navy. You must ask for either fifty-thousand or two-hundred-thousand." We chose the latter figure.

At this time, Gordon Brown added a new dimension to my life by introducing me to Susan Swett. We were married July 27, 1946.[3] My parents, Gordon Brown, and Susan are the ones to whom I owe the most for whatever I may have accomplished over an interval of seventy-plus years. Susan has given steadfast encouragement and sympathy, compensation for my frequent insensitivity to others, tolerance for my often putting work at the top of the priority list, and an uninterrupted supportive home environment.

The aircraft simulator started as an analog computer. It took a year to decide that an analog machine of that complexity would do no more than respond to its own internal idiosyncrasies. An analog computer could not deal with the problem at hand.

Still another critical break in my career came when Perry Crawford, an MIT graduate and then in the Special Devices Center of the Navy headed by Admiral deFlorez, suggested that we shift our attention to the digital computer field in which work was just beginning. Design of the aircraft analyzer was recast around the untested concept of a digital computer. But times were changing, the need for the aircraft analyzer became less pressing, and military tactics were outgrowing the capability of information handling by a human network operating through telephones.

Beginning in 1947, the MIT Digital Computer Laboratory, under my direction, designed the Whirlwind I digital computer.[4] Whirlwind was the first general-purpose digital computer at MIT. It filled two roles, as a scientific computer and as an experimental laboratory for testing the use of digital computers in military combat information systems.

The reader today with a desktop computer can hardly appreciate the skepticism in the late 1940s to a suggestion that computers could ever be made to work reliably, or that they would be needed even if they worked. One computer pioneer of that time was quoted as saying that, if all the five digital computers then under experimental development should by any chance work, they would more than saturate any conceivable need for such machines. Only the experience of having succeeded in past pioneering programs and the belief that history would repeat sustained us against the opposition of the doubters.

Robert R. Everett worked with me from 1946 to 1956 as associate director of the Digital Computer Laboratory and as associate division head in the Lincoln Laboratory. I am greatly indebted to him for his technical skill and his gift for leadership of an engineering organization. We had started together in the early 1940s in the Servomechanism Laboratory and shared the same background. After I left the computer field in 1956, Everett continued to lead the organization we had established together. That activity separated from MIT to become the MITRE Corporation, from which Everett has recently retired as president.

When development of Whirlwind began, no satisfactory devices existed for high-speed internal information storage. A few early computer projects chose one-dimensional storage, consisting of a tube of mercury, in which shock waves, transmitted and received by crystals at the two ends, represented binary digits in transit. Other computer projects based their design on two-dimensional storage in the form of cathode-ray tubes in which digits were stored as positive and negative charges on the inside faces of the tubes. But all these were slow or unreliable or both.

My invention of the coincident-current random-access magnetic computer memory in 1949 was a classic case of necessity being the mother of invention.[5] I was responsible for a computer development project and a mission in combat information systems that could not succeed with the existing technology for computer memory. The newly conceived and developed magnetic memory was fast, completely reliable, and became the standard computer memory for about 20 years until replaced by solid-state micro circuits.

Again, the slow pace of acceptance of new ideas was evident. It took us about seven years to convince industry that magnetic-core memory was the solution to a missing link in computer technology. Then we spent the following seven years in the patent courts convincing them that they had not all thought of it first.

From the Whirlwind computer program came technology for the first practical digital control of machine tools. For many years, numerical control in manufacturing operated under the patent emerging from that early work.[6]

In its final redefinition of mission, the Whirlwind computer became a laboratory for exploring how digital computers could serve as military combat information centers. At a time when no high-speed digital computer had yet operated reliably, such a proposal to use them to analyze and control military operations was met with disbelief and hostility by military officers who felt that only their training and field experience could serve as a basis for handling military situations. Such confidence in the earlier human-network handling of tactics persisted in the face of clear evidence that speed and complexity of military technology had far outstripped unaided human command and control.

By gaining the support of a few daring individuals in the military, it was possible to carry on development until the merits of these seemingly radical new proposals became evident. Professor George E. Valley of the MIT physics department, who was chairman of the Air Defense System Engineering Committee, played a key role in converging our proposals for digital computers in command and control with financial support from the U.S. Air Force, which was then seeking an improved air defense system.

Largely on the basis of this early work, the MIT Lincoln Laboratory for air defense research was formed. I headed Division 6 of Lincoln, which designed computers for the SAGE (Semi-Automatic Ground Environment) air defense system for North America. Valley headed the division handling the radar side of the system. Whirlwind grew to become the nucleus of the Experimental Cape Cod Air Defense System for demonstrating how a digital computer could analyze and coordinate radar information and issue directions to defensive weapons.

The SAGE air defense system was another of those practical undertakings where theory and new ideas were only as good as the working results. The SAGE system had about 35 control centers, each 160 square feet, four stories high, and containing upward of 60,000 vacuum tubes. Many people had criticized the concept on the basis that such a large electronic assembly would fail too often to be useful. Such a prediction was reasonable based on prior engineering experience. Vacuum tubes had a life of about 500 hours. Agreeing that such performance would make our proposals inoperative, we undertook to discover the reason that tubes had been failing, redesigned them to remove the cause, and increased the average life by a thousand fold in one design step. Even that was not enough. In addition, a "marginal checking" system was incorporated that could find any deteriorating electronic component before it reached the point of causing an error.

The SAGE computer centers were installed in the late 1950s; the last was decommissioned in 1983. They were in service about 25 years. Historical statistics show that individual centers were operational 99.8% of the time. That would be less than 20 hours a year that a center was out of operation. Even today, such reliability is a challenging record to match in military systems.

MOVING TO MANAGEMENT EDUCATION

Completion of the SAGE system design coincided with another crucial incident and the opening of another door of opportunity. James R. Killian, Jr., who was then president of MIT, brought a group of visiting dignitaries to the Lincoln Laboratory. While we were walking down the hall, Killian told me of the new management school that MIT was starting, and suggested that I consider joining. Discussions over the next several months with Associate Dean Eli Shapiro and Professor Edward L. Bowles led to my becoming a full professor in management. It was my first academic appointment; earlier work had all been on the MIT research staff.

People often ask why I made such an abrupt change as going from engineering to the Management School. There were several reasons. By 1956, I felt the pioneering days in digital computers were over. That might surprise readers looking back on the major advances during the last 35 years. But the multiple by which computers improved in speed, reliability, and storage capacity in the decade from 1946 to 1956 had been greater than the multiple in any decade since. Furthermore, moving to a management school was not a break from a purely technical background. I was already in management.

We had been running a vast operation in which we had control from basic research to military operational planning. We wrote the contracts between the participating corporations and the Air Force. We designed the computers with full control over what went into production. We defended the Air Force's budget before the Bureau of the Budget because the technology was so new that it was outside the experience of the military commands. We had been managing an enterprise that involved the Air Defense Command, the Air Material Command, the Air Research and Development Command, Western

Electric, A.T.&T., and I.B.M. The move from Lincoln Laboratory was not so much a radical change as a shift to a different perspective from which to view management.

The MIT School of Management, later to be renamed the Sloan School, had been founded in 1952 with a grant of ten million dollars from Alfred P. Sloan, Jr., the man who built the modern General Motors Corporation. The money was given with the expectation that a management school in a technical environment such as MIT would develop differently from one in a liberal arts environment like Harvard, or Columbia, or Chicago. Such a school might be better, but in any case different, and Sloan believed it worth ten million dollars to run the experiment.

In the four years before I joined the School in 1956, standard management courses existed, but nothing had been done about the concept of a management school within an engineering environment. By that time, I had 15 years of participation in the science and engineering side of MIT and bringing that background to bear on management offered an interesting challenge.

Others, and probably I also, assumed that an application of technology to management meant either to push forward the field of operations research, or to explore the use of computers for the handling of management information. My first year was free of other duties except to decide why I was at the Management School. On computers for management information, activity was growing rapidly among manufacturers of computers, and banks and insurance companies were actively using computers. It did not seem that a few of us in a management school would have major impact on the already existing momentum. Regarding operations research, it seemed interesting; it no doubt was useful; but it was not working with issues that made the difference between corporate successes and failures. Operations research did not have that compelling practical importance that had always characterized my work.

LAUNCHING SYSTEM DYNAMICS

Again chance intervened when I found myself in discussions with several people from General Electric. They were puzzled by why their household appliance plants in Kentucky sometimes worked at full capacity with overtime and then two or three years later, half the people would be laid off. It was easy enough to say that business cycles caused fluctuating demand, but that explanation was not entirely convincing.

After talking with the manufacturing people about how they made hiring and inventory decisions, I started to do some simulation. The analysis based on the feedback viewpoint from my earlier experience used very simple simulations with pencil and paper on a notebook page. The computation started at the top with columns for inventory, employees, production rate, backlog, and orders. Given these initial conditions and the policies being followed in manufacturing, one could enter how many people would be hired in the following week. Because of time delays and trend projections, production did not adjust smoothly to demand.

A fluctuating (oscillatory) response would follow a small change in demand. The internal structure and policies defined a manufacturing system that tended toward unstable behavior. Even with constant incoming orders, employment instability could result from commonly used decision-making policies. That first inventory control system with pencil and paper simulation was the beginning of system dynamics.[7]

Viewed in the context of management research, the social sciences, and economics, system dynamics differs in having been developed through intimate contact with the real worlds of practicing management and politics. System dynamics shows how structures and policies, which are well-known in the operating arenas, can produce the successes and difficulties that are being experienced.

My book, *Industrial Dynamics* (1961) first presented the philosophy and methodology of system dynamics. The book grew partly out of teaching Sloan Fellows who are managers age 30 to 40 with substantial corporate and managerial experience. Their master's theses explored many dynamic business issues, including commodity markets, evolution of nuclear energy, military research and development management, corporate growth, and design lead time and market penetration in the automobile industry. The book also benefited from our teaching two-week intensive summer session programs for managers. At the same time, we developed the systems concepts while applying them in sponsored corporate research projects that formed a meeting ground for theory and practice.

An example of the close linkage of practice and analysis arose in my early excursions into the dynamics of corporate growth.[8] At the time system dynamics was starting, I joined the board of the Digital Equipment Corporation. The founders of the company offered the invitation because they had worked with me in the Whirlwind computer days.

I did not understand the nature of high-technology growth companies as well as I felt I should as a board member. Also, if the emerging field of system dynamics was as powerful as we believed, it should shed light on why new companies exhibit such widely varying degrees of success. I undertook to model the general nature of high-technology growth companies to guide my own position on the board.

From the modeling came a number of insights about why high-technology companies often grow to a certain level and then stagnate or fail. This modeling of corporate growth moved system dynamics out of physical variables like inventory into much more subtle considerations. Over 90% of the variables in that corporate growth model lay beyond the usual tangible variables. They included the top-management influence structure, leadership qualities, character of the founders, how goals of an organization are created, and how the past traditions of an organization determine decision making. The model also dealt with the interactions between capacity, price, quality, and delivery delay.

In our corporate work on how structure and policies determine behavior, we found we could go into a troubled company and uncover the reasons for its problems. The difficulty might be falling market share, or fluctuations in production with employment varying from working overtime one year to having half the work force laid off two years later, or a lower profitability than other companies in an industry. Such difficulties are widely known to employees, the community, and the business press.

Our background about how feedback loops relate to behavior guides examination of a company. Information comes from interviewing people about how they make decisions at their individual operating points. These statements describing the basis for decisions are the rules or policies governing action. As I use the term "policy," it represents all the reasons for action, not just formal written policy.

These interviews are extensive and penetrating. There may be several sessions with each of many individuals. The discussions range widely from normal operations, to what is done in various kinds of crises, what is in the self interest of the individual, where are the influential power centers in an organization, what would be done in hypothetical situations that may have never been experienced, and what actions are being taken to help in solving the serious problem facing a company.

We find that talking to a manager can reveal a clear and comprehensive picture of the rules and conditions driving decisions at that position in a corporation. Then, when one talks to another manager about the first manager, the same picture usually emerges. In other words, people see themselves very much as others see them. There is substantial consistency throughout an organization as to the actual operational policies that are guiding decisions. Furthermore, the policies are usually justified in terms of how those policies are expected to help overcome the great difficulty that a company is experiencing.

During this interview stage, the examination of such a company follows the case-study approach used in management education. That is, a comprehensive examination of all related parts of a company is made in the context of the problem that is to be solved. The pieces of the picture are described in words. But, if left at this point, the weakness of the case-study method would intrude and dominate the outcome. A descriptive model of the company would have been assembled, but the human mind is not able to deal with the inherent dynamic complexity of such a situation.

For readers who have studied mathematics through differential equations, such a descriptive case-study type of model is equivalent to a high-order nonlinear differential equation. No scientist or mathematician can solve such a system mentally. Just as with the operation of a chemical plant, only computer simulation methods are capable of revealing the behavior implicit in the structure built from knowledge about the many local decision-making individuals and their linkages.

After obtaining a description of the important policies, information flows, and interconnections in a company, the next step translates that description into a computer simulation model. Such a model allows the computer to act out the roles of each decision point in the corporate system and feed the results to other connected decision points to become the basis for the next round of decisions. In other words, a laboratory replica of the company then exists in the computer where one can observe the behavioral consequences of the policies that were described in the interviews—policies that were intended to solve the company's problem.

To the surprise of those unfamiliar with the devious nature of such dynamic systems, a computer model, based on policies known to people in the company, will generate the very difficulties that the company has been experiencing. In short, the policies that are expected to solve the problem are, instead, the cause of the problem. Such a situation creates a serious trap and often a downward spiral. If the policies being followed are believed to alleviate the problem, but, in hidden ways, are causing the problem, then, as the problem gets worse, pressures increase to apply still more strongly the very policies that are causing the problem.

EXTENDING SYSTEM DYNAMICS TO SOCIAL AND ECONOMIC BEHAVIOR

A series of incidents in 1968 moved my work from corporate modeling to broader social systems. John F. Collins, who had been mayor of Boston for eight years, decided not to run for reelection. MIT gave him a temporary appointment as Visiting Professor of Urban Affairs to bring him into the academic orbit as a way to meet students, interact with faculty, and advise the administration on political issues.

Collins had been a victim of polio in the Massachusetts epidemic of the mid-1950s and walks with two arm canes. He needed an office in a building with automobile access to the elevator level. The building with my office was one of the few that qualified. The professor next door to me was away for a sabbatical year, so John Collins was assigned the adjacent office.

In discussions with Collins about his many years of coping with Boston urban problems I developed the same feeling that I had come to recognize in talking to corporate executives. The story sounded plausible but it left an uneasy sense that something was wrong or incomplete or being misinterpreted. So, I suggested to Collins that we might combine our efforts, taking his extensive practical experience in cities and my background in modeling, and look for interesting new behavioral insights about cities. He immediately asked how to go about it.

I told Collins that we would need advisers who knew a great deal about cities from personal experience, not those whose knowledge came only from academic study and reading. We needed people who had struggled with cities, worked in them, and knew what really happens. And furthermore, we would not know what would come of the effort, or how long it might take. The process would be to gather a group that would meet half a day a week, probably for months, to seek insights into those urban processes that could explain stagnation and unemployment.

Collins listened and said, "They'll be here on Wednesday afternoon." Collins' position in Boston then was such that he could phone almost anyone in politics or business, and get a commitment of time for a half day per week. He delivered the people. It was out of the following discussions over an interval of six months that the *Urban Dynamics* (1969) book evolved.

Urban Dynamics was the first of my modeling work that produced strong, emotional reactions. The model simulations suggested that the major United States policies all lay somewhere between neutral and highly detrimental, either from the viewpoint of a city as an institution, or from the viewpoint of low-income, unemployed residents.

Our examination of urban behavior showed that the most damaging policy was to build low-cost housing. At that time, building low-cost housing was believed essential to reviving inner cities. But the construction of low-cost housing occupies land that could have been used for job-creating structures, while at the same time the added housing draws in people who need jobs. It creates a social trap that increases unemployment, and reduces the economic vitality of both a city and individual residents.

Although I believe *Urban Dynamics* has survived the test of time, the conclusions offended many people around 1970. When the book first appeared, one faculty colleague came to me and said, "I don't care whether you are right or wrong, the results are unacceptable." So much for academic objectivity! Others, probably believing the same thing, put it more acceptably as, "It doesn't make any difference whether you're right or wrong, urban officials and the residents of the inner city will never accept such ideas." It turned out that those were the two groups we could count on for support if they became sufficiently involved to understand. That is a very big "if," if they came close enough to understand.

Three to five hours were required to understand what the urban dynamics model was revealing. Urban officials and members of the black inner city community became increasingly negative and emotional during those introductory hours. If they had not been in a captive audience, they would have walked out before they understood and accepted the way in which low-cost housing is a double-edged sword for making urban conditions worse. Constructing low-cost housing drives a powerful process for creating poverty, not alleviating it.

My first experience with reactions to *Urban Dynamics* came soon after the book was published. The Sloan School had been running a four-week program for urban executives twice a year for department-head level people from larger cities to teach various aspects of management. A group was convening shortly after *Urban Dynamics* came out and organizers of the program asked me to take a Monday afternoon and a Wednesday morning to present the *Urban Dynamics* story.

I have never had a lecture on any subject, any place, at any time go as badly as that Monday afternoon. In the group was a man from the black community in New York who was a member of the city government. He was from Harlem, intelligent, articulate, not buying a thing I was saying, and carrying the group with him.

At one point he said, "This is just another way to trample on the rights of the poor people and it's immoral." At another point he said, "You're not dealing with the black versus white problem, and if you're not dealing with the black versus white problem, you're not dealing with the urban problem." And when I explained how decay and poverty in Harlem in New York or Roxbury in Boston had been worsened by too much low-cost housing, he said, "I come from Harlem and there's certainly not too much housing in Harlem." Those are samples of the afternoon.

On Tuesday evening, the group met for dinner. Neither Collins nor I could go; but several of our students attended. One student called me at home after dinner to report what was rather obvious anyway—that the group was very hostile. On that bit of encouragement, I started Wednesday morning.

An hour into Wednesday morning, the New Yorker's comments began to change character. He was no longer tearing down what was being said. His questions began to elicit information. Two hours into the morning, he said, "We can't leave the subject here at the end of this morning. We must have another session." I ignored the request to see what would happen next. In about twenty minutes, he repeated it. I agreed to meet them again if he could find a time and place in the crowded program. I was not trying to put him off, but that usually ends such an exchange. However, he persisted and went to the administration and arranged another session.

Later the New Yorker made an appointment to come to my office to ask that I talk to a group he would invite in New York—his colleagues on his home turf. He sat in my office completely relaxed and said, "You know, it's not a race problem in New York at all, it's an economic problem." Four days earlier he had asserted that I was not even addressing the urban problem if not dealing with the black versus white issue. He gave me a report out of his brief case documenting the amount of empty housing in every borough of New York, including Harlem, and the rate of abandonment. My point in saying there was too much housing meant that there was too much for the economy of the area to support. He had all the proof right in his brief case. He simply had not realized what his knowledge meant until it was all put together in a new way.

Two years later a journalist asked me what people thought in the aftermath of *Urban Dynamics*. I suggested that he talk to others, and especially with the man in New York whom I had not contacted in the intervening two years. After the interview, the journalist phoned to say he had been told "they don't just have a solution to the urban problem up there at MIT, they have the only solution." The lesson about urban behavior had stayed clear and alive for two years even back home in his political environment. The five hours of exposure to *Urban Dynamics* had made a lasting impression. But we have not solved the challenge of how to bring enough people across the barrier separating their usual, simple, static viewpoint from a more comprehensive understanding of dynamic complexity.

Urban Dynamics led to both the *World Dynamics* and *Limits to Growth* projects and to the System Dynamics National Model program.

WORLD DYNAMICS AND THE CLUB OF ROME

The urban work initiated my contact with the Club of Rome. I met Aurelio Peccei, the founder, at a meeting on urban difficulties held in Italy at Lake Como in 1968. Later, after being asked to join, at a meeting of the Club in June 1970 in Bern, Switzerland, came another turning point in my career with system dynamics. What followed is more fully described in the introduction to *World Dynamics* (1971).

The "world problematique" discussed at the Bern meeting became the basis for the model in *World Dynamics*. In the three weeks after the Bern meeting, I created the model for *World Dynamics* and 80 pages of text. This material became the centerpiece for a two-week meeting with the executive committee of the Club of Rome at MIT in July 1970. Included in the group was Eduard Pestel, president of the Technical University of Hannover. Pestel was a very forceful person and quickly saw the power of system dynamics. The executive committee decided to finance research at MIT to go beyond the material that had been presented at the meeting. Pestel arranged for the Volkswagen Foundation to support work that resulted in the *Limits to Growth* book.[9]

The public responses to system dynamics have always surprised me. People ask what I think the reaction will be when the National Model books (discussed below) are released. I don't know. Usually I have been wrong in anticipating the effect that system dynamics books will have.

In 1971 when *World Dynamics* first appeared, the book seemed to have everything necessary to guarantee no public notice. First, it had forty pages of equations in the middle, that should be sufficient to squelch public interest. Second, the main messages were presented as computer output graphs, and most of the public does not understand such presentations. Third, the publisher of the book had published only one previous book and I doubted that *World Dynamics* had the commercial status even to be reviewed. I intended the book for maybe 200 people in the world who would like to study an interesting model on their computers. The book showed the long-term interplay of population, industrialization, resource depletion, agriculture, and pollution. But, I was wrong about the audience.

World Dynamics came out the first week of June 1971. The last week of June, it was reviewed in the *London Observer*, which then circulated around the world. A letter from a professor in New York asked for more information because he had been reading about the book in the *Singapore Times!* In August the book had the full front page of the second section of the *Christian Science Monitor*, in September a page and a half in *Fortune*, and in October a column in the *Wall Street Journal*. It was running through editorial columns of mid-America newspapers, and was the subject of prime time documentary television in Europe. It was debated in the environmental press, the zero population growth press, and the antiestablishment underground student press.

And, for those not liking their literature on either the establishment right or the establishment left, then in the middle of the political spectrum, the *World Dynamics* book was the subject of a full-length article in *Playboy*. But as a communications medium for conveying system dynamics, that magazine was a disappointment. Out of eight million copies printed, the only response I received was a request to conduct a two-day meeting for the Board of Overseas Missions after the article was read by a man at the National Council of Churches.

Nine months after *World Dynamics* appeared, *Limits to Growth* was published. The message was essentially the same, although much more research and verification had been done. The book was more popularly written, but even so, after the earlier attention from the media, it seemed that the second book could only be an anticlimax. The results showed that one can be wrong twice in succession in exactly the same way. Public attention jumped another factor of ten after appearance of *Limits to Growth*.

The two books gained wide visibility and created great controversy. *Limits to Growth* has sold several million copies and been translated into about thirty languages. Due to the system dynamics approach, the books were able to clarify issues that troubled the public and that people wanted to understand better.

As with earlier modeling, reactions surprised us. Who would react to rising environmental pressures that will progressively restrain growth of population and industrialization over the next fifty years? We assumed the subject would be anathema to chief executives of corporations. On the other hand, we expected little interest in the social sciences. Wrong on both. On the whole, the books received favorable responses from chief executives of corporations, members of Congress, and by young people. Disparagement often came from middle-level managers, the Executive Department of the U.S. Government, and economists.

Particularly surprising were the bitter and emotional attacks on the two books by many economists. We would have thought the books lay outside their area of interest until we realized that the books threatened the underlying theology supporting the belief that growth can continue forever. Even though largely unjustified, such published criticisms have left their impact, especially on people who have not read the books.

One now occasionally sees newspaper comments referring to the "discredited *Limits to Growth*," while in that paper are articles about acid rain, water shortage in California, forests dying of pollution, threatened species, and the debate about global warming; all illustrating the central message of the books about the dynamics that result from growth in population and industrialization overrunning the world's environmental capacity.

SYSTEM DYNAMICS NATIONAL MODEL

As this is written in February 1991, I am completing a long program of applying system dynamics to understanding the behavior of national economies. Two books are under way to set forth what we have learned.

The *Urban Dynamics* book led to our work on the System Dynamics National Model. After a talk at a joint NATO/US conference on cities in Indianapolis, Indiana in 1971, William Dietel, now recently retired as president of the Rockefeller Brothers Fund, came up from the audience to discuss their future programs. From that meeting came initial funding for our work in applying system dynamics to behavior of economic systems. Since then, the work continued with private-sector support from individuals and corporations.

The approach is very different from the conventional econometric models, which are structured on the basis of macroeconomic theory with parameters drawn from statistical analysis of historical data and with a heavy dependence on exogenous time-series to drive the dynamics of the model. From the system dynamics viewpoint, econometric models are essentially curve-fitting exercises. They do not contain the essential feedback structures that create the kinds of dynamic changes that are seen in real economies.

As with all my earlier work, the emphasis has been on connecting research to actual practices in the operating world. In that tradition the National Model contains policies that can be observed in managerial practice in corporations, banking, households, and government.

The results are far exceeding our original expectations. The model generates endogenously the major kinds of behavior that have been observed in actual systems—business cycles, inflation, stagflation, growth, and the economic long wave or Kondratieff cycle. Business cycles have peaks of activity three to 10 years apart. The longer Kondratieff cycle has much larger economic deviations with peaks spaced 45 to 60 years.

The National Model supplies for the first time a theory for the economic long wave, which we believe accounts for the great depressions that occurred around 1830, 1890, and in the 1930s. The long wave arises from major interactions among capital investment, saving, monetary policy, real interest rate, and speculation. It generates severe economic downturns at five-to-seven-decade intervals.

As with prior work, we can anticipate that publication on the dynamics of economic systems will generate controversy because the results differ with previous understandings about how economic behavior arises. Also the approach suggests a very different way of looking at the study of economic systems. Instead of thinking of economics as a social science, we believe that the study of economics should be seen as a systems profession comparable to engineering, management, and medicine. Like the analysis and design of a chemical plant, understanding an economy should be based on identifying the internal structure of the system. The parts can then be interrelated in a simulation model to demonstrate how they interact to generate observed, economic behavior.

GROWTH OF THE SYSTEM DYNAMICS FIELD

It is gratifying to see how the work that started in 1956 has grown into an active profession. The System Dynamics Society has a worldwide membership and publishes the *System Dynamics Review*.[10] Educational programs in the field exist in a number of countries. Annual international conferences move from country to country.

A NEW KIND OF MANAGEMENT EDUCATION

Throughout its development, system dynamics has offered a basis for a much improved kind of management education. The suggestion has been resisted for a number of reasons. It would break down the boundaries between academic disciplines. It would undermine the assumption that doing the "best" as viewed from within each separate functional area is best for the organization as a whole. It would tend to force faculty members to understand other disciplines and how those other disciplines relate dynamically to their own. Also, the approach depends heavily on knowledge about structure and policies obtained directly from participants in actual corporate practice, but in academia, such sources are often distrusted and seen as being nonscientific.

However, if the goal is worthwhile, patience and persistence prevail in time. There is clearly a movement toward seeing management success as depending on the interaction of many policies. There is a widening understanding that analysis of individual policies will not reveal the behavior of the whole.

An improved understanding of corporate systems points the way to a future advancement in management education. Beyond that, it suggests a new kind of manager for the future. One can now see clearly a kind of management education that we might call "enterprise design." And in the future there is a role for the output of such an education, the "enterprise designer."[11]

A fundamental difference exists between an enterprise operator and an enterprise designer. To illustrate, consider the two most important people in the successful operation of an airplane. One is the airplane designer and the other is the airplane pilot. The designer creates an airplane that the ordinary pilot can fly successfully. Is not the usual manager more a pilot than a designer? A manager runs an organization. Often there is no one who consciously and intentionally fills the role of organizational designer.

Organizations built by committee, by intuition, and by historical happenstance often work no better than would an airplane built by the same methods. Time after time one sees venture capital groups backing new enterprises in which the combinations of corporate policies, characteristics of products, and nature of the markets are mismatched in a way that predetermines failure. Like a bad airplane design that no pilot can fly successfully, such badly designed corporations lie beyond the ability of real-life managers.

Management education, in all management schools, has tended to train operators of corporations. But there has been rather little academic attention to the design of corporations. The determination of corporate success and failure seldom arises from functional specialties alone, but grows out of the interactions of functions with one another and with markets and competitors. Management education underemphasizes policies governing such interactions.

We need to deal with the way policies determine corporate stability and growth in an intellectual, challenging, quantitative, and effective way. Such management education leads to what I refer to as enterprise design. Such an education would combine two innovations that have developed separately in this century.

The first innovation came from the Harvard Business School, which pioneered the case-study method of management education around 1910. The case method has achieved a wide following because it addresses the problems of general management and the interactions among parts of the corporate-market-competitor system. The case method also draws great strength from being based on the full range of descriptive information and the mental data base of practicing managers. But the case method, has a major weakness. The description of a case captures policies and relationships that describe a system so complex that it can not be reliably analyzed by discussion and intuition. Such attempts often draw the wrong dynamic conclusions and fail to reveal why corporations in apparently similar situations can behave so differently.

The second innovation, the understanding of the dynamics of feedback systems, emerged from engineering to become an organizing concept for human systems as well. Feedback processes govern all growth, fluctuation, and decay. They are the fundamental generators of all change. They allow new insights into the nature of managerial and economic systems that have escaped past descriptive and statistical analysis. System dynamics modeling can organize the descriptive information, retain the richness of the real processes, and build on the experiential knowledge of managers. A simulation model reveals the variety of dynamic behaviors that follow from different choices of policies. I anticipate this will become the frontier of new developments in management education during the next twenty years.

Bringing these two innovations together offers the potential for a major breakthrough in management education. The combination will permit going far beyond the case-study method of management education by adding a rigorous dynamic dimension to the rich policy and structural knowledge possessed by managers. The difference between present and future management schools will be as great as the difference between a trade school that trains airplane pilots and a university engineering department that trains aircraft designers.

Pilots continue to be needed, and so will operating managers. But just as successful aircraft come from skilled airplane designers, so in the future will successful corporations rely on enterprise designers. Competition will force reduction in the number of design mistakes in the structure and policies of our social institutions.

Correct design can make the difference between a corporation that is vulnerable to changes in the outside business environment and one that exhibits a high degree of independence from outside forces. Correct design can improve the stability of employment and production. Correct design in the balance of policies for pricing, capital plant acquisition, and sales force, can often make the difference between growth burdened by debt and growth out of earnings. Correct design can help avoid the adoption of policies offering short-term advantage at the expense of long-term degradation. Correct design can help prevent expenditure of managerial time in debating policies that are inherently of low leverage and therefore unimportant. Correct design can help identify the very small number of high-leverage policies capable of yielding desirable change.

Future training in enterprise design will include study of a library of generic management situations combining descriptive case studies with dynamic computer models, each of which has wide applicability in business. I estimate that about 20 such general, transferable, computerized cases would cover perhaps 90% of the situations that managers ordinarily encounter. Several powerful examples already exist. They include a model of stability and fluctuation in a distribution system,[12] a model of capital investment as it often restricts growth,[13] a model of promotion chains and the evolution into a top-heavy distribution of management personnel when growth slows, and a model dealing with imbalances between design, production, marketing, and service as these influence market growth. Each such model manifests many modes of behavior ranging from troublesome to successful depending on the policies employed within it.

STARTING AT THE BEGINNING—PRE-COLLEGE EDUCATION

Slowly over the years, we have come to realize the difficulty people face in making the transition to a dynamic and systems view of the world around them. After writing *Industrial Dynamics*, I thought the task of showing how policies and structure could be analyzed to understand corporate change was finished. It seemed that managers and educators would quickly pick up and begin to apply the concepts of feedback behavior, simulation of policy interactions, and corporate design. For several years I even turned my attention to quite different activities, feeling that nothing more would be needed. Not only was that optimism unjustified, but later efforts in system dynamics have repeatedly shown the high hurdle to cross in drawing people to the dynamic viewpoint when they were already mature in established statistical, or open-ended, or static views of their surrounding environments.

Understanding dynamic behavior comes slowly. No single learning process suffices. One can encounter feedback dynamics in the form of mathematical differential equations, in computer simulations, in physical laboratory experiments, and in informed observation of surrounding natural and social processes. But no one of these suffices, and even a combination does not immediately produce insights.

In corporate consulting, it can take several years for a management to understand and accept the way in which their own policies are creating the problems that they are experiencing. By that time, the individuals have often retired or died, and one faces a new oncoming generation of managers and must start over.

It now seems clear that we are asking for a paradigm transition of the kind discussed by Kuhn.[14] Such a transition tends to be strongly resisted both because it contradicts past assumptions and because it is difficult to understand from within the prior perspective. A pessimistic, but not entirely unrealistic, picture of paradigm revision suggests that adherents to an older paradigm are seldom converted; instead, they are in time replaced.

If then we hope for a time when managers and political leaders possess a more effective grasp of how their actions affect the future, what are we to do? The educational system compartmentalizes knowledge, hides the unity of systemic interactions, and teaches facts at the expense of synthesis. By so doing, it creates a paradigm that becomes progressively harder to alter as an individual develops.

Without the cause having been clearly identified, I believe much of the current dissatisfaction with pre-college education arises from past inability to show things whole, to convey how people and nature interact, and to reveal causes for what students see happening. Education is becoming less relevant as society becomes more complex, crowded, and tightly interconnected.

Education is fragmented. Social studies, physical science, biology, and other subjects are taught as if they were inherently different from one another even though dynamic behavior in each rests on the same underlying concepts. For example, the dynamic structure that causes a pendulum to swing is identically the same as the core structure that causes employment and inventories to fluctuate in a production-distribution system or in economic business cycles. Humanities fail to relate the dynamic sweep of history to similar behaviors on a shorter time scale that a student can experience in a week or a year.

High schools teach a curriculum from which a student is expected to synthesize a perspective and framework for understanding the social and physical environment. But that framework is never explicitly taught. A student is expected to create a unity from the fragments of the educational experience. But the teachers themselves have seldom achieved that unity.

Missing from most education is a direct treatment of the time dimension. What causes change from the past to the present and the present to the future? How do present decision-making policies determine the future toward which we are moving? How are the lessons of history to be interpreted to the present? Why are so many corporate, national and personal decisions ineffective in achieving the intended objectives? Conventional educational programs seldom offer such understanding. Answers to questions about how things change through time lie in the dynamic behavior of social, personal, and physical systems. Dynamic behavior, common to all systems, can be taught as such. It can be understood.

The educational system has been teaching static snapshots of the real world. But the world's problems are dynamic. The human mind grasps pictures, maps, and static relationships in a wonderfully effective way. But in systems of interacting components that change through time, the human mind is a poor simulator of behavior. Yet, even a junior high school student with a personal computer and coaching in dynamic behavior can advance remarkably far in understanding such complex systems.

In system dynamics, understanding how things change through time is facilitated by using the process of integration (or accumulation) rather than differentiation as the foundation for dynamic behavior. Those in science and technology formulate most dynamic behavior in terms of differential equations. But a derivative is a difficult concept to understand. Differentiation is obscure because it is no more than a figment of the mathematician's imagination. Nowhere does nature take a derivative. Nature only integrates. Any child who can fill a water glass or take toys from a playmate knows what accumulation (or integration) means. By going directly in computer simulation to the real-life structures involving integration, the procedure seems entirely natural and common place.

Education faces the challenge of undoing and reversing much that a person has learned by observation of simple dynamic situations. Simple experiences in everyday life deeply ingrain lessons that are deceptively misleading in dealing with more complex social systems. For example, from burning a hand on a hot stove, one learns the lesson that cause and effect are closely related in both time and space—the hand is burned here and now. Almost all understandable experiences reinforce the belief that causes are closely related to results in time and location. But in more complex systems, the cause of a difficulty is usually far distant in both time and space—the cause lies back in time and in a different part of the system from the point where the symptoms appear.

To make matters even more misleading, a complex feedback system presents what we have come to expect, an apparent cause that lies close in time and space to the symptom. However, that apparent cause is usually only a coincident symptom through which there is little leverage for producing improvement. Education does little to prepare students for living successfully when simple, understandable lessons so often point in exactly the wrong direction in the complex real world.

In his penetrating discussion of the learning process, Bruner states, "The most basic thing that can be said about human memory...is that unless detail is placed into a structured pattern, it is rapidly forgotten."[15] For most purposes, such a structure is inadequate if it is only a static framework. The structure should show the dynamic significance of the detail—how the details are connected, how they influence one another, and how past behavior and future outcomes result from decision-making policies and their interconnections.

System dynamics can provide that dynamic framework to give meaning to detailed facts, sources of information, and human responses. Such a dynamic framework provides a common foundation beneath mathematics, physical science, social studies, biology, history, and even literature.[16]

Several high schools, curriculum-development projects, and colleges are beginning to build study units in mathematics, science, social studies, and history around a system dynamics core. These have not yet reached the point of becoming a fully comprehensive educational structure. Some other countries (Norway, Germany, Japan, and China) appear to be moving ahead in using system dynamics as a foundation for designing a more powerful educational system below the college level.

Such exposure to dynamic thinking should start at an early age before contrary patterns of thought have become inflexibly established. Apparently exposure to cause-and-effect feedback thinking and computer modeling can successfully begin in schools for students around ten years old.[17]

Through the efforts of Barry Richmond[18] and others, system dynamics is now being established in some twenty junior and senior high schools. Macintosh computers and the STELLA software are particularly user friendly and suitable for pre-college education.

I have described my introduction to feedback systems by Gordon S. Brown in the MIT Servomechanisms Laboratory in the early 1940s. Brown later became head of the Electrical Engineering Department and then Dean of Engineering before retiring in 1973. In the late 1980s, Brown completed the circle by picking up system dynamics and introducing it into the Orange Grove Junior High School in Tucson, Arizona, where he spends the winters. He started by loaning software for a weekend to Frank Draper, who teaches 8th grade biology. Draper came back on Monday to say, "This is what I have always been looking for, I just did not know what it could be."

At first Draper expected to use computer simulation in one or two classes during a term. Then he found that systems thinking and simulation were becoming a part of every class. That led to concern that he would not have time to cover all the biology subject if so much time was being devoted to the system dynamics component. But two thirds of the way through the term, Draper found he had completed all the usual biology content. The more rapid pace had resulted from the way biology had become more integrated and from the greater student involvement resulting from the systems viewpoint. Also, much credit goes to the "learner-centered learning" organization of student cooperative study teams within the classroom that was introduced at the same time.[19] To quote Draper, "There is a free lunch."

Whether we think of pre-college or management education, the emphasis will focus on "generic structures." A rather small number of relatively simple structures appear repeatedly in different businesses, professions, and real-life settings. One of Draper's junior high school students grew bacteria in a culture dish, then looked at the same pattern of environmentally limited growth through computer simulation. From the computer, the student looked up and observed, "This is the world population problem, isn't it?" Such transfer of insights from one setting to another will help to break down the barriers between disciplines. It means that learning in one field becomes applicable to other fields.

There is now promise of reversing the trend of the last century that has been moving away from the "Renaissance man" idea toward fragmented specialization. We can now move back toward an integrated, systemic, educational process that is more efficient, more appropriate to a world of increasing complexity, and more supportive of unity in life.

AWARDS

Six universities in the United States and two in Europe have recognized the work in computers and system dynamics with honorary degrees. Other awards have included the National Academy of Management Award for the *Industrial Dynamics* book (1962); National Academy of Engineering (1967); Fellow, American Academy of Arts and Sciences (1968); Valdemar Poulsen Gold Medal, Danish Academy of Technical Sciences (1969); Member, Club of Rome (1970); Medal of Honor, Institute of Electrical and Electronics Engineers (1972); Benjamin Franklin Fellow, The Royal Society of Arts, London (1972); Howard N. Potts Medal, The Franklin Institute (1974); Honorary Member, Society of Manufacturing Engineers, recognizing contribution to digital control of machine tools (1976); National Inventors Hall of Fame (1979); naming of the "Jay W. Forrester Chair in Computer Studies" at MIT, endowed by Thomas J. Watson, Jr. (1986); James R. Killian, Jr. Faculty Achievement Award, MIT (1987); Honorary Professor, Shanghai Institute of Technology, China (1987); naming the "Forrester-Yang Reading Room for System Dynamics," Fudan University, Shanghai, China (1987); U.S. National Medal of Technology (with Robert R. Everett) (1990).

PUBLICATIONS

1946

With G.S. Brown. *Remote Control System, Patent No. 2,409,190.* Washington, D.C.: U.S. Patent Office.

1948

High-speed electrostatic storage. In *Symposium on Large-Scale Digital Calculating Machinery* (pp. 125-129). Cambridge, MA: Harvard University Press.

1951

Digital information storage in three dimensions using magnetic cores. *Journal of Applied Physics, 22*(1), 44-48.

The digital computation program at Massachusetts Institute of Technology. In *Second Symposium on Large-Scale Digital Calculating Machinery* (pp. 44-49). Cambridge, MA: Harvard University Press.

1952

Digital computers: Present and future trends. In *Review of Electronic Digital Computers, Joint AIEE-IRE Computer Conference, Philadelphia, December 10-12, 1951* (pp. 109-113). New York: American Institute of Electrical Engineers.

1953

Coincident-current magnetic computer memory developments at M.I.T. In J.C. Chu (ed.), *Argonne National Laboratory Computer Symposium, August 3-5, 1953* (pp. 150-158). Lemont, IL: Argonne National Laboratory.

1956

Multicoordinate Digital Information Storage Device, U.S. Patent No. 2,736,880. Washington, D.C.: U.S. Patent Office. [Patent for the memory system used during the first 20 years of digital computers.]

1957

Systems technology and industrial dynamics. In J. Cameron (ed.), *Adventure in Thought and Action–Fifth Anniversary of the School of Industrial Management, MIT* (pp. 10-21). Cambridge, MA: MIT Office of Publications.

1958

Industrial dynamics—A major breakthrough for decision makers. *Harvard Business Review, 36*(4), 37-66. [Also appears in revised form as Chapter 2, "An Industrial System" in *Industrial Dynamics* (1961); also available in *Collected Papers of Jay W. Forrester* (1975) and E.B. Roberts (Ed.), *Managerial Application of System Dynamics.* Cambridge, MA: Productivity Press, 1978].

1959

Advertising: A problem in industrial dynamics. *Harvard Business Review, 37*(2), 100-110. [Also appears in revised form as Chapter 16 "Advertising in the System Model of Chapter 2" in *Industrial Dynamics* (1961); also available in *Collected Papers of Jay W. Forrester* (1975) and E.B. Roberts (Ed.), *Managerial Application of System Dynamics*. Cambridge, MA: Productivity Press, 1978].

New frontiers. In *Eastern Joint Computer Conference, December 3-5, 1958* (pp. 5-10). New York: American Institute of Electrical Engineers.

1961

Industrial Dynamics. Cambridge, MA: Productivity Press.

1962

Management Science: Its impact. *Technology Review, 64*(3), 27-29, 36, 38.

Managerial decision making. In M. Greenberger (Ed.), *Management and the computer of the future* (pp. 36-91). Cambridge, MA: MIT Press.

With W.M. Pease, J.O. McDonough, and A.K. Susskind. *Numerical Control Servo-System, U.S. Patent No. 3,069,608*. Washington, D.C.: U.S. Patent Office. [Patent which launched the field of digital control of machine tools.]

1963

Simulative approaches for improving knowledge of business processes and environments. In *CIOS XIII International Management Congress* (pp. 234-238). New York: Council for International Progress in Management.

New academic opportunities In management systems. *Journal of Engineering Education, 53*(10), 766-771.

1964

Common foundations underlying engineering and management. *IEEE Spectrum, 1*(9), 66-77. [Also available in *Collected Papers of Jay W. Forrester* (1975).]

A new avenue to management. *Technology Review, LXVI*(3), 9-11.

1965

A new corporate design. *Industrial Management Review (MIT), 7*(1), 5-17. [Also available in *Collected Papers of Jay W. Forrester* (1975).]

Modeling of market and company interactions. In P.D. Bennett, ed., *Marketing and Economic Development: The 50th Anniversary International Symposium of Marketing, Sept. 1-3, in Washington D.C.* (pp. 353-364). Chicago: American Marketing Association.

The structure underlying management processes. In E.B. Flippo (ed.), *24th Annual Meeting of the Academy of Management, Dec. 28-30, 1964* (pp. 58-68). Chicago, IL: Academy of Management.

Corporate structure in the age of technological innovation. In R.A. Beaumont (ed.), *Computer technology–Concepts for management, May 7-8, 1964* (pp. 61-77). Greenwich, CT: Industrial Relations Counselors.

1966

Modeling the dynamic processes of corporate growth. In *Proceedings of the IBM Scientific Computing Symposium on Simulation Models and Gaming, December 7-9, 1964* (pp. 23-42). Yorktown Heights, NY: International Business Machines Corporation.

Social structure and motivation for reducing research costs. *Research Management, 9*(1), 45-60. [Also available in *Collected Papers of Jay W. Forrester* (1975).]

1968

Principles of Systems. Cambridge, MA: Productivity Press.

Planning under the dynamic influences of complex social systems. In E. Jantsch (ed.), *Perspectives of Planning: Proceedings of the OECD Working Symposium on Long-Range Forecasting and Planning, Bellagio, Italy, October 27-November 2, 1968* (pp. 235-254). Paris: Organization for Economic Cooperation and Development. [Also available in *Collected Papers of Jay W. Forrester* (1975).]

Industrial dynamics—A response to Ansoff and Slevin. *Management Science, 14*(9), 601-618. [Also available in *Collected Papers of Jay W. Forrester* (1975).]

Market growth as influenced by capital investment. *Industrial Management Review (MIT), 9*(2), 83-105. [Also available in *Collected Papers of Jay W. Forrester* (1975) and E.B. Roberts (Ed.), *Managerial Application of System Dynamics.* Cambridge, MA: Productivity Press, 1978].

Reflections on the Bellagio Conference. In E. Jantsch (ed.), *Perspectives of Planning: Proceedings of the OECD Working Symposium on Long-Range Forecasting and Planning, Bellagio, Italy, October 27-November 2, 1968* (pp. 503-510). Paris: Organization for Economic Cooperation and Development.

Industrial dynamics—After the first decade. *Management Science, 14*(7), 398-415. [Also available in *Collected Papers of Jay W. Forrester* (1975).]

1969

Urban Dynamics. Cambridge, MA: Productivity Press.

Overlooked reasons for our social troubles. *Fortune, LXXX*(7), 191-192.

Environment and invention. *IDEA, George Washington University, 13*(2), 279-283.

A deeper knowledge of social systems. *Technology Review, 71*(6), 21-31.

Engineering education and practice in the year 2000. *Engineering Education, 60*(10), 974-979. [Also available in *Futures,* (September 1969), pp. 391-401].

Systems analysis as a tool for urban planning. In M. Goland (ed.), *The engineer and the city* (pp. 44-53). Washington, D.C.: National Academy of Engineering. [Also available in *Collected Papers of Jay W. Forrester* (1975) and N.J. Mass (Ed.), *Readings in Urban Dynamics: Volume 1.* Cambridge, MA: Productivity Press, 1974.]

1970

Toward a national urban policy. *Social Service Outlook, 5*(6), 6-7. [Also available in *Collected Papers of Jay W. Forrester* (1975) and N.J. Mass (Ed.), *Readings in Urban Dynamics: Volume 1.* Cambridge, MA: Productivity Press, 1974.]

Growth, equilibrium, and self-renewal. In *Creative renewal in a time of crisis: Report of the Commission on MIT Education* (pp. 171-184). Cambridge, MA: Massachusetts Institute of Technology. [Also available in *Collected Papers of Jay W. Forrester* (1975).]

1971

World Dynamics. Cambridge, MA: Productivity Press.

Testimony. In *Hearings before the Ad Hoc Subcommittee on Urban Growth of the Committee on Banking and Currency, House of Representatives, Part 3, October 7, 1970* (pp. 205-265). Washington, D.C.: U.S. Government Printing Office.

Counterintuitive behavior of social systems. *Technology Review, 73*(3), 53-68. [Also available in *Collected Papers of Jay W. Forrester* (1975) and D.L. Meadows & D.H. Meadows (Eds.), *Toward Global Equilibrium: Collected Papers.* Cambridge, MA: Productivity Press, 1973].

1972

Should we save our cities? *Business and Society Review, Spring*(1), 57-62.
Churches at the transition between growth and world equilibrium. *ZYGON,*
  7(3), 145-167. [Also available in *Collected Papers of Jay W. Forrester*
  (1975) and D.L. Meadows & D.H. Meadows (Eds.), *Toward Global*
  Equilibrium: Collected Papers. Cambridge, MA: Productivity Press,
  1973].
Control of urban growth. *APWA Reporter, 39*(10), 14-19. [Also available in
  Collected Papers of Jay W. Forrester (1975) and N.J. Mass (Ed.),
  Readings in Urban Dynamics: Volume 1. Cambridge, MA: Productivity
  Press, 1974.]

1973

The fledgling cheermonger. *Cambridge Review, 94*(2211), 70-73.

1974

Toward a national urban consensus. In N.J. Mass (Ed.), *Readings in urban*
  dynamics: Volume I (pp. 245-255). Cambridge MA: Productivity Press.
  [Also available in *Collected Papers of Jay W. Forrester* (1975).].
With N.J. Mass & G.W. Low. The debate on world dynamics: A response
  to Nordhaus. *Policy Sciences, 5*(2), 169-190.

1975

Collected Papers of Jay W. Forrester. Cambridge, MA: Productivity Press.
The use of data in modeling: A discussion. In W.W. Schroeder III, et al. (eds.),
  Readings in urban dynamics: Volume 2 (pp. 81-90). Cambridge, MA:
  Productivity Press.
With N.J. Mass. Urban dynamics: A rejoinder to Averch and Levine. In W.W.
  Schroeder, III et al. (Eds.), *Readings in urban dynamics: Volume 2* (pp.
  11-30). Cambridge, MA: Productivity Press.
The road to world harmony. *The Futurist, IX*(5), 231-234.
Limits to growth revisited. *Journal of the Franklin Institute, 300*(2)), 107-111.
Urban goals and national objectives. In *Collected papers of Jay W. Forrester*
  (pp. 245-253). Cambridge, MA: Productivity Press.
The impact of feedback control concepts on the management sciences. In
  Collected papers of Jay W. Forrester (pp. 45-60). Cambridge, MA:
  Productivity Press.
Understanding social and economic change in the United States. *Simulation,*
  24(4), 125-128.

Understanding social and economic change in the United States. *Simulation,* *24*(5), 129-132.

1976

Comments on national growth. In H.M. Hochman (Ed.), *The urban economy* (pp. 137-151). New York: W.W. Norton.

Testimony on the future of growth and the environment. In *Hearings, Panel on Environmental Science and Technology, Subcommittee on Environmental Pollution, Committee on Public Works, U. S. Senate, 94th Congress* (pp. 3-95). Washington, D.C.: U.S. Government Printing Office.

A new view of business cycles. *The Journal of Portfolio Management, 3*(1), 22-32.

Overlooked reasons for our social troubles. In H.M. Hochman (ed.), *The urban economy [pp. 158-163]. New York: W.W. Norton.*

Business structure, economic cycles, and national policy: Reply. Business Economics, XI(3), 74-77.

Moving into the 21st century: Dilemmas and strategies for American higher education. *Liberal Education, LXII*(2), 158-176.

Educational implications of responses to system dynamics models. In C.W. Churchman & R.O. Mason (Eds.), *World modeling: A dialogue* (pp. 27-35). Amsterdam: North-Holland.

With N.J. Mass & C.J. Ryan. The system dynamics national model: Understanding socioeconomic behavior and policy alternatives. *Technological Forecasting and Social Change, 9*(1/2), 51-68.

The validity of system dynamics: An interchange. *Technology Review, 78*(8), 2-3, 72.

Business structure, economic cycles and national policy. *Business Economics, XI*(1), 13-24. [Also in *Futures* (June 1976), pp. 195-214, Ralph Jones (Ed.), *Readings from futures* (pp. 155-174). Guildford, England: Westbury House, 1981.]

Population vs. standard of living: The trade-off that nations must decide. *The Futurist, X*(5), 246-250. [Originally given as testimony for the Panel on Environmental Science and Technology, Environmental Pollution Subcommittee, Senate Committee on Public Works, February , 1976.]

1977

Growth cycles. *De Economist, 125*(4), 525-543.

World models: The system-dynamics approach. In M. Marois (Ed.), *Volume 4: Proceedings of the World Conference: Towards a Plan of Actions for Mankind* (pp. 107-112). Oxford: Pergamon Press.

New perspectives on economic growth. In D.L. Meadows (Ed.), *Alternatives to growth–A search for sustainable futures* (pp. 107-121). Cambridge, MA: Ballinger.

1978

Changing economic patterns. *Technology Review, 80*(8), 47-53.

1979

Christianity in a steady-state world (D-3171-1). Cambridge, MA: System Dynamics Group, Sloan School, Massachusetts Institute of Technology. [Sunday sermon, Parish of the Epiphany Episcopal, Winchester, MA.]

A self-regulating energy policy. *Astronautics & Aeronautics, 17*(7/8), 40-45 and 53.

An alternative approach to economic policy: Macrobehavior from microstructure. In N.M. Kamrany and R.H. Day (ed.), *Economic issues of the eighties* (pp. 80-108). Baltimore, MD: The Johns Hopkins University Press.

Innovation and the economic long wave. *Management Review, 68*(6), 16-24.

Testimony: 'Excess' profits tax and energy policy. In *Hearings Before the Subcommittee on Energy and Foundations, Senate Committee on Finance, May 11* (pp. 239-251). Washington DC: U.S. Government Printing Office.

1980

With P.M. Senge. Tests for building confidence in System Dynamics Models. In A. A. Legasto Jr. et al. (Eds.), *System dynamics*. [Series: TIMS Studies in the Management Sciences] (pp. 209-228). New York: North-Holland.

System dynamics—Future opportunities. In A.A. Legasto Jr. et al. (Eds.), *System dynamics* [Series: TIMS Studies in the Management Sciences] (pp. 7-21). New York: North-Holland.

Information sources for modeling the national economy. *Journal of the American Statistical Association, 75*(371), 555-574.

More productivity will not solve our problems. *Business and Society Review, Fall*(35), 10-18.

1981

Inflation and unemployment. In E. Paulre (Ed.), *System dynamics and the analysis of Change: Proceedings of the 6th International Conference on System Dynamics, University of Paris-Dauphine, November, 1980* (pp. 111-135). New York: North-Holland.

1982

Global modelling revisited. *Futures, 14*(2), 95-110.

Education for the 21st century. In F.P. Davidson, & C. Lawrence Meador (Eds.), *Macro-engineering and the future: A management perspective* (pp. 239-248). Boulder, CO: Westview Press.

1983

Future development of the system dynamics paradigm (D-3454). Cambridge, MA: System Dynamics Group, Sloan School, Massachusetts Institute of Technology. [Keynote Address at the 1983 International System Dynamics Conference.]

Innovation and economic change. In C. Freeman (Ed.), *Long waves in the world economy* (pp. 126-134). London: Butterworths.

Conversation: Jay W. Forrester—Interviewed by Christopher Evans. *Annals of the History of Computing, 5*(3), 297-301.

1984

System dynamics modeling of the arms race (D-3561). Cambridge, MA: System Dynamics Group, Sloan School of Management, MIT.

Comments on system dynamics modeling of arms control (D-3544-1). Cambridge, MA: System Dynamics Group, Sloan School of Management, MIT.

Discussion notes for simple arms control model (D-3545). Cambridge, MA: System Dynamics Group, Sloan School of Management, MIT.

The system dynamics national model—Objectives, philosophy, and status. In *International System Dynamics Conference, Oslo, Norway, August 2-5, 1984* (pp. 1-16). Lincoln, MA: System Dynamics Society. [Also available as Memo D-3570 from System Dynamics Group, Sloan School, MIT.]

1985

Dynamic modeling of the arms race (D-3684-3). Cambridge, MA: System Dynamics Group, Sloan School of Management, MIT.

System dynamics in management education (D-3721-1). Cambridge, MA: System Dynamics Group, Sloan School of Management, MIT.

Economic conditions ahead: Understanding the Kondratieff Wave. *The Futurist, XIX*(3), 16-20.

"The" model versus a modeling "Process." *System Dynamics Review, 1*(1), 133-134.

1987

Thoughts on Opportunities for the MIT School of Management (D-3924-2). Cambridge, MA: System Dynamics Group, Sloan School of Management, MIT.

Comparison of the 1920s and 1980s (D-3890). Cambridge, MA: System Dynamics Group, Sloan School of Management, MIT. [Prepared for sponsors of the System Dynamics National Model Project.]

Nonlinearity in high-order models of social systems. *European Journal of Operational Research, 30*(2), 104-109.

Lessons from system dynamics modeling. *System Dynamics Review, 3*(2), 136-149.

The economy: Where is it headed? *Los Angeles Daily News* (October 25).

Fourteen "obvious truths." *System Dynamics Review, 3*(2), 156-159. [Also available in *Collected Papers of Jay W. Forrester* (1975).]

1988

Designing social and managerial systems (D-4006-1). Cambridge, MA: System Dynamics Group, Sloan School of Management, MIT. [Award recipient address, Lord Symposium, MIT.]

1989

A economics pilot plant. *CHEMTECH, 19*(1), 26-33.

1990

System dynamics as a foundation for pre-college education. In G.P. Richardson, D.F. Anderson, & J.D. Sterman (eds.), *Volume 1: System Dynamics '90* (pp. 367-380). Lincoln MA: Systems Dynamics Society. [Also available as Memo D-4133, System Dynamics Group, Sloan School, Massachusetts Institute of Technology.]

1991

Beyond case studies—Computer models in management education. In P. Milling (Ed.).

1992

Low productivity: Is it the problem, or merely a symptom? In W.F. Christopher & C.G. Thor (Ed.), *Handbook for productivity measurement and improvement.* Cambridge, MA: Productivity Press.

NOTES

1. M.M. Forrester (Marmaduke Montrose), known as "Duke," born January 3, 1883 in Emerson, Iowa, died April 19, 1975 in Portland, Oregon; and Ethel Pearl Wright Forrester, born March 16, 1886 in Hastings, Nebraska, died December 27, 1958 in Portland, Oregon. Children: Jay Wright Forrester, born July 14, 1918 at Climax, Nebraska (no longer in existence, half way between Dunning and Arnold), and Barbara Frances Forrester Sliger, born April 21, 1921, at Climax. See Susan S. Forrester, 1989, Descendants of Oliver C. Forrester, Concord, MA: 29 King Lane 01742.

2. Brown and Forrester patent (1946).

3. Our children: Judith, 1948, graduated from Goucher College, has been a teacher, world traveller, and most recently is living on and managing our family ranch in Nebraska; Nathan Blair, 1950, received a bachelor's degree from Oberlin and a Ph.D. in system dynamics from MIT and is a consultant in the field; Ned Cromwell, 1953, has a B.Sc. and M.Sc. from MIT in electrical engineering, was an engineer for several years at the Digital Equipment Corporation, and more recently an engineer on the Alvin deep-sea research submarine at the Woods Hole Oceanographic Institute.

4. For the story of this pioneering program, see Kent C. Redmond and T.M. Smith, *Project Whirlwind*. Bedford, MA: Digital Press.

5. See "Digital Information Storage in Three Dimensions Using Magnetic Cores" (1951) and *Multicoordinate Digital Information Storage Device, U.S. Patent* No. 2, 736, 880 (1956).

6. See *Numerical Control Servo-System, Patent No. 3,069,608* (1962). For a history, see J. Francis Reintjes, *Numerical Control: Making a New Technology.* New York: Oxford University Press, 1991.

7. See "Systems Technology and Industrial Dynamics" (1957); "Industrial Dynamics—A Major Breakthrough for Decision Makers" (1958).

8. See "Common Foundations Underlying Engineering and Management" (1964); "Modeling the Dynamic Processes of Corporate Growth" (1966); "Market Growth as Influenced by Capital Investment" (1968).

9. Donella H. Meadows et al. *The Limits to Growth.* New York: Universe Books, 1972.

10. Available from John Wiley & Sons, England.

11. See *Designing Social and Managerial Systems* (1988); *System Dynamics in Management Education* (1985).

12. See chapters 2, 15, and 16 in *Industrial Dynamics* (1961).

13. See "Market Growth as Influenced by Capital Investment" (1968).

14. Thomas S. Kuhn, *The Structure of Scientific Revolutions.* Chicago: University of Chicago Press, 1962, 1970.

15. Jerome S. Bruner, *The Process of Education.* New York: Vintage Books, 1963, p. 24.

16. I have recently been moved to add literature to this list after reading about the powerful impact on students from a computer simulation of the psychological dynamics in Shakespeare's Hamlet done by Pamela Hopkins, an eleventh-grade English teacher at the Desert View High School in Tucson. See P.L. Hopkins (1992). Simulating *Hamlet* in the classroom. *System Dynamics Review, 8*(1), 91-98.

17. The earliest exploration of system dynamics at the fifth and sixth grade levels was started by Nancy Roberts, "Teaching Dynamic Feedback Thinking: An Elementary View," *Management Science, 24*(8, April 1978).

18. Barry Richmond, Ph.D. in system dynamics from MIT, president, High Performance Systems, supplier of the STELLA software, 45 Lyme Road, Hanover, NH 03755.

19. See "System Dynamics as a Foundation for Pre-College Education" (1990) for a more complete description of the combination of systems thinking and learner-directed learning.

Robert T. Golembiewski

Mid-Career Perspectives

ROBERT T. GOLEMBIEWSKI

This essay delights in that it not only encourages me to look back so as to leap forward, but adds the useful discipline of making myself clear to a broad audience. Earlier reflectings have involved small cadres—family, a few colleagues and students, or clients.

But the essay also has a daunting quality, and for six reasons of which I am conscious. First, this essay fixates on "my work," and that tether is a very short one for me. Thus, "our family" has been more important, at least after I attained a substantial semblance of right reason in my early thirties under the unrelenting tutelage of my wife and especially our three youngsters-becoming-teenagers, who highlighted my central life-choice. In 1970-71, I cut my prodigiously-frequent flying by 50 percent, and kept it there.

Second, "my work" gives little direct attention to students or teaching. A few comments seem relevant, then, since I value being seen as a "good teacher," and my professed ideal is that related obligations come right after our family when priorities conflict.

Paramountly, most of what follows applies to teacher <—> learner settings, although I confess common unclarity about who is which as well as about what constitutes such a setting. I am certain that some of my "best teaching" has occurred outside of classrooms—as a major professor or on dissertation committees, as advisor to students in professional and social groups, in consulting roles, on "the circuit," or "just talking" to others. Moreover, for me really dealing with teaching <—> learning requires a detail and compass that far transcends present limitations. Finally, on this short list, the selective bibliography following this essay lists over two dozen students, conventionally defined, who were associates in particularly-intense teacher <—> learner settings.

Third, "my work" often means "our work." But the latter usage is clumsy, if not a bit imperial; and the "our" changes membership a lot. Many bibliographic references identify this protean "our."

Fourth, "my work" seems to me to have deep roots in my family-of-birth and in the Polish community in which we lived. Two sections on twig-bending summarize several resulting early choices and personal orientations. While in no sense fully autobiographical, those sections reflect a basic fact: "my work" rests on the guidance and nurturance of many, and especially my parents— John Golembiewski and Pauline Pelka, now both long gone on to better things. My sister, Helen Yarmy, was always there when it counted, and her skills and standards of performance also were my early models.

Fifth, the title's reference to mid-career is acknowledgedly hopeful. Nonetheless, let me put it the way I feel it: my work is beyond early stages, and well-started, but has a long way to go. Hence I write of mid-career, accepting at age 58 that this sense of self might change for many reasons.

Sixth, "perspectives" in the title troubles because they may really be defenses, rationalizations, idealizations, constructs based on poor data, or even delusions. A kind of inter-rater reliability will help. Thus various knowledgeable observers—my wife and our three kids-now-parents, clients, as well as others—rated the essay on the scale "asymptotic approximation of the reality you saw." Fourteen ratings averaged 9.1, with 10 being the highest.

A PROLOGUE:
"ANYTHING YOU TELL THEM IS NEWS"

So where to start? Memory leads me back to a luncheon in spring 1958 at the Yale Commons. I had just defended my dissertation, and the departmental stormy petrel was treating even though he had not been my major professor nor even on the doctoral committee. So this violation of the local norm about the social distance between faculty and student had a special quality about it, even while fully in the spirit of a man whose last (and, sadly, posthumous) book was titled *Willmoore Kendall Contra Mundum*—that is, WK Against the World.

How was I looking forward to beginning my career of teaching and research?, Kendall asked. Well, I fretted, most jobs seemed to require knowing about an incredible range of subjects, and my strong organizational interests found no ready venue. (I was a Political Science doctorate, after all, and 1958 predated the acceleration of interest in public administration. So all of us were advised, "Keep several arrows in your quiver.")

Not to worry, my norm-breaking host opined: "Anything you tell them will be news."

My host intended some comfort, and perhaps a compliment. But I remember a cold shudder.

Good grief. The man I most respected for telling the unvarnished truth as he saw it, often at very great personal cost, just advised me to expect more of what I had just barely survived. Too much of what I had been telling too many people was not the news they wanted to hear, as was exemplified by the ominous fact that my department took about a year to decide whether or not I had passed the comprehensive written exams after a year of coursework at Yale.

Details would overburden this essay, but a brief summary captures the sense of the situation after high school and through graduate study. In sum, I had an itch to do some things that were sensed only in abstract terms. Moreover, my initial choices for getting from here to there often were poorly-informed. Further, even as means-end linkages became clearer in concept, I knew of no established pathways for making them in practice, or I was in the wrong places at inopportune times. So I usually sought to invent those linkages, and collisions occurred in direct proportion to my energy level, which was usually high. Nonetheless, I survived—in part by good luck, and in part by continued optimistic effort even when an accurate diagnosis encouraged resignation.

Details follow, and they deal with four basic themes: several early choices; several pervasive personal orientations; several cycles of stuckness/progress in my research and, early on, in my person; and several perspectives on my sense of self as consultant.

AS THE TWIG WAS BENT, I:
SOME EARLY CHOICES OR REFLEXES

Looking backward, several early choices made life simple, at least in retrospect, and reflected responses to urgings whose validity I generally accepted. At times, however, these choices left me a fascinated observer of self doing what could have been finessed or simply neglected.

Four personal orientations constitute the present short-list: an early pledge, an early career choice, the tenor of my adolescent times, and a vision of *the* shining career. These orientations seem to have clear environmental roots, which get some attention here and more direct treatment in the next section. Nurture dominates in my view of the world, but does not reign.

A Pledge About the Meadowlands

My earliest sense of a direction for my machine goes back to 1943 when I was 11. For a long time, I retained the typewritten contract made with myself, but now I can only paraphrase it: "I pledge to do my best to save the people of the New Jersey meadowlands." And from what? My mind's eye can still see that interminable string of garbage dumps and assorted landfills, often smoldering and with plumes of smoke flowing upward into a very blue sky, that we encountered all along U.S. 1 on our way to see a big league baseball game in the Big Apple.

Whence came this strong and strange urge? My family, while not wealthy in this country, had an elitist sense of itself in populist service—on "doing right, not just being right." Moreover, even early on, politically-active relatives and neighbors reinforced my personal sense of responsibility. Some Polish brothers and sisters needed standing-up for, and some were better at that than others.

So it was not out of character to make the meadowlands pledge, and I am pleased that our procreated family as well as their spouses have a strong concern for social justice and the underdog. For example, our decision to leave Yale and Illinois for Georgia got crystallized in just such terms. "Where do they need you most?" With this question my wife Peggy framed *the* issue one 1964 night as we walked the beach along Long Island Sound, debating employment possibilities. She zeroed-in on a growth opportunity from a low base, not only at the university but especially in race relations. The South of the mid-1960s gave all of us—parents Peg and Bob, as well as youngsters Alice, Hope, and Geoff—ample opportunities to test our orientations to equity and justice. That part of our family history has to be reserved for another time and place, but we all cherish making a difference when it counts. Witness a recent note from one of our black "helpers," who were locally called "maids" years ago. She went on as an adult to finish not only elementary and high school but also college, and she recently tells us: "I shall always remember the warmth I felt working in your home [and] the support you gave me [and others]."

An Early Commitment to Nuclear Physics

Hiroshima had a profound effect on an early career choice—nuclear physics. With little thought, and less guidance, I enrolled as a physics major at Princeton, did nearly two years of coursework, and even got through much of Einstein's General Theory—at least to my satisfaction.

A semblance of a rationale underlay this choice. Many considered me a bit of an academic whiz in elementary and high school; nuclear physics clearly seemed *the* field of the future; and no one in my circle was prepared to tell me I couldn't do it, whatever "it" was. Paramountly, I had convinced myself that "it" was the answer to my meadowlands pledge: some kind of nuclear decomposition would deal with that blight experienced so vividly along U.S. 1, and from which so many people needed protection. Ah, youth! Ah, science!

In most other senses, however, the commitment was very strange indeed. My family favored fast cars and money-making over education. Although technical training did appear in past generations, I would be the only college attendee among my siblings. Moreover, I intended to devote major chunks of time to athletics. Although Princeton had no grants earmarked for athletes, my "total record" justified generous financial support, without which Princeton would have been impossible. This record happened to include a taste for violent physical contact in football, and was diminished not at all by a precocious ability to throw a baseball with sufficient velocity to remind even mature athletes of their mortality.

These commitments to athletics *cum* physics lasted about two years. Deep muscle tears in sophomore football put an end to serious sports, and realities also encouraged revisiting my decision about a major in college. The subsequent subsections sketch some determinants of that choice-making.

"You Didn't Have to Be A Weatherman. . ."

The days of my early consciousness were determinedly antifascist times, and that for me translated into a strong concern about the proper exercise of all authority. Local folklore powerfully fixed this concern, as in the story of a relative during the 1939 Nazi invasion. "Where is your husband?," the invaders asked about her military spouse. After each of her several truthful protestations of ignorance, one of their children was shot, beginning with the oldest. Somewhere in that grisly progression the mother snapped and remained catatonic until her death, decades later.

Such history had early personal implications, for a smallish cadre of us were being groomed for leadership, even in grade school,[1] *and we took that seriously.* For example, at our most recent reunion, my all-male high school classmates recalled my impassioned 1949 presentation about the challenges that unions raised for all of us—the many "men of action" in the workplace, and the few who would be "men of ideas" gone to university to sharpen their knowledge and skills. Violence in a factory where family members occupied central positions, and where I labored like a young bull-of-the-woods during several summers, provided a vivid experiential base for this concern. After all, I had seen crowbar meet head, and long-time friends suddenly become adversarial "management" and "labor."

The Shining Ideal

In high school and in college, public service was stereophonically emphasized as *the* employer of choice. Public coping with the depression and World War II provided me with ample evidence that government was far more the solution than the problem it recently has become portrayed as. Later, this pervasive sense was nourished by the proud motto "Princeton in the nation's service." Perhaps in largest part, this sense of government as competent problem-solver was reinforced by my growing acquaintances in the Polish community—mostly older business people and professionals, just coming of age politically, with a strong base of economic success, and with a yearning for a new generation of leadership who could consolidate recent gains and also help realize lofty communitarian ideals.[2]

Hence it was reasonable that, after embarrassment gave way to realism about what a sorry nuclear physicist I would make, late in my sophomore year I opted to major in the Woodrow Wilson School of Public and International Affairs, or SPIA. The curriculum featured several "conferences," complete with long papers by individual students on aspects of some problem in public policy. These papers—after some discussion and much politicking—variously influenced a ponderous conference report. Moreover, the SPIA curriculum permitted one to take courses across an incredible range as preparation for becoming—as we liked to joke—"an assistant secretary of something-or-the-other" with the federal government. This experience was broad rather than deep, and value-focused rather than impressed with particular "schools" or techniques or professional knowledge-bases.

Together, this combination of majors induced a definite tension—often constructive, but always a resource to be managed. Thus, I had quite a time with my 1953 SPIA conference paper, which featured a statistical analysis of voting and financial contributions that ran wildly counter to the broadly-philosophical and humanitarian currents of our curriculum. Trouble, with a capital T. A bit later—this time finding more compelling attractions in my Princeton normative orientations—I saw the "value-free science" that had become so much a part of my graduate work as procrustean and even bizarre. Again, short-run trouble for my efforts to develop "goal-based, empirical theories,"[3] along the lines of what is now known as "action research."

In quite a direct way, the two orientations—empirical and normative—are reflected in my basic concern with Organization Development. Would that "OD" had existed earlier.

My consequent research and consulting interests in government as well as business caused some pain, especially early on, for there were few academic switch-hitters in those days. On moving to a business school in 1960, I received a handwritten note from a political science savant who minced no words: "You, sir, are a TRAITOR," a reaction motivated by the difficult times then being experienced by Political Science. Practically, preserving this dual identity—while being primarily a family man, as well as a full-time-plus university administrator—led to common perceptions of my insularity, if not crabby reclusiveness. I became known as "The Ghost" in professional associations. I would do my thing at meetings, then quietly disappear, forfeiting much of that informal socialization that establishes one's professional persona and also puts analytic or methodological differences into human perspective. Something had to give, and costs had to be paid.

AS THE TWIG WAS BENT, II:
THIS PERSON AND HIS ORIENTATIONS

In addition to encouraging this range of early choices/reflexes, my environments seem to have reinforced—if they did not induce—eight elements of personal style or predisposition.

Strong Sense of Community

A complex communitarianism guides me, and that is meant in three senses. Specifically, consider community as experienced, lost, and forfeited.

As Experienced Community. Many of my positive reveries of early community go back to Top Road of the 1940s and early 1950s—a largely-Polish enclave approaching 500 square blocks in Trenton, New Jersey. There, English typically was a second-or even the third-language, and elementary education in the parochial was determinedly bilingual; a large and ornate church provided the center of collective life; a meticulous cleanliness dominated in even humble living spaces and certainly in cultural prescriptions; and the general sense was that harshness had existed but better things were happening. Roles on numerous sports teams reinforce this sense, both in Top Road and far beyond; and university clusterings and numerous intense work teams add later substance to my strong sense of *gemeinschaft*. Primarily, our family remains tight, even as our kids and their sprouts now live within a big crescent—from Pennsylvania, to North Carolina, and onto Texas.

As Lost Community. Although you can never really go back home, it is fun to try if one's expectations are not too high. Community is always being reformatted, and thus constitutes a moving target. Moreover, several developmental cycles saw changes in me and what I do, professionally and personally.

Top Road died for me twice, in effect. One time, I did the job, albeit without forethought. On announcing my intended college major to a businessman grooming me for leadership in our Polish community, I got a restrained but sad reaction: "There's not much need for nuclear physicists around here." I understood fully only as the years passed. He saw me as growing into a local power-wielder: a lawyer, perhaps, or even what he called a "silk-stockinged executive" in the several now-substantial manufacturing firms that had grown up within our community. That day, Top Road died for both of us, and more than a little.

Top Road also died in systemic ways around 1950, and quite suddenly, although clear vestiges still remain. A ratta-tat-tat of premature deaths crippled community leaders; strikes convulsed community firms;[4] and major demographic shifts occurred.

So both my shaping community and I changed or were transformed, and there would be no real going back. Especially on festive days, both the expatriates and those remaining can summon the old spirits. Our children got a sense of those high points; and it pleases me that our first grandchild was baptized in 1988 in our Top Road church. But the goings-back increasingly find shadows among the substance, and I have learned to accept both. At times, nobody seems to have forgotten anything, but I recently was introduced back home as "the best fullback Trenton Catholic ever had." I accepted that, but I had never played that position and would not have been the best ever at it if I had.

As Forfeited Community.   Because of both experience and loss by myself and others, the forfeit of community strikes me as poignant. No doubt this helps explain much of my research and especially my commitment to consultation through action research. Far beyond generous consulting fees, I have come to a growing conviction that community—for both good and ill— will be increasingly experienced and lost in organizations. Hence its forfeit there has a special saliency.

Nothing lasts forever, but over time my fellow consultants and clients have put several substantial bends in entropy's otherwise-inexorable curve. Particularly rich have been the experiences with one core-client over nearly 25 years—not straight-vanilla experience, but an indication of what can be done within and between several organizational windows-of-opportunity. This identification has led to many publications of which I am proud, and especially two McGregor Memorial Awards for Excellence in Applications of the Behavioral Sciences: "Measuring Change and Persistence in Human Affairs: Types of Change Generated by OD Designs" (1976) and "Some Effects of Multiple OD Interventions on Burnout and Worksite Features" (1987). This action research occurred at all levels: from the highest strategic levels,[5] to the lowest,[6] and all the way stations in-between.[7] All of it reflects the clarion, if boastful, call of our search for the ways-and-means of moving toward more satisfying and effective community at work: "we are not here to re-invent the *status quo.*"[8]

High Expectations About Stereophonic Nurturance

I try to make nurturance a two-way street, but I clearly have been a heavy receiver, and not only in my formative years. My wife, after all, is known as "Saint Peggy" to Georgia graduate students, for reasons that include her profuse support for children and husband.

Whence this nurturance? Family traditions prescribe plenty of hugging, squeezing, and what we indelicately call "giving a slobber." Other factors contributed. I was last-born, "the baby," and by over a decade. Hence I was (and still am) "Bobbie," with all that implies. Several years of childhood illnesses, some *very* serious, also encouraged such succorance. That my next-older brother died as a child in a tragic accident only added motivation to "take real good care of Bobbie."

Immediately, also, I had things easier than my siblings. My father had to build a life from scratch in his new country, in contrast to substantial comfort overseas. The hard times did not impact me directly, for he was doing well before I came along. Relatedly, the Polish community had built a powerful infrastructure that helped me far more than my siblings—a large elementary school of high achievers, tuition support for the expensive Catholic high school, supports for self-esteem, and opportunities for testing one's self, especially in athletics.

More broadly, those in my birth cohort (1932) constituted a sudden-bottom in birth-rates. I remember us joking that each student had two seats in elementary school, so great had been the drop in enrollment. This overbalance of resources to claimants followed my demographic cohort through life, and created a sense our children did not have. In general, the world seems more-narrowly competitive to them than to my wife or me.

These expectations could create difficulties, as with my university head football coach who was not long on nurturance. On definite balance, however, I am glad about the way it was. One has a lifetime to adjust to the non-nurturant features of the wider world.

At the same time, I was emotionally armored in one basic sense. Every ethnic kid in my neighborhood—and that was about all of us—knew in his bones that nurturance from "them" was problematic. We differed only in the frequency-of-expectation. Operationally, "them" meant all people whose first language was not Polish, and especially lower-level functionaries, from whom personal and institutional prejudice was experienced by every one of us. Consider the poor soul on a prize committee who could not accept the idea of a Pole with my SAT scores and high school average. He became comfortable with that reality only when he learned that I had Prussian ancestors, some of whom I manufactured sardonically to feed his obvious delight at discovering a pseudo-explanation for what was otherwise inexplicable to him.

This emotional armoring often overdid it—it tethered as well as motivated—and balance was always an issue. A few of my fellow footballers saw my personal ideal. They called me "Fudgehammer," partly in response to my build but also with an eye toward my strongly-nurturant side: "He's so soft and sweet, but he hits *sooo* hard." Often, the aggressive and combative side came through, especially in contacts—at times, collisions—especially with my expanding worlds but also in our expanding nuclear family.

An Easiness with Authority

Nonetheless, I experienced a substantial easiness with and about authority, and especially at more senior levels. "Easiness" refers to a low social distance or jauntiness—between myself and others who are exercising legitimate authority, and especially at more senior levels, as well as between myself and others when I am in authoritative roles. These strong tendencies both help and hinder, but they are deeply-rooted and I feel myself playacting in relation to distant authority—both as sender and receiver.

Various early reinforcers of this critical and strong predisposition—however labelled—seem clear to me. On my father's accidental death, for example, I became a young *pater familiae* at age eight, substituting for the departed head of a traditional patriarchal family in an otherwise-female household. That seemed to put them at ease, and I recall not minding at all doing the family banking from 11 or 12 years of age. Later on, I came to appreciate what this early and easy transition probably meant for my dealings with authority.

To the same effect, a group of six of us—big for our age, good students, and generally straight arrows—were co-opted as non-coms in the last three or four years of elementary school. We were major keepers-of-the-peace, a role augmented by our size as well as academic and athletic achievements, and we generally left the nuns pleased, if not beaming. (That little meritocracy was no childish flash-in-the-pan. Four of us ranked among the 10 top graduates of our high school; we gained over 30 letters for athletics there; and so on.) Even our high school football coaches—no easy riders as a categoric group, even now but especially then—gave us a long leash. One coach admitted in later years to being inhibited in language and coaching tactics by the fact that his staff were all non-Catholics coaching for a school run by Franciscan fathers. Our undefeated senior year no doubt also encouraged them to cut us substantial slack.

Massive reinforcement of this easiness with authority came from the good Franciscan fathers at our all-male private high school. They set high standards and expected balanced performance, while leaving plenty of room for personal expressions of how that was done, as well as for what was done—academics, theatre, sports, debate and public speaking, inter alia.

Although poor-fits were soon gone, the system would be characterized today as loose-tight in management terms. Race or income did not influence whether you were in or not. And a sense of fairness pervaded even the infrequent overt discipline—I remember only two or three incidents. With very few exceptions, the Franciscans had made peace with their Maker, and saw their role largely in terms of allowing their fledglings to become good flyers—if possible, excellent flyers. They lived in a community of economic poverty and spiritual humility; and public ego trips were rare, except in pursuit of seeing that "their boys made their marks."

"Easiness" with authority does not imply coziness or dependence. Quite the opposite, in fact. Easiness can be seen as presumptuous by authority figures, and it encourages an aggressive openness when "they aren't doing things right." But that aggressiveness does not intend to undercut authority, in general, but rather to help orient it.

That authority figures do not always see it my way has not deterred, in general. My expectations have been met with sufficient regularity that I seldom feel or feign an alien orientation.

In undergraduate years and early faculty experiences, especially, an aggressive reaction was triggered by faculty and administrators for whom a minority of us provided a mild basic training for what the mid-1960s would bring them. There was the shock when a university president *announced* to us assembled frosh at our opening-day orientation who our class officers would be. I uninvitedly and unsuccessfully encouraged reconsideration of what could only be a slip-of-the-mind. Similar effects ensued four years later in 1954 when, as officials of our dining club's "bicker committee," several of us tried to stand fast on our invitation of membership to the one (!) black student in the sophomore class of 800 or so.

High Marginality

While definitely "in" community, I have long and often also felt "in-between." Maybe, really feeling "in" allows one to be comfortably "between." "Marginality" seems the most appropriate term for the condition of being comfortable in multiple cultures.[9]

Low marginality does not appear ever to have been my problem. For example, as the baby-by-over-a-decade in the family, I was given unusual opportunities to chart my own course. Particularly impactful was a summer spent at Northwestern University as a "cherub"—a participant in a speech and debate program—between my junior and senior years in high school. A friendly Franciscan friar believed that would be good for me, and off I went without a familial murmur about the cost or about forfeiting a summer of American Legion baseball. As for the latter, I was silently nursing a very sore arm from many too many fastballs and sliders, thrown at too early an age, knowledge of which might have put doubts into the heads of my high school coach and even major league scouts.

Geography also contributed to marginality in that our immediate neighborhood had *no* one my age. So I either played the usual games with much-older guys, in effect taking the accelerated course; or I travelled substantial distances to play with several clusters of widely-scattered peers. I liked high marginality more than learning by failure, but both had a place.

More deeply, my early years featured marginality. Although our family relished diversity—in foods, languages, and customs—some members were very cautious about "them," and here I early took a different position. Our older daughter sharpens the point: "I think your concern for social justice grew partly as a reaction to your family's and community's rampant insularity and prejudice." Moreover, I early and increasingly ventured outside our Polish community in ways open to few of my fellow communitarians. Athletic and academic contests were a way of life, and they broadened and also toughened the ones who were locally-successful. Beyond the first round or two of competition, "they" often provided the playing fields and the *petit* officials. The former often were not level, and some of the latter were far from even-handed. So I specialized in the fine print of rule books, almost always doing better with higher-level officials.

Serendipity also played a major role in comfort-in-marginality. Thus I was born quite late in my parents' reproductive lives, and my mother was shy about this clear consequence of their behavior. Small as she was, Mama so artfully concealed the growing fact of life within her that later family gatherings were full of allusions as to how "Bobbie just appeared one day" when the next-oldest living sibling already was an adolescent. I made 4 out of 1 + 1: I was adopted, I concluded erroneously but quite firmly for a time. But not to worry. My self-ascribed adopted status only heightened my joy in and appreciation of the nurturance I received, especially during a long siege of childhood illnesses.

A Certain, Ah . . ., Expansiveness

My early days were spent in a local aura of pride in progress and achievement; our parish school and church trumpeted both high aspirations and a grandness of scale, transcending but nonetheless suffused by an ethnic one-downness attributed to us by others, which I rejected but still remained a social fact of life. Revealingly, our pastor used to remark in personal asides that there was *no* religious ceremony whose effects would not be heightened by having 30 altar boys scattered about, and 40 or 50 were even better.

So I come honestly by a certain expansiveness, especially in speech, coupled with enough personal power that many saw me in political or priestly roles. I enjoy this part of myself in its limited place, but it can get out-of-hand.

This predisposition in this regard was given awful exercise and even license by debating, which we generally considered the verbal equivalent of football, or even war; but debating also generated a useful learning experience. I recall one verbal flurry in the national high school debate finals in Kenosha, Wisconsin. We of the affirmative cited a poll, which was very powerful stuff in 1950; and the negative side cited a contradictory poll, which was the standard strategy. I scratched a counterattacking note to my partner: "AVG = 58.6 percent in the affirmative," or some such, by which I meant to convey—in a grand irrelevance—that if one averaged our poll *and* their poll, the mean (AVG) still favored our position. Hardly skipping a beat, my partner waxed eloquent about the very recent—how correct he was about that!—AVG Poll. This stunned both the opposition and me. On a long walk with myself while waiting on the judges' decision, I decided to reveal our exuberance, *if we were declared the winners*, and my partner reluctantly agreed. Fortunately, the judges made life easy for us, and I vowed never to be so vulnerable again.

My insistence on cross-checking along with even-excessive citation and documentation relate, I believe, to this experience and whatever underlies it. Hence, my active resolve to keep things balanced, as in citations of those in "other camps" when common practice often features silent neglect.

Transcending Value of Intense Work

Centrally, my early years featured a comfort with intense labor—even a taste for it. At 15 or so, I took on the work of several grown men to develop strength and stamina, and was paid for what I did—hot and heavy unloading of porcelain in the plant of our extended-family-by-marriage. Later, it was construction work.

The prime locus for this attitude seems obvious to me: my family, and especially as it reflected community values. The anti-model was "Chewing-gum Charlie"—the person looking for an edge and a way to avoid getting on with it. We had our Charlies, of course, but they paid a stiff price—first in corrective messages, and then in derision and even exclusion. I recently found evidence in a song that fits perfectly my present sense of that earlier ambiance and is even today in our church's songbook. The text announces (to that part of Beethoven's 9th Symphony known as "Ode to Joy," no less):

> Every task, however humble,
> Fills the soul with grace anew;
> . . .
> Help us all to work our best.

Somewhere, I found it harder to do less, and slower, than to work flat-out. Research is not unloading porcelain, but general principles apply: finish, then go home.

Luck in Facilitative Mentors

This good fortune has occurred so regularly and propitiously, I grew to expect that I would attract, or find, or stumble across who is needed, when they are needed.

I have never experienced a mentor whom I wanted to directly emulate or whose work I could extend, who would carry me along in the upward draft of his or her afterburners. These might be called instrumental mentors.

There have been many who opened possibilities that neither they nor I envisioned—these I call facilitative or enabling mentors. I note only a few: the late Mr. Eugene Urbaniak, who spent many evenings on our front porch testing "what I was made of"; Father Leonard, who first encouraged me to express myself in prose when the spoken word came so much more easily; the late Lt. General Harold Chase, who encouraged me into graduate study when I was disoriented; and Chris Argyris, who pointed in directions that enriched my life and expanded my professional grasp when I needed to do both.

Shorthand Sense of Human Condition

For me, life is like an artichoke or perhaps an onion—multi-layered but relatively homogeneous and yet with a core that guides growth. So let me try to provide a brief sense of *this* human condition. Five descriptors do the job, for openers, and they share the quality of forces-in-tension, or perhaps of paradoxes.

1. *A basic thrust that values or even requires options.* When I am careless, I will maintain that increasing available choices drives me. Indeed, much that I have done can be viewed as intending to expand the range of available alternatives which, pretty clearly, allows great personal investment and ownership. Life seems quite agreeable; I am usually doing what I need to do as well as like doing. That is more the case nowadays, but has been an ideal all along.

In clearer moments, however, I really mean *responsible* choices, defined as being generally consistent with one's individualized basic thrust. Choices to be the non-self get little attention from me, when I feel a oneness with myself. For me, freedom is definitely not just another word for nothing left to lose.

2. *A dynamic in-betweeness.* Blaise Pascal said it best, and maybe first. Compared to our Maker, we are not much. Compared to the bullrushes and bullfrogs, however, we constitute pretty hot stuff. For me, this sense is *vivid.*

Motivationally, such a view might cut in two ways. For some, it might de-energize. For me, I see it not only as providing a useful restraint on vaulting ambitions but also as generating a double-barreled impetus toward reducing the distance to the One and increasing the distance from the other.

3. *Active responses to fundamental inevitabilities.* Entropy has all the trump cards, I wrote elsewhere; and I see no upwardly-ascending growth curve, personally or institutionally. For me, the issue is how much you get done, overall, rather than whether regression or decay occur. They *will* occur, for each individual and organization, sooner or later. With wit and will and good fortune, however, combined efforts over the long run can keep a collective curve on the upgrade even as individual curves fade.

4. *Our vivid moments in history's broad sweep.* This constitutes another version of in-betweenness and inevitabilities, of course, but it provides a major

tether on my decision-making and hence gets separate statement. My early days reinforced this simultaneity. We were in the twentieth century, but all around us—especially in school and church—were evidences of our roots in centuries of Polish statehood and culture. Any moment was clearly in-context, even for those paying scant attention. This tendency remains strong, and at times drove to distraction fellow T-Group trainers intent on "experiencing the now."

5. *A determined balance.* In concluding a short list of personal views of this human condition, it seems that one can have too much of even the very best things. Hence my search for balance in life and work: as in the physical complements to work of the mind—hunting, fishing, jogging, softball, and (even today) a bit of basketball. Fine-tuning is the name of the game. Three years ago, I "retired" from intramural slow-pitch softball, consistent with my pledge of what I would do when my batting average fell below .500. However, the precise average was .496 which, my wife Peg reminded me, rounds-off to my personal cutting-point. So I am playing again, and the stimulus to retire has not yet reappeared.

This primacy of "balance" cuts both ways. It simplifies life, while it may tether me short of possibly-expanded orbits of personal growth.

Whence came these senses of my human condition? Certain genetic inheritances play a major role, but early experiences both reinforced and reflected these evolving orientations. Consider a strange but (to me) revealing example: between the ages of 9 and 13 or so I served as an altar boy at 100 funerals, minimum.

Not that I liked these all-morning affairs, but I found much elementary schoolwork *very* unattractive. Characteristically, I sought ways to create options—short of being really troublesome, if possible.

Funeral service also connects with other items in the short catalog above. Thus it meant confronting an elemental inevitability, and confronting vs. avoiding seems to me as generally-useful in organizations as well as in personal life. This somber forum also left me with a list of do's and don'ts for my preferred behaviors under stress. In addition, one could develop a deep spiritual balance in such settings, for they lamented death but more basically promised glorious resurrection. This "balance" might extend in cases to a certain emotional detachment, or even distaste, because some Polish funerals of that day-and-time had an unpalatable degree of theatricality about them. Hence our development of criteria for differentiating true grief from simulant behavior, details about which are better reserved for another place. In general, one learned when to activate special emotional armoring, and how, or paid high costs.

Perhaps most of all about such Stakhanovite funerary service, I remember a resolve—perhaps I only imagine it—to do whatever, flat-out, while I had the chance. This was how we all ended, no matter what, so it was best to get on with doing what one could, while one could. Pretense, persiflage, or procrastination simply distort the elementals and deflect energy.

SIX RESEARCH CYCLES:
STUCKNESS AND PROGRESS

So how does my research reflect these early choices and personal orientations? As a clumsy approximation, my research reflects six cycles of stuckness and movement. But note several caveats. Two or more of these cycles often are involved in simultaneous real-time. At times, moreover, the cycles were planned in broad terms; but some just happened as situational imperatives that were operating before their intent and effects became clearer. These six cycles can be labeled, if at the cost of ripping them out-of-context, as: normatively-guided search; tooling-up in particulars; testing in several broad applications; estimating success rates; encompassing some deviant cases by plural concept of change; and redirecting analysis and application via burnout phases.

Normatively-Guided Search

If mostly in retrospect, my early rooting-around focused on the common mismatch between work and the broadly-humanist values that became part of my personal orientations, as reinforced by the local version of the Judaeo-Christian tradition in which I had been immersed as a child. Three books came directly out of that search,[10] and they confirmed my own dour experience that serious mismatches dominated at work. With their own useful wrinkles and although guided by different biases, the three books reinforce the McGregor of *The Human Side of Enterprise* and the Argyris of *Personality and Organization*.

The search had mixed consequences, bottom-line. The three books made a real contribution to a beginning academic with a growing family, and especially by their getting a now-rounder author "on the circuit," which was an unexpected gravy train. Essentially, however, I now see this effort as another way of acting on my youthful meadowlands pledge. Practically, however, the books only hinted at operational ways of reducing the mismatch between normative ideals and the demands of work.

Retooling in Particulars

Early in the process of these normatively-guided surveys of the organizational literatures, the need for re-tooling dawned on me. This need extended not only beyond my exposure to physical science and humanistic orientations as an undergraduate, but also beyond graduate work in public administration and political science.

The retooling was quantitative and qualitative, and occasioned a planned move to business-oriented contexts—at Illinois, and then at Yale. Leaving a "dream" faculty position in Politics at Princeton seems so right today, but it was wrenching in 1960. Most observers saw me burning some very attractive bridges, but I was more interested in reservoirs—of building my own resources so as to later help accumulate collective wit and will for developing more efficient and especially more effective organizations.

Things were happening thick-and-fast in quantitative analysis, in those days. A Ford Fellowship in Mathematical Applications in Business helped fill a growing gap in my formal education and reading.

More impactfully, Steward Y. McMullen as department head of Management showed all of us at Illinois how a participative manager can make an enormous difference in a short time, and under his guidance we created courses and programs that felt good as well as proved attractive to students and managers. But that all came crashing down, as fast as it had gone up.

How could this have been prevented, based on better understanding and building? Chris Argyris became the prime agent of my unstuckness, beginning with his suggestion that I sit in for him at Yale for a year while he was on leave. A dazzling set of developments—practical and conceptual—followed a sudden distancing from the turmoil at Illinois. In close cadence, I was exposed to the "laboratory approach" and my first T-Group, to the people who were doing most with "action research," to the NTL clients who provided numerous opportunities to put new concepts into place, and especially to rich opportunities to gain new skills and orientations.

This learning centered on the self as consultant, but also helped me express the fuller range of myself. Emotionally, to put it too pithily, I always knew that I was a deep lake but saw many others as shallow puddles. I came to *really* know better.

The post-Illinois decade or so was a period of active retooling in particulars, in effect and to a degree by intent. Consulting burgeoned, and the literature also contains substantial evidence of activity on two tracks. Thus more or less consciously I sought to extend my conceptual understanding into various management functions as well as policy arenas.[11] Relatedly, growing attention went to intervention, action research, and OD consulting. A sampler of that activity includes:

- Numerous innovations in learning designs for organization development or change, both for growth,[12] as well as for cutback and decline.[13]
- Classroom resources in sensitivity training and the laboratory approach.[14]
- Summary statements concerning OD as a major way to increase value congruencies at work, both generically[15] as well as in the public sector specifically.[16]
- Developments in survey/feedback technology.[17]
- Ways of moving toward OD values. Some of these efforts deal with comprehensive social and cultural change.[18] And these extensions also involved limited-purpose efforts.[19]

Such activities increasingly moved me beyond the "organizational meadowlands of the mouth and of the mind," which was my way of expressing the limits of my early work. I remained on-the-circuit, but less frequently. "Just talking," although easy and financially rewarding, came to satisfy less and less. Despite various skill-building loops that were built into presentations, these experiences remained distal from "the action." Moreover, I worried about my over exuberance in public. "The larger the audience," I wrote, "the lower the intellectual content—especially mine." There also was the danger of becoming stereotyped as a quick and acerbic critic, an outcome that I often aided and abetted. In my ideal, however, criticism was only a mode on the way to constructive action.

Relatedly, the issue of transfer of learning came to dominate, and this mixed ethical and practical concerns. Intact work teams at systemic levels became my targets—increasingly and, as time moved on, almost always.

Testing Systemic Applications

The second cycle soon experienced its own stuckness, if a comfortable one. I saw a decade or so of it as "paying dues," but the need to "put it all together" gained urgency. Most of the work in the second cycle—both research and applications—was subsystemic, and hence even the successes there implied stuckness.

Several opportunities for comprehensive testing came along, fortunately. Most were serendipitous, but again life is like fishing. Rule 1 in both: You have to keep your lure in the water. All opportunities for systemic testing sought *the* value <---> application linkage: How to increase the opportunities for responsible freedom in organizations? And how to do so safely, which is to say with relative predictability? Examples include:

- An executive succession design, beginning with 500 system members in one large auditorium for about a week, and extending to many other contexts over several years.[20]
- An early QWL effort for an organization of 4,000, triggered by a survey and including many action-planning loops.[21]
- A multiyear effort in an R&D setting that influenced activities both small[22] as well as substantial,[23] and also saw a major product through to the marketplace—beyond that the effect culminated in setting-up the subsequent transformation of the structure and policies of that R&D enterprise.[24]
- The design, construction, and operation of a mass urban transit system, from conceptual start-up through major operating milestones.[25]
- Establishing a new culture in a growing organization, encompassing numerous activities[26] which peaked in a worldwide strategic planning exercise for the top 70 or so corporate actors.[27]

Although satisfying in deep ways, these personal experiences—both subsystemic and system-wide—implied their own stucknesss: What of their generalizability? The experiences illustrated above proved generally positive, while also establishing that nothing lasts forever. If fade-out came, however, it tended to do so after such extended-enough periods as to warrant substantial optimism about effects. But how much of this was generalizable, and how much was episodic or *sui generis?*

Estimating Success Rates

Hence the efforts to challenge stuckness in a transpersonal way: A series of success rate studies which strongly supported the generalizability of OD effects. This held for a smallish batch of public-sector OD applications[28] as well as for a batch of over 200 cases.[29] The general conclusion also held for evaluative studies in different arenas: for over 500 business applications in Western settings;[30] for 100 cases in cross-cultural settings,[31] if to a somewhat less degree; as well as for a small batch of applications in economically-deprived settings.[32] Later, with greater attention to the methodological rigor of evaluative studies, substantial success also characterized 231 QWL applications, most in business,[33] but with over two score in public settings.[34]

This summary record gets support from almost all other evaluative studies, in addition.[35] Our populations are larger, in general; and recently we have paid more attention to methodological and design rigor than others. But our bottom-line and theirs is the same.

Encompassing Plural Change

In turn, these estimates generated a fifth progress/stuckness cycle. Thus, I publicly puzzled[36] over the early general silence that greeted several of these estimates, especially during 1980-1985. One possible reason for the general silence has an ironic twist. In effect, we hoisted ourselves on our own petard in a critical regard.

To explain, an earlier analysis of a deviant case in an OD application had led us to postulate a trinitarian model of change.[37] Given the usual view of change—which we label *alpha*—a particular intervention had failed. Alpha occurs along relatively stable intervals assessing some persisting domain: it is change of degree with no change of state.

Because participants persisted in insisting on the broad success of that intervention, we came to believe "the problem" could reside in an inadequate concept of change. Hence our test for gamma change, which proposes that both intervals *and* state have changed. Beta change is intermediate in ways that can be neglected here.

Conventional measurement approaches *always* will miss gamma and, although this raises deep concerns about a vast range of research and its interpretations, the trinitarian concept of change has been accepted in principle. Thus publications for specialists usually note the concept[38] as do introductory texts.[39]

A substantial and growing volume of research also takes trinitarian change into account, as the survey by Tennis[40] shows, but references often have an "excuse me" quality, as in research reports that hedge interpretations of their results. In common, they explain what could have been done—and perhaps should have been done—but must nonetheless remain for others to do.

This conceptual acceptance fascinates and even amazes me,[41] but let me dwell on a single consequence of that acceptance. Bluntly, if plural change does apply, we created a really unexpected learning opportunity for ourselves as well as others. Consider the horns of the dilemma.

Horn 1:   Absent a demonstration of alpha-only change, no T_1 vs. T_2 comparison is strictly interpretable. This has the effect of saying that most pieces of OD research—*as well as all other pre/post comparisons in the field or in the laboratory!*—constitute ugly babies. For no one had previously tested for alpha-only, although the general issue bothered many observers. Moreover, if gamma change had occurred, there was no systematic way to establish the direction of the change. This is inelegant, because OD sees gamma as an ideal—as in creating a new and better social order at work.

Horn 2:   Our success-rate surveys of planned change did not (and could not) test for alpha-only, and hence our interpretation begged the very issue we surfaced in the concept of plural change. As the rap artist would declare: "That's cold, man."

For these and related reasons, the progress represented by trinitarian change—and I believe it to be fundamental—generated real problems. Some ODers despaired, publicly and in-print. We sought another way out of another stuckness.

Validating Phase Model of Burnout

In seeking a directional indicator of change, we struck what appears to be a rich vein for analysis and application. The search was deliberate, but began with faint heart. For we considered our first several foci as throw-aways, as a kind of warm-up for the serious analysis to come.

One of those ostensible throw aways involves "burnout," and either our presumption was very wrong or we continue to waste much time and energy. Five years have passed, a small mountain of publications has accumulated,[42] and the theoretical network continues to expand.

Although burnout seemed to mean everything to everybody and hence we doubted at first that it could mean anything very specific to anyone, we have come to view the phase model of burnout as a kind of centroid in nature. Four related features contribute to this expansive conclusion.

First, the model permits an explicit estimate of who has how much of "it," which makes the phases a rare if not unique measure of experienced stress. This improves on the typical operational definitions of stress or burnout, which deal with stressors rather than experienced strain. Among other limitations, the usual formulations neglect the crucial fact that one person's stressors can be another's motivators.

Moreover, the phase model implies a clear direction: Phase I is best, and Phase VIII is worst. As noted, our early estimates of gamma change lacked this felicitous feature.

In addition, for over 300 variables assessed so far, the phases tend to covary directly and significantly—phase by phase—with growing deficits or deficiencies. Thus, those in Phase I have higher job satisfaction than those in II, IIs report higher scores than IIIs, and so on. Exceptions exist, but few of them.

Finally, early analysis suggests that movement to advanced phases serves as a surrogate for gamma change,[43] for both individuals and collections. By definition, all burnout measures should contain at least one gamma change— that is, that between some and no burnout. Early research suggests the phase model meets this requirement, and more.[44]

However, this promising progress suggests its own potential stucknesses. In a research sense, the debate has begun about whether the phases are superior to other similar operational definitions. Our research teams are asking this central question;[45] and so are others. On balance, today we see the phase model as superior to several dozen variants, but others are not convinced[46] or remain outright skeptical,[47] and that is fair enough. We may all see.

In more complex senses, the phase model implies significant practical questions, as with regard to typical stress management workshops.[48] For example, is burnout, as the phase model requires, basically environmental and group-based? If so, experiences for intact work teams are indicated, but virtually all stress management workshops are for "strangers" who get individual inoculations, as it were, which do not and cannot reduce environmental stressors.

Relatedly, do the "wrong people" take stranger stress-management workshops? Ideally, persons with the most burnout (VI-VIIIs in the phase model) seem the most needful, but some evidence indicates attendees are largely those at low stages of burnout (I-IIIs in the phase model).

Finally, should the same workshop design be used for those in both more-and less-advanced phases of burnout? Very different needs and risks seem to characterize Is and VIIIs, but a generic stress management model tends to dominate.

So the several cycles of progress/stuckness still seem to be active in various ways and combinations. Work with burnout has clear implications for several of the cycles, and not only for plural change. Serious issues relate to appropriate learning designs, and hence to retooling for self and others. And tests of the phase model in increasingly-systemic applications also are needed.[49]

No wonder, then, that I see myself at mid-career.

SELF-PROFILE OF AN OD CONSULTANT

Research may proceed through additional stuckness/movement cycles, but I sense that my basic consulting style is quite firmly set, for good or ill. Hence the summary below. It has been shared in other forms,[50] but this consultant self-profile provides a kind of fore-and-aft perspective: it variously leaps from and contributes to the research cycles, and also is rooted in the personal orientations and choices with which this essay began. Moreover, a number of clients have reviewed the self-portrait below—both in action and in text.

Life-Training as Participant-Observer

I was born a more or less interstitial person, as the twig-bending sections reflect, and I consider the associated experiences to have been valuable in generally allowing me to make my way in organizations without being captured by them. The overall sense of it is being "in" an organization enough to understand, appreciate, learn from, and even intimately share in its culture, but not so much "of" an organization as to be a blind defender.

Perhaps even more important is the comfort in this interstitiality—no, make that joy and even freedom. Why? I typically derive great pleasure from observing myself and others, perhaps because I was always in multiple cultures, and perhaps because I am less likely to see any one as somehow sacred and thus nonobservable and immutable. Intellectually and viscerally, membership in multiple cultures seems to me a major guarantor of individual and collective freedom. The sense of simultaneity is especially delicate and delicious when there are strong pressures to respond to a single culture. I recall the preparation for a major football game. I joined in the spirit-building and tension arousal, but I also pasted the poem "Trees" by Emily Dickinson into my helmet. Often, but secretly, I compared its quiet stimulation with the boisterousness surrounding me and my teammates.

This bias toward developing and maintaining an independent-but-rooted frame of reference seems to me critical in process consulting relationships, if only because the consultant should be the most free to note that the organizational king is naked. The associated risks involve being seen as too clinical, or too distant, or both.

Our older daughter also sees other elementals at work. "Let's face it," she observes. "You're also naturally a very critical kind of guy, very self-convinced, and with what I perceive as a bit of the old chip-on-the-shoulder because of basic conflicts with some of the groups in which you've found yourself."

Moral Priority of Organizations and Institutions

According organizations a moral priority also implies the high worth of individuals, since I believe individuality can be realistically pursued by almost all people only in institutional contexts. For a few, life may perhaps be individualistic in the classic sense, but I seriously doubt this romantic option exists for very many.

A major derivative implication requires direct statement. I am deeply suspicious of this reaction to any institution or organization: "Anything would be better." This is a powerful tether on my consultative grasp, not to mention my reach.

Early experiences sketched above no doubt condition this bias concerning institutions and their underlying authority. For example, my mother and I concluded I would be a different person had my father, a towering and determined patriarch, lived beyond my childhood. Competition with a client over authority, whether overt or covert, might be more common for a consultant with a more eventful early history over such issues. I am often seen as confronting authority but (I like to believe) for the purpose of generally reinforcing it by modelling useful values for both superiors and subordinates in organizations.

I do react strongly to authority figures I perceive as misusing or corrupting their power, and thus as violating my central expectations and hopes about the general constructiveness of authority relationships. As a consultant, I seek to help inhibit such violations, or to remedy them as soon after the fact as possible.

Expectations About Ineffectiveness, Corruption

All organizations are ineffectual in variable degree, and some become unredemptively corrupt. So most organizations have to be preserved *and* saved from themselves, even at their best; but some deserve quick burials.

The ideal involves intervening before organizations cross that crucial line between needing renewal and requiring rebellion, and a high priority therefor goes to the care and feeding of semideviants. These are resource persons who are not so alienated from an institution as to be ineffective, but who are insulated enough from true believership that they can meaningfully work toward a vision of the possible that includes the existing, but yearns far beyond it. The central philosophical posture is a substantial tolerance for differences: Today's curiosity may provide tomorrow's innovative direction.

The personal ties seem obvious to me. I am one of those semideviants, and our work essentially deals with diagnosing and prescribing relevant to that crucial line described above.

Bounded Enthusiasm re Human Perfectibility

The view that improvement constitutes the essential human challenge, but that it often must be incremental and temporary, may be classified as fatalism or realism. Operationally, for me, learning and change may for a time describe an accelerating curve, but soon the appropriate symbol is a plateau for rest and consolidation, which may serve as a foundation for further learning. The basic trick is to keep this learning curve from retrogressing over the long run, or from stabilizing too soon or at too low a level.

My consulting self presses for early locating of both individuals and (more tentatively) of systems of individuals on their stepwise learning curves. Sometimes individuals and organizations are in a kind of "parking orbit"; and sometimes they are moving toward higher or lower levels of competence and insight, or seem ready to do so.

In general, I prefer situations with a strong potential for accelerated change or learning, as at the start-up of a management team—a take-off point, or a fall-flat point.

Elitism, with Pluralist and Populist Tendencies

This fifth operating belief amalgamates two tendencies in tension. Thus, small minorities tend to account for a disproportionate share of the good as well as the mischief in the world. Indeed, the world seems fundamentally shaped by elites along a huge range of criteria.

However, the world also is (and should be) ineluctably pluralist—as in implementation, which often can be provided only by broad ranges of participants in a social system. In an elemental sense, then, complex social systems should be open to populist inputs. Broad ranges of participants in any social system may be aroused only episodically, but that arousal is best allowed early expression lest it build to explosive levels. For this and other reasons, I hold as a basic good the active involvement of increasing ranges of participants in increasingly broad arenas of the governance of systems.

Determined Centrist Tendencies

The tensions above get reflected when I behave like a "determined centrist." That is, I seek to amalgamate and integrate a widening array of approaches, to seek doggedly the central commonalities or compatibilities of numerous approaches.

This exercise in balance has its costs. Life can be a bit unpredictable for the client; I may be stamped as a shallow generalist; and trying to explain to my mother what her son does as a consultant was certainly difficult.

Encompassing the Triad

I hesitate in, but do not desist from, reiterating here that effective consultation must in the long run include emphasis on a "managerial triad." This triad includes: interpersonal and intergroup interaction; organization policies, procedures, and structure; as well as technology and its impact on jobs, structures, and so on.

Many observers trace the common neglect of the triad to philosophical and life-style differences between two clusters of specialists whom the vernacular differentiates as "pushers-shovers" and "touchers-feelers." Oversimply, perhaps, each camp often seeks to protect itself against contamination by the other, but in my view thereby limits itself in a basic way.

Bias Toward Prevention

It is a useful simplification that most clients regard ODers as specialists for bringing together that which is at odds, due to misunderstandings, conflicts, and so on. As such, the integrative specialist is kept "out of the action," to be called on only when things go sour enough. The implied role is remedial or palliative, as opposed to preventative—on remedying negative consequences rather than on helping set up policies, procedures, relationships, or structures that can reduce the probability of dour consequences.

I resist specialization in being "facilitative only," despite its usefulness in many cases. It can make the consultant a mere safety valve, a dispenser of Band-Aids after-the-fact. Such a role also is fraught with professional and ethical problems. Prevention seems to me at least as significant as being facilitative or palliative, and often is more strategic.

A TENTATIVE SYNTHESIS

My life—in family as well as in research and consulting—seems to me to put into increasingly-congruent action the choices and orientations sketched above. If that sounds like I am contented-in-action, that is just how I feel most of the time.

These choices and orientations provide the basic direction and momentum for searching and fine-tuning. For example, if in surprising form, the children of my early meadowlands promise seem to me everywhere in my research and consultation, which often deal with organizational pollution control! Similarly, my early orientation to science and a later humanistic consciousness get dual reflection in action-research. Relately, my "ease" with authority seems to me to relate directly to many of my later interests, especially in consulting. And the significance of community—as both means and end—seems patent to me in both familial and professional activities.

In sum, the twig-bending seems to have clear and direct consequences, but the ways in which these basic thrusts get elaborated can surprise me, and even astound. By good fortune, dumb luck, substantial persistence, and even a bit of conscious design now and again, a trinity has substantially "come together." Personal orientations, research, and consultation have developed a kind of symbiosis or synergy. I am more and more doing what I like to do, perhaps what I even have to do. Hence there usually is no sense of effort or "pushing." My visitors can find me singing at my writing table—like now, as this essay reaches its end.

PUBLICATIONS

1958

A taxonomic approach to state political party strength. *Western Political Quarterly, 11*(3), 494-513.

1959

The small group and public administration. *Public Administration Review, 19*(2), 149-156.

1960

O & M and the small group. *Public Administration Review, 20*(3), 205-212.
The group basis of politics: Notes on analysis and development. *American Political Science Review, 54*(4), 962-971.
The Trenton milk contract. Inter-University Case Program, University, AL: University of Alabama Press.

1961

Management science and group behavior: Work-unit cohesiveness. *Journal of the Academy of Management, 4*(3), 87-99.

On authority in organizations. *Public Administration Review, 21*(2), 715-717.
On the fallacy of "Idea A." *American Political Science Review, 55*(4), 885-886.
Three styles of leadership and their uses. *Personnel, 348*(4), 34-45.
Toward the new organization theories: Some notes on staff. *Midwest Journal of Political Science, 5*(3), 237-259.

1962

Behavior and organization: O & M and the small group. Chicago: Rand-McNally.
The small group: An analysis of research concepts and operations. Chicago: University of Chicago Press.
Civil service and managing work: Some unintended consequences. *American Political Science Review, 56*(4), 961-973.
Organization as a moral problem. *Public Administration Review, 22*(1), 51-58.
Organizing work: Techniques and theories. *Advanced Management-Office Executive, 1*(6), 26-31.

1963

A behavioral approach to wage administration: Work flow and structural design. *Journal of the Academy of Management, 6*, 367-377.
Is personnel management bankrupt?: Theories and practice. *The Personnel Administrator, 8*, 18-34.
Motivation. In C. Heyel (Ed.), *The encyclopedia of management* (pp. 546-568). New York: Reinhold.
Organization structure and the new accountacy: One avenue of revolution. *Quarterly Review of Economics and Business, 3*, 29-40.
The assignment problem: Managing a management course. *Journal of the Academy of Management, 8*, 18-32.
Theory Y: A big change in purchasing management? *Purchasing, 55*, 68-71, 136.

1964

Accountacy as a function of organization theory. *The Accounting Review, 39*, 333-341.
Authority as a problem in overlays: A concept for analysis and action. *Administrative Science Quarterly, 9*, 23-49.
Innovation and organization structure. *Personnel Administration, 27*(3-4), 17-21.

Toward the management sciences: Methodological directions for public administration. *International Review of Administrative Sciences, 30*(2), 113-123.

1965

Men, management and morality: Toward a new organizational ethic. New York: McGraw-Hill.

Small groups and large organizations. In J.G. March (Ed.), *Handbook of Organizations* (pp. 87-141). Chicago: Rand-McNally.

Specialist or generalist? Structure as a crucial factor. *Public Administration Review, 25*, 135-141.

1966

With F. Gibson & G.Y. Cornog (Eds.). (1966, 1972, 1976, 1983). *Public administration: Readings in institutions, processes and behavior.* Chicago: Rand-McNally.

Personality and organization structure: Staff models and behavioral patterns. *Journal of the Academy of Management, 9*, 217-232.

Recent programs in industry and government designed to develop human potentialities. In H.R. Otto (Ed.), *Explorations in human potentialities* (pp. 505-519). New York: Charles C. Thomas.

1967

Organizing men and power: Patterns of behavior and line-staff models. Chicago: Rand-McNally.

With F. Gibson (Eds.). *Managerial behavior and organization demands: Management as a linking of levels of interaction.* Chicago: Rand-McNally.

A new "staff" model: A synthesis from behavioral research. In R.T. Golembiewski & F. Gibson (Eds.), *Managerial behavior and organization demands: Management as a linking of levels of interaction* (pp. 296-315). Chicago: Rand-McNally.

The laboratory approach to organization change: The schema of a method. *Public Administration Review, 27*(5), 21-30.

With A. Blumberg. Confrontation as a training design in complex organizations: Attitudinal changes in a diversified population of managers. *Journal of Applied Behavioral Science, 3*(4), 524-547.

With A. Blumberg. Training and relational learning: The confrontation design. *Training and Development Journal, 21*(10), 35-43.

1968

With J. Rabin (Eds.), *Public budgeting and finance: Readings in theory and practice.* Itasca, IL: F.E. Peacock. (Reprinted 1975)
Perspectives on public management: Cases and learning designs. Itasca, IL: F.E. Peacock. (Reprinted 1976)
Bear Clay's body. In R.T. Golembiewski (Ed.), *Perspectives on public management: Cases and learning designs* (pp. 228-241). Itasca, IL: F.E. Peacock.
Individual freedom in organizations: Some guidelines and one approach. Northern Illinois University, *Business Report, 5*(3), 30-48.
Integrating small behavioral groups into large organizations: Existing research as past and prologue. In B.P. Indik & R. Berrigan (Eds.), *People, groups, and organizations* (pp. 128-153). New York: Teachers College Press, Columbia University.
With A. Blumberg. The laboratory approach to organization development: The confrontation design. *Journal of the Academy of Management, 11*(3), 199-211.

1969

With W. Welsh, & W. Crotty. *A methodological primer for political scientists.* Chicago: Rand-McNally.
Laboratory goal attainment and the problem analysis questionnaire. *Journal of Applied Behavioral Science, 4*(4), 592-600.
Organization development in public agencies: Perspectives on theory and practice. *Public Administration Review, 29*(4), 367-377.
Organization patterns of the future: What they mean for personnel administration. *Personnel Administration, 32*(4), 8-24.
With A. Blumberg. Persistence of attitudinal changes induced by a confrontation design: A research note. *Journal of the Academy of Management, 12*(3), 309-318.
With A. Blumberg. Sensitivity training in cousin groups: A confrontation design. *Training and Development Journal, 23*(8), 18-23.

1970

With A. Blumberg (Eds.). *Sensitivity training and the laboratory approach: Readings about concepts and applications.* Itasca, IL: F.E. Peacock.
With C. Bullock & H. Rodgers (Eds.). The new politics: Polarization or utopia? New York: McGraw-Hill.
With M. Cohen (Eds.), *People in public service: A reader in public personnel administration.* Itasca, IL: F.E. Peacock.

Introduction. In B.W. Hawkins & R. Lorinskas (Eds.). *The ethnic factor in american politics* (pp. i-xxv). Columbus, OH: Merill.

Organizational properties and managerial learning: Testing alternative models of attitudinal change. *Academy of Management Journal, 13*(1), 13-31.

Planned organizational change: A major emphasis in a behavioral approach to public administration. In M. Haas & H. Kariel (Eds.), *Approaches to the study of political science* (pp. 394-421). San Francisco: Chandler.

With S.B. Carrigan. Planned change in organization style based on laboratory approach. *Administrative Science Quarterly, 15*(1), 79-93.

With S.B. Carrigan. The persistence of laboratory-induced changes in organization styles. *Administrative Science Quarterly, 15*(3), 330-340.

1971

With R. Munzenrider, A. Blumberg, S.B. Carrigan, & W.R. Mead. Changing climate in a complex organization: Interactions between a learning design and an environment. *Journal of the Academy of Management, 14*(4), 465-481.

1972

Renewing organizations: The laboratory approach to planned change for individuals and groups. Itasca, IL: F.E. Peacock.

A planned change in organization style: Underlying theory and some results. In J.A. LaPonce & P. Smoker (Eds.), *Simulation and Experimentation in Political Science* (pp. 369-408). Vancouver, B.C.: University of Vancouver Press.

Some problems of behavioral research in accountancy. In T. Burns (Ed.), *Proceedings of the Symposium on Accountancy* (pp. 336-346). Columbus: College of Administrative Sciences, Ohio State University.

With S.B. Carrigan, W.R. Mead, R. Munzenrider, & A. Blumberg. Integrating disrupted work relationships. In W.W. Burke (Ed.), *Contemporary organization development: Conceptual orientations and applications* (pp. 224-240). Washington, DC: NTL Institute for Applied Behavioral Science.

With S.B. Carrigan, W.R. Mead, R. Munzenrider, & A. Blumberg. Toward building new work relationships: An action design for a critical intervention. *Journal of Applied Behavioral Science, 8*(3), 135-148.

1973

With M. Moore & J. Rabin (Eds.). *Dilemmas of political participation: Issues for thought and simulations for action.* Englewood Cliffs, NJ: Prentice-Hall.

With M. White (Eds.). *Cases in public management*. Chicago: Rand-McNally.
With S.B. Carrigan. Planned change through laboratory methods: Toward building organizations to order. *Training and Development Journal, 27*(2), 18-27.
With S.B. Carrigan & A. Blumberg. More on building new work relationships. *Journal of Applied Behavioral Science, 9*(1), 26-28.
With R.F. Munzenrider. Persistence and change: A note on the long-term effects of an organization development program. *Journal of the Academy of Management, 16*(1), 149-154.

1974

"Maintenance" and "task" as central challenges in public administration. *Public Administration Review, 34*(1), 168-176.
Public administration as a field: Four developmental phases. *Georgia Political Science Association Journal, 1*(1), 21-50.
Toward tomorrow's organization development. In J.D. Adams, (Ed.), *Theory and method in organization development: An evolutionary process* (pp. 85-118). Washington, DC: NTL Institute for Applied Behavioral Science.
With P. Browne. Line-staff concept revisited: An empirical study of organizational images. *Academy of Management Journal, 17*(3), 405-417.
With R. Hilles & M. Kagno. A longitudinal study of flexi-time effects: Some consequences of an OD structural intervention. *Journal of Applied Behavioral Science, 10*(4), 503-532.

1975

With R.N. Spadaro, T.R. Dye, M.S. Stedman, & L.H. Ziegler. *The policy vacuum: Toward a more professional political science*. Lexington, MA: Lexington Books.
Public administration and public policy: An analysis of developmental phases. In R.N. Spadaro, T.R. Dye, R.T. Golembiewski, M.S. Stedman, & L.H. Zeigler (Eds.), *The policy vacuum: Toward a more professional political science* (pp. 61-134). Lexington, MA: Lexington Books.
With M. McConkie. The centrality of interpersonal trust in group processes. In C.L. Cooper (Ed.), *Theories in group processes* (pp. 131-185). New York: Wiley.
With R.F. Munzenrider. Social desirability as an intervening variable in interpreting OD effects. *Journal of Applied Behavioral Science, 11*(3), 317-332.
With S. Yeager & R. Hilles. Factor analysis of some flexi-time effects: Attitudinal and behavioral consequences. *Academy of Management Journal, 18*(3), 500-509.

1976

With A. Blumberg. *Learning and change in groups: Processes, problems, and applications of laboratory education.* London: Penguin Books. (Reprinted 1978)

With K. Billingsley. A critical decision in survey/feedback designs: To identify respondents or no. *Group and Organization Studies, 1*(4), 448-454.

With K. Billingsley & S. Yeager. Measuring change and persistence in human affairs: Types of change generated by OD designs. *Journal of Applied Behavioral Science, 12*(2), 133-157.

With K. Billingsley & S. Yeager. The congruence of factorial structures: Comparisons of four procedures and their solutions. *Academy of Management Review, 1*(3), 27-35.

With R. Hilles & S. Yeager. Some attitudinal and behavioral consequences of a flexi-time installation: One avenue for expressing central OD values. In D.P. Slevin & R.H. Kilmann (Eds.), *The management of organization design: Research and methodology* (pp. 87-120). New York: Elsevier-North Holland.

With A. Kiepper. MARTA: Toward an effective, open giant. *Public Administration Review, 36*(1), 46-60.

1977

Public administration as a developing discipline: Perspectives on past and present. New York: Marcel Dekker.

Public administration as a developing discipline: OD as one of a future family of mini-paradigms. New York: Marcel Dekker.

A critique of "Democratic Administration" and its supporting ideation. *American Political Science Review, 17*(4), 1488-1507.

Observations on "doing political theory." *American Political Science Review, 17*(4), 1526-1532.

Testing some stereotypes about the sexes in organizations: Differential centrality of work. *Human Resource Management, 16*, 21-24.

Testing some stereotypes about the sexes in organizations: Differential satisfaction with work. *Human Resource Management, 16*(2), 30-32.

With K. Billingsley & R.F. Munzenrider. Electoral choice and individual characteristics: Toward a bio-data approach. *Journal of Political Science, 4*(1), 118-133.

With R. Hilles. Flexi-time in a large firm: The first six months. *Monthly Labor Review, 100*(2), 56-59.

With R. Hilles & M. Kagno. Flexi-time and some of its consequences: A modest structural intervention. In W.W. Burke (Ed.), *Current issues and strategies in organization development* (pp. 384-423). New York: Human Sciences Press.

With R.F. Munzenrider. Some managerially-relevant covariants of hierarchical status. *Administration and Society, 9*(2), 3-12.

With S. Yeager. Fine-tuning survey/feedback interventions: Differentiating respondents in terms of performance appraisals. In R.L. Taylor et al. (Eds.), *Proceedings, 1977 Annual Meeting, Academy of Management* (pp. 348-352).

With C.C. Cotton & P.J. Browne. Marginality and the OD practitioner. *Journal of Applied Behavioral Science, 13*(4), 493-506.

1978

With W.B. Eddy (Eds.). *Organization development in public administration: OD properties and public sector features.* New York: Marcel Dekker.

With W.B. Eddy (Eds.). *Organization development in public administration: Public sector applications of OD technology.* New York: Marcel Dekker.

The small group in political science: The last two decades of development. Athens, GA: University of Georgia Press.

With F. Gibson & G.J. Miller (Eds.). *Managerial behavior and organization demands: Management as a linking of levels of interaction.* Itasca, IL: F.E. Peacock.

Managing the tension between OD principles and political dynamics. In W.W. Burke (Ed.), *The cutting edge: Current theory and practice in organization development* (pp. 27-46). La Jolla, CA: University Associates.

Mid-life transition and mid-career change: A special opportunity for a cooperative humanism. *Public Administration Review, 38*(3), 215-222.

Some correlates of commuting time. *Southern Review of Public Administration, 2*(3), 122-143.

The non-attitude hypothesis and types of change. *Georgia Political Science Association Journal, 6*(3), 103-111.

With C.W. Proehl, Jr. A survey of the empirical literature on flexible workhours: Character and consequences of major innovation. *Academy of Management Review, 3*(3), 837-853.

With F. Rauschenberg. Third-party consultation: Principles and a case study of their violation. In R.T. Golembiewski & W. Eddy (Eds.), *Organization development in public administration: Public sector applications of OD technology* (pp. 118-128). New York: Marcel Dekker.

With S. Yeager. Employee surveys and a revolution of rising expectations: Do the wrong people ask for too much? *Group & Organization Studies, 3*(1), 24-29.

With S. Yeager. Testing the applicability of the JDI to various demographic groupings. *Academy of Management Journal, 21*, 514-519.

1979

Approaches to planned change: Orienting perspectives and micro-level interventions (Vol. 1). New York: Marcel Dekker.

Approaches to planned change: Macro-level interventions and change-agent strategies (Vol. 2). New York: Marcel Dekker.

With R. Hilles. *Toward the responsive organization: The theory and practice of survey/feedback.* Salt Lake City, UT: Brighton Publishing.

Is flexi-time for employees "hard time" for supervisors?: Two sources of data rejecting the proposition. *Journal of Management, 5*(3), 241-259.

OD interventions in urban settings, I: Public-sector constraints on planned change. *International Journal of Public Administration, 1*(1), 1-30.

Perspectives on the growth and development of organizations: SPSA as a specific case of choice and transition. *Journal of Politics, 41*(3), 335-360.

Some perspectives on one consulting style. In D.P. Sinha (Ed.), *Consultants and Consulting Styles* (pp. 171-186). New Delhi, India: Vision Books.

The near-future of graduate PA programs: Some program minima, their common violation, and some priority palliatives. *Southern Review of Public Administration, 3*(4), 323-359.

With D. Sink. OD interventions in urban settings, II: Public-sector success with planned change. *International Journal of Public Administration, 1*(2), 115-141.

With J.B. Trattner & G.J. Miller. Developing an arbitration process for resolving contract disputes. *The Arbitration Journal, 34*, 14-24.

1980

Infusing organizations with OD values: Public-sector approaches to structural change. *Southern Review of Public Administration, 4*(3), 269-302.

Golembiewski, R.T. Organization development in industry: Perspectives on two cycles of progress/stuckness. In P.B. Smith (Ed.), *Small groups and personal change* (pp. 194-221). London: Methuen.

Public-sector productivity and flexible workhours: Testing three points of the common wisdom re OD. *Southern Review of Public Administration, 4*(3), 324-339.

With K. Billingsley. Measuring change in OD panel designs. *Academy of Management Review, 5*(1), 97-103.

With A. Blumberg. Training and relational learning: The confrontation design. *Training and Developmental Journal, 70*(6), 70-73.

With R.G. Fox. Diagnosis, design, and in-process adaptation in an R&D organization. In P.R. Mico (Ed.), *Visions of Tomorrow/Actions of Today* (pp. 247-254). Plainfield, NJ: Organization Development Network.

With R.G. Fox & C.W. Proehl, Jr. Flexitime: The supervisors' verdict. *The Wharton Magazine, 4*(3), 73.

With G.J. Miller. Sensitivity training. In R. Herink (Ed.), *The Psychotherapy Handbook* (pp. 652-655). New York: Meridian Books.

With C.W. Proehl, Jr. Public-sector applications of flexible workhours: A review of available experience. *Public Administration Review, 40*, 72-85.

1981

Mass transit management: Case studies of the Metropolitan Atlanta Rapid Transit Authority. Final report, U.S. Department of Transportation, Urban Mass Transportation Administration, University Research and Training Program.

Approaches to organizing. Washington, D.C.: American Society for Public Administration.

Reinforcing a reasonable caution and responding to it. *Public Administration Review, 41*(5), 603-604.

A third mode of coupling democracy and administration: Another way of making a crucial point. *International Journal of Public Administration, 3*(4), 423-454.

Small group analysis in political behavior: Perspectives on significance and stuckness. *Micropolitics, 1*(3), 295-319.

Testing for demographic covariants of a decay rate in long-run effects of flexible workhours programs. *Southern Review of Public Administration, 5*(2), 200-209.

The ideational poverty of two modes of coupling democracy and administration. *International Journal of Public Administration, 3*(1), 1-65.

With G.J. Miller. Small groups in political science: Perspectives on significance and stuckness. In S.L. Long (Ed.), *The handbook of political behavior* (Vol. 1, pp. 1-71). New York: Plenum Press.

With R.F. Munzenrider. Efficacy of three versions of one burn-out measure: The MBI as total score, sub-scale scores, or phases? *Journal of Health and Human Resources Administration, 4*(2), 228-246.

With C.W. Proehl, Jr. & D. Sink. Success of OD applications in the public sector: Toting-up the score for a decade, more or less. *Public Administration Review, 41*(6), 679-682.

1982

Do flexible workhour effects decay over time? Some warning signals and five remedial suggestions. *Public Productivity Review, 6*(3), 35-46.

Isolating some elements of victory from defeat too easily acknowledged. *Journal of Applied Behavioral Science, 18*(1), 143-148.

Organizational development (OD) interventions: Changing interaction, structures, and policies. In W.S. Paine (Ed.), *Job stress and burnout* (pp. 229-253). Los Angeles, CA: Sage.

The demotion design: An option for forward-looking organizations. *National Productivity Review, 2*(1), 63-70.

Toward democracy within and through administration: A primer to inspire and guide OD applications. In J.A. Uveges (Ed.), *Annals of public administration*, Vol. 1. *History and theory in contemporary perspective* (pp. 55-84). New York: Marcel Dekker.

With R. Hilles. Drug company workers like new schedules. In U.S. Department of Labor, Labor-Management Services Administration, *Labor-management cooperation: Recent efforts and results* (LMSA Publication 6) (pp. 80-83). Washington, DC: U.S. Government Printing Office.

With C.W. Proehl Jr. & D. Sink. Estimating the success of OD applications. *Training and Development Journal, 72*, 86-95.

1983

With J. Rabin (Eds.). *Public budgeting and finance: Behavioral, theoretical, and technical perspectives.* New York: Marcel Dekker.

Health care and organization development: In search of the ultimate treatment. *Journal of Health and Human Resources Administration, 6*(2), 4-22.

Investing in planned change in the energy industry: Features and consequences of OD approaches. *The Journal of Canadian Petroleum Technology, 22*(1), 83-87.

Professionalization, performance, and protectionism: A contingency view. *Public Productivity Review, 7*(3), 251-268.

Social desirability and change in organizations: Some surprising results and conceptual musings. *Review of Business and Economic Research, 18*(3), 9-20.

Structuring the public organization. In W.B. Eddy (Ed.), *Handbook on public organization management* (pp. 193-225). New York: Marcel Dekker.

Toward guiding small group research without hobbling it. *Politics and the Life Sciences, 2*(3), 23-26.

Two kind of romantics in planned organizational change: Insufficient inclusion or awkward exclusion? *Dialogue, 5*(3), 1-5.

With A. Kiepper. Lessons from a fast-paced public project: Perspectives on doing better the next-time around. *Public Administration Review, 43*(5), 547-556.

With A. Kiepper. Organizational transition in a fast-paced public project: Personal perspectives of MARTA executives. *Public Administration Review, 43*(3), 246-254.

With R.F. Munzenrider. Testing three phase models of burn-out: Mappings on a cluster of worksite descriptors. *Journal of Health and Human Resources Administration, 5*(1), 374-392.

With R.F. Munzenrider, & D. Carter. Phases of progressive burn-out and their worksite covariants. *Journal of Applied Behavioral Science, 19*(4), 461-482.

With M. Scicchitano. Some demographics of psychological burn-out. International *Journal of Public Administration, 5*(4), 435-447.

1984

With A. Wildavsky (Eds.). *The costs of federalism: A tribute to James W. Fesler.* New Brunswick, NJ: Transaction.

With M. Cohen (Eds.). *Public personnel update.* New York: Marcel Dekker.

Organizing public work, round three: Toward a balance of political agendas and management perspectives. In R.T. Golembiewski & A. Wildavsky (Eds.), *The costs of federalism* (pp. 237-269). New Brunswick, NJ: Transaction.

The pace and character of public-sector professionalization: Six selected questions. *State and Local Government Review, 16*(3), 63-68.

With R.F. Munzenrider. Active and passive reactions to psychological burn-out: Toward greater specificity in a phase model. *Journal of Health and Human Resources Administration, 7*(3), 264-289.

With R.F. Munzenrider. Phases of psychological burn-out and organizational covariants: A replication using norms from a large population. *Journal of Health and Human Resources Administration, 6*(3), 290-323.

With W.L. Tanner. One perspective on "Democracy vs. Efficiency": The laboratory approach as a model for testing mutuality. *International Journal of Public Administration, 6,* 125-149.

1985

Humanizing public organizations: Perspectives on doing better-than-average when average ain't at all bad. Mt. Airy, MD: Lomond Publications, Inc.

Dealing with burn-out: Emerging realities and challenges. *Corporate Commentary, 1*(5), 7-14.

Enriching the theory and practice of team-building: Instrumentation for diagnosis and alternatives for design. In D.D. Warrick (Ed.), *Contemporary Organization Development* (pp. 98-113). Glenview, IL: Scott, Foresman.

Performance appraisal and burn-out: Testing an extension of the phase model. In C. Aaron Kelley (Ed.), *Proceedings, 1985 Annual Meeting, Southwestern Academy of Management* (pp. 168-172).

With R.F. Munzenrider & M. Rahimi. Social desirability effects in simulated work teams. *International Journal of Public Administration, 7*, 1-20.
With R.F. Munzenrider & J.G. Stevenson. Profiling acute vs. chronic burn-out, I: Theoretical issues, a surrogate, and elemental distributions. *Journal of Health and Human Resources Administration, 7*(3), 107-125.

1986

With R.F. Munzenrider & J.G. Stevenson. *Stress in organizations: Research developments in mid-stream.* New York: Praeger.
Contours in social change: Elemental graphics and a surrogate variable for gamma change. *Academy of Management Review, 11*(3), 550-566.
Focusing executive power: Matching values with action. In S. Srivastva & Associates (Eds.), *Executive power: How executives influence people and organizations* (pp. 178-203). San Francisco, CA: Jossey-Bass.
Linking interaction and techno-structural emphases: A synthesis for high-performing organizations. *Public Administration Quarterly, 10*(2), 138-170.
OD perspectives on high performance: Some good news, some bad, about merit pay. *Review of Public Personnel Administration, 7*(33), 9-26.
Organization analysis and praxis: Prominences of progress and stuckness. In C.L. Cooper and I. Robertson (Eds.), *Review of industrial and organizational psychology* (pp. 279-304). London: Wiley.
Perspectives on teaching in the teeth of criticisms of the organizational sciences: Some personal reactions and an orientation for coping. *Exchange: Journal of the OB Teaching Society, 11*(1), 35-43.
"Promise not to tell": A critical view of confidentiality in consultation. *Consultation, 5*(2), 68-76.
The epidemiology of progressive burn-out: A primer. *Journal of Health and Human Resources Administration, 9*(2), 16-36.
With G.J. Deckard, & B.H. Rountree. Worksite features and progressive burn-out. *Journal of Health and Human Resources Administration, 9*(2), 38-55.
With R.F. Munzenrider. Profiling acute vs. chronic burn-out, II: Mappings on a panel of established covariants. *Journal of Health and Human Resources Administration, 8*, 296-315.
With R.F. Munzenrider. Profiling acute vs. chronic burn-out, III: Phases and life events impacting on patterns of covariants. *Journal of Health and Human Resources Administration, 9*(3), 173-184.

With B.H. Rountree. Phases of burn-out and properties of work environments: Replicating and extending a pattern of covariants. *Organization Development Journal, 9*(2), 25-30.

1987

Contextual specificity in consultation: Similarities and differences between public and private sectors. *Consultation, 6*(2), 90-101.

Counterpoint. Personnel Psychology, 40(3), 662-667.

Diagnosing health-care providers and their systems: An entry design and its supporting theory. *Consultation, 6*(4) 265-280.

Is OD narrowly culture-bound?: Prominent features of 100 third-world applications. *Organization Development Journal, 5*(4), 20-29.

Public sector management today: Advanced differentiation and early institutionalization. *Journal of Management, 13*(2), 323-338.

Public-sector organization: Why theory and practice should emphasize purpose, and how to do so. In R.C. Chandler (Ed.), *A Centennial History of the American Administrative State* (pp. 433-474). New York: Free Press.

Toward excellence in public management: Constraints on emulating America's best-run companies. In R.B. Denhardt & E.T. Jennings, Jr. (Eds.), *Toward A New Public Service* (pp. 177-198). Columbia, MO: University of Missouri Press.

With R. Hilles, & R. Daly. Some effects of multiple OD interventions on burnout and worksite features. *Journal of Applied Behavioral Science, 23*(3), 295-314.

With B.S. Kim. How the city manager sees self: Approaching the theory/ practice problem via burnout phases. *Dialogue, 9*(2), 59-70.

With R.F. Munzenrider. Profiling acute vs. chronic burnout, IV: Active vs. passive modes of adaptation. *Journal of Health and Human Resources Administration, 10*(3), 97-111.

1988

With A. Kiepper. *High performance and human costs: A public sector model of organization development.* New York: Praeger.

With R.F. Munzenrider. *Phases of burnout: Developments in concepts and applications.* New York: Praeger.

Issues and trends in public-sector OD: Doing smarter and better. In C.N. Jackson (Ed.), *Contracting for organization development* (pp. 83-86). Washington, DC: American Society for Training and Development.

OD applications in non-affluent settings: Four perspectives on critical action research. In P.N. Khandwalla (Ed.), *Social development: A New Role for the Organizational Sciences* (pp. 282-318). New Delhi, India: Sage.

Policy initiatives in worksite research: Implications from research on a phase model of burn-out. In R.M. Kelley (Ed.), *Promoting productivity in the public sector: Problems, strategies, and prospects* (pp. 209-227). New York: Macmillan.

Organization theory. In J. Rabin & M.B. Steinhauer (Eds.), *Handbook of health and human services administration* (pp. 11-43). New York: Marcel Dekker.

Working with teams in public and business sectors: Ways of dealing with major differences. In W.B. Reddy & K. Jamison (Eds.), *Team building: Blueprints for productivity and satisfaction* (pp. 124-133). Rosslyn, VA: NTL Institute for Applied Behavioral Science and University Associates.

With R.F. Munzenrider. Burnout as an indicator of gamma change, I: Methodological perspectives on a crucial surrogacy. *Journal of Health and Human Resources Administration, 11*(3), 218-248.

With R.F. Munzenrider & J.G. Stevenson. Centrality of burnout in a public agency: Multiple measurements supporting common conclusions. *Review of Public Personnel Administration, 9*(3), 28-47.

1989

Organization development: Ideas and issues. New Brunswick, NJ: Transaction.

A note on Leiter's study: Highlighting two models of burnout. *Group & Organization Studies, 14*(1), 5-14.

Anomie, resurgence, *and* opportunity: Reflections on the current state of the public service. *Public Administration Review, 49*(3), 287-290.

Burnout as a problem at work: Mapping its degree, duration, and consequences. *Journal of Managerial Issues, 1*(1), 86-97.

OD applications under economic deprivation. *Public Administration Quarterly, 13*, 31-65.

Strategy and structure. In J. Rabin, G.J. Miller, & W.B. Hildreth (Eds.), *Handbook on strategic management* (pp. 13-58). New York: Marcel Dekker.

The alpha, beta, gamma change typology: Personal reactions and progress. *Group & Organization Studies, 14*(2), 150-154.

The *Papers* and productivity: Posterity's guidance for today's challenges. *Public Productivity Review, 12*(1), 282-302.

Toward a positive and practical public management: Organizational research supporting a fourth critical citizenship. *Administration and Society, 21*(3), 200-227.

With R.A. Boudreau. Burnout and stress in American, Canadian, and Japanese work settings: Nomothetic and ideographic perspectives. *Kaihatsu Ronshu, 44*(3), 53-77.

With G.J. Deckard & B.H. Rountree. The stability of burnout assignments: Measurement properties of the phase model. *Journal of Health and Human Resources Administration, 12*(2), 63-78.

With B.S. Kim. Self-esteem and phases of burnout. *Organization Development Journal, 7*(1), 51-58.

With R.F. Munzenrider. Burnout as an indicator of gamma change, II: State-like differences between phases. *Journal of Health and Human Resources Administration, 12*(2), 245-260.

With K. Nethery, R. Hilles, and W. Shepherd. Using OD to enhance strategic planning. Organization Development Network, Annual Meeting, *Proceedings 1989*, San Diego, Ca.

With B.H. Rountree and G.J. Deckard. A causal path analysis of burnout and agitation: Human asset depletion in LTC settings. *Journal of Health and Human Resources Administration, 12*(2), 95-111.

With P. Scott. A micropolitical perspective on rational budgeting: A conjectural footnote on the dissemination of PPBS. *Public Budgeting and Financial Management, 1*(3), 327-370.

With B-C. Sun. Positive-findings bias in QWL research: A comparison of public and business sectors. *Public Productivity Review, 13*(4), 145-155.

1990

Ironies in organizational development. New Brunswick, NJ: Transaction.

Differences in burnout by sector: Public vs. business estimates using phases. *International Journal of Public Administration, 13*(4), 545-560.

Public-sector organization behavior and theory: Perspectives on nagging problems and on real progress. In N.B. Lynn and A. Wildavsky (Eds.), *Developments in Public Management* (pp. 127-156). Chatham, NJ: Chatham House.

With R.F. Munzenrider. Burnout as an indicator of gamma change, III: Differences of degree in worksite descriptors. *Journal of Health and Human Resources Administration, 13*(4), 509-523.

With B-C. Sun. Positive-findings bias in QWL studies. *Journal of Management, 16*(3), 665-674.

With B-C. Sun. QWL improves worksite quality: Success rates in a large panel of studies. *Human Resources Development Quarterly, 1*(1), 35-44.

With B-C. Sun. Situational features and QWL outcomes. *Consultation, 9*(3), 99-127.

1991

With R.F. Munzenrider. Alternative combinations of phases of burnout. *Journal of Health and Human Resources Administration, 13*(3), 489-507.

With K. Nethery, W. Shepherd, and R. Hilles. Enhancing worldwide strategic planning, part 1: An OD design and its theoretic rationale. *Organization Development Journal, 10*(3), 31-54.

With K. Nethery, W. Shepherd, and R. Hilles. Enhancing worldwide strategic planning, part 2: Some consequences at micro-and macro-levels. *Organization Development Journal, 10*(4), 57-65.

NOTES

1. "Introduction" (1970).
2. Ibid.
3. *Behavior and Organization* (1962).
4. *Men, Management and Morality* (1965, 1989); "Introduction" (1970).
5. For example, with Nethery, Hilles, and Shepard, "Using OD to Enhance Strategic Planning" (1989); Idem., "Enhancing Worldwide Strategic Planning, Part 1: An OD Design and Its Theoretical Rationale" (1991); Idem., "Enhancing Worldwide Strategic Planning, Part 2: Some Consequences at Micro- and Macro-Levels" (1991).
6. With Blumberg, "Training and Relational Learning: The Confrontation Design" (1967).
7. With Carrigan, "Planned Change in Organization Style Based on Laboratory Approach" (1970); Idem., "The Persistence of Laboratory-Induced Changes in Organization Styles" (1970).
8. See *Organization Development: Ideas and Issues* (1989, pp. 91-94).
9. Cotton, Browne, and Golembiewski, "Marginality and the OD Practitioner" (1977).
10. *Behavior and Organization: O&M and The Small Group* (1962); *The Small Group: An Analysis of Research Concepts and Operations* (1962); *Men, Management and Morality: Toward a New Organizational Ethic* (1965, 1989).
11. For example, *Perspectives on Public Management: Cases and Learning Designs* (1968, 1976); With Rabin, *Public Budgeting and Finance: Readings in Theory and Practice* (1968, 1975); With Cohen, *People in Public Service: A Reader in Public Personnel Administration* (1970, 1976); "Organization Structure and the New Accountancy: One Avenue of Revolution" (1963); "Theory Y: A Big Chance in Purchasing Management?" (1963); "Accoutancy as a Function of Organization Theory" (1964).
12. "Confrontation as a Training Design in Complex Organizations: Attitudinal Changes in Diversified Population of Managers" (1967); "Training and Relational Learning: The Confrontation Desiggn" (1967); "The Laboratory Approach to Organization Development: The Confrontation Design" (1968); "Planned Change in Organization Style Based on Laboratory Approach"(1970); "The Persistence of Laboratory-Induced Changes in Organization Style"(1970).
13. "Integrating Disrupted Work Relationships" (1972); "Toward Building New Work Relationships: An Action Design for a Critical Intervention" (1972).
14. *Sensitivity Training and the Laboratory Approach: Readings About Concepts and Applications* (1970, 1973, 1977).
15. Renewing Organizations: The Laboratory Approach to Planned Change for Individuals and Groups (1972); *Approaches to Planned Change: Orienting Perspectives and Micro-Level Interventions* (1979); *Approaches to Planned Change: Macro-Level Interventions and Change-Agent Strategies* (1979); *Learning and Change in Groups: Processes, Problems, and Applications of Laboratory Education* (1976, 1978).
16. *Public Administration as a Developing Discipline: Perspectives on Past and Present* (1977); *Public Administration as a Developing Discipline: OD as One of a Future Family of Mini-Paradigms* (1977); *Organization Development in Public Administration: OD Properties and Public Sector Features* (1978); *Organization Development in Public Administration: Public Sector Applications of OD Technologies* (1978).
17. "A Critical Decision in Survey/Feedback Designs: To Identify Respondents or No" (1976); *Toward the Responsive Organization: The Theory and Practice of Survey/Feedback* (1979, 1984).

18. "Changing Climate in a Complex Organization: Interactions Between a Learning Design and an Environment" (1971); "Enhancing Worldwide Strategic Planning, Part 1: An OD Design and Its Theoretic Rationale" (1991); "Enhancing Worldwide Strategic Planning, Part 2: Some Consequences at Micro- and Macro-Levels" (1991); *Organization development* (1989).

19. "Planned Change in Organization Stsyle Based on Laboratory Approach" (1970); "The Persistence of Laboratory—Induced Changes in Organization Styles" (1970); "Planned Change Through Laboratory Methods: Toward Building Organizations to Order" (1973); "Integrating Disrupted Work Relationships" (1972); "Toward Building New Work Relationships: An Action Design for a Critical Intervention" (1972); "Flexi-Time in a Large Firm: The First Six Months" (1977); "A Longitudinal Study of Flex-Time Effects: Some Consequences of an OD Structural Intervention" (1974).

20. For example, "Planned Change Through Laboratory Methods: Toward Building Organizations to Order" (1973); "More on Building New Work Relationships" (1973); *Approaches to Planned Change: Macro-Level Interventions and Change-Agent Strategies* (1979).

21. For example, "Changing Climate in a Complex Organization: Interactions Between a Learning Design and an Environment" (1971); *Toward the Responsive Organization: The Theory and Practice of Survey/Feedback* (1979, 1984); "A Longitudinal Study of Flexi-Time Effects: Some Consequences of an ODE Structural Intervention" (1974).

22. Ibid.

23. For example, *Approaches to Planned Change: Macro-Level Interventions and Change-Agent Strategies* (1979).

24. For example, "Diagnosis, Design, and In-Process Adaptation in an R&D Organization" (1980).

25. For example, "MARTA: Toward an Effective, Open Giant" (1976); "Lessons From a Fast-Paced Public Project: Perspecties on Doing Better the Next-time Around" (1983); "Organizational Transition in a Fast-Paced Public Project: Personal Perspectives of MARTA Executives" (1983); *High Performance and Human Costs: A Public Sector Model of Organization Development* (1988).

26. For example, "Some Effects of Multiple OD Interventions on Burnout and Worksite Features" (1987).

27. "Enhancing Worldwide Strategic Planning, Part 1: An OD Design and Its Theoretic Rationale" (1991); "Enhancing Worldwide Strategic Planning, Part 2: Some Consequences at Micro- and Macro-Levels" (1991); "Using OD to Enhance Strategic Planning" (1989).

28. "OD Interventions in Urban Settings, II: Public-Sector Success with Planned Change" (1979).

29. "Success of OD Applications in the Public Sector: Toting-up the Score for a Decade, More or Less" (1981); "Estimating the Success of OD Applications" (1982).

30. Ibid.

31. For example, "Is OD Narrowly Culture-Bound?: Prominent Features of 100 Third-World Applications" (1987).

32. "OD Applications Under Economic Deprivation" (1989); *Ironies in Organizational Development* (1990).

33. "Positive-Findings Bias in QWL Studies" (1990); "QWL Improves Worksite Quality: Success Rates in a Large Panel of Studies" (1990).

34. "Positive-Findings Bias in QWL Research: A Comparison of Public and Business Sectors" (1989).

35. For example, B-C. Sun. (1988). *Quality of Working Life Programs: An Empirical Assessment of Designs and Outcomes.* Unpublished doctoral dissertation, University of Georgia, Athens, GA.

36. For example, *Organization Development: Ideas and Issues* (1989, pp. 85-94).

37. "The Congruence of Factorial Structures: Comparisons of Four Procedures and Their Solutions" (1976); "Contours in Social Change: Elemental Graphics and a Surrogate Variable for Gamma Change" (1986); "The Alpha, Beta, Gamma Change Typology: Personal Reactions and Progress" (1989); *Ironies in Organizational Development* (1990).

38. For example, C.P. Alderfer. (1977). Organization development. *Annual Review of Psychology, 28*, 197-223; A.A. Armenakis. (1988). A review of research on the change typology. In W.A. Passmore and R.W. Woodman (Eds.), *Research in Organization Change and Development.* Greenwich, CT: JAI Press.

39. For example, W.W. Burke, (1982). *Organization Development.* Boston, MA: Little, Brown; E.G. Huse. (1980). *Organization Development and Change.* St. Paul, MN: West; E.G. Huse and T.C. Cummings. (1989). *Organization Development and Change.* St. Paul, MN: West.

40. C.N. Tennis. (1989). Responses to alpha, beta, gamma change typology. *Group & Organization Studies, 14*(2), 134-149.

41. "The Alpha, Beta, Gamma Change Typology: Personal Reactions and Progress" (1989).

42. *Stress in Organizations: Research Developments in Mid-Stream* (1986); *Phases of Burnout: Developments in Concepts and Applications* (1988); *Ironies in Organizational Development* (1990).

43. For example, "Burnout as an Indicator of Gamma Change, I: Methodological Perspectives on a Crucial Surrogacy" (1988); "Burnout as an Indicator of Gamma Change, II: State-Like Differences Between Phases" (1989); "Burnout as an Indicator of Gamma Change, III: Differences of Degree in Worksite Descriptors" (1990).

44. *Ironies in Organizational Development* (1990, pp. 257-267).

45. For example, B-S. Kim. (1990). *Alternative Models of Burnout Phases.* Unpublished doctoral dissertation, University of Georgia, Athens, GA; "Alternative Combinations of Phases of Burnout" (1991).

46. For example, R.J. Burke. (1989). Toward a phase model of burnout. *Group & Organization Studies, 14*, 1, 23-32.

47. For example, M.P. Leiter. (1988). Burnout as a function of communication patterns. *Group & Organization Studies, 13*, 1, 111-128.

48. For example, *Phases of Burnout: Developments in Concepts and Applications* (1988, pp. 164-165).

49. For example, "Some Effects of Multiple OD Interventions on Burnout and Worksite Features" (1987).

50. "Some Perspectives on One Consulting Style" (1979).

Management Laureates:
A Collection of Autobiographical Essays

Arthur G. Bedeian, *Department of Management, Louisiana State University*

REVIEW: "The collection of autobiographical essays is a creative project. No other publication in management has asked leading contributors to reflect on their experiences and the factors and forces that influenced their professional and personal development. Each essay is accompanied by a photograph and complete bibliography of each individual's work. The thirty-four autobiographies represent the editor's selection of "management laureates," those who have achieved distinction in research and publication, teaching, and consulting. These laureates are holders of distinguished professorships—almost all are Fellows of the Academy of Management, some have been presidents of the Academy of Management, and others have distinguished themselves professionally. It would be difficult, if not impossible, to read one of our scholarly journals without finding at least one of these individuals cited.

The laureates come from different disciplines and have made contributions in a variety of management related topics: leadership, motivation, human resource management, strategic management, production/operations management and systems theory. The editor suggests that those chosen represent only a sample of distinguished individuals in management. No criteria are provided for how these particular individuals were selected, but careful reading will reveal that those selected are indeed distinguished contributors to the management discipline.

The essays of these laureates will be interesting to a wide range of readers—students, academicians, and practitioners. Through the essays we get to know both the people and ideas which have influenced the course of management teaching and practice. As these individuals speak of their intellectual legacy, they are simultaneously helping to develop the researchers, teachers, and practitioners of tomorrow. Each of us can better understand the contributions of these laureates by knowing something about them as people. Most of what we know of these individuals has been gathered from the flyleaf of a book, a note at the end of an article, or the sterilized linear format of a *Who's Who. Management Laureates* provides the opportunities for in-depth, introspective revelations about individuals who are among the contemporary leaders in the management discipline."

—*THE EXECUTIVE*
Daniel A. Wren
University of Oklahoma

J A I

P R E S S

Volume 2
ISBN 1-55938-470-0   Approx. $75.00

Preface. Hapiness and Unhappiness: A Brief Autobiography, *Frederek I. Herzberg.* **Slow Learner and Late Bloomer,** *Robert J. House.* **Understanding Work Motivation and Organizational Effectiveness: A Career-Long Journey,** *Edward E. Lawler, III.* **Doing Prooblem-Oriented Research: A Daughter's Interview,** *Raul R. Lawrence with Anne T. Lawrence.* **Reflection on Leadership, Teaching, and Problem Solving Groups,** *Edmund P. Learned.* **Teacher as Leader,** *Harry Levinson.* **Principled Ambition,** *Edwin A. Locke.* **Field of Dreams: Perspectives on the Teaching of Management,** *Dalton E. McFarland.* **Pursuing Diversity in an Increasingly Specialized Organizational Science,** *John B. Miner.* **The Illusive Strategy . . . 25 Years Later,** *Henry Mintzberg.* **The Takeoff,** *William H. Newman.*

Volume 3
ISBN 1-55938-471-9   Approx. $75.00

CONTENTS: Preface. An Almost Random Career, *Charles Perrow.* **An Unmanaged Pursuit of Management,** *Lyman W. Porter.* **The Academic as Artist: Personal and Professional Roots,** *Edgar H. Schein.* **"Watch Where You Step!" Or Indiana Starbuck Amid the Perils of Academe (Rated PG),** *William H. Starbuck.* **My Roads to Management Theory and Practice,** *George Steiner.* **Spectator at the Beginning: Some Personal Notes on OB's Early Days and Later,** *George Strauss.* **Guilty of Enthusiasm,** *Eric L. Trist with Richard C.S. Trahair.* **Up the Management Mountain,** *Stanley C. Vance.* **Improvising and Muddling Through,** *Victor H. Vroom.* **Turning Context into Text: An Academic Life as Data,** *Karl E. Weick.* **From Participant Observer to Participatory Action Researcher,** *William F. Whyte.* **From Practice to Theory: Odyssey of a Manager,** *James C. Worthy.*

Future volumes will be available annually and may be ordered on a standing order basis.

JAI PRESS INC.

55 Old Post Road - No. 2   P.O. Box 1678
Greenwich, Connecticut 06836-1678
Tel: (203) 661-7602   Fax: (203)661-0792

Research in Organizational Behavior

Edited by **Barry M. Staw,** *School of Business Administration, University of California, Berkeley* and **L.L. Cummings,** *Carlson School of Management, University of Minnesota*

Volume 14, 1992, 348 pp. $63.50
ISBN 1-55938-242-2

CONTENTS: Toward a Cultural Theory of Stress Complaints, *Stephen R. Barley and Deborah B. Knight.* **Responsibility and Risk in Organizational Crimes of Obedience,** *V. Lee Hamilton.* **Job Competence and Cognition,** *Peter Warr and Mark Conner.* **A Due Process Metaphor for Performance Appraisal,** *Robert Folger and Mary A. Konovsky.* **The Algebra of Change,** *Stuart Albert.* **Learning Through Failure: The Strategy of Small Losses,** *Sim B. Sitkin.* **Structural Contingency Theory: A Re-Appraisal,** *Johannes M. Pennings.* **Organizational Determinants of Technological Change: Towards a Sociology of Technological Evolution,** *Michael L. Tushman and Lori Rosenkopf.*

Also Available:
Volumes 1-13 (1979-1991) $63.50 each

JAI PRESS INC.

55 Old Post Road - No. 2 P.O. Box 1678
Greenwich, Connecticut 06836-1678
Tel: (203) 661-7602 Fax: (203)661-0792

The Leadership Quarterly
An International Journal of Political, Social and Behavioral Science

Executive Editors: **Robert J. House,** *Wharton School of Business, University of Pennsylvania* and **Henry L. Tosi, Jr.,** *University of Florida.*

Associate Editors: **John Jermier,** *University of South Florida and* **Francis Yammarino,** *State University of New York, Binghamton*

Disciplines such as political science, organizational psychology and sociology are becoming so specialized that, for scholars and lay persons alike, the study of leadership is now highly fractionated. Studies of U.S. presidents in political science seldom make reference to the psychological literature of chief executive officers. Studies of school principals appear without attention to the impact of cultural dynamics seen in cultural anthropology. Management and administrative staffs responsible for supervisory and executive development need to scan 20 to 30 journals across many disciplines to keep current in the study of leadership.

This journal brings together a focus on leadership for scholars, consultants, practicing managers, executives and administrators, as well as those 600 or more university faculty in the United States and elsewhere who teach leadership as a college course. It provides timely publication of leadership research and applications.

Subscription Rates

Volume 4 (1993) Published Quarterly Institutions: $125.00
ISSN 1048-9843 Individuals: $60.00
Volumes 1-3 (1990-1992) $125.00 each

Outside the U.S. add $20.00 for surface mail or $30.00 for airmail.

JAI PRESS INC.
55 Old Post Road - No. 2 P.O. Box 1678
Greenwich, Connecticut 06836-1678
Tel: (203) 661-7602 Fax: (203)661-0792